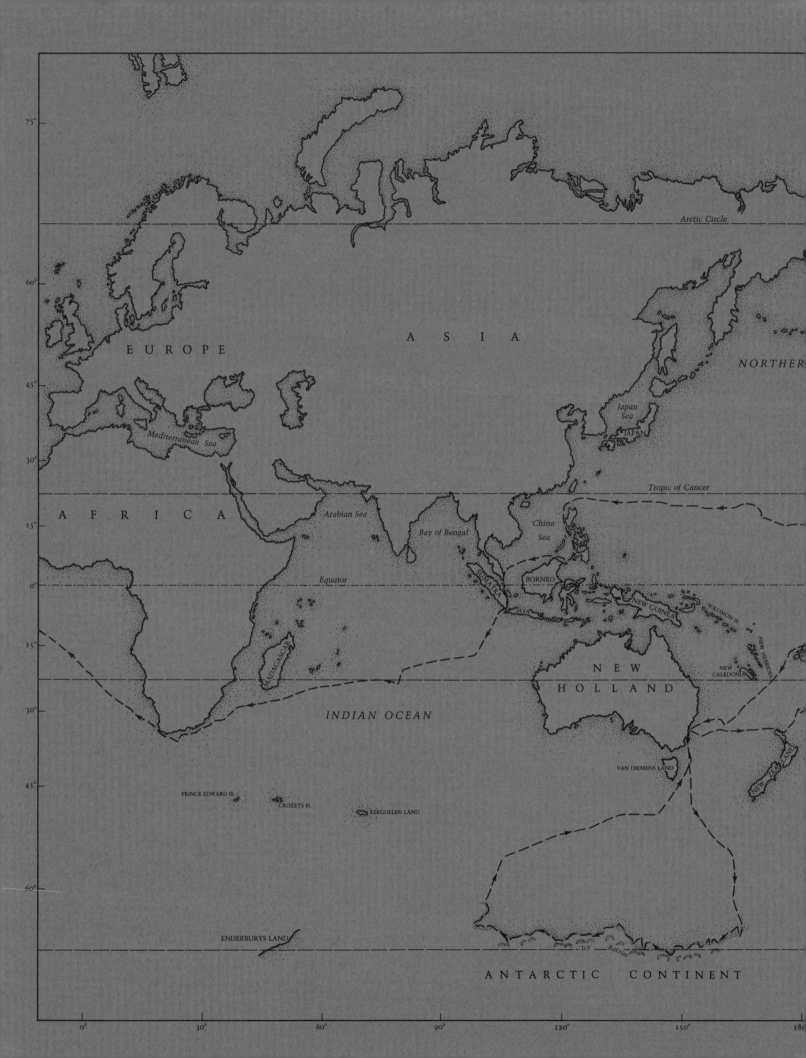

75°

60°

45°

30°

15°

Arctic Circle

EUROPE

ASIA

NORTHER

Japan
Sea

JAPAN

Mediterranean   Sea

Tropic of Cancer

AFRICA

Arabian Sea

Bay of Bengal

China
Sea

Equator

SUMATRA

BORNEO

JAVA

NEW GUINEA

SOLOMON IS.

NEW
CALEDONIA

NEW
HEBRIDES

MADAGASCAR

NEW

HOLLAND

INDIAN OCEAN

VAN DIEMENS LAND

NEW ZEALAND

45°

PRINCE EDWARD IS.

CROZETS IS.

KERGUELEN LAND

60°

ENDERBURYS LAND

Icy   Barrier

ANTARCTIC   CONTINENT

0°   30°   60°   90°   120°   150°   180°

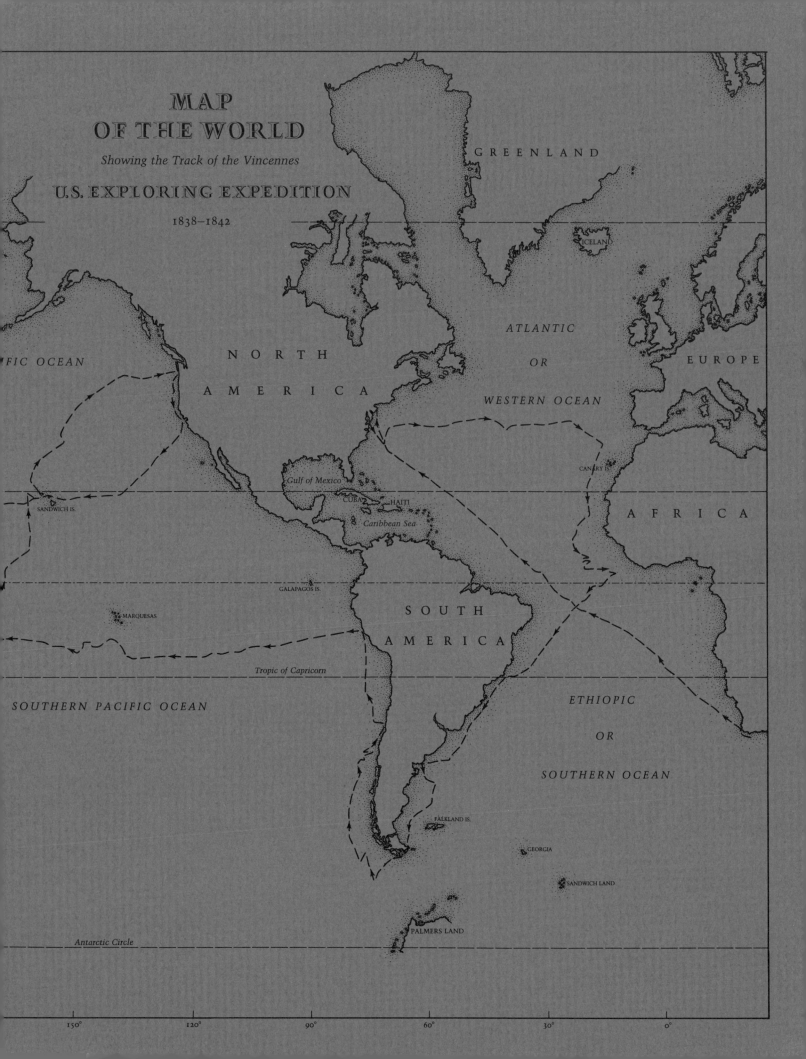

MAGNIFICENT

The U.S.

Herman J. Viola and Carolyn Margolis, Editors
with the assistance of Jan S. Danis
Smithsonian Institution Press, Washington, D.C., 1985

Printed especially for Contributing Members
of the Smithsonian National Associate Program
in honor of the seventy-fifth anniversary of the
National Museum of Natural History

VOYAGERS

Exploring Expedition, 1838–1842

Library of Congress Cataloging-in-
Publication Data
Main entry under title:

Magnificent voyagers.

Bibliography: p.
Includes index.
1. United States Exploring Expedition,
1838–1842. I. Viola, Herman J. II. Margolis,
Carolyn.
G420.U55M34 1985   973.5′7
85–40192
ISBN 0–87474–946–8
ISBN 0–87474–945–X (pbk.)

The paper in this book meets the guide-
lines for permanence and durability of the
Committee on Production Guidelines for
Book Longevity of the Council on Library
Resources.

Magnificent Voyagers is also the title of
an exhibition organized by the National
Museum of Natural History and circulated
by the Smithsonian Institution Traveling
Exhibition Service (SITES).

*Argillite carving of a sea captain
attributed to the Haida of
Queen Charlotte Island.
Presented to the Expedition by
employees of the Hudson's Bay
Company in 1841. The figure was
sent to Denmark in 1867 by the
Smithsonian as part of an early
exchange program. Height 13 inches.
Courtesy National Museum of
Denmark, Copenhagen.*

*Frontispiece, "Observatory Peak,
Feejee, Is." Drawn by Alfred T. Agate,
Narrative.*

Contents

Foreword

Magnificent Voyagers is the title of both this book and of an exhibition at the National Museum of Natural History honoring the U.S. Exploring Expedition of 1838–42, led by Lieutenant Charles Wilkes. Together, the book and exhibition represent the fruits of more than four years of research by a team of scholars from the Smithsonian Institution, the Library of Congress, the National Archives, and the Historical Division of the Navy. Headed by Herman J. Viola of the Museum of Natural History, the team located hundreds of objects relating to the Expedition and sifted through cartons of diary entries, correspondence, and official records to tell this remarkable story, a story that includes much about the early history of the Smithsonian Institution itself.

When the Exploring Expedition set sail from Hampton Roads, Virginia, in August 1838, our country did not have a national museum; and, frankly, government officials had given little thought to the ultimate disposition of the flora and fauna that the explorers were expected to bring back. This did not deter the scientists and sailors with Wilkes, however. They enthusiastically collected natural history and ethnological specimens from around the globe—two thousand birds; one hundred fifty mammals; one thousand corals, crus-taceans, and mollusks; fifty thousand plants; plus hundreds of fossils, minerals, and rocks, and more than five thousand objects of human manufacture that document the cultures of the native peoples with whom the Expedition came in contact. It was such a wonderful trove of exotica that, when the Expedition returned four years later, the specimens became the focus of a custodial tug-of-war.

The Smithsonian, you will discover after reading this book, became the reluctant recipient of this material. I say "reluctant" because a museum was not part of the great research institution on the Mall envisioned by Joseph Henry, the first Secretary of the Smithsonian. Thanks to a compromise between this predecessor of mine and the Congress, the Wilkes collection came here in 1858, and with that acquisition the National Museum of the United States was created. This important milestone in the Smithsonian's history explains why, for the seventy-fifth anniversary of the Museum of Natural History Building, we are paying tribute to those "magnificent voyagers" who sailed with Wilkes nearly one hundred fifty years ago.

Robert McC. Adams
Secretary
Smithsonian Institution

Charles Wilkes by Thomas Sully.
Courtesy U.S. Naval Academy Museum.

1 The Story of the U.S. Exploring Expedition

Few sagas of the sea embody more romance and adventure than the U.S. Exploring Expedition of 1838–42 led by Lieutenant Charles Wilkes. The history of the voyage evokes the glorious age of sail—a time when iron men in wooden ships ventured forth upon the sea, confident that wind, weather, and wits would see them safely home.

Certainly, the Expedition's accomplishments were heroic. In less than four years, this gallant naval squadron of six small ships surveyed 280 islands and constructed 180 charts, some of which were still being used as late as World War II. The Expedition mapped eight hundred miles of the coast of the Oregon territory; it explored some fifteen hundred miles of the Antarctic coast, thereby proving the existence of the seventh continent. Equally important, the Expedition collected and described natural history specimens from all parts of the globe—specimens that eventually came to the fledgling Smithsonian Institution, making it the National Museum of the United States. In a larger sense, the Expedition led to the emergence of the United States as a naval and scientific power with worldwide interests.

Despite its historical importance, the Expedition is relatively unknown today. Indeed, even the controversial and colorful Wilkes is remembered primarily for his role in the *Trent* affair during the Civil War, when he removed Confederate diplomatic agents from a British vessel in international waters.

The story of the Expedition begins in the early nineteenth century with John Cleves Symmes, Jr., a veteran of the War of 1812 from Ohio, who believed that the world was hollow and that the entrances to the inner world could be found by sailing to the South Pole. Known as the "Holes in the Poles Theory," it was not widely accepted even then. Nevertheless, New England merchants eager to find new sealing and whaling grounds allied themselves with Symmes and his friends to encourage Congress to sponsor a South Seas Exploring Expedition. The U.S. Navy welcomed the opportunity to learn more about this little-known region and to show the flag in areas where natives had taken American property and lives and had gone unpunished. Thanks to these various interests and the encouragement of President John Quincy Adams, Congress in 1828 passed a resolution authorizing the president to send one of the public ships to the Pacific to examine coasts, islands, harbors, shoals, and reefs, if this could be done without a special appropriation.

Despite the resolution, however, ten years passed before an expedition set sail for the South Seas. Officially known as the United States South Seas Exploring Expedition, it was commonly called the Exploring Expedition or the Wilkes Expedition. One

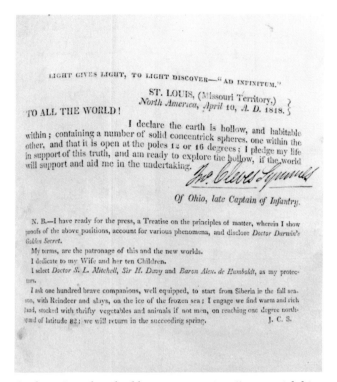

LIGHT GIVES LIGHT, TO LIGHT DISCOVER—"AD INFINITUM."

ST. LOUIS, (Missouri Territory.)
North America, April 10, A. D. 1818.

TO ALL THE WORLD !

I declare the earth is hollow, and habitable within ; containing a number of solid concentrick spheres. one within the other, and that it is open at the poles 12 or 16 degrees ; I pledge my life in support of this truth, and am ready to explore the hollow, if the world will support and aid me in the undertaking.

Jno. Cleves Symmes

Of Ohio, late Captain of Infantry.

N. B.—I have ready for the press, a Treatise on the principles of matter, wherein I show proofs of the above positions, account for various phenomena, and disclose *Doctor Darwin's Golden Secret.*

My terms, are the patronage of this and the new worlds.

I dedicate to my Wife and her ten Children.

I select *Doctor S. L. Mitchell, Sir H. Davy* and *Baron Alex. de Humboldt,* as my protectors.

I ask one hundred brave companions, well equipped, to start from Siberia in the fall season, with Reindeer and slays, on the ice of the frozen sea ; I engage we find warm and rich land, stocked with thrifty vegetables and animals if not men, on reaching one degree northward of latitude 82 ; we will return in the succeeding spring.   J. C. S.

Seeking "one hundred brave companions" to go with him to the North Pole, John Cleves Symmes, Jr., announced to the world his concentric earth theory on 10 April 1818. This copy of the announcement went to Secretary of State John Quincy Adams, who was later so instrumental in launching the U.S. Exploring Expedition. Courtesy National Archives.

wit dubbed it the "Deplorable Expedition," because of the seemingly endless delays and controversies that surrounded it. For example, there were squabbles over the number and types of ships, the choice of commander and the scope of his authority, and the size and background of the scientific staff. Typical of the bungling that beset the Expedition was the indecision of Secretary of the Navy Mahlon Dickerson, whose credo was "Be cautious not to attempt too much business in one day." [Stanton 1975:34] The general feeling of the American public about the venture was nicely summed up in 1837 by John Quincy Adams, who was now serving as a representative in Congress from Massachusetts. All he wanted to hear about the Expedition, he said, was that it had sailed. Six ships finally did depart Hampton Roads, Virginia, on 18 August 1838.

This was a young man's expedition. Passed Mid-shipman William Reynolds—an avid chronicler of the four-year adventure—wrote his sister that it was strange "to look around & find none but youthful faces among the officers—a Young Captain, with boys for his subordinates—no gray hairs among us, none of those 'hard a weather' characters. . . . We are all in the spring time of life." [1838c]

Wilkes commanded the squadron from the flagship *Vincennes.* Although not the navy's first choice to lead the Expedition—of forty lieutenants in the service, thirty-eight had had more sea duty—he had the vision, intelligence, and determination to do the job. He gave the Expedition its distinctive stamp. Aloof, stern, and resolute, he drove himself even harder than he drove his ships and men. His sense of mission and national pride dictated high standards of performance and accomplishment. Second-in-command, on the *Peacock,* was Lieutenant William Hudson. At forty-four, he was four years older than Wilkes and the senior officer in terms of service. The other vessels were the *Porpoise,* the supply ship *Relief,* and two virtually identical schooners, the *Flying Fish* and the *Sea Gull.* Modifications were made to most of the vessels to prepare them for the anticipated stresses of an expedition to polar waters and to accommodate the nine civilian scientists who sailed with the squadron.

Cut from a projected corps of twenty-five, the Scientifics, as the civilians were known, were essential to the Expedition's success. Their appointment marked the first time in American history that civilian and naval personnel combined their talents and resources in a peacetime scientific endeavor. Young—their average age was thirty-two—resourceful, and dynamic, most of them were academically trained; several went on to become giants in their fields. James Dwight Dana, the most gifted of the group and already the author of a major work on mineralogy, became one of America's most distinguished scientific leaders. The others were Horatio Hale, philologist; Titian R. Peale and Charles Pickering, naturalists; William D. Brackenridge and William Rich, botanists; Joseph P. Couthouy, conchologist; and Alfred T. Agate and Joseph Drayton, artists.

Wilkes before and had been flogged by him—unjustly, he avowed—later confessed that he planned to kill Wilkes during the Expedition but changed his mind after seeing a vision of his mother. Erskine told this story in his book, *Twenty Years Before the Mast*, which he published in 1890. Ironically, Erskine had learned to read and write during the Expedition. That Wilkes—despite his difficult personality—managed to guide the Expedition through awesome hazards, frequent privation, and occasional boredom is testimony to his considerable leadership skills.

Although denied a promotion to the acting rank of captain, which he deserved and expected, Wilkes nonetheless modeled his leadership on the precedents established by commanders of earlier overseas squadrons. From the outset, he impressed his officers and men with the demanding character of

John Cleves Symmes, Jr., the self-styled "Newton of the West." Pencil sketch by John James Audubon, dated August 1820. Courtesy The New-York Historical Society.

Scientific, commercial, and diplomatic objectives may have dominated the Expedition, but traditional naval discipline and custom—including flogging and the regular issue of grog—marked its passage throughout the cruise. Brooding, aloof, and always fearful of cabals, Wilkes was a strict disciplinarian who ran a taut ship. He later admitted that he cultivated the image of a "martinette" because it carried with it "authority" and "obedience to command." Doubtless, justice dispensed with a heavy hand contributed to the obedience that his command "induced." [Wilkes 1978:391] Navy ship captains in 1838 could authorize a maximum of twelve lashes without benefit of court, yet Wilkes often ordered more, sometimes as many as forty. One sailor, Charles Erskine, who had sailed under

Symmes used this wooden model when lecturing about his theory of the "hollow earth." Courtesy Library of the Academy of Natural Sciences of Philadelphia.

their mission and the conduct he expected of them, especially in their relations with native peoples. His men were bound by strict security policies based on previous American experience in the Pacific, and the strength of the naval contingent afforded the Scientifics a degree of protection they perhaps did not fully appreciate.

It is difficult today to imagine the stresses of shipboard life in the age of sail. The ships were small and crowded and the time between ports often weighed heavily. Since the only way to keep meat and poultry fresh in the days before refrigeration was to keep it live, the decks the first few weeks after leaving port resembled barnyards, complete with the accompanying litter and stench. The problem became even more acute when departures were delayed because the livestock usually remained on board even though, as Reynolds once grumbled, their "time would have [been] spent more profitably ashore." [1839a] Exotic fruits, native dishes, and fresh fish and game occasionally relieved the traditional shipboard diet, but short rations proved inevitable on several occasions. Not much could be done to keep drinking water tasty, for it was kept in barrels and iron tanks and, as Peale wrote his young daughters, was "very warm and . . . smells very bad." Still, "as we do not come on board ship to be comfortable we content ourselves with anything we can get." [Poesch 1961:67]

Peale seemed less "content" with his accommodations on board the *Peacock.* He went on to describe his stateroom as being about "as large as your mother's bedstead; in it I have a little bed over and under which is packed clothes, furs, guns, Books and boxes without number, all of which have to be tied to keep them from rolling and tumbling about, and kept off the floor as it is sometimes covered with water." Peale's comments in his journal were even more caustic: the ships were totally unfit for scientific service. Although staterooms had been constructed on the gun deck for use by the Scientifics, they were wet and dark and inadequate for making drawings or preparing specimens. The captain's cabin was the only appropriate space for such activities, but using it meant depriving him of privacy. They could not work on deck because of "the usual Naval etiquette," while lack of

light and air prevented their working below deck. As it was, the Scientifics ate all their meals by candlelight because the officers' wardroom was below decks.

Reynolds, on the other hand, was delighted with his quarters aboard the *Vincennes,* which he shared with another midshipman. The two officers must have gone to great lengths to make their stateroom comfortable, for little in it seems to have been navy issue. White and crimson curtains hung at the walls, while blue damask dusters covered the two couches, which ran the width of the compartment. The couches served as lounges during the day and beds at night. The bureau had a "handsome" cover and the mirror was "beautiful." In addition, the stateroom boasted silver-plated candlestick holders, a "*Brussels*" carpet as well as soft mats, and an ornamental washstand which, in "its furniture, white sprigs of green & gilt, . . . [was] in perfect taste." Completing the decor were bowie knives, pistols, and cutlasses "displayed in different places & figures [to] give the Man-of-War finish to the whole." [Reynolds 1838b]

A homey decor was no substitute for news from home, however. When mail reached a ship virtually all activity ceased until the letters had been read and reread. Reynolds once reported his pleasure at obtaining American newspapers "less than 80 days old" from a ship that came into Honolulu from Mazatlan. The vessel also carried mail for several crewmen, which made them "the envy of all the squadron." [1840c] On another occasion, only four months into the voyage, the *Vincennes* was hailed by a brig out of Boston that carried two letters for one of the passed midshipmen. His joy quickly turned to grief, however, because the letters informed him that his two infant children had died. The man's wife "even in her deep & heavy affliction had not forgotten to endeavor to afford some consolation to her equally bereaved husband," Reynolds wrote. At least three more years would pass before he could return home, "& then, when he seeks his children, he must know his way towards their graves!" [1838d] In truth, for seamen and Scientifics alike, four years of absence proved an extraordinary sacrifice, depriving their families of needed support and making particularly bitter the official indiffer-

A comic view of the U.S. Exploring Expedition. Printed in 1838, this amusing lithograph indicates that not all Americans of the day endorsed the idea of a government-sponsored exploring expedition. Courtesy Peters Collection, Division of Domestic Life, National Museum of American History, Smithsonian Institution.

ence that marked the Expedition's return in 1842.

Combining naval and scientific objectives was not always easy, but for the most part the two groups of men worked well together. The attitude of Midshipman Reynolds is probably typical of the naval personnel. "I like the associates we shall have during the cruise," he wrote home shortly before the squadron left the United States. "These enthusiastic artists, and those headlong, indefatigable pursuers & slayers of birds, beasts, & fishes & the gatherers of shells, rocks, insects, &c. . . . are leaving their comfortable homes, to follow the strong bent of their minds, to garner up strange things of strange lands, which fact proves that the ruling passion is strong in life." [1838a] A month later, Reynolds reported that the Scientifics had made "another haul." He considered it quite curious to

see them patiently toil over seeming trifles, "giving up their whole soul to their employment." On calm days they would drag scoop nets behind the ship and then empty them on deck. Because the sea was teeming with life, they would find many things "minute & beautiful to look at, and having every thing that is wonderful, in their character to hear of, by the aid of microscopes." Specimens the Scientifics considered particularly significant were immediately turned over to the artists, who copied them from life. "To watch them," Reynolds wrote, "is another source of gratification." [1838c] On another occasion, after describing the method by which the Scientifics collected and dissected fish, he wrote: "All they did was Greek to us, but . . . here's success to them, may they have a large book to publish when we return." [1838b]

Even after a year at sea, Reynolds had not lost his initial interest in the work of the Scientifics. While in Peru, he shot a white egret, the only one of its kind that had been taken thus far. It had already been described in scientific literature, Reynolds wrote, otherwise the naturalists would have named it "Rinalditis" in his honor. "Mercy! only think of the Capes & Islands & mountains, that I shall call after the names of certain individuals [on the Expedition], having them all put in bold letters on that Chart, that will be a guide to navigators forever." [1839b]

Not all the officers shared Reynolds's admiration and enthusiasm. Some derided the Scientifics as "clam diggers" and "bug catchers." Others resented the additional workload they represented, such as the need to ferry them from ship to shore so they could collect samples of the flora and fauna from the islands the squadron surveyed. Even Wilkes was vexed by the noxious odors that emanated from dissected creatures and prohibited their study below decks.

The Scientifics had complaints of their own, of course. When the squadron was actively surveying the coral islands, Wilkes sometimes did not allow them enough time ashore to do their collecting, because of the need to keep on schedule. Indeed, Wilkes insisted that the surveying duty was "a service second to none in the Expedition." [Wilkes 1844: 1, 432] Couthouy, the conchologist, later complained that the Scientifics had gotten fifty thousand specimens in well-traveled Rio de Janeiro, but what they took from the first five unexplored islands they visited would not have filled a cigar box. The Scientifics suspected that Wilkes did not want their achievements to overshadow the Expedition's naval accomplishments. Dana, writing to Asa Gray from Valparaiso, congratulated him on his decision to remain at home, thereby escaping "Naval servitude." [Stanton 1975: 137]

Wilkes did give the Scientifics reasons for suspicion, because he zealously promoted the navy's interests and he personally took charge of the studies in the physical sciences. He later explained the navy's role was not to be one of "hewers of wood and drawers of water." To Wilkes the Expedition was as much a matter of naval pride as national

pride, and he overlooked no opportunity to enhance the navy's image, even to the detriment of the Scientifics if necessary.

One area of conflict concerned the ownership of the collection of specimens. Wilkes told the officers and crews that all souvenirs obtained during the Expedition were government property and would have to be surrendered at the end of the voyage. The crew blamed the Scientifics for this decree, although in fact the Scientifics wanted the assistance of the crew in making the collections more comprehensive and planned to pay for objects retained for the permanent collections. Regardless of fault, the question of keeping souvenirs became a source of needless resentment toward the Scientifics. As it was, private collecting seems to have been common despite the strictures against it. Midshipman Reynolds, for example, told his family near the end of the Expedition that although he had been unable to bring back a live bird for his sister, he did have a dead one with plumage so brilliant it "shall exceed that of any living warbler, in all North America." [1841]

Wilkes expected his officers to take their scientific responsibilities seriously. When he learned— "with surprise & regret"—that two officers had scaled the monumental Sugar Loaf mountain that towered over the harbor at Rio de Janeiro without taking instruments with them to determine "its correct admeasurement," he shamed them into scaling the peak again, this time lugging the proper apparatus, lest their effort result "only in the idle & boastful saying that its summit has been reached, instead of [being] an excursion which might have been useful to the expedition." [Stanton 1975:90]

Midshipman Reynolds could have at times done with fewer scientific chores. While the squadron was in Rio, he had the unenviable task of tending the observatory that Wilkes established on an island at the harbor's mouth. "Every hour," Reynolds wrote, "I sally forth . . . and make the grand tour of the instruments: first a 'Barometer & Thermometer,' in the house, near the 'pendulum & clocks.' Then a diurnal variation machine, in a room alone; then the Tide Staff, then thermometer with black sheep's wool around the bulb, and another plain, both exposed to the sun's rays, 'to ascertain the solar intensity' then the Dip of the Needle; then two other thermometers in the air, but in the shade, then two other diurnal variation concerns and finally, a thermometer in the house—all these I observe and note, at the expiration of every hour in the twenty four." To make sure he kept his appointed rounds, a marine guard had the duty of calling him every hour on the hour. "My time and rest are, of course, eternally disturbed." [1838e]

Reynolds later drew the same duty in Peru, only this time he found himself and the instruments on a remote beach in an area frequented by bandits. He considered it "the most cut-throat spot . . . of the

Rare sketches of life on board ship by Agate for Palmer's Thulia.

globe." Although Reynolds feared for his life, Wilkes evidently did not think it was necessary to station marine guards at the isolated observatory. Thus, Reynolds lamented, "I am alone." For protection he set his table across the entrance to the tent "as a sort of barricade" and kept a "huge" sword in his lap and two pistols on the table. [1839b]

The first important stop for the Expedition was Orange Harbor at Tierra del Fuego, which Wilkes used as a base for his first attempt to explore the waters around Antarctica in February 1839. Leaving the *Relief* and the *Vincennes*, he took the rest of the squadron south. Peale, however, was the only Scientific to accompany Wilkes into Antarctica; the others remained in the area of Orange Harbor. Wilkes, meanwhile, was not having much luck. The weather was so bad the ships could not sail in company, and most of them returned without accomplishing anything. Wilkes, however, found enough indications of land to justify a more extended attempt the following year.

Wilkes planned to have the squadron reunite in Valparaiso, Chile, but only five ships reached port. The *Sea Gull* disappeared somewhere between Orange Harbor and Valparaiso never to be heard from again. After waiting several weeks for the missing vessel, the Expedition continued up the South American coast to Lima, Peru, where it prepared to head westward across the Pacific. Thus far, the Scientifics were generally unhappy because no

William Reynolds by an unknown artist.
Courtesy Anne Cleaver.

"View from Sugar Loaf Summit, Rio de Janeiro." This exquisite watercolor by Lieutenant John Dale documents an incident that illustrates the scientific zeal of Wilkes, who reprimanded two Expedition officers for scaling Sugar Loaf without carrying along the instruments needed for taking the mountain's "correct admeasurement." The chastened young men climbed Sugar Loaf again, this time lugging the proper apparatus, lest they be accused, as Wilkes had warned them, of accomplishing something that "results only in the idle & boastful saying that its summit has been reached, instead of an excursion which might have been useful to the expedition." Courtesy J. Welles Henderson Collection.

new or unexplored places had been visited, and Wilkes was unhappy because he suspected several of his officers were plotting against the success of the Expedition. To get rid of the supposed trouble-makers, Wilkes assigned them to the supply ship *Relief* and ordered it to return home by way of Australia, where it was to off-load supplies and equipment. Wilkes reasoned that the supply ship was too slow and would keep the Expedition behind sched-

ule. This seems to have been a valid complaint, but the lack of a supply ship caused inconvenience and difficulties later in the Expedition.

In August 1839, after almost a year at sea, the squadron reached the first Pacific islands, the Tuamotu group. The main order of business was surveying, which Wilkes developed to a fine art, using the triangulation technique he had perfected during his earlier survey of Georges Bank. The squadron gradually worked itself through the coral islands— the Disappointments, Tahiti, Samoa—completing its work by the end of November 1839.

By now the romance of the Expedition had begun to wear thin, and to add to morale problems, the explorers discovered that the islands were no longer the unspoiled paradises described by Cook and other visitors. Missionaries, a major presence everywhere in the Pacific, seemed bent on spoiling the good times the sailors had anticipated. The change, however, pleased Wilkes and his fellow officers because they expected it to mean fewer desertions.

From Samoa, the squadron went to Sydney. Leaving the Scientifics to explore Australia and New Zealand, Wilkes took the remaining four vessels— the *Vincennes*, the *Porpoise*, the *Peacock*, and the *Flying Fish*—back into Antarctic waters. The Australians, for the most part, had not been optimistic, predicting the Americans would be "frozen to death." Even Wilkes had his doubts, considering the lack of proper clothing and the poor condition of his ships, especially the *Peacock*, whose underworks were discovered to be rotted. Nevertheless, there had not been enough time to permit a major overhaul of the vessels, and four ships embarked for Antarctica on 26 December.

Despite Wilkes's best efforts, the ships were unable to sail together. The first one to become separated was the *Flying Fish*, which, unable to keep up with the larger vessels, disappeared during a dense fog. The small pilot boat was not seen again until after the Antarctic cruise and was assumed to have suffered the same end as the *Sea Gull*. Eventually, all the vessels became separated, causing many men on board anxious thoughts about each other's fate.

It was the *Peacock*, however, that came closest to a watery grave. On 23 January 1840, it went stern first into an iceberg and broke its rudder and parted the starboard wheel rope. Unable to be steered, the vessel drifted into a huge ice island and broke its stern davits, stern boat, and spanker boom. At the same time it became trapped by floating ice. Providentially, a narrow channel opened and Captain Hudson and the crew, after more than twenty-four hours of constant labor, literally pulled the stricken vessel through it into open water. Reynolds later described the effort for his family: "We toiled, toiled on, 'never say die' was the word—even the boys worked, with all the ardor of Hercules." [1840a] Although the rudder was repaired, the *Peacock* had to return to Sydney.

Despite its bad luck, the *Peacock* gets credit for the Expedition's first landfall. The episode, however, also proved to be the most controversial aspect of the Expedition. Although the landfall was officially recorded in the log of the *Vincennes* on 19 January 1840, the discovery was actually made several days earlier—on 16 January—when Midshipmen Henry Eld and Reynolds from the rigging of the *Peacock* reported distant mountains. To their dismay, the fact was not recorded in the ship's log.

This later proved to be a serious omission because a French exploring expedition under Admiral Dumont d'Urville was in approximately the same waters at the same time and recorded making a landfall on 19 January, the same day as Wilkes. To compound Wilkes's problems, his claims for discovering the Antarctic continent—based on sailing along fifteen hundred miles of the Antarctic coast and declaring the large mass to be a continent— were later contested by James Clark Ross. The British explorer had a chart of the American discoveries, which Wilkes had sent him, and reported having sailed right over the position of Wilkes's "pseudo-Antarctic continent."

Recent scholarship, however, has vindicated Wilkes. Two Australians, B.P. Lambert and Phillip G. Law, made detailed studies of the Antarctic coast and found a striking similarity between their calculations and those of Wilkes. To achieve a fit between the Wilkes chart and their own they simply shifted his features 116 miles to the south and 18 miles to the west. They pointed out that the errors in

This pencil sketch of the U.S.S. Peacock *"frozen in the ice," drawn by the ship's doctor Charles F. B. Guillou, was sent by Midshipman William Reynolds to his family after the disabled vessel returned to Sydney. "Heavens! What a hideous death we escaped!" Reynolds wrote. "It will give you of course, merely such an idea, as three inches of paper may be capable of conveying." Actually, Reynolds confided, Guillou was "the only one, who had exhibited visible signs of perturbation [during the crisis]—poor man, every one noticed his nervous anxiety—he was in every body's way & asking questions which had better not been breathed." Courtesy Anne Cleaver.*

navigation and observation were understandable given the instruments of the day and Antarctic conditions. The miracle, scholars have noted, is that Wilkes could have been as accurate as he was. Perspective is often distorted by dense clouds of snow that blow over the sea from the mountains of Antarctica and by the heavy fogs that mask the land. Furthermore, mirages are frequent, making distant objects appear near. The tricks played by Antarctic temperature inversions are now better understood. In such situations a layer of warmer air above that hugging the icy surface bends light rays

and causes a feature more than a hundred miles away to appear near at hand. This, the Australians believe, accounts for the large error in latitude in the Wilkes map.

Another dramatic moment occurred on 30 January 1840, when the *Porpoise* unexpectedly met two French vessels off the coast of Antarctica. The *Porpoise*, separated from the rest of the squadron, assumed they were the *Vincennes* and the *Peacock* but raised the American colors upon realizing the mistake. When the strangers raised the French colors, including the broad pennant of a commodore, the Americans recognized the vessels as the command of Dumont d'Urville. The *Porpoise* immediately changed course, hoping to intercept and communicate with the Frenchmen but broke off the attempt when it appeared they were trying to avoid a meeting. Unfortunately, the Americans had misinterpreted the French movements. Unduly sensitive about national honor and indignant at what each perceived to be the ill-mannered behavior of the other party, the French and American vessels went their separate ways.

The next major surveying task involved the Fiji Islands. There Wilkes investigated the murder in 1834 of ten crew members of an American ship by a Fiji leader named Vendovi, brother of the king of Rewa. To capture him, Lieutenant Hudson invited the king and his court on board the *Peacock* and then held them hostage until Vendovi surrendered, which he readily did the following day. Upon admitting his role in the murders, Vendovi was made prisoner and told he would be taken to America where, Midshipman Reynolds wrote his family, he would learn "that to kill a white man was the very worst thing a Fegee man could do." [1840b]

Shortly after Vendovi was captured, Fijians on the island of Malolo attacked a small surveying party that had gone ashore to purchase food. In the attack, two officers—Lieutenant Joseph Underwood and Midshipman Wilkes Henry, nephew of the commander—were killed. Learning of the incident, Wilkes organized a punitive assault in which the two principal towns on Malolo were destroyed and about eighty natives were killed. Wilkes buried the two slain officers on a secluded cay that he named Henry's Island; the island group, of which the cay was a part, he named after Underwood.

The Expedition remained in the Fiji Islands for three months. Despite the violence, the explorers were proud of the work done there. They corrected a number of errors on existing charts, and they made impressive additions to their growing collection of natural history specimens: Brackenridge estimated they had collected six hundred new plant species, while the corals obtained by Dana were to become the heart of the Smithsonian's coral collection, which is now among the finest in the world.

The explorers also learned firsthand about the existence of cannibalism, something about which they had heard many rumors but which they had generally discounted. The evidence was obtained by the *Peacock* during a visit to Naloa Bay in July 1840, when one of the natives in a group that came on board ship for a visit was seen eating the flesh from a cooked head. "Every one on the ship was affected with a nervous & terrible feeling of mingled horror & disgust," Reynolds recalled. [1840b] Disgusted though they may have been, the Scientifics purchased the head for their collections.

The next destination was the Sandwich or Hawaiian Islands, where the squadron enjoyed a much-needed holiday after their traumatic experiences in Fiji. The most dramatic event of the Expedition's stay in Hawaii was a scientific foray to the summit of Mauna Loa. Wilkes led a party of sixteen Expedition members and two hundred porters assembled on the authority of King Kamehameha III in an arduous nine-day trip to the summit. Interestingly, the ruins of the Expedition campsite on Mauna Loa are the only known physical remains of the U.S. Exploring Expedition in the Pacific.

Although Dana, the geologist, did not accompany Wilkes to the summit of Mauna Loa, he nonetheless made a major contribution to geology through his study of volcanoes during the Expedition. His work on Kilauea on the island of Hawaii was a principal scientific result of the Expedition, and his account of caldera formation was of great importance in the history of volcanology. Furthermore, Dana extended his ideas about volcanism to igneous processes in general. While Wilkes was engaged on Mauna Loa, the rest of the squadron was surveying various island groups in the area. The *Peacock* and the *Flying Fish*, for example, visited the Marshall and Drummond (Tabiteuea) islands, where they had a fight with natives who had killed one of the Expedition's sailors.

The squadron's next major rendezvous was to be the mouth of the Columbia River on the northwest coast of North America. Once again misfortune hampered the explorers, for the *Peacock* foundered while attempting to enter the Columbia. The crew survived, but the ship and its scientific collections were lost. Despite this setback, much was accomplished. It was here that the Expedition produced its most important map, titled "Mouth of the Columbia River, Oregon Territory, 1841." When linked to the map of the Rocky Mountains prepared the following year by Captain John C. Frémont, it enabled the United States to establish a geodetic baseline for the territory between the Mississippi River and the Pacific Ocean. After conducting extensive surveys in Oregon, Wilkes sent a party of explorers overland to California (then still part of Mexico) and took the rest of the squadron, which now included a merchant vessel named the *Oregon*—purchased in Astoria as a replacement for the *Peacock*—to San Francisco, where the entire party was once again united.

The return voyage was anticlimactic. En route, the explorers visited South Africa after the Philippines and Singapore, where Wilkes sold the *Flying Fish* because it was no longer seaworthy. The decision, though probably wise, caused considerable regret. One officer thought it deserved "a place in our National Museum—if we ever have one." [Stanton 1975: 274]

The final blow to the Expedition was the death of Vendovi, who had remained a prisoner aboard the *Vincennes* for almost two years. He survived the squadron's return to New York only by hours and died in a naval hospital. The resourceful Scientifics, although sorry to lose their living artifact, compensated by adding Vendovi's skull to their collections. A death mask was also made, which remained in the custody of the Department of the Navy until 1983, when it was transferred to the Smithsonian Institution.

Also anticlimactic was the reception the explorers received upon their return. Instead of a hero's welcome, they were met by a seemingly disinterested public, an unfriendly Congress, and doubts about their accomplishments in Antarctica. The Expedition's reputation was further tarnished by the series of courts-martial that occupied the naval officers the first weeks after their return. Most of the charges were trivial and produced more smoke than fire. Of a number of charges lodged against Wilkes by junior officers only one was upheld: he was found guilty in seventeen instances of exceeding the number of lashes commanding officers were authorized to inflict as punishment on wayward crewmen. For this, he was sentenced to a public reprimand. Mild though it was, the verdict greatly embarrassed the proud Wilkes, and it clouded the Expedition's enviable accomplishments.

Wilkes's association with the Expedition was not over, however. He was eventually placed in charge of the collections that had been acquired as well as the publications that were to document the scientific findings. He personally prepared the five-volume *Narrative of the United States Exploring Expedition*, two scientific volumes on meteorology and hydrography, and a two-volume atlas of charts. In 1848, he received the Founder's Medal of the Royal Geographical Society of London in recognition of the "zeal and intelligence with which he carried out the scientific exploring expedition intrusted to him . . . and for the volumes which he has published, detailing the narrative of that expedition."

The award was not without justification. Although Wilkes was not a profound physicist or mathematician, even by the standards of his day, his claim to the mantle of Expedition physicist is legitimate. Even though volume 24, "Physics," containing his observations of the earth's magnetic field and gravity, was not published as planned, his records were eventually recovered and studied. His magnetic data proved to be a real contribution to our knowledge of the changes with time of the earth's magnetism. His *Theory of the Winds* (1856) is less praiseworthy, however. Although his meteorological observations are excellent, his theories and explanations are generally unsound. The valuable part of this book is the "Sailing Directions" for a voyage around the world.

As will be seen in the chapters that follow, the United States was ill-equipped to receive the collections from the Exploring Expedition, and a good deal of material was lost before they came under systematic control. Almost fifteen years were consumed before their ultimate destination was determined. In 1857 the collections were finally given to the Smithsonian Institution. Wilkes and the Scien-

The author wishes to thank Daniel E. Appleman, Ann J. Brickfield, and Philip K. Lundeberg for special assistance in preparing this chapter.

This drawing by Charles Wilkes of the Vincennes *anchored near an "ice island" in Antarctica is one of the few depicting the seamen of the Exploring Expedition. The dog is "Sydney," a pet Wilkes obtained while in Australia.* Narrative.

tifics, meanwhile, had been hard at work preparing the official reports that were based on them. It was a prodigious task, because the explorers had brought back massive collections. Despite the wreck of the *Peacock,* which cost the Expedition most of its entomology collection as well as some of the material obtained in Hawaii, the trove contained more than four thousand zoological specimens including nearly two thousand new species. Of these, birds accounted for more than eleven hundred specimens and more than five hundred species. The plant specimens numbered more than fifty thousand and included some ten thousand different species. The thousands of ethnographic artifacts made up one of the most important systematic collections in the United States from the Pacific islands and the west coast of North America. Add to this the remarkable gems, fossils, and corals the explorers obtained and

the totals begin to boggle the imagination.

Therefore, the Expedition's most remarkable achievement may well be the nineteen volumes of reports and atlases published by the Scientifics, Wilkes, and their collaborators. These stand as a landmark in the emergence of the United States into international science. Certainly, scientific publication on this scale had never before been attempted in this country, while the scientific publications of European voyages—those of Cook and Dumont d'Urville, for example—were models of elegance that the young Republic sought to emulate. Although bureaucratic obstruction and congressional misunderstanding precluded publication of some of the planned volumes and limited those that were printed to an official pressrun of only one hundred copies—to make them even more important—the reports were the grandest production yet to come out of America. In spite of limited distribution, they had international impact.

Much of the credit for these publications must go to Charles Wilkes, who devoted most of his remaining life to superintending their preparation. Only during the Civil War was his attention diverted from them, yet it is for that diversion that he is best remembered. While in command of the U.S.S. *San Jacinto* he halted the British mail steamer *Trent* in international waters and took Confederate commissioners Mason and Slidell into custody. Wilkes became a Union hero, but Lincoln's government had to disapprove his action because of British protests. Wilkes did not care. As he explained to his wife shortly after the incident, "My conscience tells me I have done right and I fear nothing." [Wilkes 1861] This statement is Wilkes at his best, and it is probably the most fitting epitaph to his stormy career.

Although at Wilkes's death in 1877 the *New York Times* mentioned only his role in the *Trent* affair, James Dwight Dana had accorded him the accolade he deserved. "Wilkes," he wrote in 1846, "although overbearing and conceited, exhibited through the whole cruise a wonderful degree of energy and was bold even to rashness in exploration. . . . [and] I much doubt if, with any other commander that could have been selected, we should have fared better or lived together more harmoniously, and I am confident that the Navy does not contain a more daring or driving officer."

Wilkes and his colleagues merited more recognition from their contemporaries, for there is no question that the Expedition was a logistical and scientific triumph, a key success in the peacetime history of the U.S. Navy. Not only did it contribute to the development of the naval sciences, notably navigation, cartography, and hydrography, but it also demonstrated to European observers that the young Republic could mount and sustain a major scientific expedition overseas. It served as the model for some fourteen subsequent naval exploring expeditions before the Civil War. It also served as a floating naval academy for the midshipmen and young officers, many of whom went on to distinguished naval careers. At least eight became admirals, including Reynolds, Augustus L. Case, Thomas Tingey Craven, and Cadwalader Ringgold. Hudson, one of the U.S. Navy's premier seamen, commanded the steamer *Niagara* in laying the first transAtlantic cable; Reynolds ended his career in 1877 as commander of the Asiatic Squadron; Case concluded his long career as chief of the Bureau of Ordnance during the Grant administration; Craven became a rear admiral in 1866 and assumed command of the North Pacific Squadron; Ringgold, who commanded the *Porpoise* during the Expedition, went on to command the North Pacific Exploring Expedition, consisting of five vessels, among them the *Porpoise* and the *Vincennes*. During that expedition, the *Porpoise* was lost with all hands during a typhoon in Taiwan Strait. The *Vincennes* remained in commission until 1867 when, no match for the ironclads spawned by the Civil War, she was sold at auction in Boston for $8,600.

The accomplishments of Wilkes and his fellow explorers, though obscure today, were so important to the development of American science and so important to the history of the Smithsonian Institution, it seemed appropriate to put the best of the Exploring Expedition's scientific legacy on display in a commemorative exhibition honoring the seventy-fifth anniversary of the Natural History Building, which opened in 1910. In doing so, the Smithsonian honors not only the National Museum of Natural History, but also that band of brave young men who set sail with Wilkes from Hampton Roads in 1838.

2 Expedition Botany: The Making of a New Profession

By far the biggest collection acquired by the U.S. Exploring Expedition was its collection of pressed plants: explorers estimated they had gathered fifty thousand specimens of ten thousand kinds. These gatherings would grow to be our present national herbarium of more than four million specimens. But the Expedition's plants changed the course of science in ways not linked directly to their numbers. The Expedition launched our government's commitment to scientific work, and responsible officials had much to learn about its management. Hitherto, American science had been the purview of gentlemen—men of polite learning who had leisure for it. Problems encountered by the Expedition, especially in the writing up of findings, proved the need for trained specialists, and it was the Expedition's botany that proved it most emphatically.

Meant to bring the young Republic to its rightful intellectual place among the nations, the Expedition was the largest voyage of discovery undertaken anywhere, and the people of America had requested it. By 1825 nine petitions had been sent to Congress as a consequence of Captain John Symmes's lecturing about polar holes; Symmes had also won his most important convert, Jeremiah Reynolds, editor of an Ohio newspaper (no kin to William

Reynolds of the Expedition). In time Reynolds came to doubt the polar holes. He broke with Symmes but kept on lobbying for exploration on the grounds there might be open water at the poles, open water full of whales and seals and new discoveries like those of England's Captain James Cook. An exploring voyage by our own "hardy seamen, and scientific persons" would rival those the British had already made "and return light to them for light received." Reynolds exulted in a supporting resolution from Maryland's assembly, which bore the signature of Charles Carroll of Carrollton, sole surviving signer of the Declaration of Independence— "the only hand which death has not *palsied*, of the list of choice spirits, who pledged their lives, their fortunes, and their sacred honor, in favor of our invaded rights and liberties." [1827:62,67] As the voyage would declare our scientific independence, Reynolds's rhapsody was not off mark.

Plantsmen of the Expedition

When Reynolds finally won approval from both sides of Congress—after years of lobbying and an abortive expedition funded privately—it was understood the scientific corps would be all-American. Local societies suggested what fields to include, and interested individuals sent in names of those

Banyan tree, Upolu. Narrative.

The only known picture of Charles Pickering shows him in later years. It was published as the frontispiece to his exhaustive Chronological History of Plants. *Courtesy Library of the Academy of Natural Sciences of Philadelphia.*

thought suited to the Expedition's scientific work. The erudite Charles Pickering, capable, it seemed, of handling any branch of natural history, was highly recommended for the Expedition's zoological department. At one stage of planning he was called the Expedition's ichthyologist and herpetologist, at another, chief zoologist, but the title finally settled on was naturalist. Asa Gray was every knowing person's first choice as plantsman. Still in his twenties but already author of a botany text-book, he was the only native scientific gentleman with the credentials to be the Expedition's botanist: youth to stand the rigors of the voyage, knowledge enough to make a scientific study of the Expedition's plants, access to the specialists of Europe and their reference collections. Jeremiah Reynolds, who had lobbied with the expectation he would be the Expedition's chronicler, was destined to be left

behind. Pickering was to become as much a bota-nist as a zoologist. Gray was destined to sign on, sign off, and then sign on again as author when the man who took his place could not write up results.

Charles Pickering's scientific ardor had an early beginning. Born in Pennsylvania in 1805, he grew up in Wenham, Massachusetts, with his widowed mother and paternal grandfather, Colonel Timothy Pickering of Revolutionary fame. It was during boyhood rambles in the Massachusetts countryside that he got his love for natural history, and he sus-tained it in young manhood by exploring New Hampshire's White Mountains, where a peak now bears the family name. Attending Harvard, Picker-ing took a medical degree, as did many another naturalist before science offered ways to make a living. He then set up practice in Philadelphia and spent free time at the Academy of Natural Sciences, studying its books and specimens, serving as its librarian and later as its curator.

Asa Gray was from a farming community near Utica, New York. Like Pickering, he took a medical degree, but found he liked plants more than pills and plasters and resolved to make his living as a botanist. Though botany was not yet a paid calling in this country, he reasoned that a job might be created for him if he were to build a reputation by research and writing and by trading specimens with influential plantsmen. Accordingly, he lived fru-gally, supporting himself off and on with jobs that furthered or left time for his botanical work, in-cluding a stint as assistant and botanical apprentice to John Torrey. (Torrey, a botanist who lived by teaching chemistry, would, like Gray, figure in the compilation of the Expedition's publications.) Born in 1810, Gray was about four years older than his friend and fellow Expedition "scientific" James Dwight Dana, and the two were much alike in their abilities and zeal for science. Both had written books by the time the Expedition sailed.

Accepting Gray's application for the Expedition's botanical department, Secretary of the Navy Mah-lon Dickerson chose a second plantsman to accom-pany him. William Rich, born in 1800, was a week-end plant collector who had, with others, made a list of plants growing in the District of Columbia. His weekday work was clerking in the army pay-

nist who had served in Congress. Darlington then wrote to Dickerson with much the same argument that Torrey had advanced. Convinced, the secretary made Rich Gray's assistant. Rich apparently had no pretensions, as his note of acceptance thanked the secretary for the secondary job.

So things stood until the planning, mired in squabbles and delays, passed by presidential order to Secretary of War Joel Poinsett and to Charles Wilkes, Poinsett's choice as Expedition leader. Unhappy with an overlarge civilian corps—and there were others who agreed with him—Wilkes struck many from the list. Jeremiah Reynolds was off the list already for publicly denouncing the navy secretary's dawdling, and Wilkes was not about to put him on again. Rich was stricken from the list but went back on three weeks before the ships set sail when Gray learned his ambition had been realized:

Asa Gray in mid-life. Charcoal on paper by Garnet W. Jex. Courtesy National Portrait Gallery, Smithsonian Institution.

master's office; this paid enough for Rich, a lifelong bachelor, to live comfortably and raise plants for Washington's garden shows, of which he was the major organizer. The horticultural experience and local plant collecting fitted him, the secretary thought, to be an Expedition botanist.

American understanding of science was so rudimentary in 1836 that Secretary Dickerson first had in mind to hire Rich and Gray in parallel positions. On learning that an unknown hobbyist was deemed the equal of his protégé, Torrey wrote to Dickerson suggesting that responsibilities be split, that a plantsman experienced in research and writing be put in charge and that a plantsman with a gardening background be made assistant botanist. Gray and Torrey both appealed to William Darlington of West Chester, Pennsylvania, a respected spare-time bota-

New York botanist John Torrey about 1860. Courtesy National Portrait Gallery, Smithsonian Institution.

Wilkesia, a discovery named for the commander. Multiple labels on these Expedition specimens result from their continuing use in botanical research. Courtesy National Museum of Natural History, Smithsonian Institution.

America's first professorship of botany was being offered to him. Though Rich was hesitant to be chief botanist, Gray, eager to resign as gracefully as possible, persuaded him that he could do the job with Pickering's aid and that of an assistant. Gray then urged Poinsett to hire another plantsman charged with helping Rich and with the care and transport of live plants. The man he recommended, Scotch-born William D. Brackenridge, twenty-eight, had worked at gardening and landscaping in Europe and for about a year had been a Philadelphia nurseryman. Perhaps because Poinsett himself had botanical interests—he had introduced the poinsettia to gardens of America and Europe—he agreed to the addition. Brackenridge was not "home-grown" like other members of the scientific corps, but that was not seen as a problem because it was not thought he would take part in publishing results.

In short order, Brackenridge proved himself more than just a gardener. Pickering recorded at Madeira, the Expedition's first collecting site, that without Brackenridge's "keen eye, varied knowledge, . . . energy and endurance, our collections would have been but slender." By April 1839 Wilkes had raised Brackenridge's salary a third, and by the Expedition's end he was known not only as the horticulturist, the title that he started with, but as assistant botanist.

Wilkesia gymnoxiphium, *photographed on Kauai by Charles Lamoureux, University of Hawaii.*

Plant Collecting Prior to Fiji

The Expedition plantsmen took specimens at every stop, but some stops were too brief for adequate collecting and others were at sites already visited by able collectors. Peru was different. Climbing in the Andes, where plants had been collected rarely if at all, the explorers found new kinds in greater number than at any of their earlier sites. The names later given to the novelties sometimes show who the collector was: *Astragalus brackenridgei, Malvastrum richii, Draba pickeringii, Lupinus pickeringii, Oxalis pickeringii.* As Gray had predicted, Pickering was as much a plant collector as the official plantsmen, Rich and Brackenridge, and his

journal was to be the Expedition's premier document on plants.

The Expedition's hazards were almost everywhere as great for scientists as sailors. At Cape Horn, storms had been the biggest threat. In the Andes there were highwaymen. And in the South Sea islands there were hostile natives. The ships carried trade goods, gifts, and orders to make friends wherever possible, but some islanders did not care for friendship. Residents of Disappointment Minor (Tepoto) put a stop to plant collecting by forcibly escorting the collectors into the surf. So roughly did they drag Pickering over coral that he suffered cuts and lost his glasses. Joseph Couthouy rescued Brackenridge, a poor swimmer, with a life preserver, and Brackenridge wrote proudly in his journal that he got away with both hands full of plants. Nothing is known of Rich's adventures in the islands, as he was on a different ship from Pickering and Brackenridge and seems to have maintained no journal.

Island natives were more often friendly—sometimes even helpful. The Samoan collections included a new kind of tree belonging to the English ivy family, and Pickering recorded that "the forest-king from Interior Savaii" had brought it to him. Eventually it got the name *Reynoldsia* to honor Jeremiah Reynolds "for the unflagging zeal with which he urged upon our Government the project of the South Sea Surveying Expedition. . . ." [Gray 1854:724] Restudying this material a century later, botanists found the forest-king had actually brought branches from two species of *Reynoldsia*, one of them still known only from that first collection. Pickering had a good eye: months afterward, he came upon a like tree growing in the Hawaiian Islands and saw that it was congeneric with the forest-king's collection. Still other species of *Reynoldsia* are recognized today, each by virtue of its name a living tribute to a man who started U.S. science on its way but left posterity no picture of himself. A botanical discovery named for Reynolds is as close as we have come to Edgar Allan Poe's prediction that posterity would give the entire Expedition Reynolds's name.

While the Expedition's scientific men collected in Australia, its sailing men tried a second time to push farther south than anyone had gone. This

This detail from a crumbling oil painting owned by Helen Madine, collateral descendant of plant collector William Rich, is thought to be the only surviving likeness of Rich.

New Finds from Fiji and Beyond

Fiji, heretofore poorly charted and collected, was for three months an area of hard work and accomplishment for the surveyors and of discovery for plant collectors. When Gray rejoined the Expedition in its publication phase, he found among its Fijian plants new ones to name for its artists, *Agatea* and *Draytonia*, and for three of its scientific gentlemen: *Brackenridgea, Couthovia, Richella.* (Someone had already honored Pickering with a *Pickeringia*.) Pickering and Brackenridge, forewarned by signs from native guides that touching would cause blisters, used sticks to break a branch and take the first specimens of *Semecarpus vitiensis*, an even more poisonous relative of poison ivy. Again, we know little of Rich's adventures because he left no journal. Presumably, he sent letters to his relatives, as others on the Expedition did, but no such letters have turned up. There is an appraisal of the work of all three plantsmen in a letter Dana wrote to Gray from Fiji: "Dr. Pickering is heart and head in the botanical line, but he often wishes you were here, and speaks of your lost opportunities. . . . Rich has done so-so. . . . Brackenridge in the botanical department, is invaluable." [Gilman 1899: 118–23]

Of all the places visited, only the Hawaiian Islands matched Fiji for botanical discoveries. It was on Kauai that the plantsmen found a most distinctive plant, one that Gray eventually would name for their commander. *Wilkesia*—"iliau" to the Hawaiians—is native only to Kauai's west side, where the state now has a nature path to show it while encouraging protection. It looks much like a yucca on a yard-high pole, but in June the leaf cluster sends up a sticky stalk of blossoms that are nothing like a yucca's. Structure and arrangement of the flowers show the plant to be a member of the tarweed subgroup of the large group botanists call composites (Compositae or Asteraceae, the family of asters, sunflowers, and their kin).

Carl Linnaeus, the eighteenth-century naturalist who gave biology the Latin naming system still in use, liked a plant name that honored someone who had a trait or two in common with the plant. How Linnaeus would have loved *Wilkesia*'s connections

time they had company. Under the command of J. S. C. Dumont d'Urville, *L'Astrolabe* and *La Zélée* were also sailing south with the same goal. Frenchmen and Americans alike suffered and discovered, but the next Antarctic summer brought a British voyage of discovery to outdo them both. These deeds are of botanical interest only in that all three expeditions anchored at the Auckland Islands, where all three gathered plants. (Surgeon Silas Holmes of the *Porpoise* gathered plants for Rich.) The French came one day after the Americans weighed anchor, and the *Erebus* and *Terror* came eight months later. Among the plants that all discovered was a handsome one with round, fleshy, foot-wide leaves and umbrella-like blossoms big as a man's head. Its Latin designation, written out in full formality—*Stilbocarpa polaris* (Hombron et Jacquinot ex J. D. Hooker) A. Gray—shows botanists from three lands had a hand in naming it.

William Brackenridge before the voyage. Courtesy Smithsonian Institution Archives.

with its namesake. Does not its stickiness suggest Wilkes's tenacity? To those who worked with Wilkes, his doggedness was sometimes dazzling. It seemed to Expedition armorer William Briscoe that "a more persevering man never lived." "The more I see of him the more I am impressed with his indomitable perseverance & tenacity," Lieutenant Henry Eld wrote to his father, "like a cork he cannot be sunk." [Tyler 1968:211, 397] And is it not appropriate that *Wilkesia* is a composite? Wilkes was himself a composite, a mixture of Never Say Die and Never at Fault. Admiral J. D. H. Kane's introduction to Wilkes's autobiography summarizes his achievements but does not hide his blunt, opinionated, and self-righteous side. Dana's attempt to give a balanced view of Wilkes's mixed traits may be the one most often quoted. Writing to Gray in 1846, he remarked on the Expedition leader's skill at charting, his conceit, his daring, and his drive. Though no naval officer could have led the Expedi-

tion better, Dana thought, "He failed in never praising his officers but always finding fault with them—and often very unjustly; especially when he had prejudices the screws came down rather severely."

As the Expedition's designated plantsmen, Rich and Brackenridge went with the horseback trip from Fort Nisqually south to San Francisco. Rich sickened as they neared the California border and likely was still ailing when they reached Mount Shasta, as he does not figure in accounts of *Darlingtonia*'s discovery. It was Brackenridge who spied the previously unknown pitcher plant, and he seems always to have prized it as the Expedition's best botanical discovery. When John Torrey took the job of working up the Expedition's North American plants, he named this one for William Darlington, who was then the dean of U.S. botanists. The name was fitting for an Expedition plant because Darlington had given counsel to the Expedition's planners. Viewed today the name is apt because the Expedition marked the line between the older breed of botanist and the full-time specialist. Darlington was foremost of the botanists whose living came from such pursuits as banking, doctoring, or serving as a congressman: he did all of these. Late in life he saw botany becoming a profession and was proud to help the change occur. He was proud, too, of his pitcher plant: the stone on his grave bears the carved outline of a *Darlingtonia*.

Darlingtonia californica, sole species of its genus, is the only Expedition plant with an illustrated publication all its own. The newly founded Smithsonian Institution published Torrey's treatment in one of the early volumes in its series *Contributions to Knowledge*. Called at times the cobra lily because its leaves look like spreading cobras, the plant is now known to be an "insect eater." A secretion from the leaf's upper part attracts the insects, which fall into a pool within the tubular lower part, where they rot and thereby give up nutrients to the plant. *Darlingtonia* grows naturally only in limited areas of Oregon and California. Like *Wilkesia*, it rates a nature trail—Darlingtonia Wayside in Oregon's Honeyman State Park—for viewing and protection.

Collecting did not cease along the homeward route from California, even though the stops were brief. During their few days in the Philippines, the

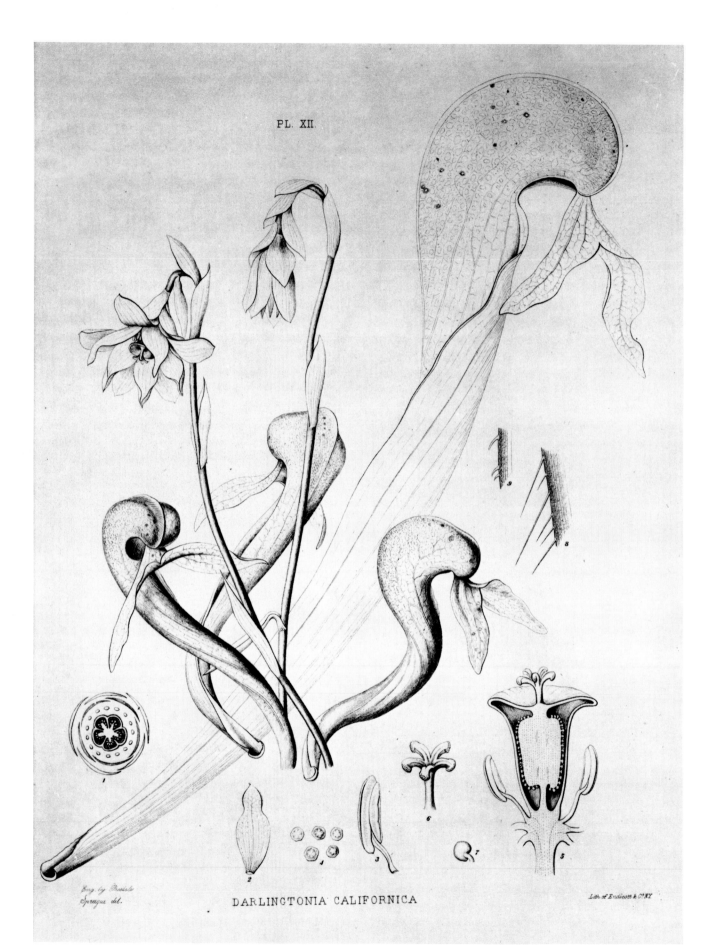

Drg by Bessie
Sprague del.

DARLINGTONIA CALIFORNICA

Lith. of Endicott & Co. NY

Leaf of Darlingtonia californica, *the cobra lily.*

Left, collected in October, Brackenridge's Darlingtonia *specimen lacked flowers. Not until 1854, after it was found in flower by a later collector, did Torrey publish his formal treatment of the new pitcher plant in* Smithsonian Contributions to Knowledge. *Courtesy Smithsonian Institution Libraries.*

plantsmen made the first collections ever of the jade-vine (*Strongylodon macrobotrys*, a member of the legume family). With its long festoons of pale green flowers it is arguably the loveliest plant discovered by the Expedition. And as things turned out, the plantsmen would have had no living plants to show the public had it not been for their work along the homeward stretch.

The Patent Office and the Garden

Tons of collections came back early, having been consigned to ships the squadron met in ports along the way. When the voyage ended, these collections were in Washington under the care of the National Institute, a short-lived but historically important society set up by Joel Poinsett and other notables to start a national museum. By agreement with the government the Institute was housing specimens— those of the Exploring Expedition and some from other sources—in the Great Hall of the U.S. Patent Office. In time, its members hoped, Congress would give James Smithson's bequest to the National Institute to support its growth. Some of the members were influential officeholders, but Wilkes had found a champion in Ohio Senator Benjamin Tappan, and the law relating to the Expedition's collections and publications put them under Congress's Joint Committee on the Library, of which Tappan was the chairman.

The Library Committee made Tappan its agent, and he arranged with the secretary of the navy to keep Pickering as superintendent of collections and of the publication work. By the first days of 1843 Pickering had called back the other members of the scientific corps. Brackenridge, like Pickering, was hired early, as his care was needed for the Expedition's living plants. There were 254 of them at first, and plant-loving citizens, on learning of the government's collection, added more. A greenhouse was built next to the Patent Office before cold weather came. It had to be enlarged as the collections grew, and in 1850, when a wing was added, the plants were moved to newly built conservatories near the Capitol. A later building program put the U.S. Botanic Garden, direct descendant of the Expedition's live collections, on its present site beside the Grant Memorial.

For shipping live plants, tightly glazed Wardian cases, or, as Wilkes called them, Loddiges cases, served the Expedition well. (The Loddiges firm had proved the worth of Ward's invention only four years or so before the Expedition sailed.) Owing to theft and other losses, however, the only Expedition plants in Brackenridge's garden were those he brought himself from stops along the home stretch.

One of two exceptions was a handsome red gloxinia grown from tubers that he sent from Rio. The other was a Norfolk Island "pine" added to the garden some years later. The only survivor of several boxed in Sydney and shipped from New Zealand, the tree was stolen and sold, then given back to Wilkes when the buyer learned its history. Grown to fifteen feet by the time it was recovered, it made a fine display in the government's botanic garden. Today the U.S. Botanic Garden has just one specimen, an old cycad (*Encephalartos horridus*), that seems to be a living relic of the Wilkes Expedition. Wilkes's *Narrative* says it was collected in Capetown, and the garden's earliest catalog explains it was a source of food—Kaffir bread—for Bushmen.

Beginning the Reports

Acting for the Library Committee, Pickering asked members of the scientific corps to estimate the size of the projected publications. Rich judged new species would fill five hundred octavo pages and one hundred plates; treating all the Expedition's plants would require a second volume of like size. Descriptions of new species should be done by the next session of Congress. In April Pickering wrote Tappan that Rich was hard at work and making progress. Pickering had a volume of his own to write on human races, but he had not seen them all, so he resigned temporarily and paid his own way to Africa and India.

Tappan now put Wilkes in charge of specimens and publications; his aide for bringing out reports would be Expedition artist Joseph Drayton. The good effects of Wilkes's management last to this day. He kept the collections together until the Smithsonian provided a hall for them and funds from Congress for their transport and care. But for his tenacity and drive the Expedition's publications would be few or none. He sustained congressional and public interest by the swift completion of his *Narrative*—all five volumes finished by the end of

Identified as pine trees in the Narrative, *these giants near Astoria are really Sitka spruce or Douglas fir.*

1844. And would anyone but Wilkes have persevered with publishing through three frustrating decades?

On the other hand, Wilkes as manager meant broils with other authors. The broils helped bring on science as we know it and bettered governmental understanding of our work, but they were no joy for those involved. It was a mark of nascent professionalization that authors balked at having someone from outside their disciplines dictate typography and editorial style. There was more than style involved, however. Wilkes and Tappan laid down rules that made good taxonomy impossible. The work was to be done in Washington, and only species gathered on the Expedition were to be treated in the Expedition's publications. Dana broke both rules successfully (not without contention), but William Rich had neither Dana's standing nor his understanding.

Problems in the Plant Department

That anyone would think the Expedition's plants could be examined, described, and the results published, without a reference collection, now almost defies belief. (Brackenridge eventually would do the ferns in Washington; however, he had just one group to worry about, and he got help by mail from Gray and Torrey.) But Wilkes was not alone in his expectation. Before the voyage, Gray had persuaded others Rich could do the job. And such was the state of plant science in America that Charles Pickering, a naturalist of awesome scope, thought Rich could do it just with books.

Washington had no scientific library of any consequence, for that matter, but Rich's work seemed to progress without one. Late in 1844 Wilkes asked for a report and Rich replied: "The Philippine and East Indian plants have been examined with the exception of three or four families . . . and more than one thousand specimens examined and over four hundred species described including several new genera." He went on to say more than three hundred species had been identified among the Fijian collections "and a great many new genera, which have been described and the drawings completed." Early in 1845 Wilkes told Congress the Expedition's botanical report, by Mr. Rich, would fill two volumes of text and two of plates. By May's end, however, Wilkes knew something was wrong. He wrote Tappan that he planned to split the work, and Rich would have to go along with it or be dismissed. Wilkes now saw he would need outside specialists—botanists who had not been on the voyage—for the algae, fungi, and the mosses, but the other work was still to be done by the explorers. Rich was to continue with the Fijian and East Indian plants. Pickering was to do the North American flowering plants (a fleeting expectation, as he had other Expedition volumes to attend to). Brackenridge would do the ferns and fern allies. Whoever finished first would take another share.

With the work divided, Wilkes did not now doubt that Rich's part would move along. In June 1846 Senator James A. Pearce, who had replaced Tappan as the Library Committee's agent, informed the Senate Rich's first volume would be ready for the press in a week or two. Six months later Wilkes told Pearce that Rich had resigned after finishing his share. The manuscript was at Georgetown College, Wilkes said, where one of the Jesuits was adding the Latin part. After that, the work would be ready for the press. The war with Mexico was on, and Rich was on his way to California as an army paymaster. He had run and Wilkes did not yet know it.

Hearing of Rich's departure, John Torrey rightly guessed that he had failed and wrongly guessed that he had been eased from the job. To his good friend Joseph Henry, who had moved to Washington to become the first secretary of the Smithsonian Institution, Torrey confided that he too hoped to move to Washington—to take charge of the Expedition's botanical department—but Henry told him Wilkes viewed the botany as "all arranged." A month or two later, Wilkes knew better. He had seen Rich's work and it was "not in any way worthy of the Expedition." It took another fortnight for Wilkes to comprehend the full extent of Rich's "consummate

Protea cynaroides, *the king protea, South Africa. Watercolor by A. Agate. Courtesy Archives, Gray Herbarium Library, Harvard University.*

Protea cynaroides.

Vanda *orchid, perhaps a garden specimen. Watercolor by
A. Agate. Courtesy Archives, Gray Herbarium Library,
Harvard University.*

*During their six weeks in New Zealand, the explorers
collected five kinds of* Metrosideros *(ironweed).
Watercolor by A. Agate. Courtesy Archives, Gray
Herbarium Library, Harvard University.*

impudence." Rich had "sought distant service to
avoid the exposé," and the descriptions would have
to be made "de novo." [1847] Wilkes approached
Torrey with the job, but Torrey told him he could
not treat tropical plants without taking them to
Europe where the reference collections were. Wilkes
would not agree to that, so Torrey started work on
just the plants from Oregon and California. After
trying several other U.S. plantsmen, all of whom
declined to take on foreign plants without comparison collections, Wilkes had to turn to Gray. Gray
said the plants should go to Europeans having special knowledge of the various groups. That was
the last thing Wilkes wanted: to go to foreigners
with what was to have been our scientific Declaration of Independence. He pressed Gray, who eventu-

ally decided he could do it. He could do it, that is,
if Wilkes would meet certain conditions, and Gray
was now in a position to make the strong-willed
Wilkes agree to those conditions. With a five-year
contract and expenses paid, Gray took the plants
abroad to be worked on at the big botanical centers.

Gray's decision was historic. Our best botanist
was moving up, so to speak, from a focus on American plants to an interest in the world's plants. After
he had worked successfully with plants from this
Expedition, Gray took on plants from later exploring expeditions. His broadened view of distribution
and dispersal readied him for Darwin and made
him evolution's most prestigious spokesman on
this side of the Atlantic.

Botany's growing pains did not end when Gray

Maniltoa grandiflora, *Fiji's thimbithimbi tree. Watercolor by A. Agate. Courtesy Archives, Gray Herbarium Library, Harvard University.*

Embothrium coccineum, *the Chilean fire tree, Tierra del Fuego. Watercolor by A. Agate. Courtesy Archives, Gray Herbarium Library, Harvard University.*

rejoined the Expedition. Further conflict in the publication program was the means of educating not just Wilkes but the congressmen to whom Wilkes answered and to whom he had to go for funds. The biggest fight was over how and whether to use Latin in a work on plants. A battle over Latin might seem a tempest in a teapot, but it was in fact a milestone in emerging professionalization. Then, as now, English-speaking botanists commonly wrote descriptions of new species in terse Latin phrases and followed with a discussion of important traits in ordinary English sentences. Wilkes said he would take Gray's Latin only with a word-for-word translation, because the Expedition was a patriotic enterprise and its reports were "for the people and not for any class of scientific

men. . . ." [1861] Gray had offered to publish entirely in English if necessary, but he would not publish a three-way treatment—Latin phrases plus translated phrases plus discussions—as the redundancy would make his work ridiculous to other botanists. He would not have his name on work that we would now call unprofessional. The battle lasted several months, Wilkes held up Gray's pay, and other researchers rallied to Gray's side. Wilkes informed Torrey he would suppress the publication rather than give in to "anti-American notions." Botany was not one of his major interests, he said, so he cared little whether the report came out or not. Of course he cared. He had confessed to Congress that he paid four years wages for a worthless work on plants. How could he not want to see the job done right? The standoff ended when Smithsonian Secretary Joseph Henry volunteered his services and arranged a face-saving way for Wilkes to yield. Henry was a physicist, but he understood the stake that all researchers had in a broil over a botanist's way of working.

The hardbitten naval officer not only yielded; in time he took a broader view. When the battle over the use of Latin opened, he had written Tappan of the "whims and caprices of the gentlemen of science," of the "follies & conceits of those who confine themselves to one branch of science." Four years later, when Tappan's successor proposed to abandon or abridge the works of Wilkes's specialists, Wilkes came to their defense, explaining that it takes a person well informed in any branch of science to determine what is new and worth publishing. "I am not prepared to take the responsibility," he declared, "of curtailing what others have written better informed than I am." [Haskell 1968:13] He meant it. He gave the job to Drayton to avoid taking part in a curtailment and resumed work (after Drayton died a few months later) only with the understanding there would be none.

Aftermath and Consequences

From the Expedition grew the comparison collection the Expedition's plantsmen had lacked. Increased by later federal expeditions, by research activities of botanists, and by exchange with other institutions, the U.S. National Herbarium has roughly 4.1 million specimens today. They occupy some thirty-five hundred cases in the National Museum of Natural History's west wing, where the more than fifty employees (including nineteen botanists with doctorates) of the Museum's Department of Botany are charged with caring for them. Smithsonian botanists not only use these specimens—the Expedition's plants and others that have since been added—in their own investigations, but through loans and visits by scholars they make the plants available to outside curators and botany professors.

That first American professorship of botany, the professorship that took Gray from the Expedition on the eve of its departure, was not a lasting one. The University of Michigan—then just forming—fell on hard times and had to let him go. But the job turned out to be a stepping stone. Harvard established a professorship for him in 1842, and that one lasted through his life. With Harvard as his base, Gray researched and wrote prodigiously, never losing his preeminence in botany. He was a founding member, in 1863, of the National Academy of Sciences and president, in 1872, of the American Association for the Advancement of Science. It was his knowledgeable support of Darwin, more than anything else, that won American acceptance of descent with modification. By 1888, the year Gray died, botany had become a profession in this country—men and women trained for it, earned a living at it, organized for its advancement—and it had become one largely through Gray's leadership.

The energetic Brackenridge wrote the Expedition's fern report (volume 16) while running its botanic garden and, in 1851 and 1852, while carrying yet another set of duties. The Mall and other public grounds of Washington were being redesigned by Andrew Jackson Downing, the noted landscape architect of Newburgh, New York. Downing came down only once a month to oversee the work; so Brackenridge was charged with many of the day-to-day responsibilities. Explaining to Torrey, with whom he had acquired deep friendship, that a Scotchman needs his independence, Brackenridge moved his family to Baltimore in 1855 and started a successful nursery business of his own. Though he never wrote another book, he was for years the gardening editor of *American Farmer* and died (in 1893) an honored member of the horticultural community.

Less is known of Pickering in later life. He moved to Boston, worked again as a physician, married, had no children, died in 1878. His *Races of Man and Their Geographical Distribution*, volume 9 in the Expedition's reports, was published in 1848. Addressing as it did a major question of the day— did the peoples of the world have one origin or more than one?—it was an important work, reprinted several times before the Darwinian revolution made the question obsolete. On the other hand, Pickering's slender *Geographical Distribution of Animals and Plants* (volume 15 of the Expedition's reports, published 1854) proved to be of little interest. It does not deal as much with distribution as with evidence for human influence on distribution, especially evidence from ancient sources. Fourteen of its 128 pages tell readers how Egyptians kept track of time. Throughout, the work shows Pickering's deep learning, but it is more a compilation from his store of facts than a report of Expedition findings. That report—actually lightly edited transcripts from his Expedition journal—are in the follow-up volume that he published privately in 1876 (as Part 2 of *Geographical Distribution*). This larger, later work was only lightly edited, no doubt, because he then was finishing a work of greater consequence. Writing *Chronological History of Plants: Man's Record of His Own Existence Illustrated through Their Names, Uses, and Companionship* filled his final sixteen years. Published posthumously by Pickering's widow, this master compilation still amazes. The text fills 1,072 large pages printed in small type; the indexes fill another 150; and the value of the information they contain is timeless. We turn to Pickering today to find a given plant in Homer or Herodotus or writings of Egyptian scribes. His master work would be his major monument were not his contributions to the national collections a more important one.

At war's end William Rich came home to Washington. He brought some dried plants from the West, but new collections did not win the friendship of established botanists. Scorned or ignored as a failure and a humbug, Rich dropped out of botany and vanished from the literature that botanists read. Details of his life before and after the Exploring Expedition came to light when research located a great-great-grandniece who still had his belongings.

After three years as a major in the army's paymaster service, Rich worked for a time as secretary to the American legation in Mexico, then lived quietly with his sister's family in Washington until his death in 1864. Dropping out of botany seems not to have troubled him, as he was also a shell enthusiast, and conchologists thought well of him and his collections. Indeed, Spencer Fullerton Baird, the Smithsonian's assistant secretary (later secretary), thought enough of them to buy them for the National Museum.

Heretofore, botanists have been severe in judging Rich's Expedition role. But the critical Wilkes, privy to Gray's last-minute encouragement of Rich, remarked in his memoirs only that Rich was a quiet gentleman ill-suited to the job. Documents indicate that Rich was not an outright fraud, that he really thought the government would print his manuscript. Looking back on Rich's failure now, we see it as part of botany's advance toward professionalization. Without the prestige gained while Rich filled in for him, Gray could not have countered Wilkes's monumental stubbornness. And Wilkes would have had no cause to let the botany be done in Europe, to give up deep-seated views about the nation's scientific independence, had he not been embarrassed and informed by Rich's failure. As things turned out, Gray got to do the treatment as it should be done. It pushed his interests into areas outside America, led him to take on plants from later expeditions, and made him receptive to the evolutionary view of life. Gray became, as his biographer A. Hunter Dupree put it, one of the generals in Darwin's army and the sole commander of the American sector. For things to happen as they did took not just the success of Gray's work but the embarrassment of Rich's.

GEORGE E. WATSON

3 Vertebrate Collections: Lost Opportunities

In July 1842, John James Audubon wrote a letter recommending nineteen-year-old Spencer F. Baird for a position "to assist in the arrangement [and] description of the species of natural history brought home by the Exploring Expedition and deposited in the National Institute for the purpose of being published and thereby rendered useful to the world of Science." [Dall 1915:79] Baird did not get the job at that time, but in 1850 he agreed to take on the task of preparing one of the reports on natural history specimens of the Expedition; and, in 1858, as head of the National Museum, he assumed stewardship of all the Exploring Expedition specimens when they were transferred to the Smithsonian Institution.

The mission of the U.S. Exploring Expedition was to collect data and specimens in support of navigation, commerce, diplomacy, and science. This charge was outlined in a letter to Lieutenant Charles Wilkes, dated 11 August 1838 and signed by James Kirke Paulding, then secretary of the navy,

One of the new discoveries of the Expedition was the many-colored fruit dove from Samoa, named Ptilinopus perousei *by Peale. His plate shows a male from Samoa (bottom figure) but the other two birds are a female and immature from Fiji that Peale was unaware belonged to a different subspecies. Cassin,* Mammalogy and Ornithology *atlas, plate 33. Courtesy Smithsonian Institution Libraries.*

although Wilkes in his autobiography said he drafted his own instructions. He reprinted Paulding's letter in his *Narrative.* The main stimulus for the round-the-world voyage that Congress authorized was the "important interests of our commerce embarked in the whale-fisheries, and other adventures in the great Southern Ocean." The purpose was to explore and survey "that sea" and "to determine the existence of all doubtful islands and shoals." The itinerary was to concentrate on the major whaling grounds in the Pacific Ocean and Antarctic seas. The "objects" of the Expedition were "to extend the empire of commerce and science; to diminish the hazards of the ocean, and to point out to future navigators a course by which they may avoid dangers and find safety. Although the primary object of the expedition is the promotion of the great interests of commerce and navigation, you will take all occasions, not incompatible with the great purposes of your undertaking, to extend the bounds of science, and promote the acquisition of knowledge."

The instructions gave no directions for "conducting the scientific researches," although they specifically did not "limit the members of the corps each to his own particular service." Wilkes was, however, to "adopt the most effectual measures to prepare and preserve all specimens of natural history that may be collected, and should any opportunities

Peale named the Society Islands pigeon from Tahiti Carpophaga wilkesii *in honor of the commander of the Expedition. Described on the basis of minor color differences, it is now considered identical with* Ducula aurorae, *a species from the Tuamotu Islands, which Peale also described. Cassin,* Mammalogy and Ornithology *atlas, plate 25. Courtesy Smithsonian Institution Libraries.*

Wilkes subsequently issued "general instructions relative to observations" in an at-sea directive 25 August 1838 to the officers and "scientific gentlemen." In addition to collecting meteorological and astronomical data, he asked that observations "of the sea, all phosphorescent lights, fishes, and all substances adhering to weeds, must not fail to claim attention, and specimens of them [should be] obtained. Fish caught must be preserved till opened in the presence of an officer, and their stomachs carefully examined, and if any thing is found, it must be taken care of. Things and animals that might in ordinary cases be deemed troublesome and useless, are not to be lost sight of, but are to be picked up for examination." [1:363–64]

The collections made during the Expedition were vast, and space aboard ship was limited. Whenever specimens could be shipped from a port of call, they were sent back from the field in installments, although not always aboard a U.S. warship. Some arrived in Philadelphia, where they were unpacked at the Peale Museum, and others came to Washington and were processed at the National Institute. Almost all were unpacked by persons other than those who had collected them.

The zoological specimens were not only the first major collections of exotic animals to come to the United States, but they were also of potential international scientific importance. Many, particularly those from islands in the Pacific Ocean, Australia, and the west coast of North America, were species totally unknown to science when the Expedition returned in 1842. Several developments, however, decreased the value and usefulness of the specimens. They were regarded as curiosities for public display as much as scientific specimens for description and publication, which was common museum practice in the first half of the nineteenth century. Preparation for exhibit by the National Institute, rudimentary labeling, careless data handling and recording, bungling and delay in publication, and the

occur for sending home by a vessel of war of the United States, copies of information, or duplicates of specimens, or any other material you may deem it important to preserve from the reach of future accident, you will avail yourself of the occasion." Furthermore, "before you reach the waters of the United States," Wilkes was "to require from every person under your command the surrender of all journals, memorandums, remarks, writings, drawings, sketches, paintings, as well as specimens of any kind, collected or prepared during your absence from the United States." [1:xxv–xxxi]

On Aurora or Makatea Island in the Tuamotus, the Expedition discovered a large, fat fruit pigeon "in great abundance in high woody districts amongst coral rocks." Cassin, Mammalogy and Ornithology *atlas, plate 24. Courtesy Smithsonian Institution Libraries.*

Oil self-portrait of Titian Ramsay Peale a few years before the U. S. Exploring Expedition sailed, painted "with a little help from his brother Rembrandt," according to notes on the frame. Courtesy Department Library Services, American Museum of Natural History.

restricted distribution and availability of the Expedition reports led to their being overlooked by many investigators. Truly our country lost many opportunities to make significant contributions to science.

The present condition of most of the bird and mammal specimens from the Exploring Expedition is woeful, even, or perhaps especially, the type specimens on which new species names were based. Some of the fish and reptiles have fared a little better, probably because they have not been subjected to so many bouts of preparation and have spent 140 years bathed in spirits; but some of them too are next to useless. Apparently the bird and mammal specimens were skinned and roughly prepared in the field; some must have been salted, others preserved in fluid. We have William Baird's testimony in a July 1841 letter to his brother, Spencer, that "the skins in the state sent in by the expedition look amazingly rough, but when mounted present a well finished appearance. I should very much like to tumble over and examine the rough skins but nothing is allowed to be touched." [Dall 1915:73–74] In keeping with the practice of the time, virtually all of the birds and mammals were mounted for display rather than prepared as study skins that could be more safely and conveniently stored. Although William Baird was impressed by the competence of the workers at the National Institute, Titian R. Peale, who collected most of the birds and mammals, was not pleased. To a Philadelphia ornithologist he unhappily reported that "one hundred and eighty specimens of birds which I collected are missing, including some new species." Peale was himself skilled at mounting animals, and, to another friend, he complained about the work of the taxidermists, "my two birds (male and female) made into one—the legs of one put on another body." [Poesch 1961:96]

The mounted specimens were on display at the U.S. Patent Office from the mid-1840s until 1858 when they were transferred to the Smithsonian Institution, where some were again put on exhibit. Beginning in the 1860s, after the reports had been published, parts of the vertebrate collections were dispersed. A small selection of birds, including some types, went to the Academy of Natural Sciences in Philadelphia as partial compensation to

John Cassin, who prepared the revised report on the birds and mammals. Later, under the Smithsonian's mandate for "the diffusion of knowledge," others were distributed to Harvard (again, including some types), the Chicago Academy of Sciences (where they were destroyed in the fire of 1871), Indiana University, and, even as late as 1962, the University of Florida. When the historic and scientific importance of the Exploring Expedition specimens was recognized by later Smithsonian scientists compiling catalogs of types, attempts were made to recover some important specimens. Those that came back from Indiana in 1919 were in wretched condition. But some of the specimens returned to government custody in 1943 from Georgetown University, which had received a small bird collection directly from Peale, apparently in gratitude for help with Latin names and descriptions, looked pristine. They had not previously been in the Smithsonian. Most of the Exploring Expedition specimens that remained in the Smithsonian have been removed from exhibit, dismounted, and installed in the study collections. Most, however, are faded, stained, and worn from long exposure on display.

The majority of the bird and mammal specimens (as well as the insects) were collected by Peale, who accompanied the Expedition as naturalist. A few bear labels with other collectors' names or, in the reports, are attributed to Wilkes, other naval officers, naturalist Charles Pickering, mineralogist James D. Dana, or the surgeons, John L. Fox and Silas Holmes, who were assigned to help the naturalists. Their contributions were later recognized when new taxa were named in their honor.

Peale, son of the artist and museum founder Charles Willson Peale, was born in Philadelphia in 1799 and was thirty-nine years old when the Expedition sailed. He had excellent credentials as a field naturalist and was a logical choice for the scientific corps. He had been a member of Major Stephen H. Long's expedition to the Rocky Mountains in 1819–20. He had spent four months in Florida with Philadelphia naturalist George Ord in 1817–18 and additional time there in 1824 collecting for ornithologist Charles Lucien Bonaparte, then based in Philadelphia. He had also collected for Bonaparte in northern South America in 1830–32. Peale

On the first leg of the Expedition crossing the Atlantic, the officers and crew were impressed with the enthusiasm and industry of the naturalists. Peale captured a migrating common wheatear, Oenanthe oenanthe, *that had landed, exhausted, on the* Peacock *off the Cape Verde Islands 19 October 1838. Courtesy Division of Birds, National Museum of Natural History, Smithsonian Institution.*

delighted in the out-of-doors and was able to take hardship. He also had a long association with museums, particularly in preserving, mounting, and cataloging specimens for his father. He had written a field manual on collecting for museums. He had been made a member of the Academy of Natural Sciences in 1817 (at the age of eighteen) and of the American Philosophical Society in 1833, and he held the position of professor of zoology and curator of the Peale Museum. Not only was he an all-around naturalist, but he was a very competent artist, a talent of great value for documenting specimen appearance in the days before photography.

Peale spent most of the Expedition aboard the *Peacock* under Lieutenant William L. Hudson, with whom he established cordial rapport, but after the *Peacock* was wrecked at the mouth of the Columbia in July 1841, he transferred for the remainder of the voyage to the *Vincennes* under the command of Wilkes.

It was naturally assumed that publication of the bird and mammal collection would be Peale's domain. He had locked horns with Wilkes several times during the Expedition, however, and only reluctantly did Wilkes finally agree to allow him to proceed. Furthermore, Wilkes, acting on behalf of the Library Committee, laid down certain ground

rules that Peale and other authors were to follow. The publications were to be monuments to American science, worked up by Americans in America, and they were to demonstrate the priority of American discoveries. Peale was also compelled to study the collection at the National Institute in Washington, a city without comparative collections and with few library resources in the 1840s. Peale's personal natural history library had been lost in the wreck of the *Peacock*, and he may not even have been able to consult regularly all the books he cited in his report. In fact, before 1846 no significant collections of exotic birds and mammals or comprehensive zoological library existed at any American institution. It would have been impossible for anyone in the United States in the early 1840s to identify and competently describe new taxa in a collection of 2,150 birds and 134 mammals from South America, the Pacific islands, Australia, Southeast Asia, and South Africa. Not only were collections and library resources yet to come, but, in contrast to Europe, there were no encyclopedists or systematists who had any experience with exotic species. Instead, American naturalists were interested primarily in life histories and distribution of American species, in the tradition of John James Audubon and Alexander Wilson. Wilkes's orders also confined Peale to describing only specimens new to science at the time of collection. Thus many of his potentially interesting observations on other species were lost to science. Peale provided names for many taxa that already had valid names; in fact, of the 129 taxa he described, only about one-third are valid today.

At the same time, personal tragedies were impeding Peale's work. He had been away from his family for four years on the Expedition, and within five years of his return his wife, a son, and a daughter died. He was disappointed in not being named curator of the Expedition collections and in being paid poorly to prepare his report and plates. Lastly, the Peale Museum in Philadelphia, of which he was still titular manager, failed to attract enough visitors to meet expenses, and in 1845 it was disposed of at a sheriff's sale to pay its debts. Nevertheless, Peale finished and handed in his report to Wilkes in June 1848, one of the early ones to be completed in the scientific series.

All this made little difference to Wilkes, who was unhappy with both Peale and his manuscript. He refused to publish Peale's apologetic and accusatory introduction because it was "objectionable & not borne out by the facts to my knowledge." He changed Peale's comprehensive intended title, "Zoology," to "Ornithology and Mammalia." He demanded a complete catalog of the specimens. He sought comments on the work from other American scientists, who criticized the syntax of Peale's Latin descriptions and ungrammatical names (which Peale stated in his suppressed introduction were furnished by Georgetown College Jesuits, but which he may have mistranscribed) and his lack of familiarity with the systematic literature. The critics pointed out that Peale had described as new some species that earlier authors had already described under other names. Inexplicably, however, Wilkes had the report printed late in 1848 and then curtailed its distribution. Of the one hundred copies of the official edition of volume 8 authorized, perhaps only ninety were actually run off. A few official copies were sent to U.S. and foreign institutions, and the remainder were destroyed in a fire in the Library of Congress in 1851. Since Peale did not avail himself of the chance to have an unofficial

edition printed at his own expense for personal distribution, as did other Exploring Expedition authors, the first edition of volume 8 is one of the rarest of natural history publications. In 1978 a reprint edition, including Peale's suppressed introduction, was published by Arno Press.

Few contemporary reviews of the 1848 report exist because it was not generally available in this country or abroad. Bonaparte, who had moved back to France, was not aware of Peale's new taxa when he published his *Conspectus Avium,* an encyclopedic worldwide review of songbird taxonomy, in 1850. William Jardine in 1852 lamented that he was unable to purchase a copy of the report from American or London booksellers, although he had earlier seen "a copy forwarded by the American Government to the British Museum." He went so far as to "almost wish that some recognized usage was adopted" for disregarding new zoological names used in such a rare work, because it was precluded "from being used or consulted generally, though

Peale confused his specimen of an unspotted crake from Fiji with another spotted species, Porzana spilonota Gould, *that Charles Darwin had collected in the Galapagos Islands. Unaware that the Fiji species had already been named* Rallus tabuensis *by Gmelin in 1788, Hartlaub and Cassin renamed Peale's bird* P. vitiensis *and* Zapornia umbrina *in 1854 and 1858 respectively. Cassin,* Mammalogy and Ornithology *atlas, plate 35. Courtesy Smithsonian Institution Libraries.*

The altered second state of the plate of the snow petrel, Procellaria *(now* Pagodroma) nivea. *Peale personally collected specimens of this species on the Expedition's first venture into Antarctic seas, although the locality he cites in the report does not agree with any of the positions Captain Hudson gives in the log of the* Peacock. *Cassin,* Mammalogy and Ornithology *atlas, plate 42. Courtesy Smithsonian Institution Libraries.*

at the same time it will be used to the annoyance and confusion of those who have no opportunity to consult it or unravel what may be quoted from it." [p. 90] Dr. G. Hartlaub sought to remedy the problem raised by Jardine and published an extensive review of Peale's new bird taxa and distributional information in a widely read German journal. And George Ord, a prominent Philadelphia ornithologist and a friend of the author, reported in a letter to Peale in January 1852 that he had "never seen any account of your book nor have I held the book myself." [Poesch 1961:102]

Wilkes searched for someone to correct the nomenclatural errors and make up a more complete catalog. In 1852, with the offer of an annual stipend

of $2,000 for five years, he finally persuaded John Cassin, a museum-oriented systematist at the Academy of Natural Sciences, to redo Peale's work. Cassin had been one of those who had reviewed the report for Wilkes and perhaps, even earlier, had offered his help to Peale directly. Cassin was by then the most competent systematic ornithologist in America. At the academy, he could work with the largest and most comprehensive bird collection in the world and an international library, both acquired by the academy between 1846 and 1848. In addition, he had access to Pickering's extensive field notes. Either Wilkes had not been willing to let Peale use Pickering's journal in preparing his text or Peale had been unaware of its potential usefulness. Apparently, however, it was available to Peale for preparing the catalog of specimens in the first edition. Cassin's report appeared in 1858 and included a lavish folio of fifty-three plates, thirty-two of which were by Peale.

False economy may have played a part in one of Wilkes's publication decisions. Wilkes told Peale to simplify his drawings for the plates. Most of his designs showed elaborate backgrounds with appropriate landscapes, habitats, or native villages or boats. The original painting of the Samoan tooth-billed pigeon, *Didunculus strigirostris,* in the American Museum of Natural History, shows a completely colored fig tree. In the published plate, only the bird is colored. Peale also produced a fine plate of a snow petrel, *Pagodroma nivea,* standing on a small cake of ice in the Antarctic Sea. The original copper plate, which is now in the Smithsonian's National Anthropological Archives, shows on the back marks of the hammering that flattened

The plate of the Samoan tooth-billed pigeon, Didunculus strigirostris, *under a huge fig tree,* Ficus sp., *which Peale said measured 102 feet in diameter. Peale's generic name for the "little dodo" survives, but Jardine had already named the species in 1845. Because they nested on the ground and were preyed upon by feral cats, Peale predicted that "the miserable fragments, now deposited in Washington" would, in a few years, be all that was known of the species. Exploring Expedition specimens are still in Washington and Philadelphia and the species persists on Samoa. Cassin,* Mammalogy and Ornithology *atlas, plate 34. Courtesy Smithsonian Institution Libraries.*

the front surface so the engraver could re-engrave the bird sitting awkwardly on the water. The first state is rare.

Some lost opportunities for solving systematic problems and describing new species of birds and mammals can be attributed to Peale's unfamiliarity with the taxonomic literature and the unavailability of comparative collections. An excellent example is provided by the North Pacific albatrosses. Three species occur in the area, the large and almost extinct short-tailed albatross, *Diomedea albatrus,* and the smaller, more abundant black-footed and Laysan albatrosses, *D. nigripes* and *immutabilis.* Peale believed that the last two represented different age classes of a single species, which he (and Cassin) called *Diomedea brachyura* (now considered a

synonym of *albatrus*). He had seen many albatrosses at sea in the North Pacific and thought that plumage varied with age "as much, or perhaps more than in the Wandering Albatross (*D. exulans*) of the Southern Ocean, and [that they] require[d] many years to attain to their perfect dress." He went on to describe presumed plumage changes from "nearly black" immatures through intermediate stages to "pure snow-like white" bodied adults. [p. 290] Although "the naturalists of the Expedition . . . for the first time, demonstrated [this species] to be entitled to a place in the Fauna of North America," [Cassin 1858:399] they found albatrosses breeding only on Wake Island during the final homebound crossing of the Pacific Ocean in December 1841. Peale found eggs of both dark sooty brown,

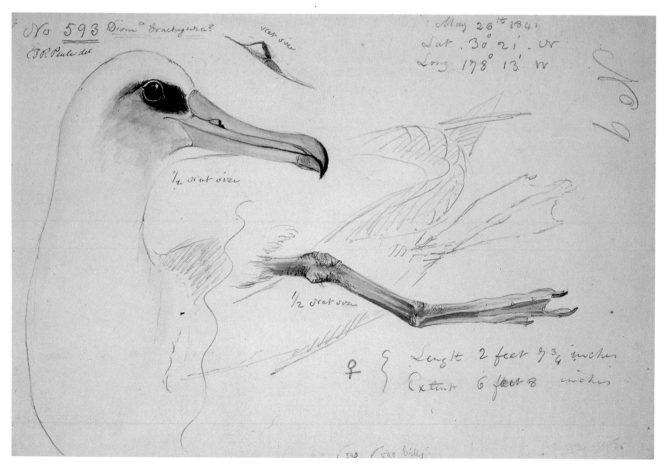

Peale's field sketch of the Laysan albatross, Diomedea immutabilis, *drawn on Wake Island, 26 May 1841, fifty-two years before the species was formally described. Courtesy American Philosophical Society.*

Peale's woodcut of an Hawaiian honeycreeper, the iiwi,
Vestaria coccinea, *feeding on nectar from a lobelia bloom.*
Peale noticed the same curvature in the bird's bill and the
corolla of the plant. Peale, Mammalia and Ornithology
report, *page 152. Courtesy Smithsonian Institution*
Libraries.

dark-billed, and black-footed birds (*nigripes*) and
white-bodied birds with pale bills and feet (*immu-*
tabilis). To confirm his observations, he sketched
both dark and light birds, but, of course, he labeled
both of his unpublished field drawings *brachyura*.
Both the short-tailed albatross, described by a Russian from seas off Kamchatka in 1769, and the
black-footed albatross, named by Audubon in 1839,
were known at the time of the Expedition. The
Laysan albatross was described in 1893, fifty-one
years after Peale drew his field sketch.

Despite his inadequacies as a taxonomist, Peale
made some remarkably astute biological observations in the field. He noted the coadaptation of a
Hawaiian *Lobelia* and a honeycreeper, the iiwi,
Vestiaria coccinea. "The singularly formed bill" of
the bird is admirably adapted "for extracting nectar
from the flower," he wrote in his report and illustrated both in a woodcut. [p. 152]

Peale described the small differences between
adult musk parrots occupying Viti Levu, Fiji, where
the species had reportedly been introduced by the
Fijians, and Vanu Levu, where it was native, and

noted that they differed but little from another
parrot already described from Tongabatu in the
Tonga island group. They are now regarded as three
of the five subspecies of the red-breasted musk
parrot, *Prosopeia tabuensis*. In his plate, Peale por-
trayed a red-breasted adult and a yellowish green-
breasted bird, which he thought was an immature
female of one of his two new taxa. The latter, it
turns out, is an adult of another species, the yellow-
breasted musk parrot, *P. personata*, native to Viti
Levu. Musk parrots are found only on the Fiji and
Tonga islands. Peale noted that the explorers had
found different species of parrots in each of the
other island groups they had visited and cited this
as possibly the "only example within our scope
of observation in the Pacific, of one species of parrot
inhabiting two groups of islands." [p. 130] Subsequent study has shown the astuteness of Peale's
zoogeographic observation. No musk parrot occurred naturally on Tonga, but apparently two subspecies of Fiji musk parrot were introduced to Tongabatu shortly before Captain Cook's visit in 1777,
and they had subsequently mixed in varying degrees.

Peale's comments on the feeding habits of the
Hawaiian io, now regarded as an endemic species of
the widespread hawk genus *Buteo*, demonstrated
the importance of his field observations: "It appears
to have all the characteristic habits of the genus;
sits solitary on dead trees, patiently watching small
birds which constitute its principal food." [p. 63]
The Expedition specimens were lost with the wreck
of the *Peacock*. The type of Peale's *Buteo solitarius*,
which is in Philadelphia, was collected by a missionary who sent it to John K. Townsend at the
Academy of Natural Sciences. It is a light phase
bird and, in color and pattern, superficially
resembles an osprey or fish hawk, *Pandion haliae-*
tus. At least that's what Cassin thought when he
called it *Pandion solitarius* in his report. A first
proof of Peale's plate, now in the Library of Congress, shows a Hawaiian honeycreeper in the hawk's
talon; the bird is crossed out and the plate bears
Cassin's annotation to the engraver to substitute a
fish.

Peale, however, misinterpreted some of his own
field observations. The overland party that traveled

from Oregon to San Francisco captured two Townsend's moles, *Scapanus townsendi,* that Peale thought were attracted to the camp supplies (tallow and peas) stored on the ground. It is, of course, more probable that rodents had eaten the camp supplies. Moles are predators, not scavengers, and feed on earthworms and beetle larvae. Cassin, commenting on Peale's observation, called eating dried peas "a habit quite unusual in an insectivorous animal" [p. 24] and suggested that the peas may have been infested by insects, which attracted the moles. Peale noted that the mole specimens were pale in comparison with other west coast specimens but attributed the color to worn pelage. Cassin, however, described one of the two as a new species, *Scalops aeneus,* even though it had been preserved in alcohol in the field and thus may have lost some of its color.

Peale also confused some data. He described as *Halichoerus antarcticus* the skin and skull of a seal "obtained on the 10th of March [1839] at Deception Island" in "the Antarctic Seas." Although Peale was the lone scientist to accompany the ships that ventured into the Antarctic seas in 1839, he was not aboard the *Sea Gull,* the only ship in the squadron that landed at Deception. In his *Narrative* Wilkes quoted Lieutenant Johnson's account of molting macaroni penguins, *Eudyptes chrysolo-*

Peale named the red-headed parrot-finch from the "open bushy grounds" of Samoa Geospiza *(now* Erythrura*) cyaneovirens (top figures), and its near relative on Fiji* G. prasina *(lower figure). Because the name* prasina *had already been used for another bird in the same genus, Hartlaub renamed it* Erythrura pealii. *Cassin,* Mammalogy and Ornithology *atlas, plate 8. Courtesy Smithsonian Institution Libraries.*

phus, and American sheathbills, *Chionis alba,* at Deception, a collapsed caldera breached by the sea, and added: "Sailing up the bay, they descried a sea leopard (the *Phoca leopardina* Jam.), which Lieutenant Johnson succeeded in taking, but by an unaccountable mistake, the skull, &c., were thrown overboard. Its dimensions were also omitted to be taken." [1:143–44]

Peale, however, figured the skull; described the teeth, body shape, and fur characters; gave measurements, even down to whiskers and eyebrow; and stated "it appears from the teeth to be an adult, and is the most perfect specimen brought home by the Expedition." [p. 31]

Cassin repeated Peale's description and data for the specimen but changed the identification and name, following Gray, to that of the crab-eater seal, *Lobodon carcinophaga.* In 1866, Gill, pointing out

Peale's plate of two species of musk parrot (right), Prosopeia *from Fiji. Peale erroneously thought that the yellow-breasted bird was an immature of his new red-breasted species,* P. splendens; *it is in reality a separate species,* P. personata, *described by J. R. Gray in the same year that Peale's report appeared. Cassin,* Mammalogy and Ornithology *atlas, plate 20. Courtesy Smithsonian Institution Libraries.*

that "Peale now doubts the correctness of the labels on the faith of which he gave its habitat," [p. 4] correctly reidentified the type specimen as a North American harbor seal, *Phoca vitulina*. Because he regarded the specific epithet as inappropriate for a northern species, he renamed it *Phoca pealii*. A penciled catalog number on the skull may refer correctly to an entry for an old west coast North American seal collected by the U.S. Exploring Expedition, which was overlooked and therefore omitted from both Peale's and Cassin's catalogs, along with an immature harbor seal skull. The skin has disappeared and the skull is broken, although both were intact in 1880 when reviewed and refigured by J.A. Allen.

Little other information about marine mammals was collected by the Expedition. Although support for the U.S. whaling industry had been a major argument for the Expedition, information about commercially important large cetaceans is absent from both Peale's and Cassin's reports. Peale described six new species of porpoises, although the collections now include only one damaged skull and one partial jaw representing two of the species. His well-executed drawings and detailed descriptions provide enough information so that all of his names can be attributed to known species. Two

other Exploring Expedition porpoise specimens were subsequently described as new species.

Although no ethnologist or specialist in material culture accompanied the Expedition, the number of ethnological specimens brought back was prodigious, and Peale's report sheds interesting light on some objects that otherwise might have been difficult to identify.

In Fiji, Peale was pestered by a Polynesian rat, an immature specimen of which he named *Mus vitiensis*. Peale had already named the Polynesian rat *M.* (now *Rattus*) *exulans*, based on a specimen from Tahiti. "Their gambols overhead in the thatch were so noisy as to banish sleep." The rats also attacked any food that was left out. "The Fijians had an ingenious contrivance to save provisions from their attacks" [pp. 49–50], an elaborately carved hanging rack, which Peale illustrated.

Peale's description and illustrations of the Samoans' method for live capture and domestication of Pacific pigeons or "lupis," *Ducula pacifica*, with a small bow and remarkably long, multipointed arrow recently helped to correct the identification of a specimen from "spear" to "arrow" and to match it to the appropriate bow. The Samoans sat in thatched blinds and shot six- or seven-foot arrows from short bows. The arrows were tipped with three

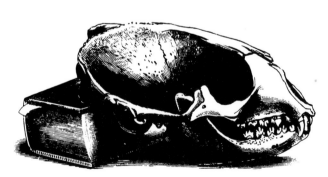

HALICHŒRUS ANTARCTICA—CRANIUM.

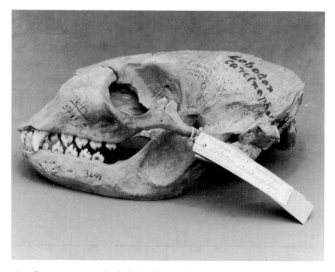

Woodcut and type specimen of the seal, Halichoerus antarcticus *Peale, erroneously labeled as collected on Deception Island by Lieutenant Johnson. The skull actually belongs to a west coast North American harbor seal,* Phoca vitulina. *Peale,* Mammalia and Ornithology *report, page 31. Courtesy Division of Mammals, National Museum of Natural History, Smithsonian Institution.*

Proof of Peale's plate of the Hawaiian io, Buteo solitarius, *showing a honeycreeper in the hawk's talons, with Cassin's handwritten instructions to the engraver to change the prey to a fish. The published plate reflects Cassin's belief that the io was a small fish-eating osprey. Courtesy Rare Book and Special Collections Division, The Library of Congress; Cassin,* Mammalogy and Ornithology *atlas, plate 4, Smithsonian Institution Libraries.*

or four flexible "barbed pieces of hard wood . . . wide enough between the points to receive the body of a Lupi. . . . The chances are in favor of the bird's being caught between the points." [p. 199] The cruel process of pigeon taming that Peale described is very similar to the practice of "bating," used by falconers to break their birds of flying off the perch.

The Expedition visited the Hawaiian Islands when some of the now-extinct native bird species were still living. Peale collected, described, and figured the first, and one of only three in the world, specimens of the honey eater *Chaetoptila angustipluma*. He was probably the only naturalist to see it alive and describe its habits. "It was very active, and graceful in its motions, frequents the woody districts, and is disposed to be musical, having

most of the habits of the Meliphaga; they are generally found about those trees which are in flower." [p. 147] So much for our knowledge of the habits of *Chaetoptila* in life!

From the large island of Hawaii, the Expedition brought back at least twelve specimens of the extinct honey eater, the o-o, *Moho nobilis*, an almost entirely black bird that furnished the small but highly valued yellow underwing plumes used in Hawaiian feather robes and ornaments. Peale told how the Hawaiians trapped the birds, removed their yellow plumes, and released them to grow back new feathers for future plucking (a remarkably sophisticated technique for conservation of a natural resource, which, alas, did not work). Apparently even in 1841 the species was rare, for Peale talked of the splendid and costly royal robes and capes

An Exploring Expedition specimen of the Polynesian rat,
Rattus exulans, *was described as a new species by Peale
(top figure), but he failed to recognize that small rats that
he named* vitiensis *from Fiji were only young specimens
of the same species (lower figure). Cassin,* Mammalogy
and Ornithology *atlas, plate 4. Courtesy Smithsonian
Institution Libraries.*

made of the feathers, which were no longer seen at
the time of the Expedition. He noted that only
"bunches of feathers called *hulu* . . . are still prepared and received in payment of a poll tax to the
king. They are made up into headbands worn by
the ladies, but few can afford to wear them." [p.
148–49] Some adult specimens of o-o that the Expedition brought home lack yellow plumes and
were probably delivered to the explorers already
plucked by the Hawaiians. The o-o survived on
Hawaii until the 1930s. Peale noted, under the erroneous name *Certhia pacifica*, that another species
of o-o, actually *M. braccatus*, whose tufts are
smaller and are on the thighs, was less exploited. It

survives today on Kauai. Although he was on Kauai
for five days and said that he collected specimens
"in the woody districts of the mountains" of Han-
alei, no specimens are in the collection. If any were
acquired, they were lost with the *Peacock*.

Peale also collected insects, particularly Lepidop-
tera, wherever he visited. These he regarded as too
fragile to send back with the other specimens during the voyage, and this collection was also lost
when the *Peacock* foundered in the Columbia
River. Peale's catalog of the butterflies survives and

*Charles Girard, who served as herpetological and
ichthyological assistant to Spencer F. Baird at the
Smithsonian from 1850 to 1861, was trained by Louis
Agassiz in Switzerland and at Harvard. He prepared
volume 20 of the Expedition reports on the reptiles
and amphibians. Courtesy Smithsonian Institution
Archives.*

is under study. Apparently, some beetles that were collected on the Expedition survived and were worked up by John LeConte in the late 1840s, but the manuscript was not published and, within a short time, all LeConte's new species had been described by others.

Peale was frustrated and embittered by his post-Expedition experiences. Along with the rest of the scientists, he was discharged after landing in New York, but Pickering asked him to come to Washington in January 1843 "to review, arrange and label the specimens." [Poesch 1961:96] He was to receive $120 per month until he finished his text and subsequently $20 for each completed plate. He was strapped for funds and sought other posts. His application for the position of curator in the fledgling Smithsonian Institution in 1846 was turned down, but in August 1848 he was named an assistant examiner in the U.S. Patent Office, where he remained until he retired in 1873 and returned to Philadelphia.

Peale had remarried in 1850, and the couple enjoyed a modest social and intellectual life in Washington before moving back to Philadelphia. He had become interested in photography and was one of the founding members of the first photography club in the United States. Many of his photographs of Washington in the 1860s and early 1870s survive. With one of his nephews, Coleman Sellers, Peale participated in the development of cinematography. He was also a founding member of the Philosophical Society of Washington. He wrote articles on butterflies and Indian artifacts for the annual reports of the Smithsonian Institution and worked on a massive illustrated monograph on the butterflies of North America that was never published. He also continued painting, mainly in oils, although it is unclear whether for pleasure or sale. Peale died at home in Philadelphia on 13 March 1885.

The reptile, amphibian, and fish collections were not worked on until ten years after the Expedition returned, when appropriate systematists were avail-

able in the United States. Charles Pickering, the Expedition herpetologist and ichthyologist, was appointed superintendent of the collections and publications in 1842, but he was more interested in human biogeography than in working up the vertebrate collections. In 1850 Wilkes approached Spencer F. Baird, then newly appointed assistant secretary of the Smithsonian in charge of the National Museum, who had himself been interested in the job of curator of the collections in 1841. Baird accepted the publication task with the understanding that the actual work would be carried out by his recently acquired but competent assistant, French-born Charles Girard. A museum-bound scientist, trained in Switzerland and at Harvard under Louis Agassiz, Girard had immigrated to the United States in 1847 at the age of twenty-five. He had worked on the systematics of fishes as well as herpetology, publishing both in association with Agassiz and alone. Baird and Girard published preliminary reports on the Expedition reptiles in U.S. journals between 1852 and 1856. In contrast to Peale's method of publication of the new mammals and birds, which of course was dictated by Wilkes, all of

In Samoa, fruit pigeons were captured live with long multi-pointed arrows shot from short bows. Captive pigeons were kept tethered on perch sticks. Peale, Mammalia and Ornithology *report, pages 199, 200. Courtesy Smithsonian Institution Libraries.*

SAMOAN PIGEON ROOST.

Cassin noted "There is not perhaps in the entire circle of Birds a genus, the species of which are more difficult to determine or more likely to be confounded, than those of the genus Todirhamphus *[now* Halcyon*]." Peale called this white-collared kingfisher from Tutuila, Samoa,* Dacelo coronata, *but because he had overlooked an earlier use of the same name for another kingfisher, Hartlaub renamed it* H. pealei. *Cassin called it* T. tuta *Gmelin. It is now considered a subspecies of the widespread species* H. chloris. *Cassin,* Mammalogy and Ornithology *atlas, plate 15. Courtesy Smithsonian Institution Libraries.*

the descriptions of new reptile and amphibian taxa thus first appeared in more easily available journals rather than in the limited-edition Expedition reports.

Girard's final report, volume 20 in the Expedition series, appeared in 1858, five years later than promised. For it and his work on western American fishes, Girard was awarded the Cuvier Prize by the Institute of France in 1861. The official edition was "prepared under the superintendence of S.F. Baird," with credit to Girard only in Baird's introduction: "Finding that other duties would interfere with the proper performance of the work, [I] was permitted to associate Dr. Girard with [me] in its execution; by whom the determinations and descriptions have been made, the drawings overlooked, and the work carried through the press." [p. v] The unofficial edition was issued the same year under Girard's name alone. The report, written in Girard's somewhat stilted English, is a fine example of contemporary systematics, with full descriptions and synonomies, comments on relationships and

Right, Péale named another subspecies of white-collared kingfisher from Fiji, vitiensis *and remarked that although he had found it in mangroves "which skirt the inner verge of the coral belts and [it] is most commonly found near salt water where fish and crabs abound, we never saw it eat anything but insects." Cassin,* Mammalogy and Ornithology *atlas, plate 18. Courtesy Smithsonian Institution Libraries.*

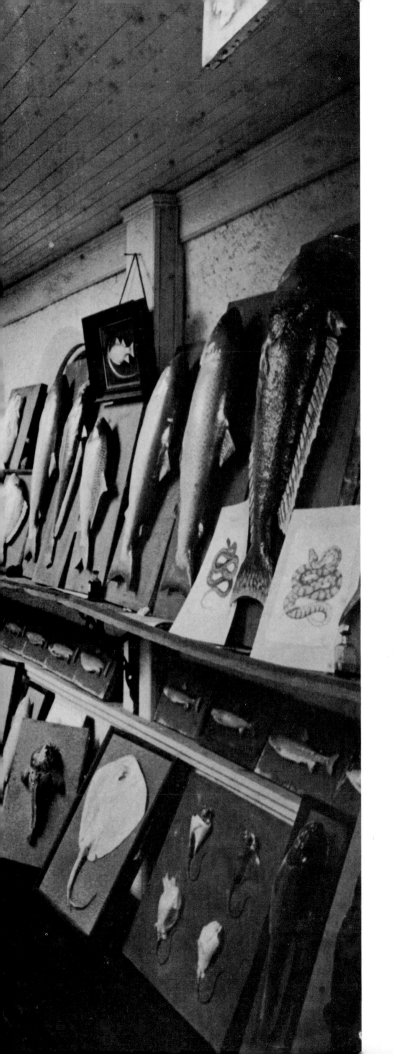

J. H. Richard in his Cambridge, Massachusetts, studio, where he drew plates showing hundreds of species of reptiles, amphibians, and fishes for Expedition reports by Girard and Agassiz. Courtesy Division of Fishes, National Museum of Natural History, Smithsonian Institution.

Richard's plates of frogs (examples shown above) and toads described by Girard appear lifelike because he had field sketches made by Joseph Drayton. Girard, Herpetology atlas, plate 3, plate 4, plate 5. Courtesy Smithsonian Institution Libraries.

Many species of geckos were collected during the Expedition: top figure Naultinus elegans, *New Zealand; middle figure,* Gekko gecko, *small island in Balabac strait, South China Sea; bottom figure,* Gehyra vorax, *Fiji, which Girard named on the basis of its "voracious disposition." He reported that the "naturalists of the Expedition state that [captives] will even spring at a person. . .and inflict a very severe bite." Girard,* Herpetology *atlas, plate 16. Courtesy Smithsonian Institution Libraries.*

Pickering's field notes on some of the Expedition lizards provide information about how they were collected. Top figure, Brachylophus fasciatus *was brought to Pickering by the natives at Fiji "and some were kept alive in my room for several days. . .They seem to be of an indolent nature and gentle disposition, never attempting to bite." Middle figure,* Hoplodactylus pomarii, *New Zealand, was "brought on board by King Pomare." Bottom figure,* Tupinambis tequixin, *Rio de Janiero. Girard,* Herpetology *atlas, plate 18. Courtesy Smithsonian Institution Libraries.*

biogeography, and exquisite illustrations in the atlas, but with virtually nothing on natural history of the species aside from a few notes on habitats quoted from Pickering's journal. Girard correctly suspected that many of the reptiles and almost all of the amphibians from islands in the Pacific Ocean had been carried about and introduced by the Polynesians. The atlas of thirty-two excellent plates by J.H. Richard is based mostly on Joseph Drayton's

drawings preserved in the Library of Congress. Girard frequently commented on the value of Drayton's drawings, particularly in showing the rotund appearance of the frogs and salamanders in life in contrast to their wizened state as preserved specimens. "A protracted immersion in alcohol is apt to contract the tissues," Girard stated, "sometimes to a considerable degree." [p. vi] Richard's herpetological plates, although artistic, are not portraits

Among the snakes were two new species described by Girard, Ahaetulla prasina, *a four-foot-long slender tree snake from Sydney, Australia, and* Philodryas patagoniensis *from the mouth of the Rio Negro. Girard,* Herpetology atlas, *plate 12. Courtesy Smithsonian Institution Libraries.*

Louis Agassiz was already a respected naturalist in Europe when he accepted a professorship at Harvard. He labored some ten years in preparing the ichthyological report on Exploring Expedition fishes that was never published. Courtesy Division of Fishes, National Museum of Natural History, Smithsonian Institution.

of single species in habitat settings, as were Peale's bird and mammal plates; they show species or age classes comparatively, with several figures on a plate. Girard's report and atlas sought to remedy the meager descriptions and poor illustrations in the older literature that made identification difficult. Throughout the report he showed his annoyance with early taxonomic publications. In discussing *Gekko indicus*, a common wall-climbing lizard, he gloated, "This species having been so often described, and so badly illustrated, herpetologists will welcome the accompanying figure," [p. 291] drawn from life in February 1842. Although the herpetological collections could be displayed in bottles without additional preparation, they too have dete-

riorated with time. A number of labels had become mixed up, much to Girard's annoyance in the 1850s, and perhaps half the specimens have disappeared from the Smithsonian collections, some without a trace.

The outcome for publication of the fish collection was far less satisfactory. On Pickering's advice and only after long negotiations over the fee and publication schedule, Wilkes persuaded Louis Agassiz of Harvard, foremost ichthyologist in America at the time, to work on the fish collection in Cambridge. Agassiz, already an established authority on zoological nomenclature, fishes, and glaciology in Europe, had immigrated to the United States from Switzerland in 1846, when he was thirty-nine, to accept a professorship in natural history at Harvard. He had brought Girard along. Until Girard joined Baird at the Smithsonian in Washington, Agassiz and he had been prolific in publishing reports on the many collections of American reptiles and amphibians that were made by expeditions exploring the newly opened West. Even without his able assistant, and in spite of his university teaching responsibilities and his efforts to establish the Museum of Comparative Zoology, Agassiz published a number of papers on fishes after 1852, including one describing some new species of Exploring Expedition fishes from the west coast. Finally, in 1861 Wilkes was able to report to Congress that Agassiz had completed a two-thousand-page manuscript. Agassiz simultaneously had been directing the work of the artist, J.H. Richard, who added to Drayton's many field sketches and drawings for the huge projected atlas of engraved plates. Wilkes, however, was unable to secure funds for publishing the ichthyological report during the Civil War and the fiscally lean years that followed.

Wilkes's *Narrative* provides information about local fishing and fish culture practices in the Pacific islands based in large part on Pickering's journals. Had this information been incorporated into a contemporary report on the fish collections, it might have had some commercial importance. As it turned out, even Drayton's observations on the great salmon runs up the Columbia River, which Wilkes quoted, were generally overlooked.

Agassiz died in 1873, his monumental work on

Drayton's field drawing of the wrasse Bodianus loxozonus *from Sertes Island, Tuamotus. The lower figure is his drawing of the labrid* Coris flavovitta *caught in nets by natives in Hilo Bay, Hawaii. Drayton's notes provide information on stomach contents. Courtesy Division of Fishes, National Museum on Natural History, Smithsonian Institution.*

Richard's engraved copper plates are remarkable for the details of fins and scales, as in this plate of Southern Ocean Notothenia. *Courtesy National Anthropological Archives.*

the Expedition fishes still unpublished. Twelve years later, in 1885, the collection, the manuscript, and 1,470 drawings and plates were returned to the Smithsonian, where the collections languished, little consulted, and Agassiz's forgotten manuscript was considered lost. Eventually, in 1920, the Smithsonian sent the entire collection and the illustrations, but not Agassiz's missing manuscript, to Henry W. Fowler, curator of fishes at the Academy of Natural Sciences in Philadelphia. He and Barton A. Bean, of the Smithsonian's National Museum, described eighteen new species and five new genera and subgenera in 1924, and Fowler produced a lengthy manuscript for publication by the Smithsonian. But Fowler's Exploring Expedition monograph also was never published, ostensibly because funds were not available. In 1940 he did publish a brief inventory of the specimens and drawings of the 588 species that he was able to identify in the extant collections and drawings, showing that had Pickering or Agassiz published promptly, 195 would have been new taxa. He reported in 1940 that, unlike some of the other Expedition collections, the century-old fish specimens were in "comparatively fair condition," and he judged the majority of the collection and its data were intact. Some specimens were badly frayed and abraded, but possibly they had been that way when collected. Only a portion of the specimens actually collected may have been preserved, and others may have been lost. A number of labels had become lost or switched, but Fowler was able to match some to locality through Dray-

ton's drawings. Localities for many, however, remain conjectural. Agassiz's manuscript has turned up recently in the Smithsonian Archives along with many of the fish drawings.

What is left of the collections and drawings of birds, mammals, reptiles, amphibians, and fishes, as well as Agassiz's and Fowler's manuscripts, now resides primarily in five places—the National Museum of Natural History, the Academy of Natural Sciences, the Museum of Comparative Zoology, the Smithsonian Institution Archives, and the Library of Congress. Other specimens that were sent to smaller museums and universities in most cases can no longer be traced, probably having been discarded after further deterioration. From time to time, individual Exploring Expedition specimens have been consulted for compiling type catalogs and special studies or for augmenting series for comparisons, but, aside from the fishes, the entire collections have not been reviewed in 120 years. Such a review would undoubtedly reveal many more instances where Expedition specimens could have extended scientific knowledge in the 1840s. As it turned out, however, many opportunities for American priority were lost as other later expeditions acquired additional specimens and scientists published the results. One can only speculate what might have been the fate of the vertebrates had Wilkes followed Audubon's recommendation and hired young Spencer Baird as curator and assistant in publishing the Exploring Expedition collections in 1842.

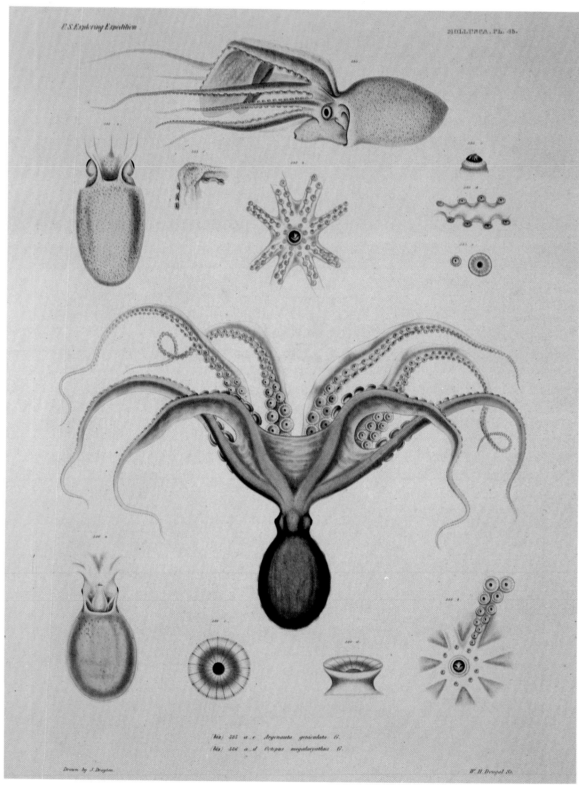

Soft-bodied animals such as these cephalopods not only were difficult to preserve in the field, but also were likely to be spoiled by evaporation of preservative while in storage in Washington. The original specimens of Argonauta geniculata *Gould from Brazil and* Octopus megalocyathus *Gould from Orange Harbor, illustrated on this plate from the atlas of* Mollusca, *have disappeared since the return of the Expedition and can no longer be traced. Courtesy Smithsonian Institution Libraries.*

4 The Invertebrates of the U.S. Exploring Expedition

The collection of invertebrates during the U.S. Exploring Expedition was largely the responsibility of Joseph Pitty Couthouy, conchologist of the Expedition, and insects that of Titian R. Peale. When Couthouy fell from grace with Wilkes, his functions were assumed by Joseph Drayton, the artist who had worked extensively with him, and by James D. Dana, the geologist.

If sampling a poorly known terrestrial biota was difficult, acquiring even a superficial representation of the marine invertebrates was a herculean task. Worse, it was obstructed by Wilkes's inability to understand the requirements of biological collecting. Early in the cruise, he forbade Couthouy to bring specimens below decks because of their smell and forced him to limit the size of his collections. Couthouy recorded the incident in his journal:

This morning after breakfast as I came on deck the Captain called me to him and stated that he could not have the whole ship lumbered up with specimens of coral and I must not bring on board so many or so large pieces. I assured him that no more than was absolutely necessary to shew the characters of the corals had been collected and as to the number, thus far we had not procured one of each species. He then mentioned the disagreeable smell produced by them and stated that in his opinion they endangered the health of the crew by producing malaria and no more specimens must be taken below the spar deck where a place would be provided for their reception. Shortly afterward an order was issued of which the following is a copy

"Hereafter no specimens of coral, live shells, or anything else that may produce a bad smell, will be taken below the spar deck, or into any of the rooms and it will be the duty of those bringing such on board to report them to the officer of the deck who will see that they are placed under the charge of a man appointed to look out for them, and that this order is rigidly enforced. . . ."

the words underlined here are so in the original. Any comments upon this order are unnecessary almost, it being obvious that if obeyed and rigidly enforced, a complete stop is put to any examinations of my collections or drawings being made of any of the objects. There is no possibility of such things being done on the spar deck amid the noise and bustle and constant change of place attendant upon the manoeuvres of the ship, and even if there was such in the day, how can it be done at night? Take for instance last evening and this—it occupied me till near midnight merely taking rough notes of such things as cannot live till morning. [p.232]

Couthouy went on to analyze Wilkes's order and to describe the captain's reaction to his arguments against limiting the size and number of specimens he was permitted to collect.

In compliance with the order of this AM. all the specimens collected today have been placed in charge of the officer of the deck—a sort of rack has been placed between the arm chests aft, about four feet long by twenty inches high and as many broad which I learn is for the reception of all the corals &c brought on board till they are cured for packing. Capt. Wilkes has directed me to procure only one specimen of each species of coral which is to be as small as consistent with the determination of its characters a regulation just the reverse of what has always been considered desirable in regard to specimens of this kind. On my suggesting that previous Expeditions had experienced no difficulty in the preservation of large and numerous specimens, he replied that he did not care a d— –n for what had been done in previous expeditions, or consider himself in any way to be governed by it, and that he should take the responsibility of deciding all matters relative to our collection according to his own views. Of course there is no reply to this. . . . I have no interest in this particular myself, beyond the wish that the Government's collection may be one of which it shall not be ashamed. [pp.233–34]

After Dana assumed responsibility for the corals in the Fijis in 1840, he obviously did not observe the restriction that Wilkes had put on Couthouy, for in many cases there are, indeed, duplicate specimens of coral species in the Exploring Expedition collection in the U.S. National Museum, and some of these same species are represented in the museums of Yale and Harvard.

In spite of the limitations the Expedition acquired a monumental collection of invertebrates that formed the basis for three landmark reports whose importance will endure as long as biological science survives. Two of them, produced in a period of ten years by the thirty-nine-year-old Dana (who concurrently wrote the report on geology), violated the dictum of the Library Committee that only scientific novelties discovered by the Expedition should be published in the reports. Dana successfully argued that he could not adequately deal with the new species of corals and crustaceans without considering those already known to science. In consequence, those two reports were, in effect, state-of-the-art monographs of the marine fauna of the regions touched by the Expedition. To a somewhat lesser extent the same can be said of the report on the Mollusca prepared by A.A. Gould.

Had all gone smoothly on the cruise, the shells (and probably most other invertebrates as well) would have been written up by Couthouy, who had been appointed conchologist, apparently through the intervention of President Andrew Jackson, in preference to the much better qualified Gould. Wilkes's comments about Couthouy's appointment show that he resented this upstart from the beginning:

This Mr. Couthouy was among the number and the only one designated as Conchologist. I had never Seen and knew little of him, and that little was by no means satisfactory. He was nothing more than a collector of Specimens, & parties were induced to sign his Recommendation. He was no man of science, had been a master of a vessel out of Boston and engaged in various other occupations of trade and merchandise. I took him very unwillingly to occupy the position. He had much glibness of tongue and very little truth or fact to accompany it, and in making the selection of his quarters, I assigned him to the Vincennes *instead of the* Peacock *where I could more readily control his peculiar disposition, as I understood it would require.* [1978:382]

Off to a bad start, Couthouy soon incurred the further disapproval of Wilkes, became incapacitated by illness, and ultimately was dismissed from the Expedition. Wilkes recalled the circumstances in his autobiography:

One of [Couthouy's] first acts shortly after Sailing was to possess himself of a Pub[lic] Doc[ument] sent me in which the correspon-

Joseph Pitty Couthouy, conchologist of the U.S. Exploring Expedition. Courtesy Boston Athenaeum.

dence of the members of the Scientific Corps had been printed from a call from Congress. Among others, several letters of his appeared and they were anything but creditable to him. This Pub. Doc. he threw overboard for several of the officers had perused it and it made a very unfavorable impression on them. This he was not slow to discover and made way with the publication. Unfortunately for him, it was soon discovered, after inquiries, that he was the last person who had it and, of course the suspicions rested on him, but what made the matter worse was his untruthfulness and direct denial that he had ever seen it . . . and in the progress of the cruize it became evident that he had not the truth in him. . . . [p.392]

Wilkes thought Couthouy "was of an irrasible and tyrannical temper and had deemed he had sole control over Mr. Drayton . . . by fair bullying and using at times indecorous language. I gave orders that the employment of the Artists was under my control . . . and that no member of the Corps would be permitted to interfere in their duties. . . ." [p. 382] Wilkes wrote that later in the cruise "the violence of this Mr Couthouy knew no bounds. He denied my authority to deal thus with him, would report me to the Govt, and even threatened a personal attack. . . . It was therefore apparent that he was a very improper person to remain with the Expedition and I decided to send him home. . . . He was the most troublesome fellow I had to deal with during the cruise but he found me equal to the task. He was a happy riddance and I congratulated myself that the Expedition had got rid of him." [pp. 480–81]

Couthouy's absence left a large part of the animal kingdom without a specialist, so Wilkes was obliged to fill the gap as best he could. "After his departure I had divided the duties and given the larger part of them to Mr. James D. Dana who had worked with great spirit and energy, not only in making collections, but in drawing & describing them and with whom the officers cheerfully assisted so that his results had been very large & important in that branch of Science, all of which it was Mr Couthouy['s] intention to appropriate to himself." [p. 480]

Augustus Addison Gould, author of the official U.S. Exploring Expedition report Mollusca and Shells. *Courtesy National Museum of Natural History, Smithsonian Institution.*

This plate from the atlas of Mollusca illustrates three new species of scallop collected by the Expedition, Pecten caurinus *Gould and* Pecten hericius *Gould from the coast of Washington, and* Pecten laetus *Gould from New Zealand. Courtesy Smithsonian Institution Libraries.*

Whatever ulterior motives Wilkes might have perceived Couthouy to have against Dana, Couthouy's journal does not reveal them. In fact, he seems clearly to have respected Dana's territory. On 7 March 1839 he wrote: "Among some kelp which I pulled up (covered with specimens of my genus Thalassina) I procured one of the most splendid Crustacea I ever beheld. It is a *Lithodes*, covering when spread out, a circumference of over 3 feet, its colour an intense crimson every where but on the

Drawn by A. F. Bellows
W. H. Bengol Sc.

under side of legs where it passes into orange. It is a brilliant addition to Mr. Dana's department." [p. 39] Again, on 12 March: "During the calm great numbers of a small cray fish (Galathea) of a deep red colour were swimming about the surface of the water of which I caught several for Mr. Dana." [p. 48]

Perhaps Wilkes's antagonism rubbed off on the other officers and crew, or perhaps memory of the "Public Document affair" lingered, but whatever the cause, Couthouy felt that his work was being obstructed. On 11 March 1839 he wrote:

It is a great loss to me that boats are so much wanted that it has almost invariably occurred when I wished for one, that none could be spared. Hitherto except in one instance, I have been obliged to depend on the shore parties & wait their time both for going & returning by which much time is necessarily lost. And yet hardly a day passes without some of the officers taking a boat for a shooting excursion. I am loth to consider this intentional, but it is too evident there is not a right feeling as to the assistance we should receive. There is no open opposition, but still I feel that an indefinable, intangible something [is] constantly thwarting my endeavors, not the less painful because I cannot bring it before me in a palpable form & grapple with it. I feel my advances checked & my motives misconstrued—yet it is shown by no open act. There are a thousand little things which disparately are nothing, but in the aggregate constitute an intolerable whole. I feel as if surrounded by a worse than Polar atmosphere—one of chilled feelings. Companionless, for the present at least that which I have anticipated as a work of pleasure, must be performed as a task of duty. [p. 47]

"Valley of Voona, Feejee Is." Narrative.

It almost seems that fate conspired against Couthouy. His journal entry for Sunday, 17 March is revealing:

A most lovely day throughout calm & pleasant with the harbour like a glassy sea. No Service. Almost all the officers & half the men on shore shooting fishing &c. A day for home musings and old letters & I have made the most of it. I trust

> *"A sadder & a wiser man*
> *To rise tomorrow morn."*

Had my philosophy (small stock have I to boast) put to a cruel test this morning. One of the boats in shoving off full of men all captains of course, in pulling round the stern, struck one of their oars against my remaining jar, containing the results of the dredging & shivered it to atoms. Happily, said I as I witnessed the catastrophe, there are duplicates of every thing in the jar laying on my Bureau. As Jacob Faithful sagely remarks "What's done, can't be helped." "Better luck next time." Bitterly was I deceiving myself. I should have remembered another adage more to the point. "Misfortunes never come singly." Going on deck I observed to my very intelligent valet pro tem, Mr James Sheafe, "James I have done, you may clean up now." Returning I found my room "swept & garnished" but the specimens were gone. With a misgiving heart, I called the rascal. "James what have you done with those shells? "Shells Sir! what shells?" "Why those on my bureau." "Oh them Sir, I thought Sir,—you was done with 'em Sir." "Well, why don't you tell me what you have done with them" I reiterated gasping for breath. "Why Sir I threw them all overboard!" All! Like the painter who despairing of his skill to represent a Father's grief, cast a mantle over his face leaving to the spectator's imagination, I stop short. There was not one left. I told him he was mistaken—and shut my door. [pp.50–51]

Although Couthouy actually began studying the mollusk collection on his return to Washington, he soon abandoned the task because of low pay and curatorial mismanagement, as well as the scant likelihood that Wilkes would accept him as author of the mollusk report in any event. After a large amount of dickering, A.A. Gould was finally commissioned to write the report on Mollusca. Recognizing the urgency of publishing descriptions of new taxa to avoid their being preempted by investigators elsewhere, Gould quickly published preliminary accounts of his new species in volumes 2 and 3 of the *Proceedings* of the Boston Society of Natural History between 1846 and 1850, before the appearance of the full report in 1852.

An outstanding contribution of the Expedition to knowledge of the mollusks was the information about life colors and the appearance of the living animals that produced the shells. Earlier works concentrated on illustrating the shells in detail, but knowledge of the organisms that made them was scanty or lacking altogether. Designed in the elegant French manner, the folio atlas accompanying the Expedition report contains fifty-two plates. Many of the drawings by Drayton show the animal in full color in great detail, but the shell in outline, so the plates may seem drab compared with some of the sumptuous European works that illustrated the colorful shells obtained by other expeditions. In its emphasis on the appearance and color in life of the soft parts of species largely unknown previously, however, the atlas of the U.S. Exploring Expedition made a greater contribution to science than did those that illustrated only the pretty shells.

The sketches and drawings of the living animals made at sea demonstrate the difficulties the Scientifics experienced in recording their observations as well as in producing the finished atlases. Without the ease and convenience of color photography, they had to draw in watercolor every specimen that might be illustrated in color when the official reports were published. The vast number of specimens precluded drawing everything in complete detail, even when the Scientifics themselves supplemented the work of the artists. Camera-ready art was not necessary, because photoengraving was as yet unknown, and much could be left to the engravers and colorists who would prepare the final plates. At Fangasar Bay, Tutuila, in the Samoan Islands, Drayton made dorsal and ventral drawings of the shell-less snail *Doris superba* but colored only enough to guide the colorist; these were supplemented by detailed drawings in pencil to guide the engraver. The finished work was a close approximation of what the artist would have produced had he taken the time to prepare a completely finished drawing in color. The three other specimens shown on the same plate were less elaborate, so Drayton colored them fully in the field.

Back in Washington, an editor (probably Drayton in this case) made layouts for each plate, using tracings of the original drawings, to instruct the engravers where to position each figure. When all the figures had been engraved, proof impressions were struck before the figure numbers and legends were engraved ("proof before letters"). At that stage, any necessary corrections were made on the figures, and sometimes the proofs were colored. Finally the engraving with letters added was proofed, and the finished plates were colored by hand from a master copy colored according to the original drawings.

Gould's text includes 443 new species, of which 308 are represented by type specimens in the U.S. National Museum. It has been impossible to trace the type specimens of 110 of the species in any museum, but of these, 57 species were soft-bodied forms without shells. It is probable that some were not preserved after drawings and notes had been made of them. It is equally probable that others dried out and eventually were discarded. This leaves 53 species, the types of which may still turn up in one or another of the museums that received sets of Exploring Expedition specimens from the Smithsonian Institution. The general collection of mollusks in the U.S. National Museum contains many of the previously described species collected during the Expedition, although in former years some were discarded on the grounds of inadequate data or better representation in the collection by other well-documented material. Seashells being virtually indestructible, the extant material is in reasonably good condition.

The same cannot be said of the specimens of Crustacea described by Dana in his report, volumes 13 and 14. Although it probably was not raided for desirable cabinet specimens as were the shells and bird skins, the collection suffered several vicissitudes. "Besides this misfortune," Dana wrote, referring to the wreck of the *Peacock*, "another befell the collections after reaching the country, before the return of the Expedition. A large part of the packages were unfortunately opened, and the specimens prepared, by drying, for exhibition. By this means, the references to the catalogues were to some extent lost, and many specimens were badly injured. Some were rendered wholly unfit for description, especially those of small size, which, without regard to their delicacy of structure, were taken from the bottles containing them and dried, and sometimes transfixed with pins, to the obliteration of many of their characters. Moreover, the larger species were rendered by this process unfit for dissection." [p. 2]

As if that catastrophe was not enough, the crustacean material suffered irreparable loss in the great Chicago fire of 1871. Virtually all of the crustacean holdings from the Expedition in the Smithsonian had been sent to William Stimpson, secretary of the Chicago Academy of Sciences, who needed the specimens for comparison with those he had collected during the North Pacific Exploring Expedition of 1853–56. The Chicago Academy had recently erected a "fireproof" building to house its collections, and in this model of modern construction the Exploring Expedition crustaceans were located. When Mrs. O'Leary's cow kicked over the lamp, the academy "went down in a fiery furnace of a magnitude which the world has never before seen, and in an intensity of heat which not even stone and iron could resist." A printed announcement dated 30 October 1871 by Stimpson and J.W. Foster, president of the academy, enumerated the losses: "The Smithsonian collection of crustacea, undoubtedly the largest alcoholic collection in the world, which filled over 10,000 jars, and contained the types of the species described by Prof. Dana and other Americans, besides hundreds of new species, many of which were described in manuscripts lost in the same fire."

As it turned out, not quite all of the Exploring Expedition crustaceans had been sent to Chicago. Some few were out on loan to other researchers, so the crustacean catalog today records ninety-seven lots collected by the Expedition. These include

*Dana's illustration of the precious coral (*Corallium secundum *Dana) discovered by the Exploring Expedition in Hawaii.*
Zoophytes atlas, plate 60, figure 1. Courtesy Smithsonian Institution Libraries.

twelve from Peru (all but one dry), twelve from Singapore (all but two still in alcohol), nine from Rio de Janeiro (all dry), and five from New Zealand (all dry). Except for seventeen without locality (examples of the mixed or lost ticketing that Dana mentioned), the rest came from scattered localities. Apart from those that have been maintained in alcohol, the specimens are in various states of deterioration, and the condition of none of them is really good.

Dana's report on the collection suffered almost as many vicissitudes as did the specimens. Many of the original drawings were destroyed by fire after the plates were engraved but before the prints could be completely colored as planned. Moreover, an intentional overrun of fifty copies of about half of the plates, made when the author's unofficial copies were printed, were damaged by fire. Somewhat more than half of them were salvaged by Dana and distributed as partial sets when an anticipated second edition of the report did not materialize.

Dana's text, which ran to 1,618 pages bound in two volumes, included more than five hundred new species. When Darwin wrote to Dana about the work, he said that if he "had done nothing else whatever, it would have been a *magnum opus* for life. . . . I am really lost in astonishment at what you have done in mental labor. And then, besides the labor, so much *originality* in all your works." [Gilman 1899:310]

Given reasonable care, corals, being durable objects, fare admirably in collections. The corals collected by Couthouy and Dana form the foundation of the Smithsonian coral collection, occupying nineteen quarter-unit cases in the Department of Invertebrate Zoology, National Museum of Natural History, eleven of them containing nothing but type specimens. The catalog records 313 specimens comprising 240 species, not considering those that may have been synonymized by subsequent revisions.

Corals may be durable, but many are fragile, some extremely so. Looking at this collection today, we can only marvel that Dana managed to collect, clean, and pack so many with so little damage. And one has to keep in mind that we are seeing only part of the collection. Some of the material was distributed to other museums in line with the Smithsonian policy at the time, and we have no record of how much.

One of the most remarkable corals collected by the Expedition was *Corallium secundum* Dana from the "Sandwich Islands," the second species of precious coral known to science. The original precious coral (also known as red coral or jewel coral), *Corallium rubrum* Lamarck, lives in the Mediterranean Sea and nearby eastern Atlantic waters and has been a prized article of commerce for millennia. Until the Exploring Expedition, precious coral had never been found in Pacific waters, and Dana could not have foreseen that the species he discovered would become the basis of a significant industry in Hawaii a century and a quarter later. It is also somewhat of a mystery how the Expedition acquired the specimen. Dana's description of it shows clearly that its delicate outer tissues were intact, so it must have been alive when collected. This species has not been subsequently obtained by exploratory vessels or by commercial operations in less than about 350 meters of water, and there is no indication that the Expedition ships had the capa-

bility of dredging that deep. Neither Dana's report nor his journals mention that the specimen was dredged, yet it must have been.

Dana's report on the zoophytes—the corals and other sessile coelenterates—the second of the scientific reports to appear (1846, atlas in 1849), was actually a synthesis of knowledge about corals and included 229 species new to science out of a total of 483. In 1850, Henri Milne Edwards and Jules Haime, the foremost European authorities on corals, called it "one of the most valuable contributions which America has yet made to Natural History." In their comprehensive review of the corals some years later, the same authors expanded their praise:

In recent years, the advances in zoophytology have been due principally to the works of Mr. Dana who, as a member of the great American expedition to the South Pole, had the opportunity to study a great many animals belonging to the class of corals, and has contributed to that study with his unique skill. Apart from the important improvements which he introduced in the natural classification of these animals, he has undertaken long and thorough studies of their morphology, and has investigated with great sagacity the way in which the aggregated individuals occur together to form composite coralla; his work is accompanied by a magnificent atlas, and the publication does honor as much to the government that sponsored it as to the author who achieved it. [1857:xxxiii trans.]

In spite of advice from Benjamin Tappan to omit the "actinias"—the sea anemones, which have no coral skeleton—Dana included them in his report. He felt that the work would be incomplete without them, and he took advantage of the notes and drawings by Couthouy and Drayton to fill this gap. In the preface to his report he clearly states that the descriptions were prepared by Couthouy or by Drayton, sometimes from Couthouy's notes, and he specifically attributes authorship of the various descriptions to them. Under the rules that govern the naming of animals, this means that Drayton and Couthouy are the authors of the new species described, not Dana himself.

The other "zoophytes"—the pelagic jellyfishes and several other phyla loosely grouped under that name—were collected by Couthouy and Drayton, and we now know what they found chiefly through their notes and drawings, for the specimens themselves did not fare so well as the corals. Many are so delicate that they are difficult or impossible to preserve under the best of conditions, which Couthouy certainly did not have. It is quite certain that he did not preserve some kinds of jellyfishes, as he remarked in his journal: "The departments under my care have this great disadvantage over all the rest—that their objects must be studied &

drawings can only be made during life. Most of the Zoophytes cannot be preserved at all." [p. 21] However, the annotated drawings of them that he and Drayton made are still preserved in the Department of Invertebrate Zoology at the National Museum of Natural History, although the location of his detailed notebooks, if extant, is not known.

The drawings and whatever descriptions there were were sent to Louis Agassiz at Harvard. Although he was commissioned to report on the fishes, no indication has been found of a formal arrangement for him to prepare a report on the "Gelly fish." Lumped under that ambiguous heading were scyphozoan and hydrozoan medusae, hy-

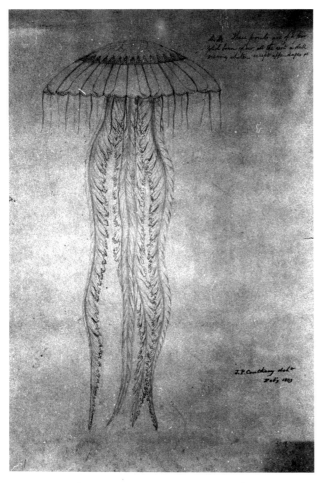

Couthouy's pencil sketch and notes on the huge jellyfish, Medora capensis L. Agassiz [now considered to be Desmonema gaudichaudii (Lesson)] collected 17 February 1839 in sight of Cape Horn by Captain Ringgold of the Porpoise. Courtesy National Museum of Natural History, Smithsonian Institution.

Couthouy's pencil sketch of a jellyfish, Diplopilus couthouyi L. Agassiz [= Cephea cephea (Forskål)], collected at Wilson's Island (Manihi) in the Tuamotus. Courtesy National Museum of Natural History, Smithsonian Institution.

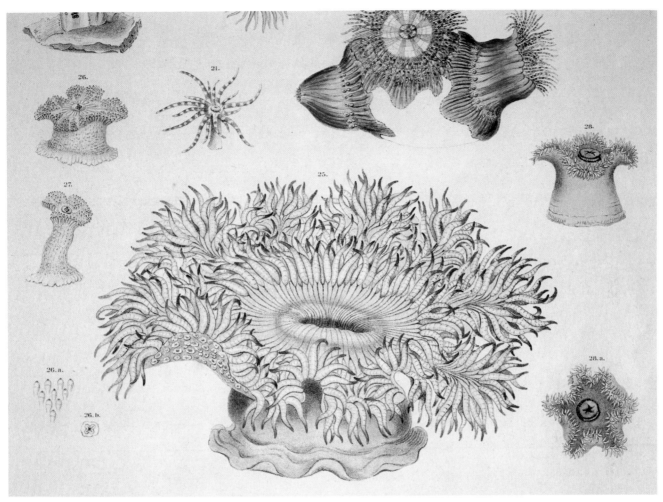

Drayton's illustration of a sea anemone, Actinia paumotensis *Couthouy.* Zoophytes *atlas. Courtesy Smithsonian Institution Libraries.*

droids, siphonophores, nemertean worms, polychaetes, nudibranchs, holothurians, crinoids, starfishes, and sipunculid worms. As was the case with the fishes, no official report on these animals was ever published, although in 1862 Agassiz commented that the drawings from the Exploring Expedition would shortly be published. This did not happen, and, unlike the fishes, not even a manuscript is known to exist.

Some of the real jellyfishes—scyphozoan medusae—drawn and described by Drayton and Couthouy were mentioned by Agassiz in enough detail to make the names he applied to them nomenclaturally available. Unlike Dana's procedure in his re-

port, Agassiz did not directly quote his source. Although he usually used the names that Couthouy had applied in the field, the descriptive or diagnostic remarks clearly are his and not Couthouy's, so Agassiz is the author of the names, not Couthouy.

One of the medusae that Couthouy described and personally illustrated in the greatest detail was found in Orange Harbor and designated *Nerinea,* "New Genus of Medusa Linn." in manuscript at the bottom of the drawing. Agassiz published the differential characters shown in Couthouy's drawings and notes and pointed out that the name *Nerinea* was already in use for a different animal. Since that name could not be used for the medusa, he

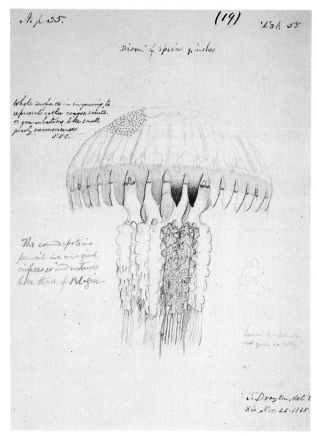

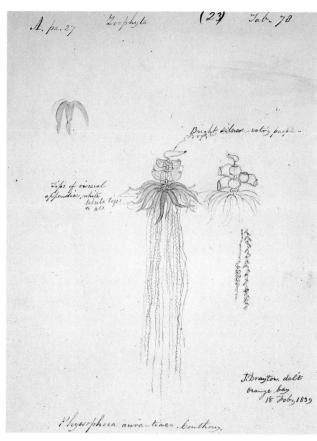

Drayton's annotated color sketch of a jellyfish, Rhacopilus cyanolobatus L. Agassiz [probably =Catostylus cruciatus (Lesson)], collected in the harbor of Rio de Janeiro, 25 November 1838. Courtesy National Museum of Natural History, Smithsonian Institution.

Drayton's color sketches of a siphonophore, Physsophora aurantiaca, Couthouy MS., collected at Orange Harbor, 18 February 1839. Courtesy National Museum of Natural History, Smithsonian Institution.

substituted *Couthouyia* for it, and in so doing he legally introduced the name *Nerinea* Agassiz for the medusa at the same time as *Couthouyia*, thus simultaneously creating a nomenclatural homonym and synonym. Today, it is chiefly a matter of historical interest, as subsequent research has demonstrated that *Couthouyia pendula* Agassiz, 1862, is the same species of jellyfish named *Chrysaora gaudichaudii* by Lesson in 1829, from almost the same locality, and the name *Couthouyia* had already been proposed for a mollusk in 1860 and therefore is a junior homonym.

Agassiz also validated Couthouy's *Medora* on the basis of his drawings of two species, one collected

"in sight of Cape Horn" by Captain Ringgold, the other at Orange Harbor. Couthouy's journal for Sunday, 17 February 1839, shows that the jellyfish from Cape Horn must have been an imposing specimen:

Shortly after Sundown a boat from the Porpoise boarded us bringing an enormous Medusoide allied to Pelagia, which Capt. Ringgold had just captured & sent for examination. It was over 9 feet in circumference, the brachia nearly 7 feet long with the buccal portion 5 & ½ inches additional. . . . All the brachiae but one are wanting, so that the weight could not be accurately deter-

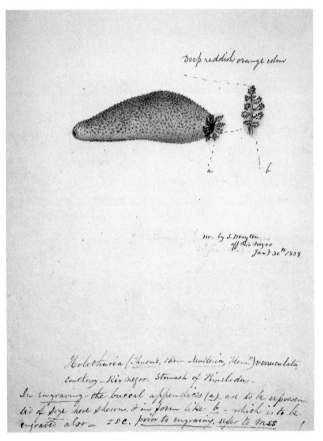

Drayton's color drawing of a holothurian, or sea cucumber, made at Valparaiso in May 1839. Neither the picture nor Couthouy's account of the animal was ever published, so the species remained unknown to science until Selenka named it Pattalus mollis *in 1868. Courtesy National Museum of Natural History, Smithsonian Institution.*

Drayton's color drawing, annotated by Couthouy, of a holothurian, or sea cucumber, that Couthouy proposed to name Thyone verruculata, *collected from the stomach of a catfish off Rio Negro in Patagonia 30 January 1839. Couthouy never had an opportunity to publish his account of the animal, which is probably the species later named* Trachythyone lechleri *(Lampert 1885). Courtesy National Museum of Natural History, Smithsonian Institution.*

mined, but it could not I think fall short of 60 pounds. It is very distinct from any known species of Pelagia. I have therefore denominated it P. capensis . . . [and] Made a drawing of it with such anatomical details as I could make out in its mutilated condition. [p.15]

Agassiz did not characterize the two species that Couthouy recognized, so the specific names he published from Couthouy's notes are not nomenclaturally available for them.

Couthouy was credited by Agassiz with solving a puzzle posed by a drawing of a jellyfish published almost a century earlier. At Wilson's Island, Couthouy drew an extraordinary medusa, which, in Agassiz's words, had a "cupola . . . made up of large conical tubercles, and standing out prominently from the upper part of the disk." [1862:157] Agassiz honored Couthouy by naming the jellyfish shown in his drawing *Diplopilus couthouyi*.

Agassiz honored Wilkes by naming a large jellyfish *Catostylus wilkesii* that Drayton found in Lake Illawarra and drew while the Scientifics were in Australia, but a later revision has shown that *C. wilkesii* is the same species that was named *Cephea mosaica* in 1824. The large and beautiful medusa

86

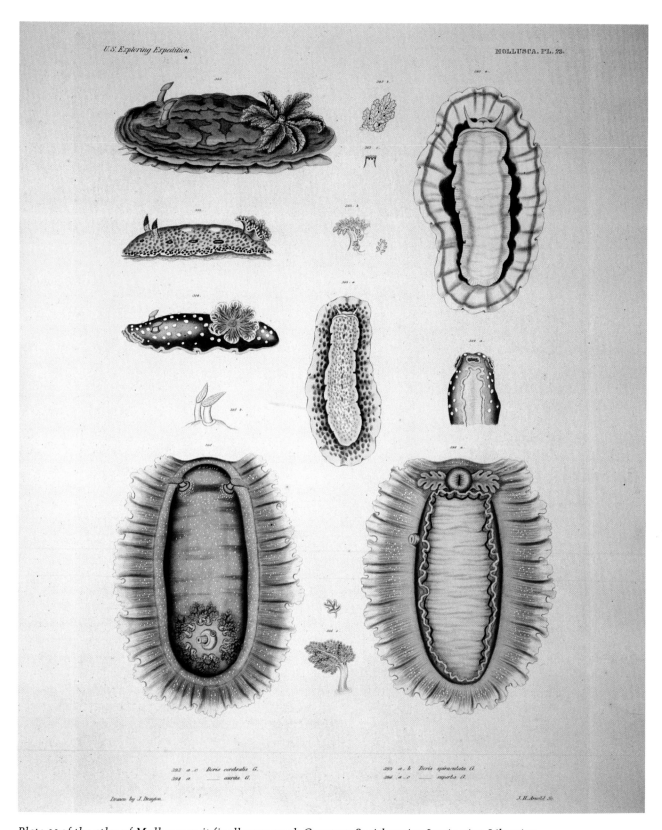

393 a.c   *Doris cerebralis G.*   395 a.b   *Doris spiraculata G.*
394 a   ———— *aurita G.*   396 a.c   ———— *superba G.*

Drawn by J. Drayton.   J.H. Arnold Sc.

Plate 23 of the atlas of Mollusca as it finally appeared. Courtesy Smithsonian Institution Libraries.

 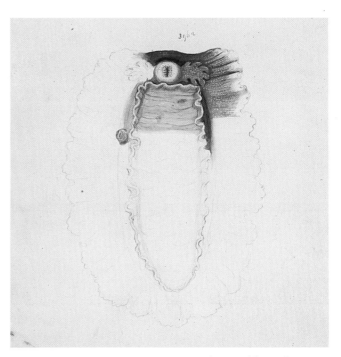

Drayton's original watercolors of the dorsal and ventral views of the nudibranch mollusk Doris superba *Gould, made at Tutuila, Samoa, in October 1839. Courtesy National Museum of Natural History, Smithsonian Institution.*

with blue marginal lobes, drawn by Drayton at Rio de Janeiro, was assigned by Agassiz to a new genus *Rhacopilus* and given the specific name *cyanolobatus* that Couthouy proposed for it.

Couthouy and Drayton drew and described many more medusae that Agassiz for some reason did not mention, probably because they were not North American. These have effectively been lost to science as have all the various worms that we know they observed.

Some of the echinoderms, such as the starfishes, brittlestars, and sea urchins, which have a substantial calcareous skeleton, have withstood the perils of mismanagement and the ravages of time. Fifty-three lots, most without precise locality records, are still preserved in the collections of the Smithsonian. Several of these have been mentioned in scattered taxonomic monographs, but for the most part their identity as part of America's first great scientific expedition has been lost. Still others, the soft-bodied holothurians (sea cucumbers) are known only from the drawings made by Drayton and Couthouy. Thanks to the detail and accuracy of their work, however, it is possible to reconstruct, albeit in a limited way, the specimens that no longer exist and thus retrieve from oblivion the work those dedicated men accomplished for their nation nearly a century and a half ago.

Dana by Daniel Huntington. Courtesy Yale University Art Gallery, bequest of Edward Salisbury Dana, B.A. 1870.

5 James Dwight Dana and Pacific Geology

The Importance of Being Dana

The most fundamental and enduring scientific contributions of the U. S. Exploring Expedition are contained in the report *Geology*, by James Dwight Dana. There are two major reasons why this should be so. One is the focus of the Expedition on the Pacific Ocean. Surrounding and scattered across this immense region, one-third of the globe, are most of the world's active volcanoes. For three years the explorers were able to study and observe volcanism in all its myriad aspects. But perhaps a more important reason resides in the character and ability of the Expedition's geologist, Dana, who proved to be the intellectual giant of the Ex. Ex. Scientifics. He became the most influential American geologist of the nineteenth century and remains a towering figure in the history of geology.

In his career Dana personified the emerging professional scientist of the future: he devoted his working life entirely to scientific research, writing and teaching as a geologist. His single-minded pursuit of this goal contrasts sharply with the lives of his Expedition colleagues. His "professionalism" was not acquired by accident. Dana owed both his excellent scientific training and his intensely professional approach to scientific research to the extraordinary school of natural sciences established at Yale College by Benjamin Silliman. Indeed,

Dana's life and career are inextricably linked to Silliman and Yale.

James Dwight Dana was born in 1813 in Utica, New York. As a boy he collected rocks and minerals, but his serious interest in natural history began at Utica High School. This private boarding school, highly advanced for its day, emphasized the natural sciences—Asa Gray taught there after Dana left. In 1830 Dana went on to Yale College. Already determined on a career in the natural sciences, he was attracted to Yale by the presence of Benjamin Silliman, then America's most eminent teacher in the field.

As his graduation approached in 1833, Dana realized that jobs for natural scientists were almost nonexistent. The minuscule number of college teaching positions available in any field remotely resembling natural history led him to look elsewhere. He sought and received an appointment as instructor in mathematics to midshipmen in the U. S. Navy, on board the ship of the line *Delaware*, cruising to the Mediterranean. Such appointments were commonly used in the navy for providing officers with necessary academic training in the days before the establishment of the U.S. Naval Academy. After crossing the Atlantic to Minorca, Dana transferred to the frigate *United States*, on which he cruised the Mediterranean ports.

The Mediterranean cruise was in a real sense

Dana's first "exploring expedition." His duties were sufficiently light to leave plenty of time for scientific pursuits. In Italy he ascended the famed volcano Vesuvius, then in an active phase, and made detailed geological observations. He wrote these up and sent them home to Silliman, who promptly published them in his *American Journal of Science.* Made shortly before an eruption in 1834, Dana's notes on Vesuvius constitute the first description of an active volcano by an American geologist, and surely make him the first American volcanologist.

Dana returned from his Mediterranean cruise at the end of 1834, more determined than ever to make his career in geology. Back at Yale, he eventually obtained a position as Silliman's assistant. This position launched his career as a professional geologist; it also served him as postgraduate training, perhaps the closest approach to a modern graduate school then available in the United States.

Benjamin Silliman was one of the true pioneers of American science. Among his most important achievements was the establishment of the *American Journal of Science*—the first national scientific journal published in the United States. By thus bringing American research to the attention of the international scientific community, Silliman as much as anyone promoted the "coming-of-age" of American science. Under Silliman's tutelage, Dana acquired the lifelong habit of rapid and voluminous publication of his research.

While working with Silliman at Yale, Dana published his first book, *A System of Mineralogy* (1837). A landmark in the systematic classification and description of minerals, the *System* immediately brought Dana considerable renown. In this first edition, Dana introduced a "natural" classification and binomial Latin nomenclature similar to those used in botany and zoology, in an attempt to remedy what he perceived as deficiencies in the rudimentary chemical classifications of previous workers. In the third edition (1850) he completely abandoned the "natural" system and returned to a chemical classification based on more advanced chemical and crystallographic principles. Regardless of these changes of direction—or perhaps because his book moved with the times—Dana's *System* was tremendously successful. It went

through six editions in his lifetime (the last revised by his son Edward), and in its seventh edition remains the authoritative reference in its field. It is ironic that Dana is most widely known today as the author of *A System of Mineralogy,* this work of his youth which he revised throughout his life as a duty rather than an enthusiasm. At any rate, by the time of the organization of the Exploring Expedition in 1836, Dana was already a rising young scientist with an established reputation. This led to the invitation from Jeremiah Reynolds, its chief promoter, to join the Expedition.

Overture: South America

As the Expedition made its way slowly around South America en route to the South Pacific, where its real objectives lay, Dana was all too conscious of following in the wake of Darwin and the *Beagle.* On the entire west coast of South America, where Darwin had made some of his most important geological observations, Dana was allowed only a few brief days ashore. Thus South America contributes little of importance to the *Geology* report. However, Dana had sufficient self-confidence to differ with his distinguished predecessor over the interpretation of sea-level changes at San Lorenzo Island, off the coast of Peru. Here Darwin, who spent an inordinate amount of effort on such changes, had postulated an uplift of eighty-five feet "since *Indian man inhabited Peru.*" [Darwin 1846:49] He based this conclusion on a thick accumulation of recent shells, mixed with man-made "Indian" relics, on a supposed wave-cut terrace eighty-five feet above sea level. Dana pointed out rather tartly that the supposed beach is probably just a sandstone layer more resistant to erosion, and that the shells were most likely accumulated there by the Peruvians themselves, along with the relics. The incident shows refreshing skepticism as well as keen geologic observation.

Eimeo (Moorea), Society Islands, by Agate, shows extreme dissection of the original shield volcano. Narrative.

The Origin of Coral Islands

In July 1839 the Exploring Expedition left Peru and sailed westward. For four months it explored three of the most important coral and volcanic island groups of the South Pacific: the Tuamotus (they called them the Paumotus), the Society Islands, and the Samoan group. Dana found himself in the middle of a classic geologic problem: the origin of coral islands and atolls. How could reef-forming corals, which can grow only in shallow water, form islands in the deep ocean? Why did they often have peculiar, ringlike shapes, enclosing central lagoons? Dana was familiar with the various theories advanced to answer these questions, and he had ample opportunity to test them against his careful observations of a great many islands. But none of the theories seemed to fit the facts.

When the Expedition reached New South Wales, Australia, at the end of November, Dana saw in the newspapers a brief account of Darwin's theory of the origin of atolls. "The paragraph threw a flood of light over the subject," Dana wrote, "and called forth feelings of peculiar satisfaction, and of gratefulness to Mr. Darwin." [1872:7] Dana immediately saw that Darwin's hypothesis explained his own observations as no other theory had. When the Exploring Expedition reached the Fiji Islands in 1840, Dana found still better evidence for the validity of Darwin's ideas, better even than Darwin himself had been able to adduce.

Darwin's hypothesis is set forth with great simplicity in his *Structure and Distribution of Coral Reefs*, first published in 1842. It is based on observations that a continuous evolutionary sequence exists, from volcanic islands with fringing coral reefs, through volcanic islands with surrounding barrier reefs separated from the island by a deep lagoon, to circular atolls surrounding a deep lagoon with no central volcanic island. The key is gradual subsidence.

The stages of development of a coral atoll are well illustrated by Dana with examples, mostly from Fiji.

Stage 1: A volcano erupts on the sea floor, eventually building a volcanic island. While the island is actively growing, little or no coral reef development can take place around it. Example: the island of Hawaii.

Stage 2: Volcanic activity ceases. Corals build a fringing reef in the shallow waters around the island. Example: Chichia Island, Fiji group.

Stage 3: The sea floor beneath the island begins to subside. As the island slowly sinks, the coral reef continues to grow upward, especially on the outer side exposed to wave action. This leaves a lagoon between the reef and its central island; it is now a barrier reef. Example: Matuku Island, Fiji group.

Stage 4: As the sea floor continues to subside, the central island eventually sinks beneath the waves. The reef continues to grow upward, keeping pace with the slow subsidence; it is now a roughly circular lagoon. Example: Nanuku Island, Fiji group.

Darwin had thought that direct proof of subsidence of volcanic islands was almost impossible, but Dana recognized two distinct lines of geologic evidence, both based on the shapes of volcanoes. He noted that the slopes of basaltic shield volcanoes, where unaffected by erosion, seldom average more than eight degrees, and that on any reasonable assumption of submarine slope the minimum thickness of many barrier reefs must exceed a thousand feet. Since reef corals rarely grow below 120 feet, subsidence of the order of a thousand feet must have occurred.

A second line of reasoning was based on Dana's observations of erosion on Pacific islands, of which we will hear more later. Dana recognized that islands such as Tahiti, in the Society Islands, had once had the characteristic low domelike shape of young shield volcanoes like Mauna Loa. The extremely rugged, dissected present topography of Tahiti he correctly attributed to subaerial erosion

Map of Tahiti, "an admirable model of a deeply denuded or water-sculptured mountain cone." [Dana 1890: 374] Courtesy Smithsonian Institution Libraries.

by running water. He realized that if a dissected island like Tahiti were partially submerged, its deep valleys and narrow ridges would form an extremely irregular, deeply embayed coastline. Such a coastline would be virtual proof of submergence, as the sea was incapable of eroding the shore in this way. Darwin, who thought the sea was the chief agent of erosion of such landforms, never understood or appreciated the power of Dana's reasoning. Today, deep drilling on coral atolls has largely confirmed the Darwin-Dana hypothesis.

Dana made another significant contribution to geology by recognizing that reef-forming corals are extremely sensitive to cold. They cannot exist where the water temperature falls below a critical value for even a short time, which effectively restricts their growth to tropical waters. Dana attempted to outline rather precisely, on his chart of the Pacific Ocean, the region of coral reef development, showing the effects of cold currents in certain regions such as the west coast of South America.

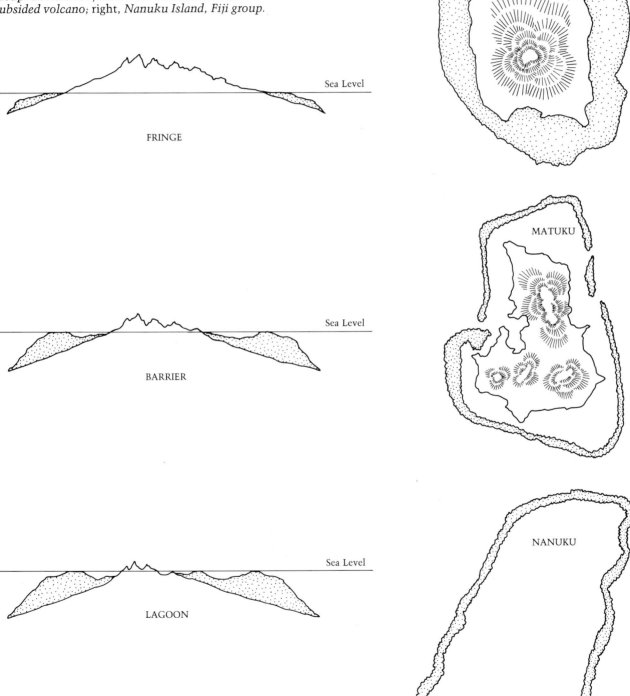

Diagrams after Dana; maps from Exploring Expedition reports and atlases. Top left, fringing reef around a volcanic island; right, Chichia Island, Fiji group. Center left, barrier reef, lagoon, and fringing reef around a subsiding volcanic island; right, Matuku Island, Fiji group. Bottom left, atoll with central islets over a subsided volcano; right, Nanuku Island, Fiji group.

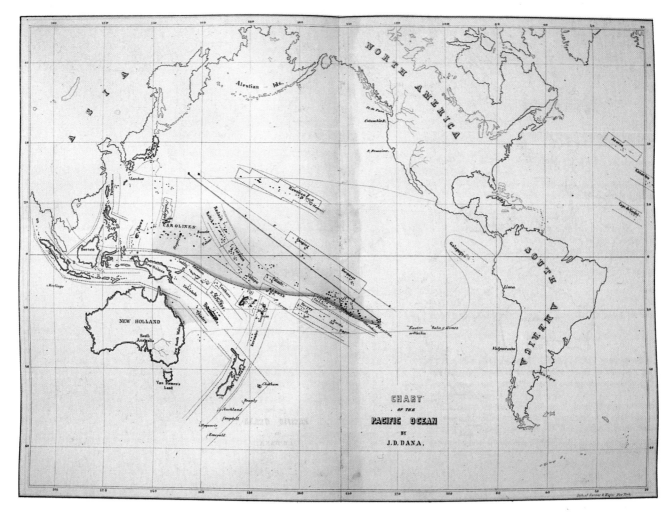

Chart of the Pacific Ocean. Green*: atolls, region of subsidence.* Red*: areas of non-subsidence.* Dotted line AB*: axis of greatest subsidence from positions of island chains.* Green line AB*: axis of greatest subsidence from study of coral islands.* Solid line*: limits of coral reef formation.* Dashed lines*: island chains.* Dotted lines*: trends of island chains.* Dana, Geology, *after page 352. Courtesy Smithsonian Institution Libraries.*

He noted that fossil coral reefs are found in ancient rocks on the continents in latitudes far outside their present range. This fact is used today as evidence for continental drift, but Dana instead assumed that the ancient corals had possessed a much greater temperature tolerance.

Originally, the zoological study of corals on the Exploring Expedition was to have been done by Joseph P. Couthouy, the Expedition conchologist. When Couthouy fell ill in New South Wales, and ultimately had to leave the cruise, Dana took over this work. Thus it was Dana, not Couthouy, who studied the lush coral reefs and islands of Fiji and who eventually wrote the *Zoophytes* report. Back in Boston in 1841, Couthouy learned of Darwin's theory of the origin of coral islands from a series of lectures by the great British geologist Charles Lyell. In a long paper presented to the Boston Society of Natural History and published in 1842, Couthouy developed an origin for coral atolls very similar to Darwin's, based on his own detailed observations during the Exploring Expedition. More remarkable, he set out a theory of the temperature dependence of coral reef growth almost identical to Dana's.

Both Dana and Couthouy thus differed sharply (and correctly) with Darwin, who insisted that temperature could not explain the absence of coral reefs in areas like the Galápagos. However, Darwin refers to Couthouy's article often and very favorably in his own book on coral reefs, published in 1842, because it strengthens his theory with numerous striking examples.

Dana rather surprisingly reacted with fury to Couthouy's article and publicly accused him of plagiarism, on the grounds that he had been privy to Dana's notes during the Expedition. The fight raged in the pages of the *American Journal of Science*. Poor Couthouy, deeply shocked at this attack from one he had considered a friend, was hard-pressed to defend himself, because all of his notes and journals had been removed to Washington by order of Wilkes. Eventually, he found proof of his originality in letters he had written during the cruise, and Dana was forced to apologize. The truth very likely is that the two had often discussed their observations and deductions during the voyage and had not unnaturally come to rather similar conclusions. Dana's intemperance seems to have had its origin in the urgency he felt to establish his professional reputation, knowing that writing the Expedition reports would require many years of his labor before publication.

Australia

In Australia, the explorers found themselves back in Civilization. In this most distant outpost of English-speaking culture, they were welcomed enthusiastically by the local naturalists. The continent, isolated for sixty million years, was a treasure trove of unique plants and animals. The Scientifics did full justice to it in their collections. Freed for two glorious months from the discipline of navy life, they accomplished some of the most interesting field work of the Expedition.

The study of natural history was well established in Australia by the time of the Exploring Expedition visit in 1839–40. At that period, however, the focus of organized scientific investigation had shifted from New South Wales to Van Diemen's Land (Tas-

mania). The Tasmanian Society of Natural History was founded in 1837. Meanwhile in New South Wales, as an Australian historian has written, "the cause of science was kept alive by the individual efforts of such men as Clarke." [Hoare 1969:33] This was the Reverend W. B. Clarke, a pioneering figure in Australian geology. Clarke was a graduate of Cambridge University, where he had studied geology under the great Adam Sedgwick. He had immigrated to New South Wales just eight months before the Exploring Expedition arrived, and as the first trained geologist to settle in Australia was eager to begin exploring the new land.

Clarke met Dana shortly after the Expedition's arrival, and the two men, enjoying similar interests, became lifelong friends. Together they roamed the countryside, making large collections of rocks and fossils and trying to interpret the geology of the coastal regions of New South Wales. Most of what we know about Dana's travels in Australia comes from Clarke's journals. The two months Dana spent doing geologic field studies in New South Wales represent far more time than he was allowed at any other single place during the Expedition. He was among the first to study Australian geology seriously, and his accomplishments here far outshadowed those of earlier visitors such as Paul de Strzelecki and even Darwin.

One of Dana's major contributions was the description and geologic mapping of the rock formations between the Hunter and the Shoalhaven rivers. He visited—mostly with Clarke—the sandstones around Sydney and Paramatta, the beautiful Illawarra District and Kangaroo Valley sixty miles to the south, and the country around Newcastle eighty miles to the north. He journeyed 120 miles up the Hunter River Valley, from Newcastle to Puenbuen, his farthest trip into the interior. In all these areas he carefully measured stratigraphic sections and collected numerous fossils to help correlate the sedimentary rocks from region to region.

Dana mapped and studied three major sedimentary units throughout the area he investigated: the coal formation; the sandstone above the coal, which he called the Sydney Sandstone; and the argillaceous sandstone below the coal. These are

Glossopteris ampla *Dana, 1849. Neotype specimen NMNH 41296; drawing by Dana,* Geology atlas, *plate 13, figure 1b. The description of this new species was typical of Dana's careful study of the plant fossils from the coal formation. Courtesy Smithsonian Institution Libraries.*

well shown on his geologic map of the Illawarra district; but he also correlated them with equivalent rocks in the Sydney and Newcastle regions. The Sydney Sandstone was virtually nonfossiliferous; the coal formation had abundant plant fossils; and the sandstone below the coal yielded a rich fauna of fossil marine invertebrates, especially bivalved mollusks. Through careful study of the fossils, Dana was able to show that the lower sandstone and the coal were of Permian age; and the conformable nature of the sequence led him to the belief that the Sydney Sandstone was also Permian or a little younger. Modern restudy of these fossils, now in the Smithsonian collections, confirms Dana's work.

The fossil plants collected by Dana from the coal formation at Newcastle and Illawarra are particularly interesting. They compose a distinctive group called the "Glossopteris Flora," after the striking plants most abundant within it. The British paleontologist J. Morris had examined some of these fossils, sent to him by Strzelecki. He had noted that they resembled those found in coal measures in India, but differed from the flora found in rocks of similar age in North America and Europe. Agreeing with him, Dana wrote: "Morris concludes from the facts that the Flora of the southern hemisphere

differed from that of the northern at the 'carboniferous period.'" [1849:495].

Later workers confirmed that the Glossopteris Flora is common in Permian (280–225 million-year-old) rocks in India, South Africa, South America, and Antarctica, as well as Australia; but is not found in Permian rocks of North America or Eurasia. This led early twentieth-century geologists to speculate that the southern continents were joined during the Permian Period into a supercontinent, which they called "Gondwana" after a locality in India. This was one of the earliest pieces of evidence for continental drift. Dana's plant fossils are significant as one of the earliest published records of the Glossopteris Flora; they have recently been restudied in great detail because of their importance to modern paleobotanists.

The most striking feature of the Australian landscape noted by Dana was the great gorges that dissect the sandstone, such as Kangaroo Valley, near Illawarra, which he visited with Clarke. Darwin had equally been impressed by similar valleys in the Blue Mountains west of Sydney. Darwin could not believe that these immense gorges had been eroded by running water; he called the idea "preposterous." [1851:II,136] Instead, he proposed that the sandstone had been deposited in heaps by current action on an irregular sea bottom, and that the valleylike spaces between heaps might have had their walls worn into cliffs during uplift, either by the retreating sea or by streams.

Dana argued on the basis of solid geological reasoning that the gorges were indeed due to subaerial erosion by running water, acting over the immensity of geologic time. The original continuity of the sandstone layers was obvious, and the sea did not erode valleys out of coastlines. Dana patiently outlined again, as he had in his observations on the Pacific islands, the evidence that running water is the major force in shaping landscapes. He showed that while the sea can form wave-cut platforms along the coast, the valleys are stream-carved and do not extend below sea level. He explained the effects of mass-wasting and discussed the carrying power of streams and the importance of floods. It was a powerful performance and effectively disposed of Darwin's objections. While this may seem ob-

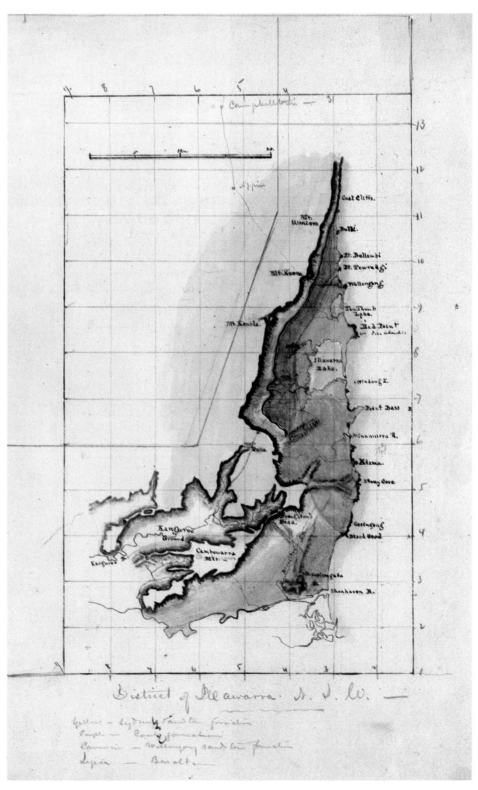

Map of New South Wales, 1848. Dana, Geology, after page 448.
Courtesy Sterling Memorial Library, Yale University.

vious today, it was challenging and original then. Dana's conclusions on erosion of the gorges of New South Wales were a major contribution to geology.

Although not a region of active volcanoes, New South Wales has its share of ancient volcanic rocks. Dana carefully studied basalt layers interspersed between sandstone beds and noted the evidence of heat alteration of the underlying sandstone and its irregular surface, which led him to interpret the basalt as flows, not intrusions. He mapped dikes and showed alteration effects in the surrounding sandstone and coal. And he sketched and described spectacular columnar jointing at Kiama, which he said "will bear comparison with the rocks of Staffa" [Dana 1849:496] As usual, Dana went beyond mere description and tried to correlate the degree of perfection of the columnar jointing with the cooling

rates of the flows, and to explain the direction of columns by the geometry of the underlying surface.

Intermezzo: New Zealand

At the end of February 1840, the scientific party arrived in New Zealand. Here they were to rendezvous with Wilkes and the fleet, back from their exploration of the Antarctic coast. Although New Zealand is a land of active volcanoes, Dana was not able to visit them or to see the famed geyser and hot-spring regions. The explorations of the Scientifics were limited instead to the region around the Bay of Islands, at the northern end of North Island. Here he was able to visit an area of extinct cinder cones and some modest hot springs; but most of

Sketch by Dana of basaltic columns at Kiama in Illawarra, New South Wales.
Courtesy Sterling Memorial Library, Yale University.

his knowledge of volcanic activity on New Zealand came from a published work by Dr. Dieffenbach and from a local missionary, the Reverend Mr. Williams.

It is not clear why Dana and his companions did not attempt to see more of North Island in the six weeks or so they spent in New Zealand. Perhaps it was because this was still a rather wild and unexplored part of the world, and they had no Clarke to guide them. In one of his most myopic statements, Wilkes said: "I believe that no person in the squadron felt any regret leaving New Zealand, for there was a want of all means of amusement, as well as of any objects in whose observations we were interested." [1844:II,3]

Hawaii

From New Zealand the Exploring Expedition proceeded slowly to Tonga, thence to Fiji. The Tonga group added still more varieties of coral islands to Dana's growing list. For Dana, the Fiji group was primarily a place to collect and observe living corals, since that task had fallen to him when Couthouy was invalided to Hawaii and home. These islands also offered, of course, superb examples for the study of atoll development; we have seen that Dana took full advantage of them. Finally, in late September 1840, the Expedition arrived in the Hawaiian Islands, and Dana the geologist came into his own.

The Hawaiian group, he wrote, is "the key to Polynesian Geology," [Dana 1849:156] and so it proved. Here on the island of Hawaii the explorers were to make the first accurate scientific studies of the active volcanoes Mauna Loa and Kilauea, one of the great scientific achievements of the Expedition. Their work laid the foundation for a century and a half of research, which has made Kilauea the most studied volcano in the world.

Kilauea is also one of the most active volcanoes in the world and the explorers recognized that it was an ideal "natural laboratory" for studying volcanic processes. It was easily accessible, even in 1840. It erupted often, indeed, for long periods almost continually. And its generally quiet, nonex-

plosive style made it possible to approach and study it closely during eruptions and even to sample the molten lava.

Kilauea is a typical shield volcano—a broad dome of basalt with very gentle slopes, built up over many thousands of years by innumerable flows of highly fluid lava. It rises to a height of just over four thousand feet, twenty-two miles east of lofty Mauna Loa. At its summit is a steep-walled oval depression about two by three miles across; this is the summit crater or caldera, in which summit eruptions take place. Such an eruption was in progress when Dana visited in November 1840. However, the volcano was not quite the same in appearance as it is today.

A major eruption early in 1832 had filled the entire caldera to within about 600 feet of the top with "solid lava." [Martin 1979:55] Later in that year the central portion of the caldera floor collapsed, leaving a wide ledge completely around the basin. By 1839 continued summit eruptions had refilled the basin, obliterating the ledge, but during the great flank eruptions of May–June 1840 the center again collapsed and the ledge reappeared. At the time of the Expedition's visit, this "Black Ledge" was about 650 feet below the caldera rim and about 340 feet above the floor of the inner pit where the eruptions were taking place.

The outer walls of the caldera look almost the same today as they did then, but the Black Ledge is gone. By 1886 the basin had filled pretty much to the level we see now. The caldera floor is now less than five hundred feet below the rim, burying the Black Ledge. The inner pit has been reduced to the present "fire-pit" of Halemaumau, about three thousand feet in diameter.

When Dana and Titian Peale saw Kilauea, the inner pit occupied most of the caldera. On its floor were several erupting lava pools, the largest one at the present location of Halemaumau. The depth of the inner pit in 1981 was about 260 feet. Since the main caldera floor today is not very different in position from the Black Ledge in Dana's time, the general features of Drayton's sketch are still recognizable.

Dana was allowed to spend only five days on the island of Hawaii; most of them on a tramp from

Kealakekua on the west coast, around the southern tip of Mauna Loa and up to Kilauea, thence down to Hilo. Much of his route closely paralleled the modern Highway 11. Though he had only one full day at Kilauea, he gathered all the information he could about prior eruptions and all the observations of his Expedition colleagues, as well as his own data from visits to Kauai and Oahu and his shipboard observations of the other islands.

In the Hawaiian group Dana refined his observations on the shapes of volcanoes and their eruptive styles. Here he noted three major types. Most important were basaltic shield volcanoes like Kilauea and Mauna Loa. These were formed by rather thin flows of highly fluid basaltic lavas that were erupted quietly and often went for long distances.

A second type, "cinder cones," were steep-sided conical hills of basaltic fragments, formed by more violent ejection of lava into the air so that it fell in a shower of cooled fragments around the vent. A few hundred feet high or less, they were especially abundant as the last eruptive phase of the great shield volcano Mauna Kea on Hawaii.

The third major type, "tufa cones," were formed of finer fragmented material, volcanic "ash," blasted into the air when molten lava came into contact with water and erupted explosively. Diamond Head near Waikiki on Oahu is the best-known example. Dana also saw littoral cones that had formed just before his arrival, south of Hilo, where the 1840 flank eruption entered the sea.

In his description of Kilauea in summit eruption, Dana strongly emphasized the quiet eruptive style; he particularly delighted in countering the rather fervid accounts of many earlier visitors. He clearly recognized the way in which a huge edifice like Mauna Loa can be built up by a combination of summit eruptions and fissure eruptions from the flanks of the growing volcano. In the process he did in once and for all the popular, but erroneous, elevation hypothesis of von Buch, who thought that volcanic cones were punched up by forces below

Summit caldera of Kilauea, 1840, by Joseph Drayton. This view was drawn with the camera lucida for greater accuracy. Narrative.

Field sketch for West Crater from the Black Ledge. Courtesy Department Library Services, American Museum of Natural History.

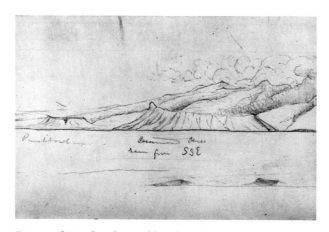

Diamond Head and Punchbowl on the island of Oahu: typical tufa cones. Sketch by Dana. Courtesy Sterling Memorial Library, Yale University.

the center after the lavas had been erupted more or less on a plain.

The influence of Kilauea upon Dana's thinking was fortunate in another way: it led him to appreciate the importance of collapse. Dana saw clearly that the steep-walled pit craters and summit calderas of Hawaiian volcanoes are caused by collapse of the volcanic edifice, when molten lava is drained from below by eruption through fissures. Ultimately, he was able to explain correctly the great Krakatau eruption of 1883 as due to the explosive eruption of volcanic ash, followed by collapse of the cone into the space left empty by the discharge. This "explosion-collapse" theory is now accepted as the general origin of calderas in explosive, non-Hawaiian types of volcanoes, such as Crater Lake in Oregon. Before Dana, many volcanologists had

West Crater "Kaluea Pele" from the "Black Ledge" Nov. 22, 1840, by T. R. Peale. The outer caldera wall, inner ledge, and main "fire pit" Halemaumau are well illustrated. Courtesy Department Library Services, American Museum of Natural History.

thought that the entire mountain was blown away to form such calderas.

Dana noted one historical exception to the quiet "normal" eruptions of Kilauea. In 1790 a devastating explosive blast killed a large party of Hawaiian warriors near the summit and deposited a thick blanket of volcanic ash and other ejecta over a large area to the south and southeast. Dana observed these deposits; the devastation was apparent even then, fifty years later—it is well shown in Peale's painting of Kilauea from the side of Mauna Loa, looking southeast. Dana records an account of the eruption given by a missionary who had

interviewed survivors years earlier.

In 1890, Dana explained such rare explosive eruptions as the result of ground water penetrating to the molten lava deep within the volcano and flashing into steam. This explanation is still accepted, with some modifications. The phenomenon occurs when the level of molten lava within the volcano is drastically lowered by voluminous flank eruptions. The latest explosive eruption occurred in 1924; though much smaller than the 1790 eruption, it caused the only death recorded at Kilauea in modern times.

Ultimately, his observations of Hawaiian volcanoes were crucial to Dana's work because they yielded the knowledge of the processes by which volcanoes are built and the kinds of edifices that result. This in turn enabled him to recognize these edifices, even when they had been degraded by later erosion or collapse, and to estimate the relative degree of modification. By this method he was able to predict the relative ages of volcanoes in an island chain, and his knowledge of their original shape led him to appreciate the immense power of erosion by running water.

The major scientific effort of the Exploring Expedition on the island of Hawaii was the ascent of Mauna Loa. In one of the most dramatic episodes of the entire voyage, Wilkes led a party of sixteen explorers and two hundred Hawaiian porters to the 13,679-foot summit. On this windswept spot in midwinter he established an observatory and spent three arduous weeks making meteorological, gravity, and magnetic measurements and mapping the summit caldera. At this camp, which the explorers called "Pendulum Peak" after the most cumbersome of their instruments, they erected large stone walls to protect both instruments and men from the biting winds. The ruins of these walls are still visible—the sole remaining evidence of the Exploring Expedition in the Pacific.

Wilkes had anointed himself physicist to the Expedition, and the Mauna Loa observatory was his proudest effort in that direction. His ship, the *Vincennes*, remained at Hilo for three months; during this time, the explorers made detailed maps of the summit regions of Kilauea as well as Mauna Loa. These maps formed a baseline for all subsequent scientific observation of the evolution of the craters. Meanwhile Dana, the Expedition geologist, had been allowed a meager five days on the island. This was not, however, because of any malevolence on the part of Wilkes—Dana just happened to be on the wrong ship. The *Peacock* was to finish charting the South Pacific islands; Dana was assigned to the *Peacock*, not the *Vincennes*; therefore Dana would look at coral islands (and lots of ocean). This was, after all, a Naval Expedition.

Kilauea, Night Scene, by T. R. Peale. Courtesy Bernice Pauahi Bishop Museum.

Perhaps it was for the best. Having seen the Hawaiian group, Dana approached the volcanic islands of the South Pacific with a new understanding. During this cruise he first formulated his ideas about island chains, one of his most significant contributions to science.

Island Chains: The Key to Practically Everything

In introducing this section, we can do no better than use Dana's own introduction to his report *Geology*. "The epithet *scattered*, as applied to the islands of the ocean, conveys a very incorrect idea of their positions. There is a system in their arrangement, as regular as in the mountain heights of a continent. . . . Even a cursory glance at a map is sufficient to discover a general linear course in the groups, (as was long since remarked by Malte Brun and other geographers,) and a parallelism even between those in distant parts of the ocean." [p.12] As a member of an Expedition principally devoted to charting the South Seas, Dana was in an enviable position when it came to systematic description of the islands, and he did a remarkable job. He sorted out the various chains, defined their trends, and grouped them accordingly. But this was only the beginning.

Dana's key contribution was to recognize a systematic age progression within the island chains. In the Hawaiian group, he saw that the northwestern-most island, Kauai, was the oldest. The islands became progressively younger to the southeast, until at the southern tip of the last island, Hawaii, were the only active volcanoes.

Dana established this age sequence by looking at the relative degree of erosion of the different islands. He knew what a young, still-active shield volcano looked like: Mauna Loa or Kilauea. The 13,796-foot

Volcano of "Kaluea Pele" as seen from the side of "Mauna Loa," looking S.E. Nov. 21, 1840, by T. R. Peale. Note the abundant silverswords now extinct in this area. Peale and Rich, with a local companion named Hall, were on their way across the island. Courtesy Department Library Services, American Museum of Natural History.

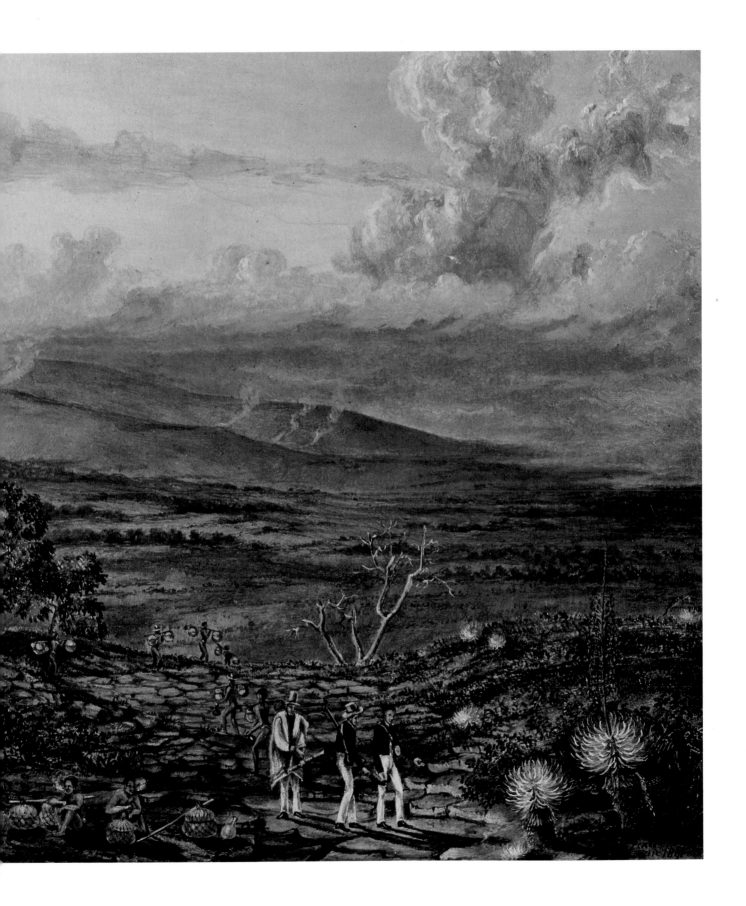

The camp on Pendulum Peak, atop Mauna Loa. The largest tent is the pendulum house. Narrative.

Mauna Kea, slightly to the north on Hawaii, was clearly another huge shield volcano like Mauna Loa, but it was now extinct. Its eastern side, exposed to the trade winds, was gullied with huge ravines; the protected western side still had much of its original form. Thus the ravines must be due to erosion by streams, working since the volcano became extinct. On Mauna Loa, active lava eruptions kept such valleys from forming. Therefore, reasoned Dana, the degree to which a shield volcano was eroded was a measure of the time since it had become effectively extinct.

Applying this reasoning to other chains, Dana suggested that the Society Island group, which is parallel to the Hawaiian Islands, showed the same age progression: older toward the northwest. The Samoan chain was parallel to the Society and Hawaiian chains, but seemed to have the opposite trend in ages; the islands were apparently youngest at the northwestern end. For the other chains parallel to the Hawaiian group, Dana felt he lacked the data to make an age estimate. He did estimate an age progression in the Ladrones (Mariana) Islands, but this north-south trending chain belongs to a different class; Dana thought it became younger to the north where there were still active volcanoes.

To understand the significance of Dana's observations it is necessary to refer to the modern concept of plate tectonics. Geologists now believe that the earth's outer crust is divided into a number of separate, rigid plates. There are several minor plates and eight or nine major ones, of which the Pacific plate is the largest. These rigid plates of the lithosphere move relative to each other by sliding over a partially molten inner layer of the earth, the asthenosphere. The plates are basically composed of basalt and other heavy rock materials; on some of them, the continents, which are made up of lighter rocks, ride like passengers on a raft; this process causes "continental drift."

The Pacific plate has no continents riding on it, but it does encompass numerous island chains. The simplest interpretation of these chains of volcanoes is that they are caused as the plate moves over several fixed heat sources, called "hot spots," arising from much deeper within the earth. As the plate moves over a particular hot spot a series of volca-

Malatta, opposite Mount Fao in Fagaloa Bay, island of Upolu, Samoa. This sketch by Dana shows extreme erosion of the old Fagaloa shield volcano, here not covered by more recent lavas. Courtesy Sterling Memorial Library, Yale University.

noes is generated, forming a line in the direction of plate motion. The volcanoes will then be successively older in the direction of this motion, away from the hot spot. Each hot spot will generate a separate line of volcanoes, and these lines will be parallel if they are on the same plate.

The agreement between this model and the arrangement of Pacific island chains is among the most convincing pieces of evidence for plate motion. Thus Dana's observations on the Exploring Expedition turned out to be fundamental to one of the great unifying concepts of modern geology. Today it is possible to make direct radiometric age measurements on rocks. Such measurements have confirmed the age progression suggested by Dana and extended it to the other island groups parallel to the Hawaiian trend.

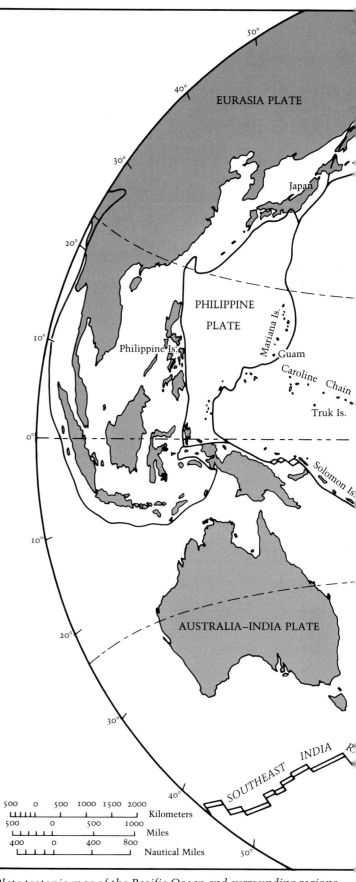

Plate tectonic map of the Pacific Ocean and surrounding regions.

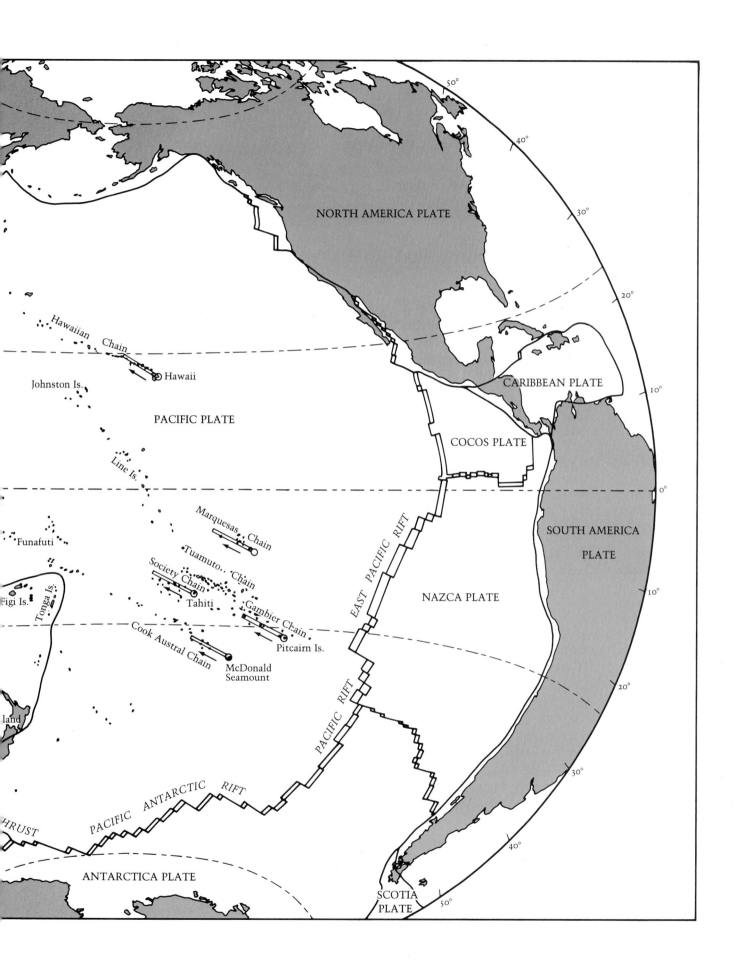

NORTH AMERICA PLATE

CARIBBEAN PLATE

COCOS PLATE

SOUTH AMERICA
PLATE

NAZCA PLATE

PACIFIC PLATE

Hawaiian Chain

Johnston Is.

Hawaii

Line Is.

Marquesas Chain

Tuamuto... Chain

Society Chain

Tahiti

Gambier Chain

Pitcairn Is.

Cook Austral Chain

McDonald
Seamount

Funafuti

Figi Is.

Tonga Is.

land

EAST PACIFIC RIFT

PACIFIC RIFT

PACIFIC ANTARCTIC RIFT

HRUST

ANTARCTICA PLATE

SCOTIA
PLATE

50°
40°
30°
20°
10°
0°
10°
20°
30°
40°
50°

What about Samoa, which Dana and all subsequent workers thought showed a reverse age progression? Recent studies by Natland and Turner show that the shield volcanoes of Samoa do indeed become younger to the southeast, just like the Hawaiian islands. However, the older islands to the northwest, after they had been deeply eroded, were subjected to voluminous renewed lava outpourings that covered the old shield volcanoes and gave them a youthful appearance. This recent volcanism, which continues today, is probably related to the position of these islands at the very edge of the Pacific plate.

The island chains that Dana placed in groups not parallel to the Hawaiian trend represent "island arcs" and arise at the plate boundaries from a different cause. The material that forms the Pacific plate is generated by upwelling from the mantle, deep within the earth, along the line of submarine volcanic fissures called the East Pacific Rise. The plate then moves in a northwesterly direction across the Pacific basin, as determined from the trend of island chains, and finally sinks back into the mantle in the series of deep ocean trenches which line the western margin of the basin. As the plate sinks it is partially remelted, and generates curved lines of volcanoes called "island arcs." Dana distinguished island arcs from linear island chains by trend, but he did not realize that they had a different origin.

The simple picture of fixed hot spots generating straight lines of volcanoes in plates moving across them is, as one might expect, too simple. Although Dana recognized two thousand miles of the Hawaiian chain, including the atolls out to longitude 175°E, he did not know about the Emperor seamount chain. This is the submerged continuation of the Hawaiian chain with a sharp bend to the north, indicating a change of direction in the motion of the Pacific plate about forty-three million years ago. Such bends should occur at the same time in all contemporaneous linear chains on the plate. Dana's map shows some hints of this, but age determinations sufficient to confirm it are still lacking.

The real complexity comes in the actual arrangement of the islands. Dana devoted pages of painstaking observation and analysis to this question. He showed that the "linear chains" were actually broken up into short, overlapping segments arranged in quasi-parallel fashion along the trend of the chain. He attempted to relate this arrangement to an oceanwide or even worldwide fracture pattern. Some modern workers, notably Jackson and Shaw, agree with his observations and contend that the pattern is related to stress in the Pacific plate, a view which would certainly have appealed to Dana.

Perhaps the most severe limitation of Dana's concept of island chains was his insistence that the age progressions he observed on Hawaii (and elsewhere) represented only the age of extinction of the volcanoes, not their age of formation. "From Kauai to Mauna Loa all may have thus simultaneously commenced their ejections, and have continued in operation during the same epoch till one after another became extinct," he wrote in the report *Geology*. "No facts can be pointed to, which render it even probable that Hawaii is of more recent origin than Kauai, though more recent in its latest eruptions." [p. 280] This overly rigorous interpretation of the evidence of erosion led Dana to a static model for the origin of the volcanoes by rupture of fissures; he had to explain the age progression by assuming that the fissures were "widest in the southeast portion." Who knows what he could have accomplished had he realized the dynamic age progression of volcanic activity from one island to the next.

Ironically, someone did realize the truth: Dana's much-maligned colleague, J. P. Couthouy. Once more, as in the case of the coral islands, Dana had to give Couthouy credit in print for independently originating a fundamental idea. He quoted a manuscript sent to him by Couthouy and apparently never published: "The foregoing observations are applied to the course of volcanic action at the islands taken separately, with a view to show that it has been successive in each, from the western to the southeastern extremity of the group, and the possibility that they were also forced up in regular succession by the subterranean fire. The phenomena they present seem to point to such an origin. . . ." [Dana 1849: 283] Indeed they do. Dana never did accept the idea of sequential origin of the volcanoes. One begins to think that Couthouy was a scientific observer of extraordinary talent.

Foothills, Mount Rainier, by Joseph Drayton. Dana saw that these immense cones represented an entirely different type of volcanism from the broad domes of Hawaii. Courtesy Oregon Historical Society.

In all fairness, determining the "age" of a volcano is still a tricky business. The later, post-erosional volcanism that confused Dana in Samoa occurs in Hawaii and on other island chains; and it can lead to erroneous radiometric ages for an island just as certainly as to bad erosional ages. Even more difficult is the problem of what part of a shield volcano is being dated. Whereas one can sample the older interior flows of a deeply eroded island, this is not always possible on an active shield like Mauna Loa, where mostly young flows are exposed. Finally, submerged parts of the chains can only be sampled accurately by deep ocean drilling, an extremely expensive and complicated undertaking.

The detailed interpretation of Pacific island chains, and their significance to understanding both global tectonics and the physical and chemical origins of volcanoes, are still the subject of intense scientific activity. Much of this current research attempts to explain the very complexities that Dana so carefully recorded, as well as his general observations.

In reading Dana's report on Pacific geology, the modern reader is continually struck by the relevance of his work to plate tectonics. For example, the subsidence theory of the origin of coral islands led Dana to attempt a structural map of the entire Pacific. Here, following Darwin's lead, he mapped out the regions of subsidence and elevation and tried to correlate them with the island trends. He looked on the subsidence as a global phenomenon; but as to elevation he recognized (as Darwin had not) that "we cannot . . . distinguish any evidence that a general rise is or has been in progress; yet some large areas appear to have been affected, although the action has often been isolated." [p. 412] Today it appears that the general subsidence may be due largely to the sinking of the Pacific plate as it moves away from the East Pacific Rise and cools off, a truly global effect. Elevation is indeed probably due to more local effects.

Dana was obviously quite skeptical about reported examples of large recent uplifts, especially in chains like Hawaii and Tahiti where he himself failed to find such evidence. While he recognized isolated instances such as Metia in the Tuamotus, which had coral reefs uplifted several hundred feet, he hesitated over similar reports from Maui and Molokai, which he did not visit. Couthouy was similarly doubting. Recent studies by Moore and Moore show that all reported coral occurring at a high level in the Hawaiian Islands is probably debris deposited by a giant ocean wave. Thus there is no evidence for large uplift in the Hawaiian chain.

Leaving the Pacific islands, Dana wrote, "The truth forces itself upon the mind, in view of these facts, that some universal cause has operated in producing results so general, and so mutually dependent. . . ." [1849: 426] The validity of this statement has only become apparent within the last two decades. While his global interpretations may be out of date, Dana in the Pacific made a quite remarkable number of the right observations.

Oregon and California

On 14 June 1841 the *Peacock*, with Dana on board, returned to Hawaii after six months in the South Pacific islands and in a week sailed for the Columbia River. The arrival, on 17 July, was inauspiciously marked by the total wreck of the ship on the bar at the river's mouth. Although all hands were rescued, it is probable that some of Dana's notes and specimens were lost.

The Pacific Northwest at that period was as little known and as unexplored as New Zealand. Dana's personal experience was confined to the region around the mouth of the Columbia at Astoria, and an overland trip from Fort Vancouver, near the mouth of the Willamette, to San Francisco. A considerable section of his report *Geology* is devoted to a summary of the geography of the entire region, mostly gleaned from the observations of other members of the Expedition.

In Oregon Dana was thrown into the midst of some of the most complicated geology in the world. The product of some two hundred million years of collision between the Pacific plate and the North American continent, the region offers a bewildering variety of rocks and geologic structures. Wisely, Dana concentrated on what he understood: volcanoes. In the vicinity of the Columbia he recognized the huge outpourings of fissure basalt and remarked on the tremendous extent of these flows. He later observed (in 1890) that this type of eruption was characteristic of highly fluid basalts rather than of more viscous felsic (silica-rich) lava such as rhyolite. The "rhyolite flows" that he thought existed in western North America are probably welded tuffs.

South of Astoria, Dana explored the prominent peak of Saddle Mountain, which he called by its Indian name, Swalalahos. He correctly described its rocks as basaltic breccia and noted its feeder dikes. He also observed its surprisingly limited extent—it is actually an eroded remnant of a once-continuous extensive formation.

At Astoria, Dana collected numerous fossil mollusks from the thick sequences of sedimentary rocks now known as the Astoria formation. These mollusks were identified and described for Dana by T. Conrad, then the leading American expert, and illustrated by Dana in the atlas of the *Geology* report. They form an important collection of type specimens, housed today in the National Museum of Natural History. Conrad established the age of the Astoria fossils as Miocene. From the geologic relationship between the Astoria rocks and the basalts of the region, Dana concluded that the Columbia River basalts were the same age. Modern radiometric dating confirms the Miocene age of the lavas.

The most spectacular features of the Northwest landscape are the great volcanoes of the Cascade Range. Dana saw them only from a distance—he got a little closer to Mount Shasta—but he recognized from their steep-sided form that they had more in common with Vesuvius and the Andean volcanoes than with Mauna Loa. He discussed the composite nature of these cones—a mixture of lava flows and fragmented deposits—and the more viscous nature of their lavas, trachyte rather than basalt. (In the *Geology* report "trachyte" is often used for andesite, rhyolite, dacite—anything more felsic than basalt.)

Dana knew that these were very recent volcanoes and that Mount St. Helens, at least, had been active within the past few years. When he wrote the report, he had seen Frémont's notice of an 1842 eruption of Mount St. Helens, and he also mentioned a trip made by an Expedition party under Lieutenant Johnson to the missionary station of Chimikaine near the present city of Spokane. Here the party met Chief Silimxnotylmilakabok (also known as Cornelius) of the Spokane tribe, who gave them

an account of a singular prophecy that was made by one of their medicine-men, some fifty years ago, before they knew anything of white people, or had heard of them. Cornelius, when about ten years of age, was sleeping in a lodge with a great many people, and was suddenly awakened by his mother, who called out to him that the world was falling to pieces. He then heard a great noise of thunder overhead, and all the people crying out in terror. Something was falling very thick, which they at first took for snow, but on going out they found it to be dirt: it proved to be ashes, which fell to the depth of six inches, and in-creased their fears, by causing them to suppose that the end of the world was actually at hand. The medicine-man arose, told them to stop their fear and crying, for the world was not about to fall to pieces. "Soon," said he, "there will come from the rising sun a different kind of men from any you have yet seen, who will bring with them a book, and will teach you every thing, and after that the world will fall to pieces." . . . There is little doubt that the fall of ashes took place. . . . [Wilkes 1844, 4:339]

This must have been the great eruption of 1800.

On the overland journey from the Columbia to San Francisco, some 750 miles, the party followed a route that must have been close to the modern Highway I5. The pace was too severe to allow for more than the most hurried geologic observations. Dana faithfully recorded the various rock types he encountered, but he did not try to make much sense out of their distribution.

In the Sacramento Valley, Dana did succeed in making a significant, and virtually unregarded, contribution to volcanology. He made the first geological observations on the "Sacramento Bute." This striking edifice, rising improbably from the flat alluvial plain of the valley, was later known as the Marysville Buttes and is now called the Sutter Buttes. Dana correctly identified it as an extinct volcano and did a surprisingly accurate job of describing its curious features. They are well shown in sketches in his notebook: the outer gently sloping "ramparts," the inner "moat," and the central craggy core. He even identified a rhyolite dome in the "moat" as one of the last eruptive centers. All of this—done in one day—agrees very well with the classic studies of Williams; but Williams refers only to Lindgren, who did a brief study of the volcano published in 1895, and neither refers to Dana.

Conclusion

This chapter has treated the geological results of the Exploring Expedition primarily as they were

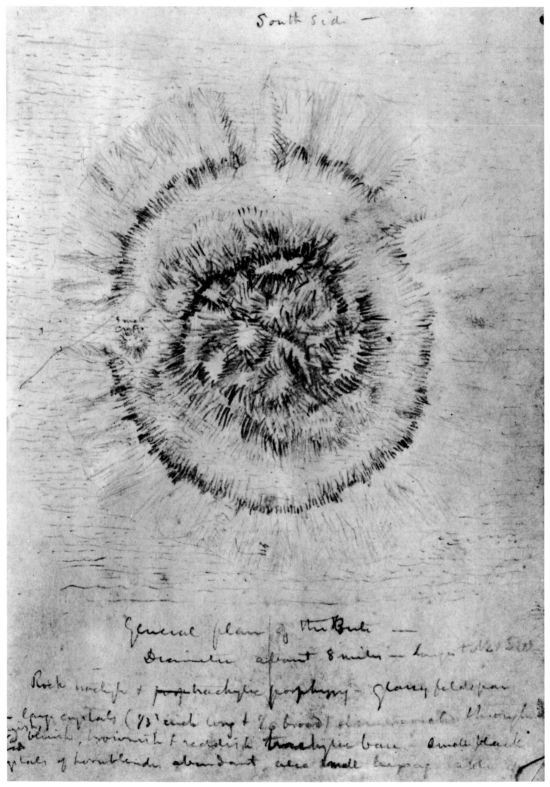

Plan of "Sacramento Bute" (Sutter Buttes), California, by Dana. Courtesy Sterling Memorial Library, Yale University.

published by Dana in 1849 in the report *Geology*. Regardless of their influence on Dana's later work, these results can stand by themselves as major contributions to geology. This achievement is truly remarkable, when one realizes that in less than ten years Dana produced the monumental reports *Zoophytes* (1846), *Geology* (1849), and the two-volume *Crustacea* (1852–53)—each with large atlases of plates for which he did most of the drawings—at the same time publishing furiously in the *American Journal of Science*. Dana's zoological work has been well described by Bartlett. It was of the same high caliber as his geologic studies and remains largely valid today.

The parallels between the lives and achievements of Dana and Charles Darwin are numerous and instructive. Close contemporaries, both launched their careers with years-long global expeditions, then based their entire subsequent work on their experiences with these expeditions. Both were superb observers and describers of nature; but both were also superb synthesizers and theorists, drawing on their observations to deduce great general forces and principles. Both were geologists and biologists, though Dana moved more and more into geology as Darwin moved more and more into biology. The parallel extends even to their personal lives: each developed a mysterious quasi-invalidism.

True, Dana never produced as grand and fundamental a synthesis as Darwin's—the geologic equivalent would have been to propose the theory of plate tectonics. Since he lacked the knowledge of the interior of the earth that seismology would later furnish, this was probably not possible. Yet as we have seen, Dana made many fundamental observations which would ultimately bear upon modern global tectonic theory. Above all, he recognized—in 1849—the profound differences between the ocean basins and the continents: that these basins were not merely flooded low-lying regions of the earth but differed in fundamental ways, in composition and structure, from the higher-lying continental terrains.

Dana exerted a tremendous influence on American geologic thought, through his many scientific papers and textbooks which trained generations of geologists. His ideas entered the intellectual baggage of every geologist—ideas with a global viewpoint, the result of his four remarkable years of cruising to the far corners of the earth. "If this work gives pleasure to any," he wrote in 1890, "it will but prolong in the world the enjoyments of the 'Exploring Expedition.'"

6 Anthropology and the U.S. Exploring Expedition

In 1838, and during the long planning stages of the U.S. Exploring Expedition, anthropology was not considered a separate scientific subject. At that time the study of human society and culture was largely an amalgam of observations made by navigators, missionaries, and other travelers that had been processed by philosophers, historians, and adventure writers, all of whom had distinct preconceptions about non-Western peoples that affected the selection and presentation of information about them. The study of language, which had been viewed as a means of discovering relationships between peoples, was beginning to develop into a science of linguistic structure, so much so that a linguist was appointed to the Expedition. Horatio Hale, whose title was the older term philologist, rather than linguist, was to gather information on the languages encountered and eventually wrote one of the final reports, volume 6, *Ethnography and Philology*. The study of people as living organisms and their racial variation was considered an extension of biology, and much information on this subject was collected and published by Charles Pickering in *Races of Man*. Both of these volumes included observations and some insights about the

society and culture of the people who spoke the languages and inhabited the physical forms that Hale and Pickering studied, but they also contained remarks and conclusions that reflected the attitudes and style of the age in which they were written and are today considered subjective and unscientific.

No one was assigned the specific duty of investigating the ways of living and thinking of the peoples they would meet during the voyage, but many Expedition members recorded observations in their diaries and journals. Much of this information about the societies and cultures encountered became part of the five-volume *Narrative* published by Captain Charles Wilkes. The numerous illustrations by Joseph Drayton depicting people, architecture, clothing, household objects, canoes, and objects collected, as well as his musical notation, are invaluable records for studies of these societies, as are the drawings and oil paintings by A.T. Agate and the vignettes of human activity included by Titian R. Peale in his drawings and oil paintings.

The numerous ethnographic objects collected during the voyage by Wilkes, the officers and men, the Scientifics, and other Americans and Europeans encountered during the voyage form an especially significant collection that helps to document the material culture of the areas visited. Except for Peale, who was actively collecting ethnographic

Forest Illawarra N.S.W. Narrative.

(and natural history) specimens for his father's "American Museum"—the Peale Museum—in Philadelphia, most of the objects were collected primarily as curios and as evidence for the prevailing evolutionary view of culture. Detailed information about where the objects were collected or how they were made or used was often not recorded and kept with the objects. Besides the large number of artifacts that became the "official collection" now in the Smithsonian, personal collections were retained by many individuals on the voyage. These are particularly difficult to trace today. Titian Peale's collection, for example, went to the Philadelphia Academy of Natural Sciences and to his father's museum. The ethnographic objects from the academy are now on permanent loan to the University Museum, Philadelphia, while those from the Peale Museum were dispersed in 1849, primarily to the collections of P. T. Barnum and Moses Kimball. The collection that went to Barnum was lost in fires in 1851 and 1865, while those to Kimball were amalgamated with his previous collections. In 1899 Kimball's heirs presented his ethnographic collections to the Peabody Museum of Archaeology and Ethnology, Harvard University, where, because of information lost in the various transfers, they are almost impossible to isolate. The collection made on the voyage by Lieutenant George F. Emmons was inherited by his son G. T. Emmons, who also collected objects, especially on the northwest coast of North America. G. T. Emmons did not keep records that specifically identified which objects had come from his father. Eventually he dispersed the artifacts, now intermixed, to numerous collections, including the Princeton Museum of Natural History, the American Museum of Natural History, the Smithsonian Institution, and the Vancouver Museum. Some collections still remain in private hands, such as the one made by William Rich (now in the custody of his great-great-grandniece, Helen Caulfield Madine) and the one of Midshipman George Colvocoresses (now owned by his great-great-grandson, Harold Colvocoresses). Other personal collections from the Expedition have entered public museums in this country and abroad.

The "official collection" of more than twenty-five hundred ethnographic pieces from the Expedition became one of the early collections of the Smithsonian Institution. This collection was a nucleus for what would eventually become a separate department devoted to the study of people and their material culture. Before the anthropological collections were separated, they were exhibited in the U.S. Patent Office and in the Smithsonian Castle. Along with natural history specimens many were distributed to public institutions and private individuals in the United States and abroad between 1859 and 1920 in keeping with the Smithsonian mandate "for the diffusion of knowledge." Indeed, some twenty-five "sets of duplicates" ranging from twelve to twenty-five pieces were given away. Two larger groups were sent to the National Museum of Ethnography in Copenhagen, Denmark (about one hundred pieces), and the Chicago Academy of Sciences (about fifty pieces). The former collection is still in Denmark, while the latter was destroyed in the Chicago fire of 1871. Sixteen other sets have been located, but we are still searching for the rest. Of the eighteen hundred objects that remained in the Smithsonian after the distribution ended in 1920, nearly sixteen hundred have been located.* Many had lost their numbers and were incorrectly identified; many were in very bad condition and have undergone conservation and restoration.

The ethnographic collection made by the Exploring Expedition appears to be the largest ever made by a single sailing expedition. At least four thousand pieces, it outnumbers the total ethnographic collections made by the three Pacific voyages of Captain Cook by at least one third (see Kaeppler 1978 for an inventory). The collections from Cook's voyages form the most important baseline collection for the Pacific islands and the areas of the northwest coast of North America he visited. The U.S. Exploring Expedition collection, made some sixty years after the first contacts with Europeans, illustrates the changing relationships of indigenous

---

*Jane M. Walsh, museum specialist in the Department of Anthropology, National Museum of Natural History, carried out a two-year search of the anthropology collection to locate these objects.

A full catalog of all the ethnographic objects collected during the voyage and now located in the Smithsonian and elsewhere is being prepared for future publication.

peoples with the gods, with outsiders, and among themselves. It forms one of the first and most important American collections from the Pacific islands and the west coast of North America.

The most important sections of the anthropological collection are from Fiji and Polynesia, while other objects are treasured pieces or groups of objects from California, the Oregon territory, and the northwest coast of North America. A manuscript catalog of the collection prepared by Titian Peale came to the Smithsonian. A breakdown of the collection entries by area is as follows:

1 Fiji 1,202
2 Polynesia 679
3 Micronesia and Melanesia 110
4 Australia 12
5 North America 300 (including 85 bows and arrows)
6 South America 91
7 Other 52
8 Human remains 63

Because such collections are by their very nature selective—depending on the quality of contact as well as the length of time spent in an area—a complete statement about the society or culture of any group visited during the voyage cannot be made. Even the Fijian collection, which is by far the largest, lacks many objects of everday and ceremonial life.

At the end of the voyage in 1842, Horatio Hale observed that

One of the sciences which have of late years attracted an increasing attention, and one which from the subject would seem to claim a peculiar regard, is what may be termed the natural history of the human race, or as some have named it, anthropology. It divides itself naturally into various branches, possessing distinct names of interest, and requiring different methods of study. One of them, and that perhaps to which the [National] Institute will be able to contribute most largely, treats of the manners and customs of the various nations and tribes of mankind, as indicating the character and the grade of

civilization which is to be ascribed to them. . . . Among the collections of the exploring expedition . . . will be found nearly all the articles of native manufacture in use among two tribes of distinct races, the New Hollanders [Australian Aborigines] and the Fijians; those of the former number about a dozen, while the latter yield several hundreds. A single glance at the two collections will give a clearer idea of the wide differences existing between these tribes than any description.

This ethnological conclusion illustrates mid-nineteenth-century ideas about the nature of man and culture, when it was more or less assumed that a restricted range of material culture meant an impoverishment of the rest of society and culture. With the hindsight of history such ideas can now be seen as erroneous, but during the 1840s, when the study of non-European cultures was in its infancy, these were important considerations. Nevertheless, we can appreciate the wonder felt by the young American scientists and sailors on their first meeting with peoples very different from themselves and at the same time appreciate the creative genius of those who made the objects, which are some of the ethnographic treasures of the Smithsonian Institution.

Australia

As noted by Hale, the Australian Aborigines had only about a dozen types of articles of native manufacture, and examples of the major categories were collected. These included clothing and ornaments, a few household objects, weapons, and the enigmatic boomerang. Drayton depicted a man with weapons and boomerang and Pickering in his journal noted that the boomerang is "entirely unique, and its performances were for a long time doubted by the Professors. This is a carved flat stick which when thrown by a skillful hand may be made to return to the place of starting, hit an object behind a tree, or assume the most unexpected directions at the will of the thrower."

The most important object collected in Australia

Decorated skin rug from New South Wales, Australia. Dimensions 57 × 58.5 inches. Courtesy National Museum of Natural History, Smithsonian Institution.

was a skin rug worn as a protection from cold or rain. These rugs were also used for burial, which may help to explain their rarity. Indeed, according to Mountford only seven such rugs exist today—five in Australian museums, one in Berlin, and the one collected by the Exploring Expedition, which is one of the most elaborately decorated. The skins were stretched on a sheet of bark until dry, and some were handsomely engraved, using a sharpened stone or shell, with the personal symbols and totemic designs of the owner. The designs were darkened by rubbing them with a mixture of fat and pigment, and the skins were sewn together and worn as a cape. Made of twenty-three opossum skins and one kangaroo skin, the Smithsonian rug was collected by Hale near the Hunter River in New South Wales.

Although individuals on the voyage made some important observations on the native manufactures of the Aborigines, not until much later was the complex nature of their kinship systems understood by the outside world. Although Expedition members probably had occasions to question the Aborigines on these matters, prevailing notions about the interrelationships of physical, technical, and mental capacities probably prevented them from pursuing this sort of inquiry.

Fiji

The Fijian collection made during the Expedition is one of the three most important in the world and the only large one that can document a specific time period, having been collected during a few short months in 1840. Some of the oldest Fijian objects are in the collection of the Peabody Museum, Salem, Massachusetts, consisting of items acquired in the early nineteenth century by sandalwood and bêche-de-mer traders and other early visitors to Fiji. Another important collection, in the University Museum of Archaeology and Anthropology in Cambridge, England, was collected primarily in the 1870s. It was brought together by Anatole Von Hügel (the first curator of that museum, 1883–1921) and includes objects obtained by himself, Sir Arthur Gordon (the first British governor of Fiji), and members of his staff. The Smithsonian collection was made between these two collections and at a crucial period of increasing influences from the Western world. Thus, it not only documents traditional Fijian life during 1840, but also is crucial for understanding the earlier and later traditional collections and serves as a reference collection for all other Fijian material in the world.

Fijian mask collected during the Expedition is one of only two known examples of historic "clown" masks worn during ceremonial dances. Height and width each 11 inches. Courtesy National Museum of Natural History, Smithsonian Institution.

The original Fijian collection from the Exploring Expedition that came to the Smithsonian comprised some twelve hundred pieces, of which nearly four hundred were distributed during the 1859 to 1920 dispersal, including sixty pieces to the National Museum in Copenhagen. Among the remaining eight hundred pieces are numerous examples of objects from three important aspects of Fijian culture—ritual, everyday life, and warfare. In addition, there are some unique items, which are the only known examples of these artifacts.

Although Fiji is often included with the cultures of Melanesia, many social and cultural characteristics were closely related to West Polynesia, where whole societies showed a remarkable homogeneity. However, Fijian social and cultural institutions varied considerably from island to island and between coastal and inland tribes, and there was an absence of centralized authority. Most of the objects acquired by the Expedition were from coastal areas.

At Ovalau the Expedition witnessed a large entertainment that included the performance of a *meke wau* or club dance. This men's standing dance, based on the manipulation of heavy war clubs, consisted of an entrance section, the dance proper, which included a masked "clown," and the presentation of the clubs used in the performance. These complex performances depicted historical and mythical battles with offensive and defensive actions. Such *meke* (performances of sung poetry accompanied by dance) were considered by Fijians to be the essence of their culture and were presented as gestures of friendship from one sovereign nation to another. On this occasion a "very large pile" of clubs was presented to the Expedition. Also acquired were two "clown" masks, the only two historic Fijian masks known to exist.

Other important groups of Fijian objects from the Expedition include four carved wooden figures, which are the earliest known examples in museum collections; eighty women's skirts (*liku*), intricately plaited from the dyed inner bark of the hibiscus tree; a large collection of ornaments for the hair, neck, and arms, made of plant materials, shells, ivory, pig tusks, human and dog teeth, snake vertebrae, and imported glass beads; a large collection of bark cloth used for clothing, household furnishings,

Fijian War Clubs. Short round-headed throwing or missile clubs such as the two at the top and one in the foreground were used to stun an enemy. The tooth embedded in the club in the foreground was a war trophy. The larger two-handed clubs have different functions. The center club was said to slice and snap through bone, while the pointed battle hammer on the right made a neat hole in the skull. Courtesy National Museum of Natural History, Smithsonian Institution.

"The Club Dance." Drawn by J. Drayton and engraved by Rawdon, Wright, and Hatch, Narrative. *The entrance section of the club dance and the masked clown are illustrated along with a number of long and short clubs which were given to the Expedition.*

and ceremonial gifts; twenty envelope baskets of pandanus; and a very large collection of weapons, including a gun decorated with Fijian carving. The large number of some of the artifact types makes the collection an important corpus of material for studying variation and uniformity within artifact types collected at a single time period as well as the creative variety developed in genres of useful artifacts. It is also a valuable study collection for analyses of Fijian design motifs and aesthetic use of two-dimensional space.

A unique fragile headdress was presented to the Expedition by the king of Somo Somo. Its catalog number had been lost, and after 140 years it was in extremely bad condition and unrecognizable as a headdress. It was identified and entirely reconstructed by comparison with the woodcut and the description from the *Narrative*.

Another important chief met during the voyage was Tanoa, chief of Bau. Agate depicted him wearing an ivory and shell breast plate, which appears to be the earliest illustration of this type of ornament. The Expedition did not acquire it, but Sir Arthur Gordon did, about 1875, and it is now in the collection in Cambridge, easily identifiable as Tanoa's because of Agate's illustration (see page 204).

Agate made an exquisite drawing of the tombs at Muthuata Island, and Hale was given permission to disinter some skeletons. Despite permission to collect a skeleton in Fiji, no complete one seems to have entered the Smithsonian collection. Apparently only skulls were brought back, in keeping with the nineteenth-century notion that the skull gave the most important scientific information. The human remains acquired by the Exploring Expedition were cataloged, along with other skeletal remains in the mammal department, in 1862. They were subsequently transferred to the Army Medical Museum but were returned to the Smithsonian in 1904 after the appointment of Aleš

Carved wooden female and male figures from Fiji. These, along with two others collected during the voyage, are the earliest known Fijian figures in museum collections. Height 18.5 inches (left) and 17 inches (right). Courtesy National Museum of Natural History, Smithsonian Institution.

Hrdlička as the Institution's first physical anthropologist. Pickering's *Races of Man* was one of the earliest American works to treat the subject of physical variability and inheritance. A recent study of the skull of one Fijian chief by T. Dale Stewart suggests a close cranial relationship between it and Polynesian skulls. This is of interest because studies of living populations of Fijians, Polynesians, and Melanesians often focus on skin color and hair form, which suggest a closer relationship between Fijians and Melanesians.

Polynesia

The similarity of culture among many of the islands in the eastern Pacific had long been recognized, but the extent of this similarity and its coherence was not fully realized until well into the twentieth century. The large collection of ethnographic objects made by the Exploring Expedition and the associated information form significant basic data for further study of Polynesia as a culture area, of the creative exploitation of limited resources, and of objects as material manifestations of changing social relationships. Polynesia is a geographic and culture area consisting of many island groups stretching from Hawaii in the north to Easter Island in the southeast to New Zealand in the southwest. The societies were highly stratified chiefdoms with complex social structures and well-developed material cultures that were integrally associated with social rank and prestige.

By 1838 Polynesians had been subjected to more than sixty years of European and American influence. These outsiders had introduced new tools, powerful weapons, jealous gods, different perceptual categories, unknown diseases, and different value systems. No Polynesian was untouched by these encounters; their way of life was in transition. Thus, in addition to illuminating indigenous traditions, the Expedition collections illustrate traditions in transition as well as the development of new genres of objects made specifically for trade— the forerunner of the tourist market.

Polynesia is a relatively homogeneous culture area but can be subdivided into West Polynesia and

Polynesian women beating bark cloth. Sketched by A. T. Agate and engraved by J. J. Butler, Narrative.

East Polynesia. These island groupings are based primarily on social and cultural factors and reflect migration patterns as well as prehistoric interaction. The subdivisions are not strictly geographic; New Zealand, which is geographically the most western of the Polynesian islands, is culturally part of East Polynesia. The varied environments of the Polynesian islands influenced relative social stratification as well as material culture. Thus, high volcanic islands could support a denser population than low coral atolls. Natural resources influenced the availability of raw materials. For example, on volcanic islands an efficient tool was found in basalt adze blades, while on low coral islands shell adzes were a less efficient substitute. Interisland voyaging, however, was important within some island groups for trade in raw materials.

The subareas of East and West Polynesia can be well illustrated by differences in bark cloth, of which the Expedition made a large collection. In West Polynesia separate sheets of bark cloth were pasted together to form large sheets resulting in easily separated layers (for example, Samoa, Tonga, and Futuna), while in East Polynesia sheets of ret-

ted bark cloth were pounded together to form a felted fabric in which the layers could not be peeled apart (for example, Hawaii, the Austral Islands, and Tahiti). The designs on Polynesian bark cloth are equally important for localizing material culture to specific islands or island groups. The designs, in fact, are cultural signatures (for example, Austral Islands, Tahiti, Hawaii, Samoa, Tonga, Futuna, and Lau). Agate's sketch of women beating bark cloth illustrated the communal nature of this essentially female activity, while the description from Wilkes's *Narrative* illuminated differences in method of fabrication. In Polynesia bark cloth was used for bed coverings, room dividers, wraparound skirts, loincloths, shoulder coverings, and ponchos, and huge pieces were used for ceremonial presentation.

The importance of fish in Polynesian diets led to the development of efficient fishing equipment.

Polynesian bark cloth. Top to bottom: *Futuna; Lau, Fiji; Tonga; Hawaii. Courtesy National Museum of Natural History, Smithsonian Institution.*

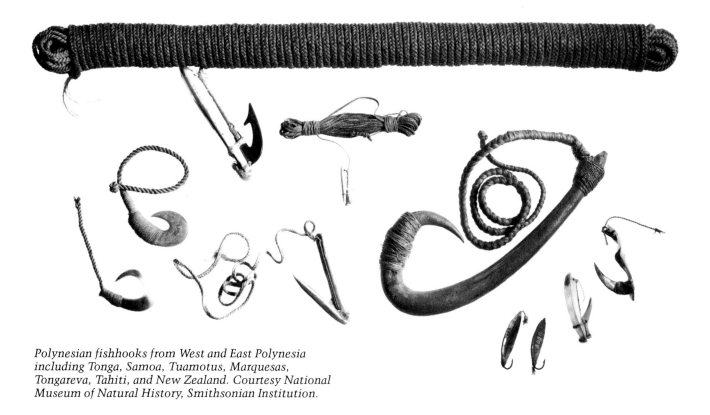

*Polynesian fishhooks from West and East Polynesia
including Tonga, Samoa, Tuamotus, Marquesas,
Tongareva, Tahiti, and New Zealand. Courtesy National
Museum of Natural History, Smithsonian Institution.*

Styles differed between East and West Polynesia. West Polynesia developed large and small two-piece hooks consisting of ivory or shell shanks and turtle-shell points (for example, Tonga and Samoa), while East Polynesia developed one-piece pearl shell hooks, one-piece turtle-shell hooks, and two-piece hooks with shell shanks and bone points (for example, Tahiti, Tongareva, New Zealand, the Tuamotus, and the Marquesas Islands). There was also sporadic use of large wood revetus hooks for obtaining large fish (for example, Tongareva and Fakaofo).

One of the most useful plants to Polynesians was pandanus, which was used for mats, clothing, fans, and baskets. Two charming illustrations by Agate depicted pandanus trees and their environments in Tahiti and the Tuamotu Islands. In Fakaofo, Tokelau, pandanus mats were used to protect the god images while they were not in use, also illustrated in an oil painting by Agate.

The most elaborate Polynesian basket-making techniques were specific to Tonga. These baskets were made of specially prepared plant materials other than pandanus. In this highly stratified society, specialized baskets were used during wedding and funeral ceremonies. The highest-ranking basket was *kato mosi kaka*. Fibers obtained from the fibrous integument at the top of coconut palms, *kaka*, were dyed black and intertwined with those of natural color into triangular designs outlined with shell beads. A number of such baskets were obtained in Tonga during the visits of Captain Cook, but their fabrication had declined by the 1830s. Only one such basket was obtained by the Exploring Expedition, and it is the only known basket of this type in the United States. Tongans also made *kato alu* baskets by encircling a vine called *alu* around a coil of midribs of coconut leaflets. Such baskets were lined with fine pandanus or hibiscus fiber mats and used to hold gourd containers of scented coconut oil used to anoint the living or dead.

Polynesians made ornaments from the human, animal, and natural environment. Traditionally these special ornaments were worn primarily by chiefs. Ornamental hair combs were made from the midribs of coconut leaflets (Tonga and Samoa); necklaces were made of human hair and ivory (Hawaii), shell and crabclaws (Tuamotus), human hair and fingernails (Tongareva); other ornaments were made from feathers (Tuamotus), shark teeth (New Zealand), wood and bark cloth (Tuamotus), greenstone (New Zealand), and imported European beads (Samoa).

At the time of the visits of the Expedition many of the Polynesian islands were engaged in intertribal warfare. Although European and American guns were part of the armory, clubs and spears were still made and used. Often elaborately carved, these weapons illustrate the artistic skill of the Polynesians and the time lavished on utilitarian objects to give them beauty and power.

Household furnishings in Polynesia were few. Those collected by the Expedition included neckrests, wooden bowls for food and scented coconut oil, as well as large vessels for mixing *kava*—an infusion of the root of a pepper plant often mixed and drunk with great ceremony.

Fly whisks of braided coconut fiber attached to a handle were used by orators in West Polynesia (Samoa, Tonga) as an insignia of their office. They were held and manipulated in a specific manner that took practice and deftness of hand. Fly whisks in East Polynesia became more and more elaborate, having carved images on the handles and evolving into feather *kāhili* in Hawaii. An Austral Island fly whisk, the only one of its type acquired by the Expedition, was collected and retained by Titian Peale; it did not become part of the national collection.

View in Tahiti with pandanus tree in the foreground. Drawing by A. T. Agate. Courtesy Peabody Museum of Salem.

Hawaiian stone tools including basalt adzes and pounders, reef rock game stones, and weights for fishing equipment. The unique pounder with human head is 6.5 inches high. Courtesy National Museum of Natural History, Smithsonian Institution.

Carved war clubs from Samoa and Tonga. Courtesy National Museum of Natural History, Smithsonian Institution.

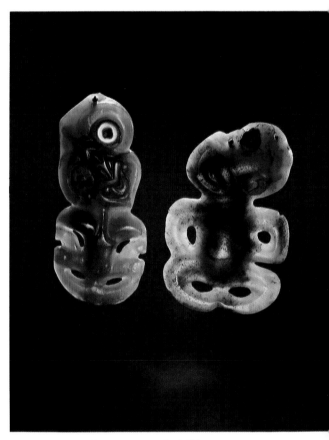

Tongan Baskets. Left, kato mosi kaka, *height 11 inches, width 14 inches;* right, kato alu, *height 6.5 inches, width 14 inches. Courtesy National Museum of Natural History, Smithsonian Institution.*

Greenstone neck ornaments, heitiki *(above), were sacred objects to the Maori of New Zealand. The Maori chief Pomare would not even take his off to enable Expedition members to look at it. Height 3¾ inches (left), 3½ inches (right). Courtesy National Museum of Natural History, Smithsonian Institution.*

Carved wooden figure from New Zealand (at left). Such figures represented Maori ancestors and were kept in sacred meeting houses. Height 10¾ inches. Courtesy National Museum of Natural History, Smithsonian Institution.

The environment of New Zealand was considerably different from tropical Polynesia, and although the culture and physical appearance of the New Zealand Maori were undoubtedly Polynesian, the objects made and used by them illustrate the modifying influence of environment on culture. Warmer clothing and more substantial houses were a necessity. Pandanus was absent and paper mulberry did not grow well, thus baskets and clothing were made from flax and other nontropical plants.

Flax baskets with black-dyed geometric twill decoration collected before 1850 are extremely rare in museum collections. One such basket acquired by Peale was apparently the only one collected during the Expedition. It is one of only three known early baskets of its type in the United States and one of the largest known in the world. After 145 years the basket was very fragile and required extensive conservation.

Fine cloaks were made of flax with an elaborate finger-weaving technique, representing one of the high technical achievements of the Maori. The cloaks were warm and versatile and were made to fit by inserts of various sizes and shapes. Cloaks of chiefs often incorporated a finely woven *taniko* border. Drayton illustrated a Maori with facial tattoo wearing a cloak with a black tag decoration, probably one of the cloaks collected and now in the Smithsonian.

The Maori are best known for their excellent woodcarving, and many of their prized possessions were decorated with finely carved designs. Carved wooden objects collected during the voyage include a figure, ornament boxes, a canoe prow, and hand clubs and staves used in combat and for ceremonial confrontation.

At the opposite end of Polynesia is Hawaii, which had been known to the Western world since 1778

Flax basket of the New Zealand Maori. Height 15 inches, width 26 inches. Courtesy National Museum of Natural History, Smithsonian Institution.

*Maori chief with tattoo and cloak. Drawn by A. T. Agate
and engraved by V. Balch,* Narrative.

King Kamehameha III of Hawaii. Watercolor by A.T. Agate. Courtesy National Anthropological Archives.

Day View of Kilauea Volcano with a vignette of Hawaiians wearing feathered cloaks and helmets. Oil on canvas by Titian Ramsay Peale. Bernice Pauahi Bishop Museum.

when it was visited during the third voyage of Captain Cook. In the intervening sixty-two years change had been far-reaching, especially since the arrival of Protestant missionaries from New England in 1820. Nevertheless, a number of interesting ethnographic objects were acquired by the Expedition that reveal both persistence and change in nineteenth-century Hawaiian life.

The most prized objects collected in Hawaii by European and American ship captains were feathered cloaks, capes, and helmets. But by the time of the Expedition's visit most feather pieces had already been given away, except for a few sacred pieces regarded as the crown jewels of the Hawaiian kings. Indeed, Peale noted that feathered cloaks were not even seen during the Expedition's visits. Peale's

painting, *Day View of Kilauea Volcano,* however, features a vignette illustrating individuals wearing feathered cloaks and helmets. But Peale's reconstruction of Hawaii's past in this painting was not simply based on fancy. The illustrated objects were in his father's museum in Philadelphia. The feathered helmet, for example, had been acquired in Hawaii by Captain Gray of the *Columbia* in 1790. It had been given to President Washington, who in turn gave it to Charles Willson Peale for safekeeping. It is now part of the collection of the Peabody Museum, Harvard University.

Although Peale noted that feather cloaks were not to be seen during the Expedition's visits, Captain Aulick, a great adversary and rival of Wilkes's, managed to acquire one at approximately the same

time. A very important cloak, it was worn during the warfare that broke out between two Hawaiian factions after the overthrow of the traditional gods in 1819. This cloak was worn by the loser, Keku-aokalani, and was taken as a battle prize by King Kamehameha II. It was given to Captain Aulick by Kamehameha III. Apparently the only Hawaiian featherwork collected by the Expedition was a staff (*kāhili*) and a tuft of feathers prepared for presentation as a tax.

By 1840 many Hawaiians wore European-style clothing or a combination of cotton clothing with some traditional pieces made from bark cloth. Missionaries introduced the "Mother Hubbard," a dress that hung free from the shoulders without a yoke and became the prototype for the *mu'umu'u*, still a popular style of dress among Hawaiians. Clothing of the chiefs, however, emulated European high fashion with elaborate Western-cut dresses for women and military-style dress for men.

Kamehameha III, the ruling monarch in 1840, was depicted in a watercolor by Agate in full dress uniform. An impressive figure, Kamehameha returned from the neighboring island of Maui specifically to meet with Wilkes and the American consul. Agate also depicted the high chiefess Kekauluohi and her young son Lunalilo, who, related to the Kamehameha line and a high chief in his own right, would become the first elected Hawaiian monarch in 1873. Wilkes stayed at the home of Lunalilo and Kekauluohi while on shore in Honolulu.

Missionary influence was apparent in the bark cloth clothing, as noted in the *Narrative*:

On the 1st of November they attended Mr. Alexander's church [on Kauai]. The congregation was composed of about four hundred. They were all much struck with the dress of the native women, its unusual neatness and becoming appearance. It seemed remarkable that so many of them should be clothed in foreign manufacture, and that apparently of an expensive kind; but on a closer examination, the dresses proved to be tapas, printed in imitation or merino shawls, ribands, etc. [4:77]

A number of the shawls were acquired as were

Gourd container with fiber carrying net. The nets were hung from the ends of a carrying pole. Height 18 inches. Courtesy National Museum of Natural History, Smithsonian Institution. Left, the Pali, Oahu, with Hawaiians and gourd containers by Agate. Narrative.

loincloths and multilayered bark cloth skirts of traditional style that were probably worn for dancing. These skirts incorporate the characteristic Hawaiian double layer of design—a "watermarked" design was pounded into the fabric with a beater carved with intricate incising, while a second design was "printed" on the upper surface. Under the direction of missionary wives, Hawaiians raised cotton, spun it into fine thread, and made cloth and stockings.

Other important groups of objects collected in Hawaii include ornaments, stone tools, and gourd containers. A charming picture by Agate illustrated how gourd containers were carried in the Hawaiian way—that is, encased in a fiber net and hung from the ends of a carrying pole.

Following pages, masks and headdress frontlets from the northwest coast of North America. They were presented to the Expedition by employees of the Hudson's Bay Company near the mouth of the Columbia River but were collected farther north. They have since been attributed to Haida, Tsimshian, and Kwakiutl tribes. Courtesy National Museum of Natural History, Smithsonian Institution.

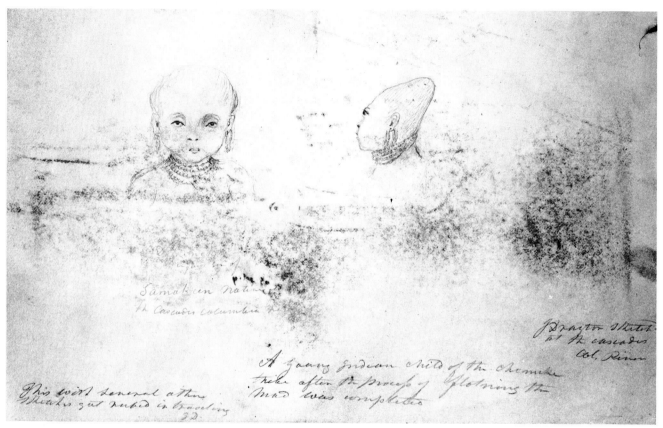

Sketches of a Chinook child by Joseph Drayton. Courtesy Smithsonian Institution Archives.

Oregon Territory

After spending nearly two years in the Pacific, the Expedition sailed to the west coast of North America where it spent six months traveling from the Columbia River to San Francisco overland as well as by sea. Although the ethnographic collections made were not nearly as extensive as in the Pacific islands, some two hundred important objects became part of the National Museum. Unfortunately, precise area identifications were not noted, either by those on the voyage or by individuals who gave artifacts to the Expedition.

One of the important series of contacts made in Oregon territory was with the Chinook Indians, a tribe with only a few living members today. While in Oregon territory, Horatio Hale, the Expedition linguist, made a study of "Chinook Jargon," a simplified hybrid language that had emerged on the

northwest coast during the late eighteenth century in the contacts between European sailors and traders and the Indians of the area, who spoke numerous diverse languages. Hale's chapter, "The 'Jargon,' or Trade-Language of Oregon," was the first account of this language, which has intrigued linguists ever since. Hale also collected vocabularies of many of the languages of the Northwest and collected information on the highly complex grammar of the Chinook Indians' own languages, which except for contributing some words to the jargon are entirely distinct from it. Other Expedition members interested in the natural history of the human race were intrigued by the Chinook fashion of artificially flattening the cranium, and they collected skulls that illustrated it as well as a model of a child in a cradle that showed how the effect was achieved.

Also collected in this area were Chinook clothing and ornaments, a paddle, bow and arrows, fishing equipment, combs, and an excellent series of baskets.

A fine cuirass made of wooden rods, fiber, and hide obtained from the Shasta Indians was presented to the Expedition by John McLoughlin, chief factor of the Hudson's Bay Company. This rare piece is one of only a few such objects known in museum collections today. Henry Eld noted in his diary that on Youngs River Expedition members were visited by an individual who "had on a Coat of Mail to protect himself from the arrows, the garment if it may be so called is more like a straight jacket, protecting the body only, the arms being at liberty, and is made of sticks about as large as a man's thumb, woven together so closely as to resist effectually their bows and arrows. They are in two parts fastened together by shoulder straps at the top & secured in like manner at the bottom."

California

Objects collected by the Expedition in California are especially important for the study of the material culture of this area because of the many changes that came shortly after, with the gold rush of 1849. Although significant collections were made previous to those brought back by the Expedition, they are primarily in Europe—Spain, England, Germany, and Russia.

Among the rare objects acquired by the Expedition were two feathered cloaks, which appear to have been collected in the area of Sutter's Fort. About a dozen of these cloaks exist today, and all seem to have been acquired between the 1820s and 1842. Another ceremonial dress, made of the feathers of crow, turkey vulture, and white swan or goose, is even more rare; as it is one of only two known cloaks of this type (the other is in Leningrad).

The baskets collected by the Expedition are important because they were acquired from central California groups that are not otherwise well documented, and they antedate the majority of California basket collections in American museums today. One particularly fine basket is covered with bands of feathers and though similar to Pomo baskets probably came from a neighboring tribe.

Northwest Coast of North America

Objects acquired by the Expedition from the area north of Oregon territory were presented to the Expedition by employees of the Hudson's Bay Company. The collection includes examples of new genres of objects apparently made for trade to Europeans, such as argillite dishes, figures, and especially pipes made of argillite, wood, and ivory. Some important traditional objects were also acquired. These included magnificent basketry hats, masks, cedarbark cloaks, and a fine painted rattle. Although these types of traditional objects were known since Captain Cook visited the area in 1778–79, this group constitutes the first significant collection of such pieces for an American collection.

Tierra Del Fuego

The inhabitants of Tierra del Fuego were the first group of people met on the Expedition who were very different in culture from the Americans. The Western world had been aware of this group of people since Captain Cook's first voyage in 1769, and when the U. S. Expedition visited, some seventy years later, little had changed. Exploring Expedition members, like their predecessors, were struck by similar things—the seeming poverty of the material culture, insubstantial houses, and lack of clothing in this relatively cold climate. Interesting items of hunting equipment were acquired, including sealskin quivers, bows, arrows, and very long fish spears.

Chile and Peru

The items brought back from Chile and Peru by the Expedition, principally by Hale, are few and, while interesting, not ethnographically important. The objects are of the sort that would fill the South American corner of almost any nineteenth-century cabinet of curiosities. The local costumes of a man and woman from Lima and various riding accoutrements illustrated the Spanish influence in countries

Baskets from Oregon territory and California. Although unprovenanced when collected, the baskets have been attributed by researchers to tribal groups including Tillamook, Quinault, Cowlitz, Clatsop, and Clallam. The feathered baskets are from central California groups. Courtesy National Museum of Natural History, Smithsonian Institution.

that had freed themselves from three centuries of Spanish rule less than two decades before. The ceramic vessels from various locations in Peru and Chile represented the pre-Columbian peoples and cultures and may have been of scientific interest to the naturalists on the voyage, in that their shapes were based on plant and animal forms including a shell, cherimoya, snake, and opossum.

The only attempt at a scientific collection was made by Pickering during his visit to the ruined city of Pachacamac on the outskirts of Lima. His effort to describe a somewhat hurried excavation of pottery, cloth fragments, and vegetable and dietary remains record an early archaeological excavation. Unfortunately most of the excavated items were either discarded or separated from the identifying data.

Other Collections

A number of important ethnographic objects were acquired by the Expedition from areas to which it did not travel. In addition to those given by the Hudson's Bay Company, others were acquired from expatriate Americans or ships in the same ports at the same time, while still others were obtained from natives who had themselves acquired them when traveling abroad or from earlier visiting ships. A Kamchatka sled was acquired in Hawaii from Captain Joy of the ship *Hero.* An Easter Island figure was acquired at the Bay of Islands, New Zealand. A paddle, a club, and numerous bows and arrows from Bougainville, Solomon Islands, were acquired in New Zealand from a whaling ship that had visited the area. A Javanese kris was presented by Captain Lewis of the barque *Java* during the Expedition's stop at Singapore in February 1842.

One of the most remarkable objects that seems to have been collected "out of place" was an Aleut gut skin garment made in the style of a Russian cloak. The Expedition did not travel to the Aleutian Islands but the cape may have been acquired in Eimeo, Society Islands. On September 25, 1839, at Eimeo, Pickering noted that "One of these Natives who came on board this evening had on one of those thin dresses manufactured on the North West Coast, from the internal membrane of some animal." Although a few examples of such capes are known in European museum collections their place of manufacture has not been securely documented.

Argillite pipes from the northwest coast of North America presented to the Expedition by employees of the Hudson's Bay Company. Pipes of this sort, as well as ones made of wood and bone, were a new genre of object made during the nineteenth century. Traded to visitors, rather than used by their makers, they might be considered early "tourist art." Courtesy National Museum of Natural History, Smithsonian Institution.

Raven rattle from the northwest coast of North America. Such rattles were used by shamans. This nineteenth-century example is similar to those collected during the eighteenth century except for an elaboration of the painting. Height 8½ inches, length 17¼ inches. Courtesy National Museum of Natural History, Smithsonian Institution.

Another group of objects is interesting as one of the pre-Perry Japanese collections that reached an American institution. Collected thirteen years before Commodore Perry visited Japan to establish formal relations with the United States, the collection has historical as well as ethnographic interest. The objects, including an "apron" and gaiters, were given to the Expedition in Hawaii by Dr. J.P. Judd, who obtained them from a group of Japanese whose ship, the *Chōja Maru*, had been disabled in the North Pacific. Rescued by Captain Cathcart on the American whale ship *James Loper*, which took them to Hawaii, Maui, and finally to Honolulu, they stayed for nearly three months (in 1840)

with Dr. Judd, a missionary from the United States. After returning to Japan, Jirōkichi (called Ijirō by Judd) dictated his story to a scribe who wrote and illustrated a manuscript titled "Bantan," which is now in the Bishop Museum, Honolulu. In this manuscript which details his adventures in foreign lands, Ijirō notes,

The minister in Oahu was Mr. Bingham. The second leader was called "Mr. Kaoka" (kauka means doctor in Hawaiian), and he was a medicine man. After going ashore with the letter of introduction from Mr. Baldwin [a missionary in Maui], the guest (Jirokichi) and his group were

taken to Kaoka's house, with their belongings on a cart. That house was facing the minister's residence and on its left there was a printing house.

These places were included in Jirōkichi's schematic watercolor illustration of Honolulu, which showed a Japanese view of the same area the Expedition saw in 1840. In his diary Dr. Judd noted that on 30 September 1840 the *Peacock* arrived, and he had "looked up books and Japanese curiosities for the Squadron." Dr. Judd was extremely helpful to Captain Wilkes and the Expedition in organizing and accompanying the ascent of Mauna Loa in Hawaii and treating the climbers for the ill effects of elevation and weather.

Anthropological Legacy of the Expedition

The anthropological legacy of the Expedition includes detailed observations, illustrations, and original linguistic research as well as the ethnographic and physical anthropology collections. The linguistic research of Horatio Hale on the Pacific islands and in Australia was a significant synthesis of information on languages that had for the most part already been extensively studied by other scholars. In northwestern North America, in contrast, Hale obtained the first information of any kind on many of the numerous Indian languages there, and on the basis of these materials he published the first linguistic classification of the Indian groups of this large and important area. The linguistic map of Native North America, which had previously had a large blank in the West, was now substantially filled in.

The human skeletal specimens acquired by the Expedition, although not numerous, formed an important early part of what eventually became one of the largest physical anthropology collections in the world. The Smithsonian skeletal collection has provided data for numerous scientific studies that have helped to clarify problems of human biological history and medicine.

The ethnographic collection forms one of the most important systemic collections in the United States from the Pacific islands and also includes significant material from the west coast of North America. In addition to much traditional material the collection also includes new cultural forms that had been stimulated by the tools and visual images acquired through interaction with Americans and Europeans. Study of these materials today, in association with other museum collections in the United States and elsewhere, illustrates persistence and change and makes it possible to assess sixty years of previous European influence on the cultures visited by the U.S. Exploring Expedition.

The hazards of navigating amid icebergs and heavy seas during foggy weather were first encountered and sketched by Wilkes on his initial Antarctic reconnaissance early in 1839 with the Porpoise and Sea Gull. As ice rapidly built up on their decks and rigging, it became virtually impossible for his half-frozen men to work the vessels' sails, inducing Wilkes to order the 110-ton tender back to safe haven at Orange Harbor. Narrative.

7 Ships and Squadron Logistics

The selection and outfitting of men-of-war suitable for the peaceful mission of the U. S. Exploring Expedition proved of critical importance for the ultimate outcome of that pioneering naval venture. In the tradition of earlier European voyages for scientific investigation of the Pacific, the Wilkes undertaking was being dispatched to those distant waters "not for conquest but discovery," in the benign phrase of Secretary of the Navy James Kirke Paulding. Primary emphasis in the secretary's formal instructions of 11 August 1838 was placed on the survey and exploration of selected islands and groups in the South and Central Pacific, most particularly the Samoan Islands and the Fijis, where American whaling crews had repeatedly been lost on uncharted reefs and hostile shores. Insofar as possible, during these hydrographic efforts, projected to the high latitudes of the south polar seas, the ill-defined coast of the Pacific Northwest, and westward to the Sulu Sea and Sea of Japan, Lieutenant Wilkes was enjoined to assist the Expedition's scientific corps of naturalists and artists in the collection and documentation of a broad range of natural phenomena.

Conventionally outfitted men-of-war were clearly unsuited for this ambitious four-year mission. The long-range security of the Expedition's scientific and survey parties required not only a modest armament allowance for individual vessels but also a sufficient number of seaworthy ships to ensure their effective mutual support, particularly when the squadron broke company to carry out simultaneous surveys of widely separated island groups. Early in the planning of this complex undertaking, when veteran Captain Thomas ap Catesby Jones attempted to organize the Expedition, it had been determined that two ships, long the standard on European exploring ventures, would be inadequate. Memories remained of the disappearance in 1788 of the ill-fated La Pérouse expedition, a mystery only partially explained by the discovery of remains of its two frigates by Dumont d'Urville on the reefs at Vanikoro in 1828.

As envisioned by Jones in 1836, the Expedition required no fewer than five vessels—the 36-gun frigate *Macedonian*, the brigs *Pioneer* and *Consort*, schooner *Pilot*, and storeship *Relief*—all recently designed for an exploring expedition by Naval Constructor Samuel Humphreys. The small, clipper-lined *Macedonian* was badly matched with the *Pioneer*, *Consort*, and *Pilot*, which proved unacceptably slow in sea trials conducted early in 1837. The 230-ton brigs, relatively short, deep-drafted, and heavily timbered for service mainly in south polar waters, were thereupon drydocked at the Norfolk (Gosport) Navy Yard in an effort to improve their freeboard and sailing qualities. Only the packet-hulled *Relief* survived the ensuing months of preparation, during which Jones finally resigned the Expedition command, in frustration and ill health, following further unsuccessful sea trials off Norfolk. In seeking to reconstitute the squadron, the Board of Navy Commissioners sought vessels that combined proven sea-keeping qualities, more adequate accommodation for the scientific corps, and capability for survey operations among coral-fringed Pacific islands.

In trying to outfit the Expedition, Jones had drawn on European experience as well as his own Pacific service, recognizing that adequate accommodation for both scientific and survey activities could be achieved by reducing armament tonnage for greater provision-carrying capacity and by adding stern cabins of the type long used in the European trade with the East Indies. These modifications, as well as the installation of stronger spars and rigging, were applied to the four principal men-of-war finally assigned to the Exploring Expedition in 1838. In addition to the 468-ton storeship *Relief*, the commissioners designated two sloops of war with previous Pacific service, the 700-ton *Vincennes* and 559-ton *Peacock*, as the Expedition's most substantial vessels. They were supplemented by the 224-ton brig *Porpoise*, which had served Wilkes well during his notable survey of Georges Bank in 1837. In August 1838, as alterations were being completed at Norfolk on Wilkes's principal ships, two former New York pilot boats were added to the squadron, the 110-ton *New Jersey* and 96-ton *Independence*, which were hurriedly refitted for more extended sea service and rechristened the *Sea Gull* and *Flying Fish* respectively. Although redesignated as tenders, these handsome schooners were intended primarily to conduct shoal-water surveys in the South Pacific. Manned by hardy crews of ten

U.S.S. Vincennes *in "Disappointment Bay," January 1840. The acquisition of fresh water proved a recurrent logistical preoccupation of the Exploring Expedition, as recorded in this painting, attributed to Wilkes, of the flagship* Vincennes *watering from an iceberg near the Antarctic barrier. The painting represents the most detailed depiction of any of the squadron's ships by Expedition artists. Courtesy Peabody Museum of Salem.*

bluejackets and five young officers, the graceful *Sea Gull* and *Flying Fish* aroused both admiration and deep anxiety about their chances of survival south of Cape Horn. Indeed, on his departure from Orange Harbor in Tierra del Fuego, the smaller schooner's skipper, Lieutenant William Walker, was genially advised by fellow officers that she "would make him an honourable coffin." Yet the gallant *Flying Fish* was destined to survive three years of arduous and hazardous service, eventually to be celebrated in a modest epic poem, *Thulia*, published by James C. Palmer at New York in 1843, shortly after the Expedition's return.

As Charles Wilkes's flagship, the *Vincennes* merits comparison with at least three renowned European exploring vessels, including H.M.S. *Endeavour*, the indomitable 369-ton bark in which Captain James Cook carried out his celebrated first Pacific voyage of 1768–71; the 306-ton Spanish corvette *Descubierta*, flagship for the epochal five-year expedition of Alejandro Malaspina in 1789–93; and the 380-ton French corvette *L'Astrolabe* (so rechristened in memory of La Pérouse's flagship), the durable veteran of Admiral Dumont d'Urville's three trans-Pacific cruises. Fitted with stern cabins to accommodate hydrographers and naturalists, these vessels were seaworthy craft yet modest performers from the standpoint of speed under sail. *Endeavour*, a bluff-bowed ex-collier scarcely one hundred feet in length, lodged Cook's surveyors, two artists, and three scientists, headed by Joseph Banks, in the after cabin. The 109-foot *Descubierta*, whose plan survives in the Museo Naval in Madrid, had been specifically designed, with her sister *Atrevida*, for the Malaspina expedition to the Pacific and included a laboratory and studio rooms as well as a library in her commodious stern cabin. When Dumont d'Urville refitted *L'Astrolabe* for her third voyage to the Pacific in 1837, he extended her existing cabin farther forward and embarked two naval officers doubling as scientists and one artist on the flagship, while finding room for additional savants on board her consort, the corvette *La Zélée*.

The military characteristics of Wilkes's vessels were similarly modified, through the addition of living quarters, drafting space, and preparatory room for the scientists and their collections, as well as

through reduction of their heavy armament allowance. Though a larger scientific corps had originally been recruited for the American expedition, Wilkes initially assigned four scientists, an artist, and an instrument maker to share his new cabin in the 127-foot *Vincennes*. Additionally two scientists, including James Dwight Dana, sailed with Captain William L. Hudson in the 118-foot *Peacock*; the 109-foot *Relief* embarked a botanist and an artist. As revealed in plans for the alterations of the *Vincennes* at Norfolk, the 36-foot stern cabin actually included staterooms for seven scientists and guests, an adjoining dining room for the scientific corps, Wilkes's own stateroom and pantry, and a large reception room that accommodated drafting tables and a library of charts and scientific works, as well as the ample conference table and sideboards customary in small frigates. Here, at the center of squadron activities, its commanding officer received native potentates, interrogated a steady stream of ships' officers, conferred with accompanying naturalists, directed the daily program of his cartographers, consulted charts and accounts of previous Pacific voyages, and planned the squadron's varied operations.

The addition of stern cabins and forecastles in Wilkes's larger vessels not only required some modifications in the belaying arrangements for their rigging plans but also necessitated changes in some of the conning and steering arrangements, matters significant to effective navigation. Plans for refitting of the 88-foot *Porpoise* reveal that a large cockpit was constructed well aft, three feet below the level of the new poop deck, providing a seaworthy conning station somewhat higher than the more exposed cockpits in the *Sea Gull* and *Flying Fish*. In the *Peacock* the wheel remained on the weather (spar) deck, being located forward of the mizzen mast. On board the *Vincennes* the installation of a stern cabin, extending forward of the mizzen mast, appears to have required relocation of the wheel on the spar deck just forward of that cabin's doors. This arrangement, evident in the accounts by Wilkes and Midshipman George Colvocoresses of King Tanoa's visit to the flagship in the Fijis, would have preserved close visual communication between the helmsmen and the watch officer conning

Brig Porpoise *in Antarctic waters, 1840. This 88-foot vessel proved a weatherly explorer in the heavy seas and gale force winds encountered during Wilkes's second approach to the polar ice barrier early in 1840, as depicted by Passed Midshipman George M. Totten.* Narrative.

the ship from the forward end of the quarterdeck (poop deck).

In outfitting his squadron at Norfolk, Wilkes reduced the armament on board the *Vincennes, Peacock,* and *Porpoise,* while adding weaponry useful for conducting modest demonstrations in force, in accordance with his instructions. His flagship's normal allowance of two long 9-pounders and twenty-two 24-pounder carronades was modified to two long 9-pounders and only eight 24-pounder carronades. The *Peacock,* which carried two 12-pounders and twenty 32-pounder carronades in normal service, was rearmed with two 9-pounders and eight 24-pounder carronades; the *Porpoise,* with previous survey service, continued to mount

two 9-pounders and only two 24-pounder carronades.

For landing operations on hostile beaches, the squadron was supplied with two particularly potent side arms, the breech-loading 1819 Hall rifle produced at the Harpers Ferry armory and the intimidating Elgin cutlass pistol, in addition to more traditional swords, pistols, dirks, and cutlasses. Most unusual in the squadron's armament was the inclusion of 24-pounder Congreve rockets; these were pyrotechnic weapons of the combustible type used by British naval forces during the War of 1812. Rigged for firing from high launching frames, they could be discharged not only from Wilkes's larger ships and shallow draft tenders but even from his

Orange Bay near Cape Horn Sa.
25th February 1839.

The relative size of ships in Wilkes's squadron is clearly illustrated in this sketch by Lieutenant George Emmons of the Expedition anchored in Orange Harbor on Washington's Birthday 1839. The small tenders, the Flying Fish *and* Sea Gull, *lie astern the* Peacock, Vincennes, *and* Relief, *while Ringgold's* Porpoise *lies off their bows. Courtesy Beinecke Rare Book and Manuscript Library, Yale University.*

highly prized survey launches, 27-, 29-, and 32-foot craft originally designed for the *Peacock*'s earlier survey operations in the Pacific. Informally dubbed "Leopard," "Albatross," and the like, these single-masted boats proved themselves capable of independent survey operations during the squadron's brief stay at Tierra del Fuego and later were to participate in both survey activity and punitive rocket attacks in the Fiji Islands.

Owing to the Board of Navy Commissioners'

evident displeasure with the selection of Lieutenant Wilkes for its command, the squadron received less than wholehearted assistance in its final outfitting at Norfolk, thus creating inevitable and foreseeable logistic problems on the long voyage. The commissioners had been reluctant to fit out the *Relief* at more than minimal expense, while the well-worn *Peacock*, though generously coated with fresh paint, was, as Wilkes and her able skipper, Lieutenant William L. Hudson, soon discovered, "in a wretched state to go to sea," with rotten masts and spars, a leaky hull and defective, rusted pumps. Determined to avoid lengthy delays in his departure, Wilkes overcame many bureaucratic obstructions in provisioning his squadron. It was a measure of his ambition and confidence that, notwithstanding his responsibility for some 680 officers, scientists, and men, he did not also resign the command but instinctively followed the classic navy dictum: "Do the best you can with what you've got."

The comprehensive itinerary for the Expedition derived from Captain Jones's earlier plan. In helping to draft the instructions that directed operations, Wilkes undertook not only to schedule survey and exploring activities at realistic seasons for particular areas but also to provide Navy Department officials with a firm schedule for systematic replenishment of his force during its prolonged cruise. The navy's well-established system for routine supply and overhaul of its Mediterranean, South Atlantic, and Pacific squadrons could be exploited to a limited degree, but the wide-ranging circumnavigation projected for the Exploring Expedition required supplementary arrangements. Initially, resupply was envisaged at Rio de Janeiro, Tierra del Fuego, Valparaiso, Sydney, the Sandwich Islands, San Francisco, and Singapore. Wilkes was further authorized to arrange supplementary replenishment and overhaul as occasion required, utilizing drafts on Baring Brothers of London, the banking house through which the U.S. Navy cleared its overseas purchases. In addition, the squadron included the storeship *Relief*, an auxiliary with sufficient stowage capacity to supply the Expedition's most urgent requirements including anti-scorbutics between scheduled ports of call. Although the U.S. Exploring Expedition indeed accomplished its far-flung mission with rather remarkable precision, its energetic commanding officer found frequent occasion for logistical extemporizing.

Intending its initial probe of south polar seas early in 1839 (the summer season in those forbidding waters), the Expedition departed Hampton Roads on 18 August 1838, heading eastward from the Chesapeake capes for Madeira on the outward leg to Rio, in order to clear the track of hurricanes spawned in the West Indies. As time had not per-

mitted sea trials for Wilkes's ships in company, the outbound passage to the South Atlantic served necessarily as a shakedown cruise for ships and men alike, enabling the Scientifics to gain their sea legs. Sailing astern the flagship, the heavy-laden *Relief* soon proved unable to keep pace with the swifter men-of-war and was detached by Wilkes four days out and ordered to rendezvous with the others in the Cape Verdes. The squadron entered Funchal Roads at Madeira on 16 September, affording the scientific corps an initial collecting opportunity ashore, while the seamen painted the ships and took on water, fruit, and fresh vegetables. During the ensuing passage to Rio, the *Peacock*'s deficiencies became alarmingly apparent, obliging Wilkes to extend the visit at that hospitable Brazilian entrepot by nearly a month to enable Hudson to carry out extensive repairs to the spars, masts, and hull before attempting the stormy Cape Horn passage. *Relief*'s tardy appearance on 24 November, three days after the squadron arrived at Rio, meanwhile had convinced Wilkes of its inability to operate in close support of his ships, leading him to send the *Relief* southward in advance of the squadron, which departed for Tierra del Fuego on 6 January 1839, now weeks behind schedule.

Proceeding southward, the Expedition rounded Cape Horn in heavy weather and reached Orange Bay, Tierra del Fuego, late on 17 February, finding it a well-sheltered advance base for the challenging operations ahead. Wilkes prudently directed the *Relief* to supply all ships with a year's provisions, in the event any found themselves caught in the polar ice fields. Wilkes's initial reconnaissance of Cook's "Great Icy Ocean," undertaken with the *Peacock, Porpoise*, and the two frail tenders, encountered the same difficulties that had befallen Dumont d'Urville in those stormy waters a year earlier. Detailing one of the survey launches to chart the Hermite Islands east of Orange Harbor, Wilkes sailed in the *Porpoise* on 25 February, in company with the *Sea Gull*, intent on probing the icebound coast of Palmer Land (Peninsular), while the *Peacock* and *Flying Fish* cruised westward to Cook's "Ne Plus Ultra." Buffeted by heavy gales as they probed the massive ice barrier, the *Porpoise* and *Sea Gull* reached 63° 10' South Latitude before

Wilkes ordered the ice-burdened schooner back to Orange Bay. The brig pressed eastward toward the South Shetlands, being obliged by heavy gales to take shelter in Good Success Bay. Efforts to land a reconnaissance party under Lieutenant John Dale on those storm-battered shores soon taught all hands a sobering lesson in polar survival. Though Dale successfully conned his launch through the breakers, he found his party marooned for five days by gale-force winds that meanwhile swamped a rescue boat sent to his assistance. Shaken by the incident, Wilkes sternly suspended Dale for his failure to attempt an earlier passage back through the daunting breakers. Beneath this exacerbated misunderstanding, one of several that made the early months of 1839 doubly tortuous for the squadron, there loomed for Wilkes the haunting question of how far men's lives might be hazarded to attain the Expedition's most heroic objective, ascertaining whether there was indeed a south polar land mass.

Unknown to Wilkes, meanwhile, the *Flying Fish* had separated from the *Peacock* in a gale and, despite mounting injuries to her crew, forced her way through fog and heavy ice fields to reach 68° 08′ South, well beyond Cook's most southerly penetration, before rejoining the *Peacock*. It was indeed a superb, even miraculous achievement that Lieutenant William Walker and his hardy crew had successfully navigated the diminutive craft through such berg-strewn polar seas. Surgeon Palmer well epitomized the gallant venture in the quaint verses of his "Antarctic Mariner's Song":

Benighted in the fleecy shower,
Wee Thulia slowly southward creeps;
Now overhung by tottering tower—
Now all becalmed 'neath jutting steeps.

More fortunate than her larger sister, the *Flying Fish* rejoined the squadron early in April at Orange Bay, there to recover from the Antarctic ordeal before setting out with the *Sea Gull* on 28 April to join the main body at Callao. Early the following morning, the schooner's lookouts lost sight of the *Sea Gull* off False Cape Horn, laboring in a heavy gale that claimed her shortly thereafter with the

loss of her entire fifteen-man crew. For Wilkes, embroiled in mounting disciplinary problems with his officers, the tragic loss of the *Sea Gull* reduced the Expedition to but four vessels, for he had determined, after studying the report of the *Relief*'s nightmarish experience in attempting to traverse the Straits of Magellan, to detach the storeship from his squadron and send it home after depositing a final cache of provisions in Australia.

Happier prospects lay to westward, and on 12 July 1839 the reduced squadron departed Valparaiso for exotic ports known only to Wilkes. During the ensuing four months, the *Vincennes* and company conducted surveys through the Tuamotus, Tahiti, and the Samoan Islands, affording the *Flying Fish* and the survey launches their first opportunity for coral reef hydrography. Among these friendly islands the Expedition found fresh breadfruit, oranges, and coconuts and an agreeable introduction to the native culture of the Central Pacific. Less amiable experiences lay ahead.

As specified by the Expedition's instructions, however, a more immediate objective late in 1839 was to mount a conclusive assault on the south polar barrier, in reality the objective as well of both French and British expeditions then at sea. Accordingly, the squadron directed its course to Australia, entering Sydney late on 29 November for major replenishment before the Antarctic venture. While the scientists scattered for extended studies of natural phenomena, Wilkes's ships reprovisioned from stores deposited earlier by the *Relief*, and urgent repairs were carried out on the *Flying Fish* and *Peacock*, the latter now suffering from such widespread timber decay topside that Captain Hudson had grave doubts of her surviving the approaching mission. No less disturbing were the frank comparisons offered by knowledgeable Australians between Wilkes's unreinforced vessels, particularly the vulnerable *Flying Fish*, and the heavily built ships recently used by Russian and British explorers in South Pacific waters.

Leaving the scientists to explore Australian natural phenomena, the squadron sailed from Sydney on 26 December 1839 and headed slowly south for Macquarie Island to enable the *Flying Fish* to keep in company. The schooner lost touch on New Year's

As graphically depicted in Voyage au Pole Sud, *warmly clad seamen struggle to free* L'Astrolabe *from an ice floe during d'Urville's first probe of Antarctic waters early in 1838. Courtesy The George Peabody Library of the Johns Hopkins University.*

Day, however, after sustaining sail damage in heavy weather, and the main body continued southward in intermittent fog, signaling with horns, bells, and guns to keep contact. Late on 11 January the *Porpoise* reached the ice pack, subsequently heading west with the *Peacock* in search of open leads in the seemingly unbroken barrier. On 16 January 1840, Passed Midshipmen Henry Eld and William Reynolds of the *Peacock* excitedly reported sighting land beyond the long barrier. "The Mountains could be distinctly seen," Eld recorded in his journal, "towering over the field ice & bergs in the back ground stretching to the S & W as far as we could discern anything." The young officers' superiors failed to investigate personally this first American sighting of the Antarctic land mass, which was not

confirmed until 19 January, when the *Peacock's* lookouts, eventually including Captain Hudson, confirmed the appearance of distant land. During the ensuing week, observers in the *Vincennes* also reported land, leading Wilkes to continue westward in search of passages to the land mass.

At the same time corvettes *L'Astrolabe* and *La Zélée* under the veteran Dumont d'Urville reached the polar ice barrier east of the Americans in 140° East Longitude, sighting the Antarctic highlands on 19 January. Launches from both vessels succeeded in working through the less massive ice barrier in those waters two days later and planted the French tricolor on a rocky islet off the Antarctic mainland, which Dumont d'Urville named Adelie Land in fond recollection of his wife. Wilkes, unaware of the French presence in those waters though the *Porpoise* encountered Dumont d'Urville's corvettes late in January, meanwhile continued westward in the *Vincennes* for a month, to 105° East Longitude, occasionally sketching the distant continental highland and collecting birds and rocks but finding no passages that permitted landings on the tantalizing Antarctic land mass. Finally, on 21 February with thirty men on the flagship's sick list, Wilkes mustered the crew for words of appreciation for their hardy endurance and then directed the course for Sydney, toward which the *Peacock* was also proceeding after a harrowing encounter with the massive ice barrier.

Following repairs and replenishment from the *Relief's* remaining stores in Australia, where Wilkes's and Dumont d'Urville's accomplishments were simultaneously reported, the American expedition headed late in March for New Zealand before undertaking difficult survey operations in the inhospitable Fiji Islands to the northward. Wilkes's huge task in charting the reefs and shoals of this labyrinthine group proved the most challenging of his hydrographic career, owing not only to the treacherous character of those waters but also to the patent hostility of its inhabitants, many practicing cannibals. As the *Flying Fish* and the survey boats from the larger vessels were alone suitable for this painstaking, tedious work, their crews were pushed to the limits of their endurance in completing extensive surveys that Wilkes planned during the Expedition's subequatorial summer of 1840.

Untitled oil by Agate depicting the Flying Fish *in heavy seas off the coast of Antarctica. Courtesy Alfred T. Agate Collection, Naval Historical Foundation.*

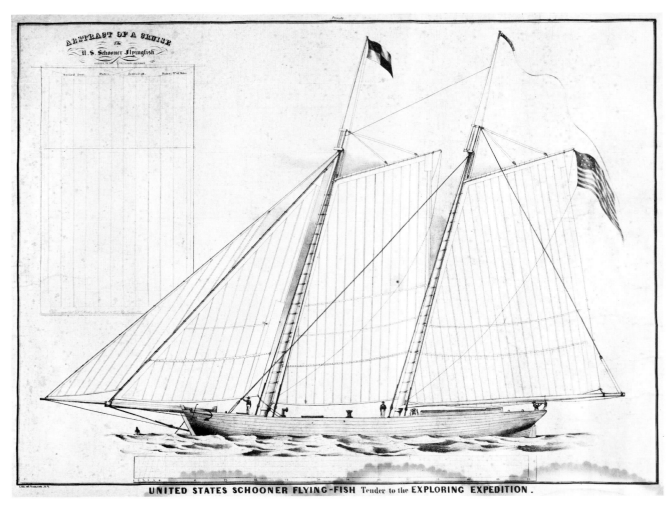

UNITED STATES SCHOONER FLYING-FISH Tender to the EXPLORING EXPEDITION.

A former New York pilot boat of seagoing design, this handsome 96-ton schooner was armed with two small cannon at Norfolk and fitted with reduced canvas. The Flying Fish *survived two harrowing probes of the Antarctic barrier and conducted extended shoal water surveys in the South Pacific. Courtesy Peabody Museum of Salem.*

Operating in groups of three, the launch crews had to remain constantly on the alert during the long, hot months and found it necessary to employ the traditional hostage system when bartering with the Fijians for local pork and vegetables. Notwithstanding the loss of two officers in a tragic instance when the hostage scheme broke down, the Expedition substantially completed the congressional mandate to chart this dangerous island group, while assisting the scientific corps in acquiring major botanical, coral, and ethnographic collections. A tall order indeed!

Some three months behind schedule as it headed for the Sandwich Islands, the Expedition had by now virtually exhausted the *Relief*'s provisions and reached friendly Oahu on short rations. During the ensuing winter, the squadron refitted and replenished from chartered storeships and sent a shipment of scientific specimens home by the *Lausanne*. Wilkes established a temporary meteorological station atop Mauna Loa and conducted a wide range of land surveys that contributed significantly to the emerging science of volcanism. For the brig *Porpoise*, a late arrival from extended surveys in the Fijis, there was little respite. In mid-November it departed Honolulu for four months' additional charting operations under the dependable Lieutenant Cadwalader Ringgold in the Central Pacific.

U.S.S. Peacock Ex. Ex. Antarctic Sea 1839.

Geo. F. Emmons

Peacock *working clear of the ice barrier, 1840. By means of ice anchors, Hudson's men managed, as recorded by Lieutenant George Emmons, to extricate their damaged vessel from almost certain disaster. This drawing illustrates the limited technical detail provided by Expedition artists on the appearance of Wilkes's ships. Courtesy Beinecke Rare Book and Manuscript Library, Yale University.*

Through such independent cruises, as well as the subsequent operations of the *Peacock* and *Flying Fish* in the Samoas, Kingsmill group, and Marshall Islands, the Expedition largely fulfilled the ambitious program outlined in its instructions, not without considerable privation among the crews.

These far-ranging Pacific explorations were but the prelude to the Expedition's most significant geopolitical undertaking, a comprehensive survey of the Oregon territory, extending from the Strait of Juan de Fuca to the Columbia River valley. Equipped with George Vancouver's accurate coastal charts of the Pacific Northwest, Wilkes departed Honolulu on 5 April 1841 with the *Vincennes* and the freshly coppered *Porpoise* and headed directly northeast for the mouth of the Columbia, leaving instructions for the *Peacock* and *Flying Fish* to follow. Arriving off Cape Disappointment some three weeks later, the veteran navigator realized the entrance to the Columbia was too treacherous for

the deep-drafted sloop-of-war and accordingly headed north to begin his surveys in Puget Sound. The *Vincennes* and *Porpoise* entered the Strait of Juan de Fuca on 1 May, anchoring at Port Discovery near the entrance to Admiralty Inlet the following day before proceeding south in intermittent fog to Fort Nisqually, a venerable outpost of the Hudson's Bay Company on the southern reaches of Puget Sound. Notwithstanding the political implications of the squadron's appearance in the heart of the disputed Oregon country, the British traders offered the weary explorers a hearty welcome and badly needed provisions, including much appreciated sides of beef.

During ensuing weeks the *Porpoise* surveyed Admiralty Inlet, the eastern arm of Puget Sound, while launches from the *Vincennes* explored from the Hood Canal to the mouth of the Fraser River. From Fort Nisqually Wilkes sent Lieutenant Robert E. Johnson across the Cascade Range with an over-

This model of the Porpoise, *constructed by Dr. William Brown, illustrates the major alterations made in Wilkes's ships, including the addition of forecastles, stern cabins, iron trusses, heavier spars, and larger survey launches, balanced by reduction of their heavy armament. In particular, note the rectangular cockpit located well aft. Courtesy Division of Transportation, National Museum of American History, Smithsonian Institution; gift of Dr. William Brown.*

Wreck of the Peacock *off Cape Disappointment, 1841. Alfred T. Agate, a survivor of this disaster at the mouth of the Columbia, recorded the sloop of war's disciplined abandonment on the morning of 19 July, as the* Flying Fish *cruised warily off the treacherous bar.* Narrative.

land party charged with surveying the upper Columbia Valley, while leading yet another party himself south to the primary headquarters of the Hudson's Bay Company at Fort Vancouver on the lower Columbia. From that equally hospitable entrepot, parties explored the Willamette and ultimately undertook the long and hazardous overland trek to San Francisco Bay, thus rounding out a historic cartographic venture that furnished Washington a superb representation of the Oregon territory at a critical juncture in its border negotiations with Great Britain. The *Peacock* and *Flying Fish,* overdue and a cause for mounting concern, had meanwhile reached the mouth of the Columbia and stood offshore awaiting a favorable tide across the treacherous bar. Shortly after noon on 18 July, Captain Hudson attempted to negotiate the shoal passage off Cape Disappointment, only to feel his sloop run aground, to be broken up in the agonizing hours that followed. Through good seamanship and disci-

pline, Hudson got his entire crew safely ashore, but invaluable scientific collections, including extensive entomological acquisitions and some of Dana's notes and specimens, had been irretrievably lost. Temporary quarters for the survivors, happily again on native soil, were established near Fort Clatsop, while the *Flying Fish* and two of the *Peacock*'s veteran launches doggedly began surveys of the lower Columbia.

Learning belatedly of the *Peacock*'s total loss, the squadron commander ordered the *Vincennes* to the Columbia mouth, subsequently directing the flagship to proceed to San Francisco Bay rather than risk destruction on the bar. By way of replacing the gallant Pacific veteran, Wilkes purchased the 250-ton Baltimore brig *Thomas H. Perkins,* which, rechristened U.S.S. *Oregon* and armed with two guns, thereupon assisted the *Porpoise* and *Flying Fish* during their final survey of the lower Columbia. Much surveying work remained on Wilkes's agenda for the Western Pacific, including the Sea of Japan. After major refits, replenishment, and further surveys at San Francisco Bay, the *Vincennes, Porpoise,* and *Oregon* departed Golden Gate late in October 1841, while the *Flying Fish,* obliged to refit off the Oregon coast, proceeded directly to the Oahu rendezvous. Reaching Honolulu midway in November, the Expedition braced for an arduous homeward passage, initially involving surveys of the northwest reefs and islets of the Sandwich Islands as well as lonely Wake Island en route to the Philippines. Though heavy weather frustrated all but the Wake survey, the *Vincennes* and *Flying Fish* charted Mindoro Straits and the extensive Sulu Archipelago late in January 1842, in passage from Manila to Singapore. Not undertaken on the long westward voyage was the intended reconnaissance of the Sea of Japan, which Wilkes prudently judged to be beyond the capacity of his well-worn squadron.

During replenishment at Singapore, Wilkes carried out a methodical survey of the faithful *Flying Fish,* now weakened in her frame, and determined with regret that he could not risk the lives of her crew in crossing the Indian Ocean or rounding the Cape of Good Hope in the approaching monsoon season. Thus denied a share of a triumphal return to its native New York, the gallant pilot boat was sold, shortly to enter a new and no less hazardous career in the booming opium trade, under the name *Spec.* The Expedition departed Singapore on 26 February 1842, proceeding through anticipated violent gales, with waves up to twenty-three feet in height, to temporary haven at Capetown, where provisions were secured with the assistance of the American consul. For Wilkes, the brief visit afforded an opportunity to visit the Cape Observatory, renowned for the studies of Sir John Herschel on the southern constellations. The naturalists had a re-

warding tour of Baron von Ludwig's Botanical Garden, from which numerous specimens were obtained. In retrospect, the Expedition's logistical career since the detachment of the *Relief* had benefited not only from the assistance of American consular and naval agents but also from the ready availability of provisions and repair services in far-flung British entrepots from Australia and the Far East to the Cape Colony, this during a period of heightened diplomatic tension between Great Britain and the United States over the Canadian borders. Thus happily continued the peaceful scientific tradition stemming from the era of Cook's voyages.

At Capetown the Exploring Expedition broke company for the homeward passage, the brigs in advance of the *Vincennes* sailing at Wilkes's orders to Rio de Janeiro to secure a final consignment of scientific specimens, thereby being denied a share in the flagship's homecoming reception at New York. Wilkes was not sanguine regarding the likelihood of a grand official welcome and appears to have been determined not to stage a return in the heroic pattern of the squadron's departure from Hampton Roads some three years and ten months earlier. Departing Capetown on 17 April, the *Vincennes* made a twelve-day passage to Saint Helena, tarried there briefly and proceeded under favorable trade winds to the American coast, arriving off Sandy Hook on 10 June 1842. Pausing not for the *Porpoise* and *Oregon,* which arrived shortly before the Fourth of July, Wilkes mustered the flagship's crew for final words of appreciation off the battery, fired the national salute, and ceremoniously hauled down his command pendant with the realization that, notwithstanding the inevitable coolness of forthcoming official interviews, the curious contents of his ships' holds and chart cabinets contained the ultimate vindication of America's first great overseas exploring expedition.

this mode of explanation to the eye
rather than troubling the reader with
a long written explanation, red
& black represent the two diversi

The Tangents are not marked in this diagram
as they would render it too confused

RALPH E. EHRENBERG, JOHN A. WOLTER, *and* CHARLES A. BURROUGHS

8 Surveying and Charting the Pacific Basin

A major objective of the U.S. Exploring Expedition was to survey and chart large portions of the Pacific Ocean for the American shipping industry, which was concerned about dangers to navigation. Before 1790 American merchant vessels were braving the hazardous passage around Cape Horn and crossing the Pacific Ocean to ports in the Sandwich Islands and China. The whalers and sealers followed the traders, and by 1835 Jeremiah N. Reynolds could call the South Pacific "our field of fame" and report no fewer than two hundred American whaling ships sailing in the area. The logbooks of these vessels make fascinating reading today. Most are illustrated, with varying degrees of artistic success, and several include sketch maps and charts of Pacific islands. But Reynolds knew American seafarers lacked adequate knowledge of winds and currents and the location of many islands, rocks, and reefs, and he pleaded for better aids to navigation. The only charts available, he said, had been based on "loose accounts from whalers, who were careless in some instances, and forgetful in others, and which were seized with greediness" by European mapmakers, who then put the information on their charts "as an important acquisition to geography,

Drawing by Wilkes illustrating procedures for conducting a "running survey" of an island. Courtesy Manuscript Division, The Library of Congress.

but without mentioning the names, or alluding to the nation of the discoverers." [Reynolds 1835, 1841]

Despite Reynolds's critical appraisal of Pacific charting, Europeans had sent many expeditions into the Pacific Ocean, beginning with the famous voyages of Ferdinand Magellan in 1520–22. Sixteenth-century exploration and discovery was dominated by the Spanish, who eventually established a successful eastward passage along the northern fortieth parallel. Methodical Dutch navigators in the seventeenth century made significant discoveries in the East Indies.

Geographical knowledge of the Pacific island groups and the northeastern and southern continental margins was greatly increased by the British voyages of Captains James Cook and George Vancouver in the eighteenth century. Meticulous observation and technological developments finally brought accuracy to hydrographic and topographic surveying in the Pacific. The invention of the Hadley octant in 1731 enabled navigators to obtain both vertical and horizontal angles of measurement on the heaving deck of a sailing vessel. The subsequent invention and perfection of the chronometer, a reliable timepiece with a known rate of gain or loss, and the publication of the *Nautical Almanac* allowed accurate determination of the all-important longitude.

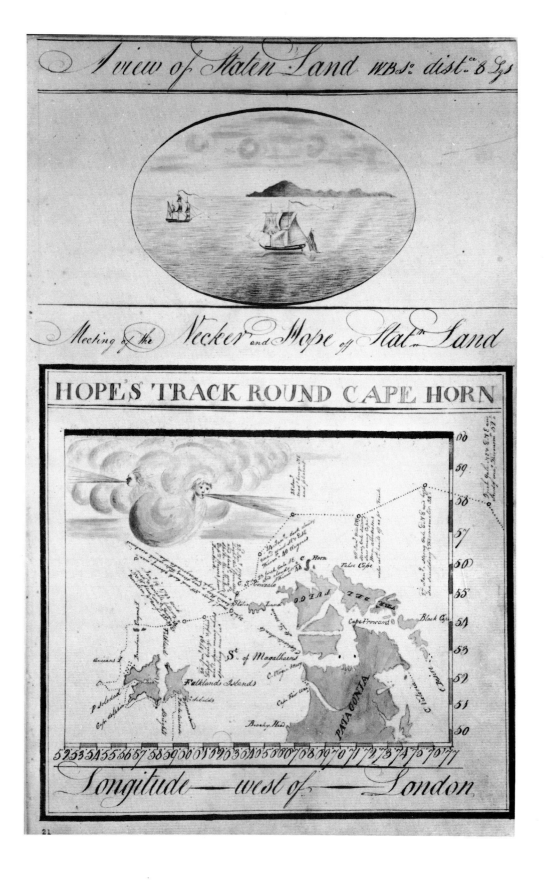

The first reasonably accurate large-scale chart of the Pacific Ocean was compiled by Aaron Arrowsmith, the great British mapmaker. Its title describes the sources used in its compilation: "Chart of the Pacific Ocean. Drawn from a great number of printed and Ms. Journals. By A. Arrowsmith, Geographer, No. 24 Rathbone Place, London 1798." The chart shows a rather sketchy outline of the islands in the Western Pacific, for Arrowsmith included only information of reasonable accuracy. The chart depicts the tracks of many explorers and notes of their discoveries, "I. Jesus of Mendana, 1567," for example, or "saw a seal" and "saw rock weed and penguins" along Cook's 1773 track south of New Zealand. Arrowsmith's chart was one of those ordered for the Exploring Expedition, and, although the 1814 edition is listed, one can assume his later "Chart . . . [with] additions to 1826" was available to Wilkes and his navigators. Examination of the 1826 edition reveals the increasingly accurate portrayal of the Pacific as the results of European exploration and discovery became available through narratives and hydrographic and topographic surveys and, as noted, the results of the voyages of whalers and other commercial vessels.

On the list of books purchased for the Exploring Expedition can be found the most important records of European voyages of exploration and discovery of the seventeenth, eighteenth, and early nineteenth centuries, along with the geographical compendia so popular at the time. Of particular importance were the recently published Freycinet's *Narrative* with excellent illustrations and an important atlas; Duperrey's *Voyage*; Dumont d'Urville's *Voyage* with a folio atlas of sixty-nine plates; reports of

Cook's three voyages; Beechey's *Narrative* with the three important maps; and Vancouver's *A voyage of discovery* with an atlas of plates with ten folding charts. The list also refers to one French and five English sets of official hydrographic charts. The last may well have included charts not just from the latest English voyages of exploration but from the French, Dutch, and Spanish where only their charts existed.

Wilkes obtained his training as a navigator and surveyor largely through his own initiative long before leading the first American marine surveying and charting effort beyond the waters of the United States. As a young student he had studied mathematics and drawing, and by the time he first went to sea at seventeen he "had become quite a good navigator, understood the use of the instruments, could readily make all the calculations [and had become] familiar with all the tables & solutions of the various formulae of navigation and the construction of charts." [Wilkes 1978:16] Subsequently, he learned from Ferdinand Hassler the fundamentals of triangulation and hydrographic surveying and studied with the famed mathematician Nathaniel Bowditch.

Wilkes gained practical experience as a junior officer with the survey of Narragansett Bay in 1832, a position he had sought hoping it would lead to an appointment with either Hassler's Coast Survey or "the contemplated Exploring Expedition to the South Seas." [Wilkes 1978:285] Since the U.S. Navy then lacked proper equipment, Wilkes used a theodolite he ordered made in New York from drawings of Hassler's instrument. The charts were drawn in a cottage in Newport, Rhode Island, which Wilkes and his wife occupied that summer, where he had a "table & draughting boards constructed for the Making of our charts." [Wilkes 1978: 290]

Wilkes's assignments through the mid-1830s—to direct the Navy Depot of Charts and Instruments, to purchase the scientific instruments for the planned Expedition, to survey the shoals of Georges Bank and the entrance to the Savannah River— further broadened his experience. The survey of Georges Bank, a large and dangerous shoal area lying off the coast of New England and threatening all vessels bound for Boston, produced the first set

This is one of thirteen beautifully drawn manuscript charts that enhance Joseph Ingraham's Journal of his fur trading voyage to the northwest coast of North America and China *between 1790 and 1792. Charts such as this one were often prepared by merchant ship masters to record their voyage before the advent of published charts. This chart shows the passage of Ingraham's brigantine* Hope *around the Falkland Islands, where it stopped for provisions, and the treacherous Cape Horn. Above is a view of the* Hope *and* Necker, *an American-built whaler which accompanied the* Hope *during this passage. Courtesy Manuscript Division, The Library of Congress.*

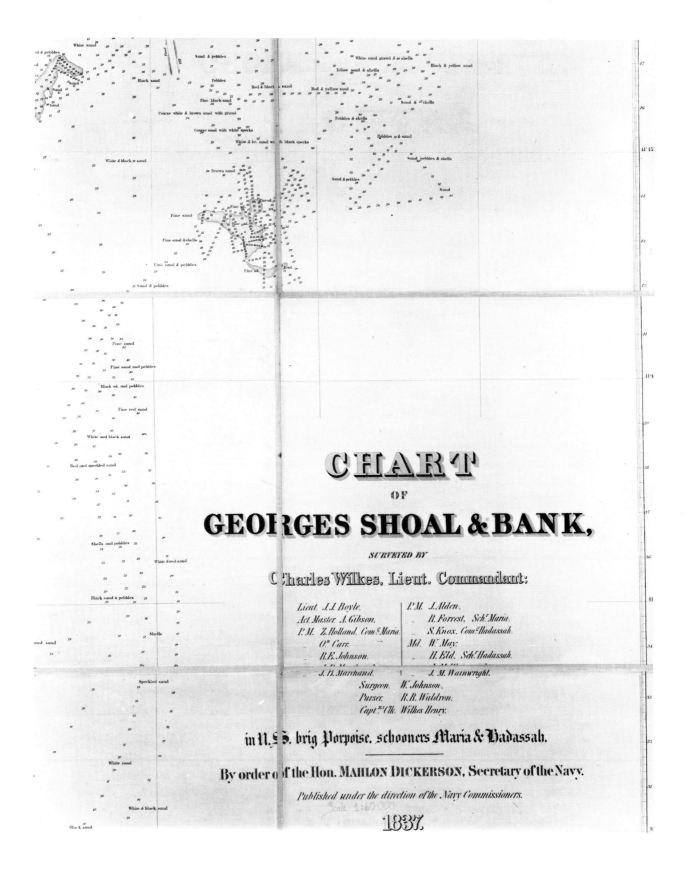

CHART
OF
GEORGES SHOAL & BANK,
SURVEYED BY
Charles Wilkes, Lieut. Commandant:

Lieut. J.J. Boyle.	P.M. J. Alden.
Act Master A. Gibson.	R. Forrest. Sch. Maria.
P.M. Z. Holland. Com. Maria.	S. Knox. Com. Hadassah.
O. Carr.	Md. W. May.
R.E. Johnson.	H. Eld. Sch. Hadassah.
J.B. Marchand.	J.M. Wainwright.

Surgeon. W. Johnson.
Purser. R.R. Waldron.
Capt.ns Clk. Wilkes Henry.

in U.S. brig Porpoise, schooners Maria & Hadassah.

By order of the Hon. MAHLON DICKERSON, Secretary of the Navy.

Published under the direction of the Navy Commissioners.

1837.

of charts prepared under the authority of the Depot of Charts and Instruments. Wilkes used the quincunx system for triangulating the survey, a system he later used in the Pacific.

Appointed to lead the Exploring Expedition in 1838, Wilkes was specifically instructed to explore and survey "the great Southern Ocean . . . as well as determine the existence of all doubtful islands and shoals [and] discover and accurately fix the position of those which lie in or near the track of our vessels in that quarter, and may have escaped the observation of scientific navigation." His surveys during the Exploring Expedition were of several basic types: those along unbroken coastlines, most of which were studded by reefs and islands; those of singular islands or reefs, such as those found in the Western Pacific Ocean; and those offshore encompassing a reported shoal, perhaps reported by some previous navigator.

For a coastal survey, or that of an area surrounding an island, common practice was to build up a framework of triangles over the region to be surveyed, forming the basis for "controlling" the area to be sounded. The construction of this "triangulation" ranged from the rough triangles of a "running survey"—where the side (or base) measurements were obtained by determining distance by sound and the angles were horizontal sextant angles, taken on board from a by-no-means-stationary position—to the almost exactly formed triangles of a detailed survey, where observations with carefully leveled theodolites on shore established a regular trigonometrical network, which covered the whole portion to be charted.

Wilkes's surveys used gunfire to determine "base line" distances between the ships and horizontal angular measurements by sextant to fix geographic positions. He described the process in the *Narrative* as firing guns alternately in quick succession from each vessel, "noting the elapse of time between the

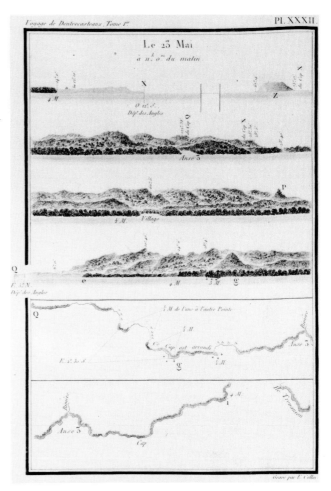

A plate from Charles-François Beautemps-Beaupré, Methodes Pour la Levée et la Construction des Cartes et Plans Hydrographiques *(1808), one of several contemporary manuals on marine surveying and charting which Wilkes and his officers procured for the expedition. Courtesy General Collections, The Library of Congress.*

During the hydrographic survey of Georges Bank, off the coast of Massachusetts, Wilkes first used the quincunx system for triangulating the survey. His chart of the region was the first published by the Depot of Charts and Instruments, the predecessor of the U.S. Hydrographic Office. Courtesy Geography and Map Division, The Library of Congress.

flash and report." [1:384] During this gunfire, officers measured the angles between the ships and the shore. This operation continued around the island, with the ships changing their positions, until an entire circuit had been made and a network of triangles established to "control subsequent survey work." At the same time, observers were also placed on prominent points on the island to determine precise geodetic positions of latitude and longitude by astronomical measurements.

After delineating the island and establishing points of known location along its perimeter, the officers would then deploy survey boats along a systematic lattice of sounding lines radiating from its shores. Using their sextants, two officers in each boat would simultaneously measure off horizontal angles to the known points on land (or perhaps include an anchored vessel of known location offshore), while at the same time the leadsman measured the depth of water using a long line weighted with lead. In so doing, one of the points in common to both angles, generally referred to as the "center object," thereby produced a left angle and right angle from which the boat's position could be accurately located. Such locations, commonly called "fixes" or "fixed positions," were normally taken at convenient time intervals along the sounding lines so as to coincide with lead line measurements of depth, as well as to mark major changes in course.

Describing this "excruciating and unceasing" work on a twenty-seven-foot survey boat on a long cruise, Midshipman William Reynolds, in a letter to his mother, wrote that "surveying keeps the mind on the utmost stretch of attention, & a moment given to relaxation might spoil or injure the whole." Reynolds, like the other surveyors, was particularly concerned about accuracy. "There is a responsibility attached to the duty that forces one to be keen, watchful & correct, if a ship trusting to your chart, gets into danger, *who* is to blame? We had much to do, knew nothing of the hidden shoals & the intricate passages that were to be found & laid down, & were limited to weeks to perform that which required months. We did as well as we could, but sometimes I was so perplexed that my brain was all in a whirl." [Reynolds 1840]

Upon completion of the survey work each day, the ship and shore observations were recorded on the "deck-board" of each ship or survey boat, copies of which were sent to Wilkes along with a copy of the surveyor's work, and a diagram or survey chart constructed to show all the basic control points at a convenient scale. The compilations were then calculated and plotted by Wilkes and his associates in preparation for the later printing of the charts.

The Expedition produced some 241 separate charts and maps. As a mariner, Wilkes was acutely aware of the value of accurate charts and maps for navigating and as aids for depicting geographical

information. In his famous lecture describing the Expedition before the National Institute in June 1842, Wilkes first brought to public attention the cartographic results of his surveys, illustrating his talk with numerous manuscript maps and charts to give the public "some idea of our work." [p. 29] The earliest printed maps of the Expedition were incorporated in his five-volume *Narrative* and accompanying five-sheet atlas, published by C. Sherman in Philadelphia in 1844. Wilkes's monumental two-volume folio *Atlas of Charts*, also published by Sherman, followed in 1850 and 1858. In addition, maps were used to illustrate the following scientific publications: Horatio Hale's *Ethnography and Philology*; Charles Pickering's *Races of Man*; James D. Dana's *Geology*; Wilkes's *Meteorology*; Dana's *Crustacea*; Pickering's *Geographical Distribution of Animals and Plants*; and Wilkes's *Hydrography*.

Basically, three types of charts and maps are found in the reports and atlases of the Exploring Expedition: nautical charts, topographic maps, and thematic maps. Small-scale maps were also used by Wilkes to provide basic locational information for readers of his *Narrative* and in some of the scientific reports. For the most part, these maps were reduced versions of maps and charts found in the atlases.

The nautical charts were designed to serve as navigational aids for whalers and merchant vessels. Based on surveys of some 280 islands, eight hundred miles of coastal and inland waterways of Oregon territory, and fifteen hundred miles of the Antarctic continent, these charts represented a major contribution to the geographical knowledge of the Pacific basin. Much of the original plotting was done immediately following the survey work, but some of the survey sheets were drawn in Honolulu, where Wilkes reported "part of the officers were employed in bringing up the work of our charts." [1842:30–31] It was demanding, difficult work often done under the most adverse conditions.

After the original survey sheets were compiled, they were sent to Wilkes, along with the work notes, for his inspection and approval. Some of these initial charts were drawn by Lieutenant James Alden (later chief hydrographer for the survey of the west coast during the 1850s); Passed Midship-

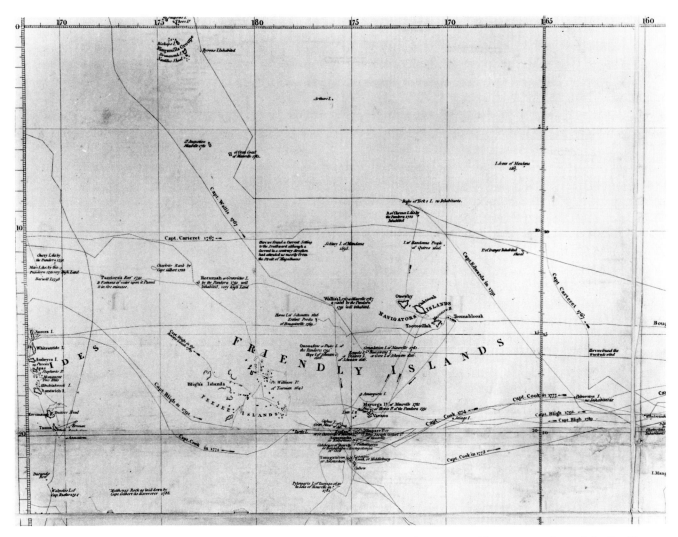

A section of Aaron Arrowsmith's "Chart of the Pacific Ocean" (1798). The first reasonably accurate chart of the Pacific Ocean, it was based on logs and journals of James Cook, William Bligh, and other contemporary mariners, whose tracks of exploration are denoted on the chart. Courtesy Geography and Map Division, The Library of Congress.

man William May; Captain's Clerk Frederick D. Stuart; Lieutenant Robert E. Johnson; and artist Joseph Drayton. All were accomplished mapmakers, experienced in surveying, determining projections, and drawing. Alden and May had served before with Wilkes and had drawn his charts of Georges Bank and, with Johnson, of the Savannah River. Most of the nautical charts, however, are not attributed to any one surveyor or draftsman because Wilkes firmly believed that the surveying and charting work was a team effort and "should be credited to

the whole" rather than to any single person. Wilkes established this policy early in the cruise when he reprimanded Lieutenant William Walker of the *Peacock*, who had directed the compiler of the chart of a harbor in Tahiti to add the note "Surveyed by Lt. Walker, U.S.N." "I felt really ashamed to think that any officer should so far forget himself as to permit this act of selfishness," Wilkes later observed in his autobiography. "So I at once determined to teach them all a lesson and deliberately took my pen and drew it through his name and wrote above it 'by the Exploring [Expedition]' and returned it to have another copy made." [p. 428]

After the squadron's return, Wilkes directed the preparation of the charts and maps for publication. The final calculations and drawings were done in Washington by Stuart and his assistants. Several copies of each chart were prepared, not only to prevent loss or destruction by fire or accident, but also to serve later as a check against the proof sheets pulled from the engraved plates. This very exacting work, requiring close attention to detail and accuracy, was hindered during the winter months by the cold, damp climate of the nation's capital. "Since Monday I have not been able to get the room at the office warm," Stuart lamented to Wilkes on 9 January 1856, "water froze on the drafting table yesterday and this morning much to my surprise the dividers stuck to my fingers, good fire in the stove notwithstanding."

The final manuscript charts were then sent to copper engravers in New York, Philadelphia, and Boston by Drayton, who was responsible for all engraving work. Although the Depot of Charts and Instruments had purchased a lithographic press in 1835, the navy continued to engrave its charts from copper plates until after the Civil War, using private

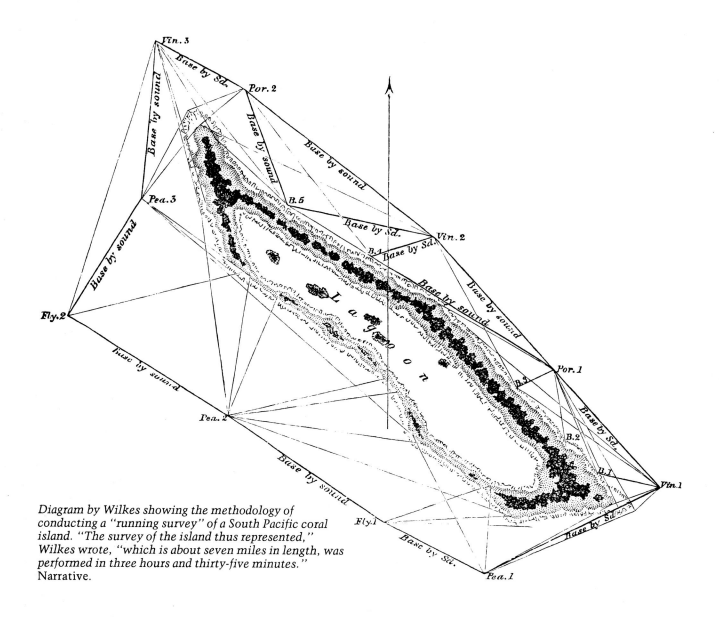

Diagram by Wilkes showing the methodology of conducting a "running survey" of a South Pacific coral island. "The survey of the island thus represented," Wilkes wrote, *"which is about seven miles in length, was performed in three hours and thirty-five minutes."* Narrative.

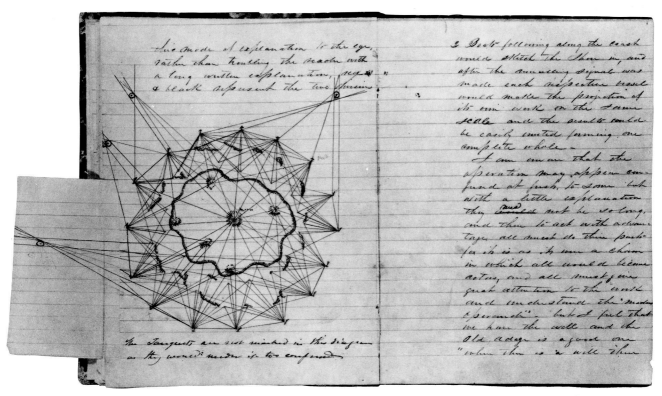

This drawing is from Wilkes's unpublished instructions to his new officers showing his procedures for conducting a "running survey" of an island. "I have made a diagram to illustrate it, preferring this mode of explanation to the eye," he wrote, "rather than troubling the reader with a long written explanation." Courtesy Manuscript Division, The Library of Congress.

printing companies under contract. At that time, the quality of copper engravings was much higher than lithographs, ensuring the reproduction of the detailed bathymetric features recorded by Wilkes and his officers. Drayton, who took his responsibility very seriously, carefully inspected the work of each firm before letting a contract. To ensure the highest quality, he required that only master engravers work on the chart plates, avoiding what he termed "Engraving factories," which employed large numbers of young men and apprentices. [Drayton 1843]

Incised copper plates were returned to Drayton, who had an office in Philadelphia near C. Sherman, the publisher. Proof sheets were then pulled from each plate and sent to Stuart and Wilkes in Washington, where they were checked against the original drawings. Corrections were noted on the proofs and returned to Drayton, who apparently made minor corrections directly on the copper himself, probably with a burnisher; for major corrections, plates were returned to the engraver to be pounded out and reengraved.

The corrected plates were then printed on a rolling press by C. Sherman. A major problem that sometimes delayed production was acquiring suitable paper that would remain stable through the four-step process of dampening, inking, pressing, and drying. The lack of good engraving paper plagued American cartography during the first half of the nineteenth century. "The paper shrunk so much in one direction," Wilkes wrote, "that it made all our scales erroneous either in Latitude or Longitude." [Wilkes 1845] Not until about 1855, when he began acquiring paper from the Millton Mills in Boston, was Drayton fully satisfied.

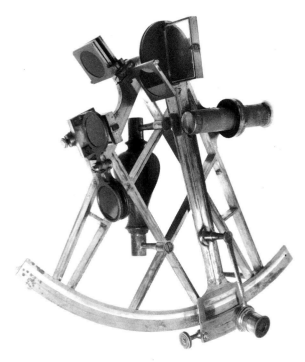

Sextant, an optical instrument for measuring angular distances at sea, either vertically between the horizon and stars for purposes of celestial navigation, or horizontally between identifiable objects on shore for purposes of charting coastal waters. Courtesy Division of Physical Sciences, National Museum of American History, Smithsonian Institution.

The navigational charts were printed between April 1843 and March 1856. The atlas for the *Narrative* was completed in December 1844. One year later Wilkes reported that one-third of the plates for volume one of his large atlas were engraved. In September 1845 single sheets of the plates already engraved were made available to navy commanders and merchant marine officers "at the cost of paper and press work." [Bancroft 1845] Double-page sheets sold for twenty-five cents, single-page sheets for thirteen cents. Eventually some fifty thousand charts were printed and distributed in this manner. These first printed sheets were received with much praise. "The charts and surveys which have already appeared are pronounced by competent judges to be unrivalled excellence," the *North American* noted in 1846, "and reflect the highest credit on the commander and his subordinate officers." When finally issued in 1858, Wilkes's masterful two-volume atlas

illustrated 236 distinct surveys made by the Expedition. Altogether, his atlas contains 109 sheets embracing four large general charts of the oceans; 85 charts of harbors, bays, coves, and anchorages; 112 coastal charts of islands and island groups; and 12 charts of canals and rivers.

Although all of the navigational charts contributed greatly to expanding the geographical knowledge of the Pacific Ocean, several are particularly noteworthy.

Wilkes's "Chart of the Antarctic Continent Shewing the Icy Barrier Attached to it" documented the existence of that continent. Indeed, Wilkes was the first to show the vast extent of the coastline and to identify it as a continent. His printed chart depicts the tracks of his ships; the general extent of the pack ice; the coastline from 160° to 100° East Longitude, covering more than fifteen hundred nautical miles; and the positions where land was sighted. In addition, six panoramic views as seen from the *Peacock* and *Vincennes* show the pack ice and, more significantly, land covered with snow. The first is dated 19 January 1840, "the day on which we felt confident the land existed, in 154°30′ east Longitude." [Wilkes 1842] Although Wilkes's claim was challenged for almost seventy-five years, expeditions by Mawson in 1911–14 and 1930–31 finally verified that land existed along most of the coastline Wilkes charted.

The five views of headlands appearing on the Antarctic chart were probably drawn with the aid of a camera lucida, an optical instrument used by nineteenth-century artists and explorers to record landscape features accurately. Listing necessary instruments for the Expedition, both Wilkes and Drayton included the camera lucida. Of the more than five hundred views of headlands and harbor entrances made during the cruise, forty were reproduced on the printed charts. On Drayton's manuscript drawing of Serle's Island, which was sketched in August 1839, he depicted three separate views of

A detail of Wilkes's chart of the Fiji Islands shows several of the 154 islands and 50 detached reefs of this island group which the Exploring Expedition surveyed and charted during a three-month period in 1840. Courtesy Geography and Map Division, The Library of Congress.

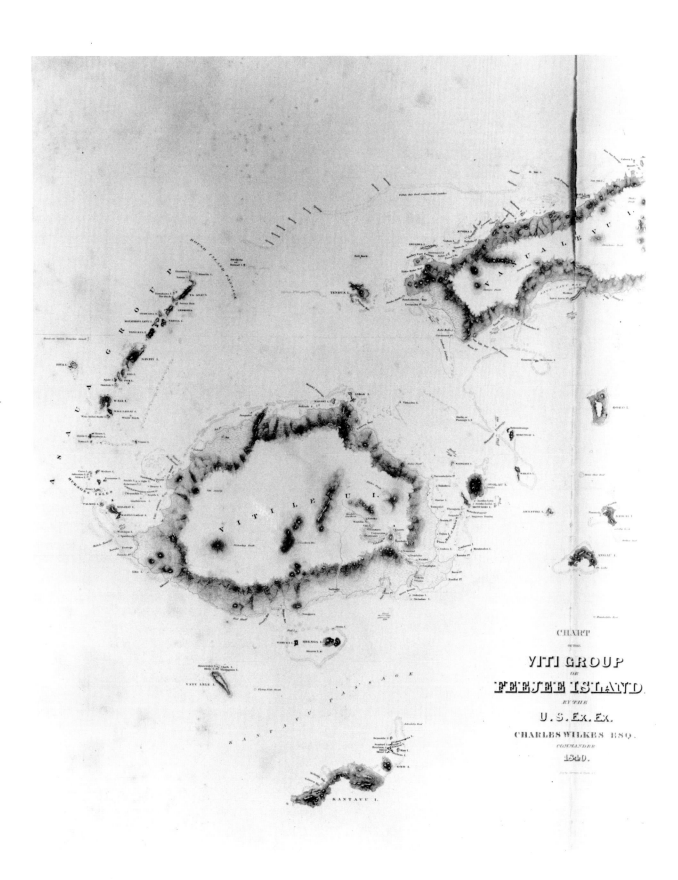

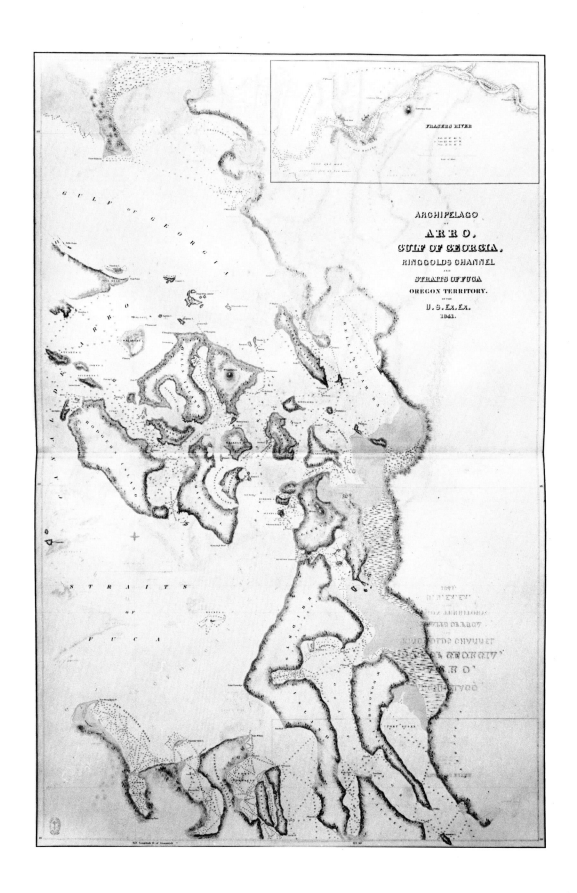

Chart of Wilkes's San Juan Island region in the Pacific Northwest with inset detail showing "Gordon" and "Adolphus" islands, which were determined by the U. S. Coast Survey in 1853 to be nonexistent. It is believed they had been deliberately added to the original survey by a disgruntled midshipman. Courtesy Geography and Map Division, The Library of Congress.

Detail below showing "Gordon" and "Adolphus" islands.

the island as seen from 5 miles, 12 miles, and an unspecified distance. "The trees loomed up nearly as high when 12 miles off as when we were 5 miles," he noted on the chart.

The charts of the Fiji Islands were far superior to any earlier charts of this region, and their exquisite engraving by Sherman and George E. Smith evoke picturesque images of the Central Pacific. These detailed charts were based on the surveys of 154 islands, detached reefs, and "numerous harbors

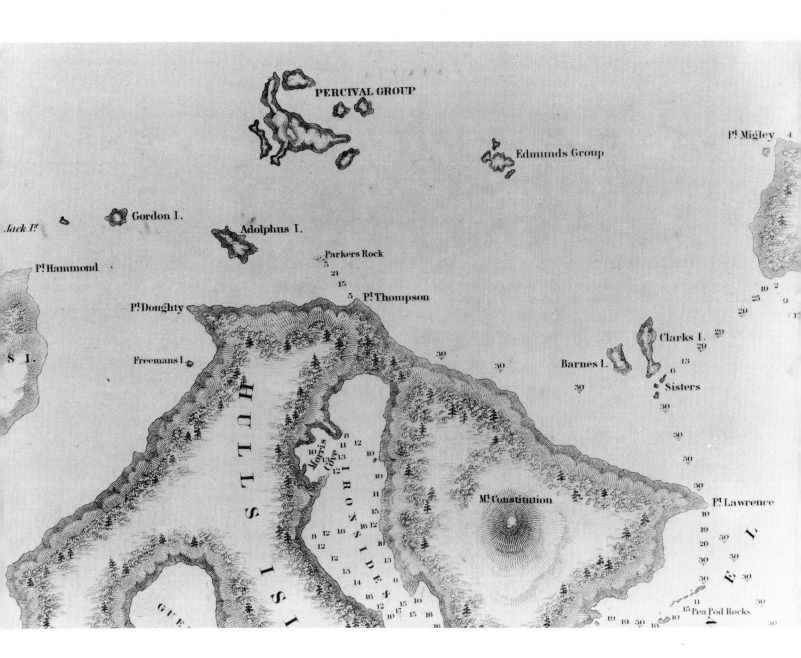

surveyed and sounded out" over the course of three and one-half months. Obviously proud of this achievement, Wilkes exhibited his charts, the "Viti Group or Feejee Islands," at the National Institute in 1842. On the general chart, each island, reef, and harbor of the archipelago is clearly depicted in its approximately correct position and named, some for the first time. "It will be sufficient to inform you," Wilkes remarked, "that every exertion was made both by the officers, scientific gentlemen, and crews, to obtain accurate results and information useful to our whaling interests, navigation, and scientific departments; in which we succeeded to my fullest gratification and anticipation." [p. 29]

A series of forty-six harbor and river charts of the American west coast are included in volume 2 of the *Atlas of Charts*, covering the area from the Strait of Juan de Fuca south to San Francisco. These large-scale harbor charts depict soundings along systematic diagonal lines, following the standard

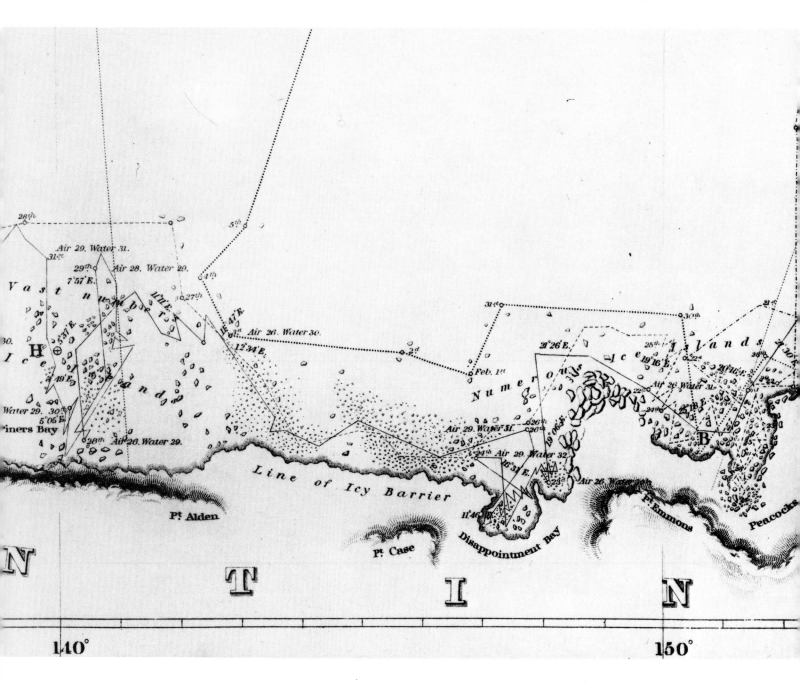

method for determining depth in those days, and show the vegetation and relief features along the coastlines. As the historian H.H. Bancroft observed some forty years later with respect to the Wilkes Expedition, these charts helped to authenticate the west coast. "These shores, which hitherto were little more than myths in the world's mind, were now clothed in reality." [Henry 1982: 164] The most intriguing chart of this series is Wilkes's "Chart of the Archipelago of Arro, Gulf of Georgia," based on

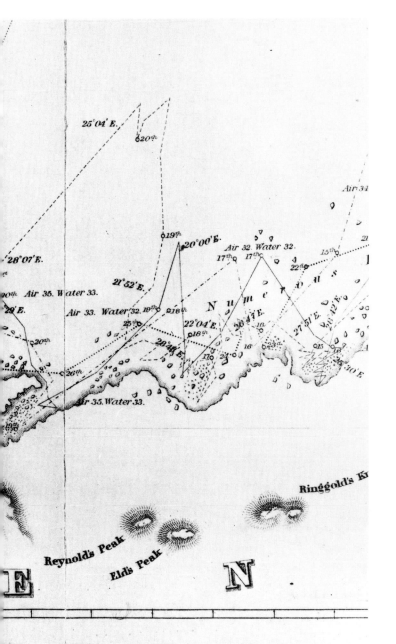

a survey of the San Juan Islands, which shows two nonexistent islands. These false islands were apparently added to the chart by Midshipman May, who had become a disgruntled officer, twice recommended for court-martial by Wilkes. The two carefully drawn fictitious islands—Gordon and Adolphus—were located north of Hulls (Orcas) Islands, seemingly to embarrass Wilkes, who placed so much emphasis on accuracy. Another name appearing on this chart has a more melancholy history. Vendovi Island, one of the last islands to be surveyed by the Expedition in Puget Sound, was named after Wilkes's Fijian prisoner, who died upon the Expedition's arrival in New York. Despite the minor errors that invariably found their way into these charts, their value as navigational aids was of the greatest significance.

The Expedition also compiled and printed topographic or "geographical maps," as Wilkes called them, including several of Hawaii, Oregon territory, and Upper California. In addition to charting harbors during the stay in Hawaii, a number of which "were surveyed at the desire of the King" [Wilkes 1844:180], Wilkes visited the island of Hawaii where he and Drayton made topographical drawings. The result was their "Map of Part of the Island of Hawaii Sandwich Islands Shewing the Craters and the Eruption of May and June 1840," engraved by Sherman and Smith in 1843. The map embraces the southeast corner of the island and is dominated by the smooth dome of Mauna Loa and the nine distinct cones of Mauna Kea. Both mountains are depicted by a series of concentric circles of hachures suggesting the succession of lava flows that formed these majestic peaks. These volcanic mountains awed Wilkes and his companions. While measuring the height of Mauna Kea from the highest point of Mauna Loa, Wilkes related in his *Nar-*

Detail of Wilkes's "Chart of the Antarctic Continent Shewing the Icy Barrier Attached to it," which documented the existence of that continent for the first time, depicts the tracts of his ships and the general extent of the pack ice. Headlands sighted by the explorers are identified by the names of Wilkes's senior officers. Courtesy Geography and Map Division, The Library of Congress.

rative that he was so taken with the "bold relief" of the former mountain "covered with its snowy mantle" that it briefly interfered with his surveying work. [4:160]

Wilkes's "Map of the Oregon Territory" was a major contribution to the cartography of the American West. First issued with his *Narrative* in 1844, it was the most detailed map of the region north of the Sacramento River up to that time and provided Americans with a new image of an area "then almost . . . incognite to the people of the United States." [Wilkes 1978: 506] The map was based in part on a two-month overland expedition from Fort Nisqually on Puget Sound, across the Cascades near Mount Rainier, to the middle course of the Columbia. Wilkes directed the expedition leader, Lieutenant Robert E. Johnson, to "keep an accurate map of your route, noting on it the latitude and longitude of all your stopping-places, from which position you will take the bearings and angles on all distant hills and mountains, direction of ranges, courses of rivers, &c." The map was to be drawn in his journal, with the ruled lines serving "as a convenient scale of miles" on which he could mark "the mountains, hills, woods, rivers, brooks, and plains, within your horizon." [Wilkes 1844:4: 529–30]. Another overland party led by Lieutenant George F. Emmons was sent up the Willamette Valley and then south to the Sacramento River and San Francisco Bay, with similar instructions to map the water courses and mountain ranges. Wilkes and his survey parties obtained additional information of the interior from officials of the Hudson's Bay Company, particularly Peter Skene Ogden, an experienced explorer who had prepared many sketch maps used by the famous English mapping firm of Arrowsmith. References on Wilkes's map also suggest that Ogden either talked with the American mountain man Jedediah Smith or had access to his 1831 map, which no longer exists. Smith was the first American to explore great areas of the American West. The region east of the Rockies was derived from John C. Frémont's map of 1842.

Completing Wilkes's general map of Oregon was a large inset map of the Columbia River from its mouth to the Walla Walla, compiled by Drayton from his detailed survey of the 120-mile portion of the river. A prominent feature on this map is Mount Saint Helens, which, Wilkes wrote, "may be seen from the sea when eighty miles distant."

The impact of Wilkes's map was direct and immediate. Using Drayton's survey of the Columbia River, Frémont was able to prepare and issue in 1845 the first scientifically constructed map of the trans-Mississippi West. It "fills up the vast geographical chasm between the two remote points," Frémont wrote, "and presents a connected and accurate view of our continent from the Mississippi river to the Pacific Ocean." Frémont also relied heavily on Wilkes's work for his map of Oregon and Upper California, published in 1848. Reflecting the importance and timely nature of Wilkes's map, it was revised and reengraved in 1856 by George E. Smith for volume 2 of the *Atlas of Charts*, the only one of the five maps appearing in the *Narrative* atlas to be completely updated. Although much of the new information was obtained from Frémont's maps of 1845 and 1848, Wilkes also added coastal features derived from other sources.

The third class of map produced by the Expedition was the thematic map, which focuses on the distribution or variation of phenomena rather than the assemblage of features. Thematic maps also differ from nautical charts and topographic maps in their smaller scale; their color; their scope, covering either the entire world or a large portion of it; and their widely varied sources of data. Thematic maps generally illustrated the scientists' reports, often in the form of large fold-out sheets. Although the development of thematic maps dates from the latter half of the seventeenth century, their real growth began during the first half of the nineteenth century, coinciding with the emerging study of the physical and cultural environment, advances in map printing, and large, government-sponsored scientific expeditions sent out to collect sufficient data to be mapped.

An incomplete manuscript draft of Wilkes's "Map of the World Shewing the Extent and Direction of the Wind and the Route to be followed in a Circumnavigation of the Globe," designed to support his theory of the winds, appeared in his volume Hydrography (1861). Courtesy Geography and Map Division, The Library of Congress.

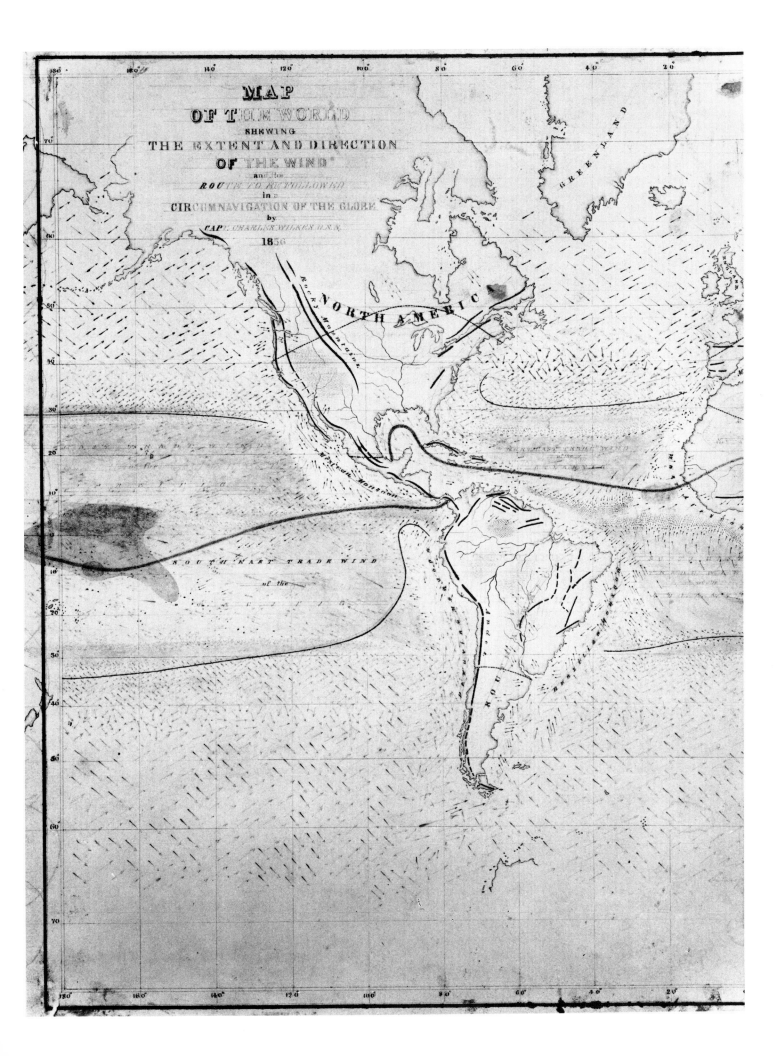

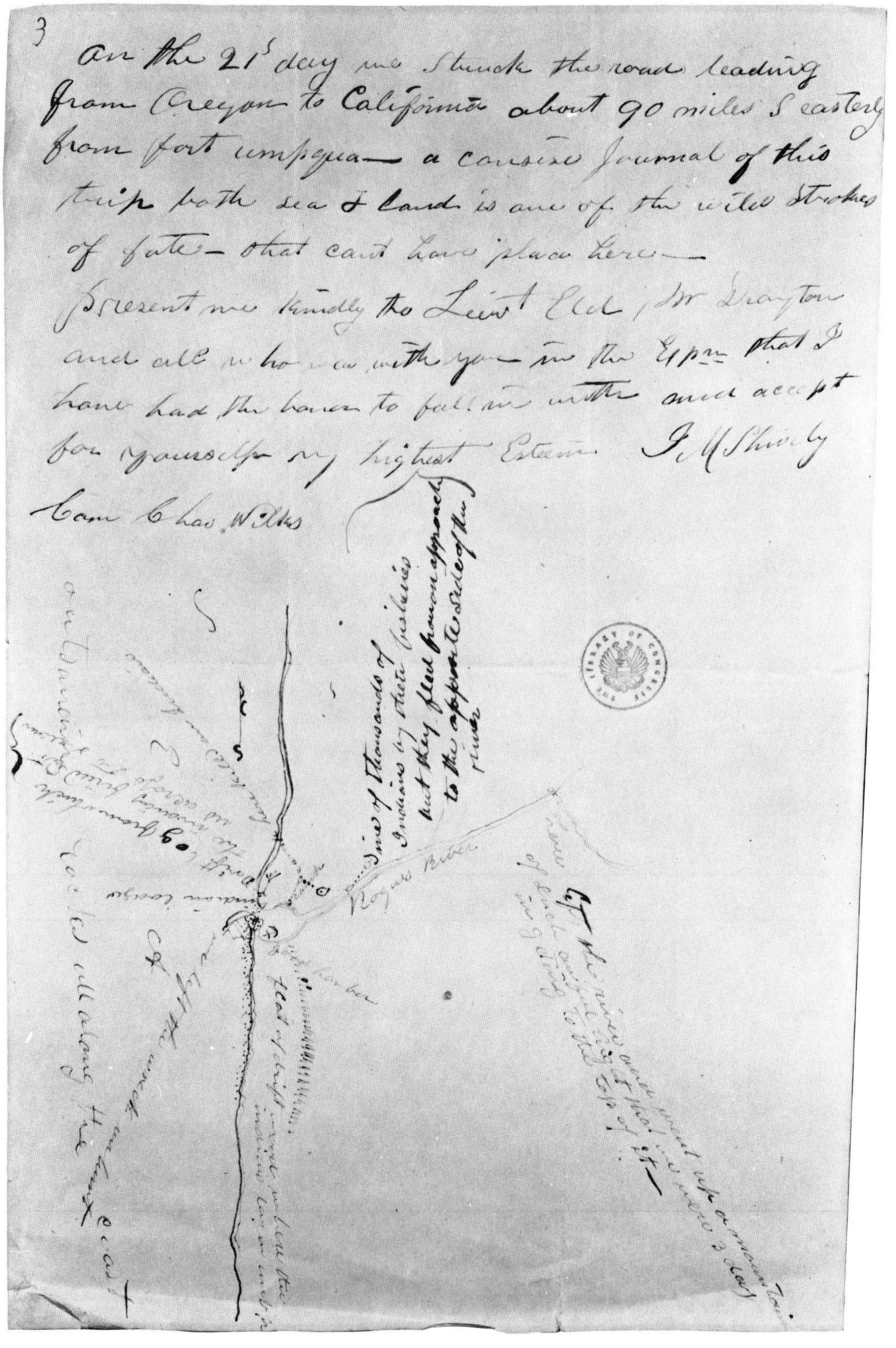

3

On the 21st day we struck the road leading
from Oregon to California about 90 miles S easterly
from fort umpqua — a concise Journal of this
trip both sea & land is one of the wild strokes
of fate — that can't have place here —

Present me kindly to Lieut Eld, Mr Drayton
and all who was with you — in the Up— that I
have had the honor to fall in with — and accept
for yourself my highest Esteem. J M Shively

Capn Chas Wilkes

Rogues River

The thematic maps produced by the Expedition can be divided into two groups: maps of the physical world and maps of people. The first and largest example of the first group was Wilkes's "Chart of the World Shewing the Tracks of the U.S. Exploring Expedition," published by Sherman and Smith in 1844 to accompany Wilkes's *Narrative.* In addition to delineating the courses of the various vessels of the squadron, this chart was designed to show the interrelationships between the direction of the winds (illustrated by arrow heads placed along the ships' tracks), the directions of the currents (noted by arrows crossing these tracks), the velocity of the currents (indicated by the length of the arrows) and isothermal lines (represented in colors) for every five degrees of temperature. The technique for mapping isothermal lines was first devised by the great German geographer Alexander von Humboldt in 1817 and adopted for a world map in 1838, which appeared in Heinrich Berghaus's *Physikalischer Atlas,* published in 1845. The first map of the Pacific showing both currents and temperature was compiled by Duperrey in 1831 and served as a model for Berghaus. Berghaus's monumental work was revised and translated into English by A. K. Johnston in 1848. Wilkes's chart is more detailed and comprehensive than the Berghaus-Johnston models, but the technique for illustrating the data is similar. Johnston's 1848 edition of this work contains two maps—a current and temperature chart of the Pacific Ocean and a world map of isothermal lines—which show the Antarctic coastline based on Wilkes's observations. They are accompanied by the notes "Coast seen by Wilkes 1840" and "Coast of the Southern Continent (?) seen by Lieut. Wilkes of the American Navy in 1840." We believe that this was based on information transmitted to Johnston by Captain James C. Ross, the British explorer who followed Wilkes to the Antarctic, since these maps do not incorporate any of

A sketch of the Rouge River, Oregon, sent to Wilkes in 1849 by J. M. Shively, a west coast merchant who had been shipwrecked near the mouth of this river, in response to Wilkes's request for information on the correct location of the river. Courtesy Manuscript Division, The Library of Congress.

Wilkes's wind and current data. Wilkes wrote in his *Synopsis* that he made a tracing of his chart of Antarctica and forwarded it to Ross on 5 April 1840.

A similar concept was employed in Wilkes's "Map Exhibiting Areas of Temperature of the Ocean and the Isothermal and Isocheimal Curves of the Continent," published as a fold-out map in his *Meteorology.* The map, comprising two hemispheres, is designed to show the general influence of the ocean temperature (illustrated by lines based on mean annual temperature) on the climates of the continental land masses (shown by lines of equal value based on the mean winter temperatures). For his *Crustacea,* James Dwight Dana constructed a world map showing the relationship between cold water (depicted by lines showing the mean temperature of the coldest month) and the distribution of marine species.

Wilkes's *Hydrography,* which was not published until 1873, contains a large folded map entitled "Map of the World Shewing the Extent and Direction of the Wind and the Route to be Followed in a Circumnavigation of the Globe." Drawn by Stuart in 1856, the map shows the general directions of the prevailing winds by arrows during various types of weather conditions and the most advantageous routes for vessels within these conditions.

No true geological maps were prepared by the Expedition, although they were probably the most advanced type of thematic map then being produced. Accompanying Dana's *Geology* are little more than locational maps or maps showing the forms of craters and coral reefs. Two maps are color coded to show the generalized extent of surface rock formations, but neither one contains a color key; the reader must search Dana's lengthy descriptions to learn, for example, that yellow on the map of Oahu indicates coral formations. Both maps were lithographed by the New York firm of Sarony and Major and then hand-colored under the direction of Drayton. The cost of coloring maps varied from five cents to twenty-five cents per map, and one of Drayton's major problems was finding skilled colorists.

Charles Pickering's *Geographical Distribution of Animals and Plants,* published in 1863, contains four beautiful maps showing the geographical dis-

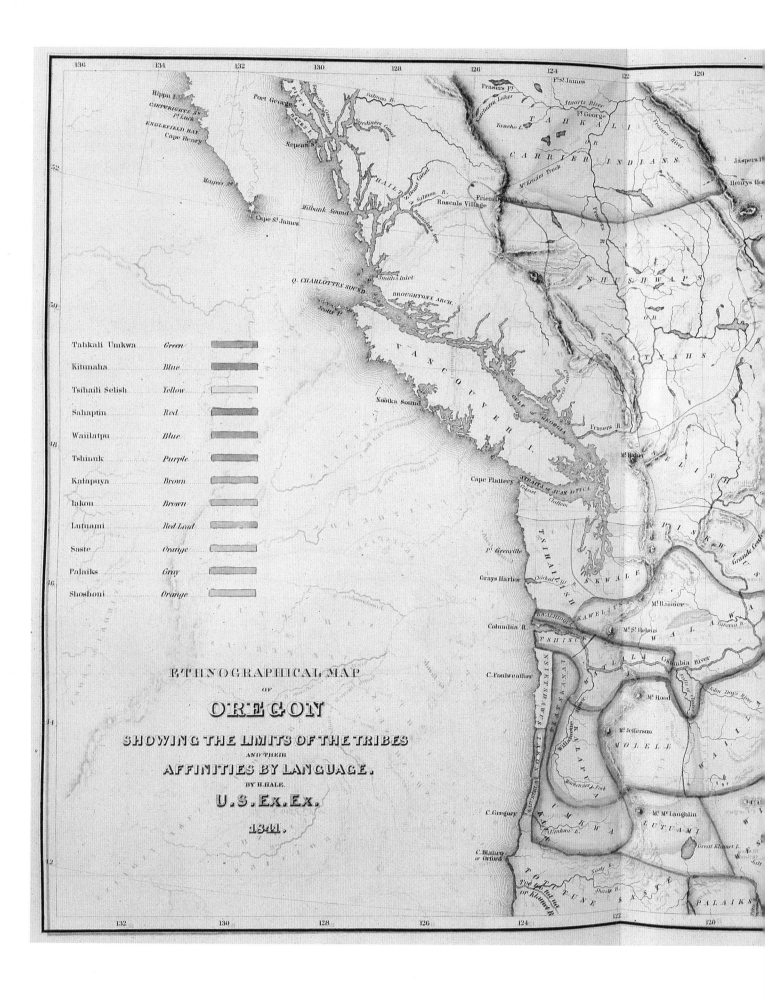

ETHNOGRAPHICAL MAP
OF
OREGON
SHOWING THE LIMITS OF THE TRIBES
AND THEIR
AFFINITIES BY LANGUAGE.
BY H.HALE.
U.S. Ex. Ex.
1841.

Tahkali Umkwa	Green	
Kitunaha	Blue	
Tsihaili Selish	Yellow	
Sahaptin	Red	
Waiilatpu	Blue	
Tshinuk	Purple	
Kalapuya	Brown	
Iakon	Brown	
Lutuami	Red Lead	
Saste	Orange	
Palaiks	Gray	
Shoshoni	Orange	

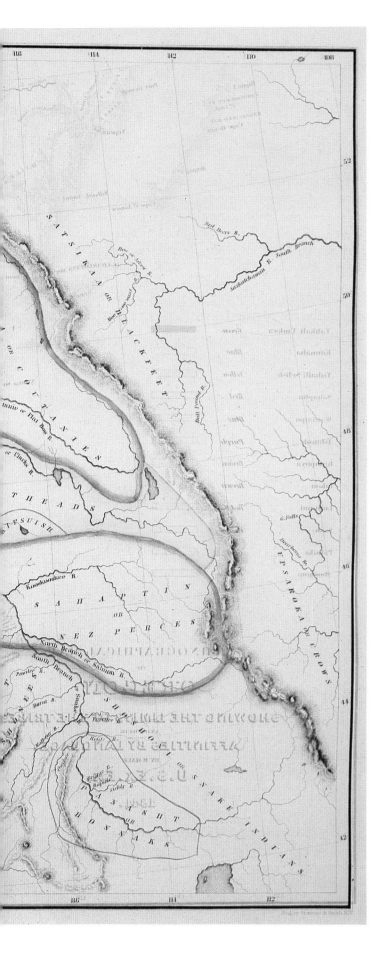

tribution of ground mammalia, plants, fluviatile animals, and marine animals in relation to eleven color-coded climatic regions. Pickering's maps, which are closely related to the text, were designed as a "pictorial representation of the Earth's surface."

Two of the scientists produced thematic maps relating to the distribution and characteristics of peoples. To illustrate his *Races of Man*, Pickering used a double-page hemisphere map to display the geographical distribution of eleven races by different colors. The map was printed in 1845 and is one of the earliest ethnographic maps of the entire world, the first appearing only two years before in J.C. Pritchard's *Natural History of Man*. Pickering used an equal-area projection to exhibit "at one view, the true area of the surface of the globe, or in other words, the relative size of the different countries." More significant for the development of ethnographic mapping in the United States was Horatio Hale's "Ethnographical Map of Oregon Showing the Limits of the Tribes and Their Affinities by Language," published in 1846. This double-page map complemented Albert Gallatin's 1836 classic "Map of the Indian Tribes of North America," which had left the northwestern territories blank. Much of the information for Hale's map was obtained from officers of the Hudson's Bay Company, particularly Ogden, and from the Indians themselves. Hale's *Ethnography and Philology* also contains a fascinating double-page document "Chart of Oceanic Migrations" that records the migration routes of Polynesian tribes westward from Micronesia to the Paumotu Group and eventually the Hawaiian Islands. This map was derived in part, according to Hale, from a native chart drawn by Tupaia, a Polynesian who had accompanied Cook.

The final cost for the compilation, engraving, and printing of the charts and maps produced by the Expedition came to about $15,000 or 17 percent of

An important contribution to ethnographic mapping, this hand-colored map showing the distribution of Northwest Indian tribes appeared in Horatio Hale's report on Ethnography and Philology. *It was based on interviews with Indians and officers of the Hudson's Bay Company. Smithsonian Institution Libraries.*

the total publication budget. Their value to mariners in general and to the United States, however, was much greater and was the one area in which the achievements of the Expedition can be said to have been immediately recognized. The secretary of the navy in 1843 deemed the charts of the Pacific Coast alone to have been worth the full cost of the Expedition. Perhaps more importantly, Wilkes's work established the precedent of federal government responsibility for charting foreign waters for the safety of American commercial and naval interests, which led eventually to the establishment of the U.S. Hydrographic Office in 1871. The surveys of Antarctica established American interests in that continent and its right to carry out scientific research, which continues to this day. Wilkes's pioneering work in charting sailing directions led to great savings in the time of ocean passage.

Wilkes's major legacy, however, remains his nautical charts. Their wide distribution through the British Admiralty Hydrographic Office and later the U.S. Hydrographic Office perpetuated the achievements of the Expedition among mariners and naval officers throughout the seafaring nations for more

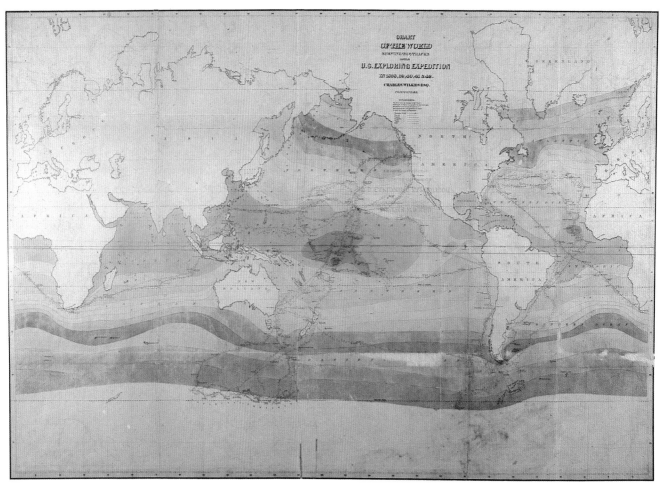

Wilkes's "Chart of the World Shewing the Tracks of the U.S. Exploring Expedition" is an early example of an isothermal map, designed to show the gradients of temperature. The map also depicts the direction of the winds and the direction and velocity of the currents. Courtesy Geography and Map Division, The Library of Congress.

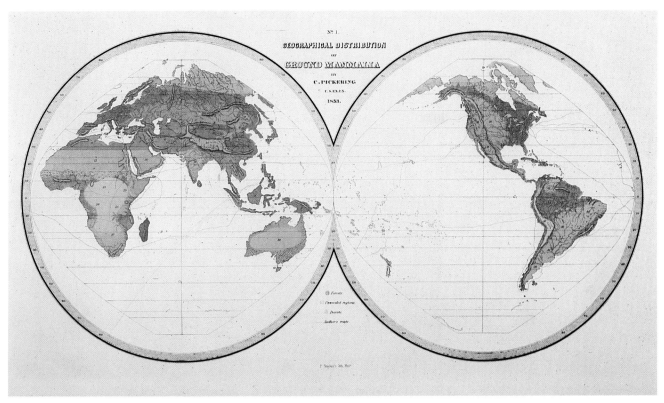

One of four hand-colored double-hemisphere maps that appeared in Charles Pickering's volume Geographical Distribution of Animals and Plants *(1861) showing the distribution of ground mammalia in relation to climate. Courtesy Rare Book and Special Collections Division, The Library of Congress.*

than one hundred years. The engraved copper plates of the surveys of the Expedition formed the nucleus of the chart collections of the U.S. Hydrographic Office. They were corrected as new information was acquired, but many continued to be used as late as the 1940s. Wilkes's great-grandson, for example, upon graduation from the U.S. Naval Academy at Annapolis during the 1920s found that the chart he used for his first cruise in the Pacific had been made by the Expedition. Twenty-some years later, in preparation for the invasion of Tarawa during World War II, Wilkes's chart of that island was the only one available to the invasion forces. The value of Wilkes's charts can also be seen in their use by the British and French hydrographic offices, which incorporated Wilkes's surveys into their standard chart series. British admiralty charts of the Pacific islands carried the credit "Surveyed by Commander Charles Wilkes, U.S.N. 1839" well into the twentieth century.

9 Charles Wilkes: A Biography

Charles Wilkes was only a junior lieutenant in the U.S. Navy when he commanded the U.S. Exploring Expedition of 1838–42 on its spectacular cruise around the world. Although eminently qualified to be in charge of the naval sciences on the Expedition, Wilkes was initially precluded from command because of his junior rank. However, in March 1838 the preparations for the Expedition were in such complete disorder that no senior officer could be found willing to undertake the duty. At this point President Martin Van Buren, under pressure to launch the Expedition, approved the appointment of Lieutenant Wilkes to the command. Wilkes immediately set to work to bring organization out of chaos and in less than six months was ready to set sail. This was a remarkable feat considering the constraints he had to overcome. This same drive and perseverance enabled him to return from the four-year cruise with the unsurpassed accomplishments that marked the entry of the United States into the international community of science and exploration.

Charles Wilkes was born on 3 April 1798 in New York City. The Wilkes family had been based in

Wilkes was promoted acting rear admiral on 8 September 1862. He was not permanently appointed to that rank, however, until 6 August 1866. Courtesy Naval Historical Center.

London where his great-grandfather, Israel, had been a prominent distiller. His great-uncle John is best remembered as "Wilkes No. 45" for his attacks on British government policy in the *North Briton* in the 1760s. His father, John Deponthieu Wilkes, immigrated to this country during the Revolutionary War. After successfully establishing himself in business in New York City, he married Mary Seton, the daughter of a business partner, and at the time of Charles's birth was able to provide generously for his family.

Charles was the youngest of three boys and one girl and enjoyed a comfortable, secure childhood until the death of his mother in February 1801. Afterward he was consigned to the care of various female relatives and friends. Among these was his aunt, Elizabeth Seton (canonized in 1974 as the first Roman Catholic American saint); he did not live long with her before she left the country to join her husband in Italy. Another, whom Wilkes described as his nurse and foster mother, was Mammy Reed, who cared for him with as much affection as a natural mother. She was the one who prophesied that he would follow the sea and become an admiral, although the rank did not then exist. Wilkes remained fond of her and continued to visit her until her death.

Upon reaching an appropriate age, Wilkes was sent with his brothers to various boarding schools,

where he received a sound preliminary education in mathematics, drawing, and modern languages. About this time his father remarried. The former Mrs. John Rogers was apparently a kind stepmother to Wilkes, but he keenly felt the loss of intimacy with his father.

When about fifteen years of age, while he was attending a preparatory school for Columbia College in New York City, Wilkes's predilection for a naval life surfaced. His father was initially adverse to such a career and installed him in his own offices while continuing his studies with tutors. The desire for adventure proved too strong, and his father finally consented to help him make an application for a midshipman's warrant in the U.S. Navy. Before acceptance, however, Wilkes was advised to obtain some practical experience in the merchant service. In 1815, when about seventeen years of age, he joined the *Hibernia*, bound on a cruise to France, rated as a boy on the ship's book. Wilkes described himself at this time as "a rosy cheek boy, a pretty Sailor, . . . with a high idea of my consequence." [1978:17]

The voyage in the *Hibernia* was not in the least what Wilkes had expected. The rough, uneducated sailors hazed him mercilessly. So harsh was his treatment that he was tempted to jump ship in France, but the return trip found him still on board. His appearance on his homecoming reflected his initiation into the sea service: "I was a very different looking boy from my appearance when I left a natty sailor boy. My clothes were well tarred and worn, my hands olive brown, and the beauty spots of my cheeks had disappeared for months. . . . I had grown considerably and lost all the freshness of an English boy. . . ." [pp. 27–28]

His enthusiasm for a naval career remained undiminished, and his father procured another ship for him, the *Calpi*, bound first to North Carolina, then Europe. The ship was unexpectedly delayed at Wilmington and Wilkes was recalled to New York City by his father to continue his studies. Eventually

Wilkes's father, John Deponthieu Wilkes, initially disapproved of his son's choice of a navy career, but later relented and helped him to secure a midshipman's appointment. Courtesy Gilbert Wilkes III.

another ship was selected—the *Emulation*, then outfitting for France. With the influence of his father, Wilkes was able to obtain the rating of third mate. The cruise proved uneventful except Wilkes returned to New York with a promotion to second mate. Several weeks later, on 1 January 1818, he received confirmation of his appointment as midshipman in the U.S. Navy, obtained through the intercession of the French minister in Washington, a family friend.

Wilkes's first orders, dated 26 January 1818, were to the *Independence* based at Boston as a naval school. Under Captain William Bainbridge, Wilkes and about fifty other midshipmen were instructed in the technical and social aspects of naval life. Although he remained on the *Independence* for only six months, he formed indelible impressions about the unenviable aspects of life in the navy:

> *A midshipman's life on board a American Man of war was a dog's life, and in many respects acts of tyranny and a total disregard to the feelings of the young officers were lost sight of. Some of the older officers ruled through intimidation and coertion by punishment—totally inconsistent with the rules and regulations of any service. The Midshipmen were placed under the fostering care of the commanders and were treated with parental hardship. Captains thought that they were above the law and no regulations bound them to observe a proper regard for the feelings and sensibilities. The Commander was supreme over all. The men were harshly treated, nay, often cruelly, and all were made subservient to the pleasures, caprices and gratifications of this irresponsible authority. [p. 45]*

On 21 July 1818 Wilkes was assigned to the *Guerriere*, then outfitting at Boston for Russia and the Mediterranean, under the command of Captain Thomas Macdonough. One purpose of the cruise, a typical navy duty, was to carry diplomats and their families to Russia and Sweden. This was Wilkes's first introduction into life at sea on an American naval vessel, and he took every advantage on the cruise to increase his knowledge of the practical workings of the navy. At this time, also, his talent for intelligent observation, which was to serve him so well on the Exploring Expedition, was developed. Every country and port visited by the *Guerriere* found Wilkes eager to explore, not only the government buildings and museums, but also the life styles of the general population.

The *Guerriere* returned to Norfolk in October 1819, and Wilkes was relieved of duty to recuperate from the malaria he had contracted off the African coast. He returned to New York City to stay with his brothers, his father having died in February 1818. Wilkes, anxious to advance his education, immediately engaged tutors in mathematics, engineering, and drawing and attended lectures at Columbia College. On 26 May 1821 he received orders to join the *Franklin*, under Captain Charles Stewart, on a South American cruise.

The cruise in the *Franklin* proved instructive in many ways. One particular highlight for Wilkes was to be introduced to General Simón Bolívar at Guayaquil, Ecuador. Wilkes was generally impressed by Bolívar and became acquainted with several of his officers, characteristically endeavoring to learn all he could of the revolutionary movement.

In early 1822, when the *Franklin* was off the coast of Chile, Captain Stewart determined to build two tenders. Wilkes was ordered to superintend their construction. The first, built at Arica, Chile, was named *Waterwitch*. The second, built at Quilca, Peru, was considerably larger and named *Peruviana*. Upon its completion in July, Wilkes was named second-in-command of the *Waterwitch*, and in September he was put in command of her when the officer in charge was transferred to the *Peruviana*. Wilkes, finally experiencing his first command, dealt effectively with many problems, including navigational procedure in foreign waters, difficulties with customs officials and port authorities, and the usual drunkenness of the crew.

He arrived at Valparaiso, Chile, in March 1823 and was offered the command of the merchantman *O'Cain*, whose master had recently died from fever. The owner had applied to Captain Stewart for an officer to take charge of her on the return voyage to Boston. Stewart offered the command to Wilkes, who accepted with the proviso that it not harm his standing in the navy. He arrived with the *O'Cain* at

Jane Renwick was Wilkes's first wife. They were married on 26 April 1826, just two days before he was promoted to lieutenant. Courtesy Naval Historical Center.

Boston on 15 October 1823.

Wilkes returned to New York City and immediately proposed marriage to Jane Renwick. The Renwicks were family friends, and Wilkes had known Jane since they were children. In fact, an understanding had existed between them before his cruise in the *Franklin*. The wedding took place on 26 April 1826. At this time Wilkes was also involved in his preparations for his lieutenant's examination. Financially, his ability to support a wife rested on this promotion. His knowledge, however, was so extensive that he was congratulated by the board of examiners on his proficiency and informed he "had passed No 1." [Wilkes 1978: 211] His promotion to lieutenant was dated 28 April 1826.

Wilkes now began a period of several years when he was officially on leave awaiting orders. This was a common practice in the peacetime navy. Wilkes took advantage of the opportunity to continue his studies, most notably in hydrography. His teacher was Ferdinand Hassler, first superintendent of the U.S. Coast Survey. Wilkes studied with him for about three years and gained much practical experience in the new triangulation method of surveying by accompanying Hassler on his official field work. This technique he later employed to great success on the Exploring Expedition. Wilkes regarded Hassler as the most competent scientist to head the U.S. Coast Survey, and in later years he actively supported Hassler's programs in the agency.

On 21 May 1828, Congress passed the initial legislation for an exploring expedition, providing for one ship to explore the Pacific. In September the sloop of war *Peacock* was launched at the New York Navy Yard, and Secretary of the Navy Samuel Southard appointed Captain Thomas ap Catesby Jones to command. Wilkes immediately requested duty with the expedition and even drew up a list of instruments required for such a project. Enthusiasm was high among officers of the U.S. Navy and the scientific community. But in February 1829 Congress reevaluated its support and decided that domestic exploration should take precedence, if funds were available. Besides, Congress reasoned, individuals with commercial interests could more adequately direct and finance such endeavors. Consequently the expedition was shelved.

Wilkes continued his sea duty in April 1830 with a cruise in the *Boston*, bound to the Mediterranean, and in November at Port Mahon transferred to the *Fairfield*. On 10 May 1831 Wilkes was detached from the *Fairfield* at Norfolk and again placed on leave awaiting orders. This cruise, though brief, provided Wilkes with needed sea experience.

Wilkes now began in earnest to concentrate his career in fields of naval science—hydrography, geodesy, and astronomy. From May 1832 to early 1833 he was engaged in the survey of Narragansett Bay. Ostensibly under the command of Captain Alexander Wadsworth, Wilkes in reality organized the survey work since he was the most qualified of the officers assigned to the duty. He arranged for the loan of a theodolite, a sophisticated instrument used by Hassler, and proceeded competently to direct the field work. The resultant chart was presented to Congress and eventually published.

Wilkes returned to Washington in March 1833 to take charge of the Depot of Charts and Instruments, which had been established in 1830 under Lieutenant Louis M. Goldsborough. (It was the predecessor of the Navy Hydrographic Office, today called the Navy Oceanographic Office.) Wilkes's first official action was to move the depot to a new site, originally selected by Hassler, and then to erect, in 1834 at his own expense, an observatory mounted with a transit made by Edward Troughton in England for the U.S. Coast Survey. The next year he installed a press, and chart production was begun.

As superintendent of the depot one of Wilkes's greatest contributions was to establish standardized procedures for rating and testing chronometers. He would obtain chronometers on loan and test them for one year, a plan demanding meticulous supervision and detailed daily records for each instrument. If they passed the test period they were purchased by the U.S. Navy; unsatisfactory instruments were returned to their makers at no cost to the government.

The long-awaited legislation for the U.S. Exploring Expedition was finally passed by Congress on 14 May 1836. The responsibility for outfitting the Expedition was initially placed in the hands of Secretary of the Navy Mahlon P. Dickerson. Following his predecessor's 1828 choice, Dickerson selected Captain Thomas ap Catesby Jones as its commander. Enthusiasm for the project was again widespread in naval and scientific circles. The Expedition would consist of at least five ships, providing ample room for a large scientific contingent. In the midst of all the preparations Dickerson requested Wilkes to compile a list of necessary instruments and to arrange for a European trip to purchase them.

Wilkes sailed for Europe in August 1836. In his primary duty, to purchase instruments for the Expedition, he was at first thwarted. Every reputable instrument maker in London had a large backlog of orders, which they attributed to the current popularity of conducting private observations. Wilkes, however, went to great lengths to explain the purposes of the Expedition to the manufacturers and their clients. His persuasiveness secured top priority for the construction of his instruments in the

Wilkes studied survey methods with Ferdinand Hassler, first superintendent of the U. S. Coast Survey, for several years. Courtesy National Oceanic and Atmospheric Administration.

allotted three months.

On this trip Wilkes met many of the most important men of science in Europe. One in particular with whom he developed a very close relationship was Francis Baily, vice-president of the Royal Astronomical Society. Wilkes assisted Baily in conducting pendulum experiments and was even guest of honor at a dinner meeting of the society. This honor, combined with other important contacts he made, enabled Wilkes to present the Expedition's scope and purpose to the European scientific community, and, consequently, his name became associated with the Expedition before he was even appointed to it.

Wilkes returned from Europe in January 1837 and

found the organization of the Exploring Expedition in a shambles. The ships still needed major work, the equipment and provisions were not yet prepared, the officers and scientists were at odds, enlistments were one-third over, and Congress was on the verge of withdrawing support. Wilkes, who had entertained hopes of an appointment as astronomer, decided to absent himself from the turmoil. Since the vast fishing grounds east of Cape Cod were of great commercial value, an accurate chart was needed, so from 14 June to 20 October Wilkes was engaged in the survey of Georges Bank in the brig *Porpoise.*

While headquartered at Boston on this survey Wilkes became acquainted with Nathaniel Bowditch, the distinguished mathematician, astronomer, and author of the *New American Practical Navigator.* Wilkes, on his many visits to Bowditch, explained his method of surveying and, in return, was taught some of the practical aspects of advanced mathematics. Wilkes believed this experience influenced his appointment to command the Expedition.

In October 1837 Wilkes continued his field work in South Carolina with surveys of the Savannah River and Calibogue Sound. He returned to Washington in the spring of 1838 to find that Jones had resigned the command of the Expedition the preceding December, and that in the interim several other commanders had been appointed and relieved of the duty.

On 20 March 1838 Wilkes was offered command of the Exploring Expedition by Secretary of War Joel R. Poinsett, who was in charge at Van Buren's request because of Dickerson's poor health. Wilkes accepted on the condition that he have total control over the outfit and organization. Mismanagement had in the past seriously hampered the preparations, and Wilkes was determined to brook no interference with his plans. The president approved his appointment on 20 April. The selection of so junior an officer to such a command sparked a stream of protests to the Navy Department and even to the president, and suddenly there was a wealth of volunteers for the command. Wilkes's scientific accomplishments, combined with Poinsett's emphasis on the nonmilitary character of the Expedition, soon quieted the open resentment, but dissatisfaction was still pronounced in navy ranks.

One of Wilkes's most pressing duties was the selection and outfitting of his squadron. The sloops of war *Vincennes* and *Peacock* were the first choices. Wilkes also requested and received the brig *Porpoise*, which he had used on his recent survey duties. Two New York pilot boats were purchased, refitted, and renamed the *Sea Gull* and *Flying Fish*. The final selection was the storeship *Relief*, the only ship of the original squadron to be retained. The opposition to Wilkes's appointment put many obstacles in his path in the outfitting of these ships for the cruise and the procurement of the necessary supplies. Wilkes even found it necessary, on occasion, to appeal to the president for assistance in obtaining crucial items.

Simultaneously Wilkes was selecting his officers and arranging the ships' crews. His choice for second-in-command was Lieutenant William L. Hudson, who at first declined, not wishing to serve under an officer several numbers below him on the lieutenants list. Hudson finally consented upon being persuaded of the nonmilitary character of the Expedition. The other selections of officers reflected this same difficulty; Wilkes's junior status in the navy precluded many experienced senior officers from serving. The ships' crews presented an additional dilemma. Most of the seamen had been assigned to the Expedition from the beginning and their enlistments were rapidly expiring. Some had already deserted, and those that remained were bored and dissatisfied with the long delays. Wilkes personally visited the seamen at Norfolk and explained his resolve to perform the duties of the Expedition to the best of his abilities; he expected the same from all crew members. He then shrewdly gave them liberty, assuring them of the imminent sailing of the Expedition.

Wilkes next turned his attention to the scientific corps. He was firm in his decision to limit the participation of civilian scientists and to retain as many scientific duties within the ranks of the navy as possible. After his final selections, only seven scientists and two artists remained. Wilkes appointed himself in charge of all departments pertaining to physics, surveying, astronomy, mag-

Nathaniel Bowditch, author of The New American Practical Navigator, *instructed Wilkes in the practical aspects of advanced mathematics. Courtesy Peabody Museum of Salem.*

netism, and geodesy and chose junior officers as his assistants. He made no secret of the fact that he considered the naval sciences the most important on the Expedition—an opinion that did not endear him to the civilian scientists.

Wilkes was disappointed in one of his requests—acting appointments to captain for Hudson and himself. He considered this rank essential for the proper discipline of the squadron and was under the impression the appointments would be forthcoming. The new secretary of the navy, James Kirke Paulding, had already approved acting lieutenant's commissions for the squadron's passed midshipmen. However, Paulding would not approve acting appointments for Wilkes and Hudson. Perhaps he feared adverse political repercussions. Wilkes, totally disregarding established navy policy, then proceeded under his own authority to assume the rank and directed Hudson to do the same

and to maintain it as an inviolable secret. . . . It would seem to have been a bold and unwarranted stroke of policy on my part to overcome the difficulties I anticipated might arise and, so far as he was concerned, I should stand all the odium that might be attached to it. We accord[ing]ly adopted the uniforms which had been prepared and without any further explanations or developement, the temporary promotion was acceded to, and in this manner my object was attained & I saw no further difficulty and took the responsibility of those conferring upon us, and without presumption of extra authority above that which I already possessed as the Commander of the Expedition. It certainly had its moral effect and elevated us above those who were placed under our orders, and I came to the conclusion it was justified under the necessities of the case. [Wilkes 1978:377]

The six ships of the U.S. Exploring Expedition finally set sail on 18 August 1838. Wilkes at this time was forty years old and his wife had just given birth to their fourth child, a daughter Eliza, on 19 July. His three other children, John, Jane, and Edmund, had been born respectively on 31 March 1827, 3 January 1829, and 4 February 1833. Wilkes's qualifications for this command were without parallel in the U.S. Navy. He had studied with many of the great scientists of the day. His brother-in-law James Renwick, a noted chemist and engineer, stated that Wilkes's abilities already exceeded those of his teachers. On a personal level, he was not, however, likeable or friendly. He was conceited, domineering, and arrogant. On the cruise he was a stern disciplinarian and almost fanatical about the observation of his orders and regulations. His aloof manner, which resulted from his determination to keep his own counsel, alienated his officers. This, in part, can be attributed to his nervousness as a young commander striving to exert authority. It cannot, however, be disputed that his driving ambition and almost limitless energy enabled the squadron to accomplish the near impossible, and it is

doubtful if any other naval officer could have surpassed Wilkes in his performance of the difficult duties required on the cruise.

The ships returned to New York in summer 1842 after a cruise of almost four years and more than eighty-seven thousand miles. Ships of the squadron explored South Pacific islands, Australia and New Zealand, the Hawaiian Islands, and the Oregon territory and California. The accomplishments were overwhelming. In addition to circumnavigating the globe, the Expedition identified Antarctica as a continent, surveyed many islands in the Pacific for the first time, and collected specimens in all branches of the natural sciences. Nearly two hundred charts were prepared as a result of the surveys. The charts of Oregon territory stimulated American settlement and suggested points of military interest, and the charts of the Pacific islands were in use as recently as World War II.

The spectacular accomplishments of the Expedition were, unfortunately, initially overshadowed by accusations leveled at several of the junior officers by Wilkes and his own subsequent court-martial. On 15 June 1842 Wilkes brought charges against Passed Midshipman William May, Lieutenants Robert E. Johnson and Robert F. Pinkney, and Assistant Surgeon Charles B.F. Guillou. In return these officers filed charges against Wilkes. His trial was convened on 20 July and of the eleven charges brought against him only two proved substantial. One, conduct unbecoming an officer, questioned Wilkes's sighting of land in Antarctica, and was eventually disproved through witnesses and evidence. The second, illegal punishment, was upheld, and on this charge alone Wilkes was sentenced to a public reprimand by the secretary of the navy on 7 September. Wilkes justified his exceeding the prescribed twelve lashes on several occasions by the necessity for strict discipline.

These were court martial offenses, but the duties of the squadron would not permit me to order a court for their trial, without great loss of time and detriment to the service. To let such offenses pass with the ordinary punishment of twelve lashes, would have been in eyes of the crew, to have overlooked their crime altogether.

Wilkes was awarded the Founder's Medal of the Royal Geographical Society of London for his discoveries on the U. S. Exploring Expedition in 1848. Courtesy National Museum of American History, Smithsonian Institution.

I was, therefore, compelled to inflict what I deemed a proper punishment, and ordered them each to receive thirty-six and forty-one. . . . This was awarding to each about one tenth of what a court-martial would have inflicted; yet it was such an example as thoroughly convinced the men that they could not offend with impunity. [Henderson 1975:75]

Wilkes was placed in charge of the Expedition's collections, and the subsequent reports, on 1 August 1843. Public interest in the results of the Expedition was growing, in part because of Wilkes's lecture to the new National Institute in Washington about the squadron's accomplishments and the immense number of specimens obtained. The collections were displayed in the Patent Office Building in Washington, D.C., until their final home at the Smithsonian Institution was decided by Congress in 1857. Wilkes's responsibilities during his custodianship were basically twofold: prepare the specimens for exhibit and protect the specimens from the public. Some previous attempts to arrange displays had been disastrous; specimens were lost or irreparably damaged. At the same time, members of Congress and other public figures had openly taken specimens as souvenirs. Wilkes proceeded to bring some measure of organization to the exhibit and absolutely refused to allow any more "mementos" to be taken. This course antagonized many influential people, including Mrs. Tyler, the president's wife.

There were many annoyances attending the preservation of the Plants. No sooner had it become known that the Govt had a green house of very moderate size than application was made for flowers and plants, and had these demands been acceeded to, in a very short time we should not have had a plant remaining. To obviate this I gave Mr. Brackenridge orders that no flowers & plants should be cut or given away under any call for them by those in official station, many of whom deemed they had a right to them. . . . In several instances Senators and Members of the house were really excited & swore they would make no appropriation for the care of the collection, and even Mrs. Tyler, the President's lady, made him a visit and demanded both plants & flowers. She was met with a positive denial and left in a huff & made complaint to the Commissioner of Patents that she had been refused and rudely, as she said, denied by one of the workmen. This proved to be Mr Brackenridge himself who was working among his plants with his coat off. It was soon put an end to as I assumed the responsibility and stated that no one could be permitted or had any privilege to the flowers or plants. It was soon known that the President's wife had been refused and much exaggeration of the circumstances, but I stood firm in defense and it became to be known that refusal would attend any application by whomsoever made. [Wilkes 1978:529–30]

Still, it was largely due to the careful and meticulous custodianship of Wilkes that so many Expedition plants survived this initial chaotic period.

His duties in publishing the Expedition reports were no less arduous. They included not only overseeing the scientific volumes but also preparing the official narrative. Congress had appropriated money for one hundred copies of the total set to be printed, mostly for presentation. Wilkes, under the direction of the Joint Committee on the Library, devoted himself to writing the narrative. He even moved temporarily to Philadelphia to supervise the printing and to correct the proofs as they came off the press. When released the five-volume *Narrative of the United States Exploring Expedition During the Years 1838, 1839, 1840, 1841, 1842* was not, however, a total success. Many commented on the great disparity in writing styles, implying that Wilkes

had copied verbatim from the logs and journals of his officers, which were in his possession. Thirteen of these officers submitted a memorial to this effect to the Library Committee. Wilkes managed to have it dismissed and, audaciously, applied for and received a copyright on the *Narrative*.

The *Narrative* went through three additional printings before the end of 1845 and a total of fifteen editions before the last one in 1858. Popular authors, from Herman Melville to James Fenimore Cooper, relied on it for authentic background for their stories.

In addition to the *Narrative*, Wilkes's other contributions to the Expedition publications included *Meteorology*, published in 1851, a two-volume *Atlas of Charts*, 1858, and *Hydrography*, 1861. He also published, as a result of the Expedition, *Western America, Theory of the Zodiacal Light*, and *On the Circulation of Oceans*. In 1848 he was awarded the Founder's Medal of the Royal Geographical Society of London for his discoveries.

Wilkes continued to rise through the ranks of the U.S. Navy. On 13 July 1843 he was promoted to the rank of commander. He requested active duty in the Mexican War in 1846, although he was deeply immersed in the Expedition publications. His request was denied. On 14 September 1855 he was promoted to captain. In 1858 he was temporarily detached from the Expedition reports and ordered to survey the natural resources of the Deep River country of North Carolina. His personal life also underwent drastic changes. His wife, Jane, died at Newport in August 1848, and six years later he married his second wife, Mary Lynch Bolton. In 1859 they had a daughter, Mary.

The outbreak of the Civil War suspended work on the Exploring Expedition reports, and Wilkes was ordered to command U.S.S. *Merrimack* on 19 April 1861. When he arrived at the Norfolk Navy Yard to assume command, he found the ship scuttled and a general destruction of the yard underway. Several weeks later, on 14 May, he was ordered to command U.S.S. *San Jacinto*. His subsequent ac-

Wilkes with his daughter Mary by his second wife Mary Lynch Bolton. His first wife died suddenly in 1848. Wilkes remarried in 1854. Courtesy Gilbert Wilkes III.

Confederate commissioners Mason and Slidell were enroute to England on the British mail packet Trent *when captured by Wilkes on the* San Jacinto. *Courtesy Naval Historical Center.*

tions while in this command initiated the famous international incident called the *Trent* affair.

Returning from the African coast in the *San Jacinto* in September 1861 to join Admiral Samuel F. DuPont's attack on Port Royal, South Carolina, Wilkes decided to detour to the West Indies in the hopes of capturing Confederate privateers. Upon reaching the West Indies he learned of the escape of the Confederate commissioners, James Mason and John Slidell, from Charleston. They were then at Havana awaiting final transport to England. Wilkes, after a hasty study of international law, determined to attempt their capture. There was insufficient time to obtain the official sanction of the Navy Department, and, having served in distant stations, Wilkes was used to making his own decisions. On 7

November the commissioners and their families sailed from Havana on the British mail packet *Trent*. The next day in the Bahama Channel, Wilkes in the *San Jacinto* forced the packet to heave to. Lieutenant Donald McNeill Fairfax was ordered to board the *Trent*, remove the commissioners, and seize the ship as a prize. Fairfax returned to the *San Jacinto* with the commissioners and their secretaries, but, disobeying orders, he had not seized the ship. He justified his action on the grounds that a prize crew would seriously weaken the *San Jacinto*. Surprisingly Wilkes agreed, and with the commissioners safely on board he proceeded immediately to Port Royal. He arrived, however, too late for the battle. After a short stop at Norfolk, he continued to New York, where he was ordered by Secretary of the Navy Gideon Welles to deliver his prisoners to Boston. On 24 November, Mason and Slidell were removed from the *San Jacinto* and placed in custody at Fort Warren. The *San Jacinto* was then decommissioned at the Boston Navy Yard on 30 November.

Northern public reaction to the capture of Mason and Slidell was jubilant, and Wilkes was hailed as a hero.

Unknown to myself a public reception had been decided upon, and my officers and self were escorted to the Fanueil Hall and underwent the ordeal of shaking of hands from a large number of citizens. The crowd was very great, and my hands showed the effect of shaking of hands by the blisters raised on my fingers which remained for a couple of weeks afterwards—a pretty severe punishment for the honor of a public reception continuing several hours. [*Wilkes 1978: 775*]

Additional ceremonies followed. At New York he was paraded down Broadway to a reception at City Hall. Officials in Washington were equally enthusiastic. Secretary of the Navy Welles sent him a congratulatory letter, the House of Representatives voted him their thanks, and President Lincoln publicly voiced his approval.

Reaction in England was exactly the opposite. There the public was outraged by the insult and demanded restitution. Ultimately the British government based its decision more on the current political climate than on the precepts of international law. On 17 December the British formally requested the release of the prisoners and a suitable apology. President Lincoln met with his cabinet on 26 December and, after careful deliberation, decided to risk popular disapproval and release the prisoners to avoid the possibility of war with England. Many were incensed by this decision, and criticism of the Lincoln administration was rampant. Wilkes was

The Trent *affair made Wilkes a national hero, although pressure from the British government eventually forced the return of Commissioners James Mason and John Slidell. Courtesy Naval Historical Center.*

Secretary of the Navy Gideon Welles ordered a second court-martial of Wilkes for disobedience of orders, among other charges, in the spring of 1864. Courtesy Naval Historical Center.

characteristically outspoken in his denunciation.

> *The idea of delivering these prisoners up was disgraceful in any light it can or was viewed. . . . It is almost impossible to conceive how Great Britain could have had the impudence to have made the demand of us and still more how we could [submit]. . . . [1978:845]*

After service on the James and Potomac rivers, on 8 September 1862 Wilkes, with an acting appointment to rear admiral, was transferred to the West Indian Squadron to operate against Confederate privateers and blockade-runners. In this com-

mand Wilkes was moderately successful against blockade-runners, but he failed totally in his attempts to capture Confederate commerce raiders, most notably the *Alabama* and *Florida*. He also, typically, managed to offend the governments of Great Britain, Spain, France, Denmark, and Mexico by his complete disregard of the rights of neutrals. He further alienated the secretary of the navy by blatantly disobeying or ignoring his orders, and on 1 June 1863 he was recalled and placed on "awaiting orders" status. He did not see further service during the war.

Wilkes was also at this time engaged in a dispute with the Navy Department over his promotion to commodore. He had received notification of his promotion on 4 August 1862, with the rank retroactive to 16 July 1862. However, due to a mix-up with his records the rank was rescinded in November. In March 1863 he was able to have the rank restored, again retroactive to July 1862. Unfortunately the consequent frustration, combined with the intense disappointment of his failure in the West Indies, brought him into conflict with Secretary of the Navy Welles. The dispute became public when a private letter from Wilkes to Welles, concerning his actions in the West Indies, was printed in the newspapers. A court of inquiry determined that Wilkes had prior knowledge of the publication of the letter, which was against navy regulations. This resulted in a second court-martial for Wilkes in the spring of 1864.

The court was ordered convened in Washington, D.C., on 27 February 1864. The five charges brought against Wilkes were disobedience of orders, insubordinate conduct, disrespectful language, disobedience to a general order or regulation, and conduct unbecoming an officer. On 26 April he was found guilty on all counts and sentenced to a public reprimand and a three-year suspension from the navy. Wilkes considered the proceedings a mockery of justice and the sentence a result of Welles's personal antipathy. On 30 December 1864 President Lincoln reduced the suspension to one year, and only eighteen months later, on 6 August 1866, Wilkes was promoted to rear admiral on the retired list.

For several years after his court-martial Wilkes,

while on the retired list, turned his attention to business. In 1865 he purchased a 14,000-acre property named High Shoals in Gaston County, North Carolina, hoping to establish an iron works. Unfortunately Wilkes lacked sufficient ready cash to make the works profitable, and he was subsequently unable to involve other investors in a Southern enterprise during Reconstruction. In January 1874, after nine years of desperate attempts to succeed at the works, Wilkes was forced to sell the property at auction.

At this time Wilkes also suffered a personal tragedy when his infant son, Charles Wilkes, Jr., born on 25 May 1865, died after only a few weeks of life. Wilkes, sixty-seven years old and a devoted family man, was particularly affected by the infant's sudden death.

The early 1870s found Wilkes on special duty in the navy, attached to the Library Committee, to continue work on the Exploring Expedition reports, particularly his volumes on hydrography and physics. Although the hydrography volume was virtually finished by 1861, it was not distributed until 1873; the volume on physics was never published. The reluctance of Congress to fund the reports was again a major stumbling block, and at one point, in 1871, Wilkes offered to pay for it himself. On 17 March 1873, when he was seventy-three years old, Wilkes was detached from active duty for the last time, although until his death he lobbied for the publication of the final volumes.

Wilkes began writing his autobiography in 1871 and devoted the final years of his life to the project. Although he used it as a vehicle to explain and justify his controversial career, it also provides a fascinating picture of life in the U.S. Navy in the nineteenth century. Wilkes initially hoped to find a publisher for his memoirs, but this was not realized in his lifetime. The autobiography was, however, finally published in 1978 by the Naval Historical Center.

Toward the end of his life Wilkes became discouraged over his many battles, and his opinion of the navy reflected his disillusionment: "The service to one's country is one of forebearance and without thanks or consideration." [diary 1871] He was in poor health, suffering from debilitating migraine headaches, and in 1873 a fall resulting in a serious leg injury made his life increasingly difficult. He died on 7 February 1877 at his home in Washington, D.C. He was buried at Oak Hill Cemetery, but in August 1909 his remains were moved to Arlington National Cemetery.

For more than a century Wilkes has been best remembered for his role in the *Trent* affair. His more enduring contribution to history was, however, his association with the U.S. Exploring Expedition, not only his command of the Expedition, but also his steadfast devotion and commitment to the publication of its remarkable achievements.

204

TANOA, KING OF BAU.

E. JEFFREY STANN

10 Charles Wilkes as Diplomat

One day in June 1840 on Ovalau in the Fiji Islands, Charles Wilkes looked up from his astronomical observations to see the approach of a massive canoe powered by dozens of paddles and a sail of bark cloth. That the canoe carried Tanoa, king of Ambau, and his retinue was clear from its very size and the pennants on the yard.

> On the following morning . . . everything was prepared to give them a most marked reception, excepting the salute. Tanoa was the first to mount the side of the ship, where I was ready to receive him, with the officers at the gangway. When he reached the deck, he was evidently much astonished, particularly when he saw the marines, with their muskets, presenting arms, and so many officers. . . . After presenting him to the officers, and receiving the rest of his suite, I led him to the after part of the deck, where mats were laid down, and we all seated ourselves to

King Tanoa of Ambau, drawn by Agate. Because Tanoa was the most powerful Fiji chief, Wilkes first gained his approval of proposed commercial regulations before approaching other chiefs in the islands. A great warrior in his youth, Tanoa was, according to Wilkes, "about sixty-five years old, tall, slender, and rather bent by age; . . .his countenance was indicative of intelligence and shrewdness. . .; he is about five feet ten inches in height, and of small frame; his features are rather inclined to the European mould . . . ." (Wilkes 1845, 3: facing p. 56, 56)

> hold a council; for I was anxious to finish first the business for which I had particularly sought the interview; this was to procure the adoption of rules and regulations for the intercourse with foreign vessels, similar to those established in the Samoan Group the year preceding. [Wilkes 1845, 3: 55–56]

The king had some difficulty understanding the purpose of such port regulations, until a visiting Tongan chief in his party explained the concept. Tanoa then listened as the regulations were translated and approved their adoption, returning to the *Vincennes* the following day to sign the prepared document.

In this manner did the head chief of the Fijis sign the first agreement regulating commerce with Westerners. For years, New England sea captains and merchants had sought protection from attack by Fiji Islanders, as American shipping spread across the Pacific during the early nineteenth century in pursuit of whales and in search of sandalwood and other products for the China trade.

Pressure from New England shipping interests was a principal stimulant in getting the Exploring Expedition approved—so much so that the promotion of commerce and navigation was the principal purpose of the Expedition, ahead of the advance of science.

Nowhere in Wilkes's instructions was he specifically ordered or authorized to conclude treaties or practice other diplomacy. Yet, the commander drafted and signed two commercial agreements and appointed two U.S. consuls to improve trade in the Pacific islands, signed the first trade agreement between a Western power and the sultan of Sulu in the Philippine archipelago, mediated a number of disputes among natives or between natives and Westerners in the Pacific, and became involved in the delicate balance between U.S. and British interests in Oregon territory. Wilkes, with Lieutenant William Hudson, punished those guilty of violence against American sailors and, where diplomacy failed, quickly took the initiative with superior military power.

Such initiative was not unusual for Western navies in those years, nor was Wilkes's role as diplomat. Between 1801 and 1830, U.S. Navy commanders in the Mediterranean had combined diplomatic and naval duties, enforcing treaties with the Barbary states and trying to negotiate one with Turkey. Naval officers negotiated many of this country's first diplomatic agreements in West Africa and the Pacific, operating on instructions or as opportunity and judgment dictated in regions beyond the reach of a still-limited diplomatic corps. Captain Thomas ap Catesby Jones was sent to Hawaii with the *Peacock* in 1826 to conclude a treaty of friendship, commerce, and navigation; to negotiate debt payments; and to make peace between pro- and anti-missionary factions. In 1830, Wilkes's future flagship the *Vincennes* had been the second U.S. warship to visit Chinese waters, on a mission to deal with Chinese authorities in suppressing piracy against American shipping.

Wilkes's instructions directed him to avoid unnecessary hostility or situations which might lead to misunderstandings. At Fiji, he was told only "to make such arrangements as will insure a supply of fruits, vegetables, and fresh provisions, to vessels visiting it hereafter, teaching the natives the modes of cultivation, and encouraging them to raise hogs

Meeting house, Kingsmill group (Wilkes, 1845, 5: facing p. 56)

in greater abundance." In the Sulu Sea he was to "ascertain the disposition of the inhabitants of the islands of this archipelago for commerce, their productions and resources." [U.S. Navy Dept. 1838]

While these instructions were not explicit, Wilkes was not operating in a vacuum. As early as June 1837, Thomas ap Catesby Jones (then Expedition commander) had prepared a list of eleven matters needing decision by the secretary of the navy, which was sent to the president. In addition to questions about the purpose and route of the Expedition, appointments of the scientific and naval complements, budget, collections and publications policies was this one: "How and by whom is intercourse to be held, Treaties or commercial regulations to be made with such of the Native tribes of the South Sea Islands, as it may be found expedient to treat with?" [Jones 1837] Beyond Van Buren's notation—"Refd to the Secy of the Navy"—there is no evidence that action was taken. Nor is there any evidence of other instructions, written or unwritten. But these documents, together with Wilkes's familiarity with prior diplomatic correspondence, strongly suggest that he was expected to conduct diplomatic tasks. Characteristically, Wilkes pursued these tasks with energy and perseverance.

The State Department did not consider it necessary to inform other governments that an expedition was being despatched to their shores, even when extensive exploring and surveying were to be carried out in their waters or territory. Surprisingly, American consular and diplomatic officers abroad were not alerted either. Thus, the Expedition was placed in at least one delicate situation, otherwise avoidable, and Wilkes's strong leadership and confident sense of righteousness had to carry them through.

During the first year after leaving Norfolk, diplomatic dealings were minimal. In Rio de Janeiro, Wilkes petitioned the imperial government of Brazil, through U.S. chargé d'affaires William Hunter, to grant him use of a nearby island for magnetic observations. Dealings with the Platine, Chilean, and Peruvian authorities were similar; the main problem was explaining why, because of their cargo of delicate instruments, the squadron's ships did not fire the customary courtesy salutes upon arrival

in harbor. Diplomatic and consular reports to Washington from these three countries barely mention the Expedition. The squadron must have kept a fairly low profile altogether, for, in all the South American cities visited, only the newspaper *O jornal do comercio* in Rio gives more than passing reference to the squadron's presence, printing on 21 January 1839 a lengthy and favorable article about the great purposes of the Expedition. By contrast, *El Mercurio* in Valparaiso only listed the arrival of each of the ships and mentioned Lieutenant Hudson among the foreigners offering a toast to the President of Chile during a large banquet given in his honor in that city.

Once away from South America, things took on a different character. As the squadron departed Peru—leaving behind the more European cultures and the more established network of State Department representation—in July 1839, Wilkes assumed a more active role in diplomatic matters.

Protecting American Commerce: The Commercial Regulations

The Society Islands were a popular resort for American whalers during the 1830s. Some seventy-five vessels—mostly whalers—visited Tahiti every year to provision and to rest their crews, some of whom promptly jumped ship. The previous American consul had been replaced after a dispute with the government over the lawlessness on the island and the excessive influence of British missionary George Pritchard.

Commercial regulations signed at Samoa, November 1839. The regulations were signed at a grand concourse of chiefs and officers in dress uniform and were witnessed by the British and American consuls. No original version exists. This broadside was printed for distribution either in Samoa or in U.S. ports to set forth the rights and obligations of both captains and the government. A copy of the regulations dating from 1853, signed by the head chief of Pago Pago, testifies that the regulations "have been carried out in this port since their first adoption [in] 1839 and will continue to be observed." (Commercial Regulations 1839; Commercial Regulations 1853) Courtesy Beinecke Rare Book and Manuscript Library, Yale University.

Commercial Regulations, made

by the principle chiefs of the Samoa Group of Islands, after full consideration in Council on the fifth day of November, 1839.

I.

All Consuls duly appointed, and received in Samoa, shall be protected both in their persons and property, and all foreigners obtaining the consent of the Government, and conforming to the laws, shall receive the protection of the Government.

II.

All foreign vessels shall be received into the ports and harbours of Samoa, for the purpose of obtaining supplies, and for commerce; and with their officers and crews, so long as they shall comply with these regulations, and behave themselves peaceably, shall receive the protection of the Government.

III.

The fullest protection shall be given to all foreign ships, and vessels, which may be wrecked; and any property saved shall be taken possession of by the Consul of the country to which the vessel belongs; who will allow a salvage, or portion of the property so saved, to those who may aid in saving, and protecting the same; and no embezzlement will be permitted under any circumsatnces whatever. The effects of all persons deceased shall be given up to the Consuls of the nation to which they may have belonged.

IV.

Any person guilty of the crime of murder, upon any foreigner, shall be given up without delay to the commander of any public vessel of the nation to which the deceased may have belonged, upon his demanding the same.

V.

Every vessel shall pay a port charge of five dollars, for anchorage and water, before she will be allowed to receive refreshments on board; and shall pay for pilotage in and out, the sum of seven dollars, before she leaves the harbour: and pilots shall be appointed subject to the approval of the Consuls.

VI.

No work shall be done on shore, nor shall any natives be employed on board vessels on the Sabbath Day, under a penalty of ten dollars, unless under circumstances of absolute necessity.

VII.

All trading in spirituous liquors, or landing the same is strictly forbidden. Any person offending shall pay a fine of twenty-five dollars; and the vessel to which he belongs shall receive no more refreshments. Any spirituous liquors found on shore will be seized and destroyed.

VIII.

All deserters from vessels will be apprehended, and a reward paid of five dollars to the person who apprehends him; and three dollars to the chief of the district in which he may be apprehended, shall be paid on his delivery to the proper officer of the vessel. No master shall refuse to receive such deserter under a penalty of twenty-five dollars. Deserters taken after the vessel has sailed, shall be delivered up to the Consul, to be dealt with as he may think fit. Any person who entices another to desert, or in any way assists him, shall be subject to a penalty of five dollars, or one month hard labor on the public roads.

IX.

No master shall land a passenger without permission of the Government, under a penalty of twenty-five dollars, and no individual shall be permitted to land or reside on the Samoa Group of Islands without the special permission of the Government. Any one so landing shall be compelled to leave by the first opportunity.

X.

If a sick person be left on shore from any vessel for the recovery of his health he shall be placed under charge of the Consul, who shall be responsible for his sick expenses and will send him away by the first opportunity after his recovery.

XI.

Any seaman remaining on shore after 9 o'clock at night shall be made a prisoner until the next morning when he shall be sent on board, and shall pay a penalty of five dollars.

XII.

All fines to be paid in specie or its equivalent, or be commuted by the Government at the rate of one months hard labor on the public road for five dollars.

XIII.

Should the master of any vessel refuse to comply with any of these regulations, a statement of the case shall be furnished to the nation or the Consul of the nation to which he belongs, and redress sought from thence.

XIV.

All Magistrates or chiefs of districts where vessels or boats may visit, shall enforce the rules and regulations relative to the landing of foreigners, and apprehension of deserters, or pay such a fine as the Malo shall impose.

XV.

For carrying into effect the foregoing rules and regulations the chiefs and tula fale of the respective districts shall meet and elect one of their number to act as Magistrate or Judge, to execute the laws.

XVI.

These regulations shall be printed, promulgated, and a copy furnished to the master of each vessel visiting these Islands.

The foregoing rules and regulations having been signed by the King and Chiefs in my presence, and submitted to me, I consider them just and proper, and shall forward to the American Government a Copy of the same for the information of all Masters of Vessels visiting the Samoa group of Islands.

CHARLES WILKES,
Commanding U. States
Exploring Expedition.

In presence of

WILLIAM L. HUDSON,
Commanding U. S. Ship Peacock.
CADR. RINGGOLD,
Commanding U. S. Brig Porpoise.
R. R. WALDRON, U. States' Navy.
B. VANDERFORD, Pilot.

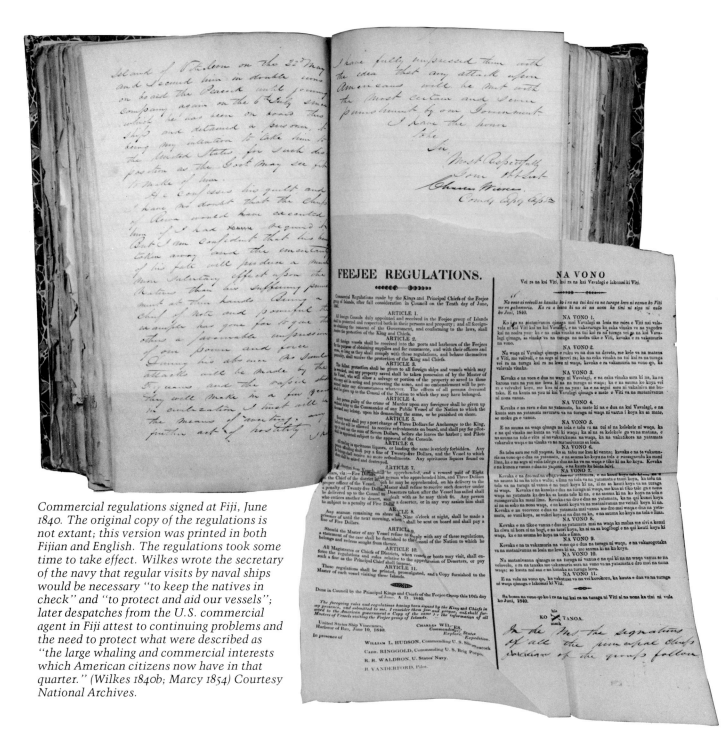

Commercial regulations signed at Fiji, June 1840. The original copy of the regulations is not extant; this version was printed in both Fijian and English. The regulations took some time to take effect. Wilkes wrote the secretary of the navy that regular visits by naval ships would be necessary "to keep the natives in check" and "to protect and aid our vessels"; later despatches from the U.S. commercial agent in Fiji attest to continuing problems and the need to protect what were described as "the large whaling and commercial interests which American citizens now have in that quarter." (Wilkes 1840b; Marcy 1854) Courtesy National Archives.

When the Exploring Expedition arrived in Tahiti in September 1839, Samuel Blackler, the new consul who had been in Papeete only six months, visited the squadron at Matavai Bay to request Wilkes's help with the government. The consul described the seizure of an American whaleboat and ill-treatment of the crew, fines unjustly imposed on seamen, and lack of cooperation in returning deserters and in providing a site for a consulate. Wilkes responded by calling a council of the chiefs. A French commander, not long before, had exacted a large cash retribution payment; Tahitians had seized two French Catholic missionaries from their asylum in American consul J.A. Moerenhout's

Kingsmill warriors, drawn by Agate. In the Kingsmill or Gilbert Islands (now the republic of Kiribati), the squadron had to contend with a war party such as this armed with weapons edged with shark teeth and protected by cocoa-fiber vests. After a pleasant visit to the town of Otiroa on Drummond Island (Tabiteuea), the hospitality of the natives turned to treachery as one of the sailors of the Peacock *disappeared. The kidnapping triggered an attack by the U.S. Navy. (Wilkes 1845, 5: 48)*

house and set them adrift in a small boat. But Wilkes reminded the chiefs of Queen Pomare's letter to Andrew Jackson in 1829, inviting Americans to visit and promising her protection. Wilkes accepted their explanations and promises to reform, believing both in their good will and in their fear of foreign men-of-war.

All but Blackler were satisfied. The consul wrote Washington to complain that Wilkes had naively showered the natives with gifts. He was typical, Blackler thought, of naval commanders "who in a praiseworthy, though mistaken exercise of forbearance towards those whom they consider a harmless people, are too apt to be contented with kind assurances & oft repeated promises." [Blackler 1840: 3] Further, Wilkes had not allowed him to speak at the council, while Pritchard—now the British consul— had taken an active role and was generally turning the government against Americans. Wilkes very well may have tried to shut Blackler out of the discussions. The captain found in Blackler's house six or seven dozen jugs of gin, which he was illegally selling, and he also learned Blackler was taking it upon himself to punish cruelly sailors accused of minor offenses. Hudson, who had discovered Blackler's liquor operation when some of his crew turned up drunk, wrote that the consul had brought some seventy cases of gin ashore by telling authorities that it was for the Exploring Expedition and would not be sold on the island. Wilkes recounted in his autobiography that he tried to get Blackler removed from office—without success, as the latter stayed at his post until he died a few years later.

The results of Wilkes's activities are disputed. When Lieutenant Cadwalader Ringgold visited Tahiti again in the *Porpoise* in early 1842, he found curfews against sailors being enforced and conditions improved. Yet, Blackler at this time was still complaining to Washington of the government's abusive practices and criticizing Wilkes. The situation in the Society Islands was to change soon anyway, in the face of competing imperial designs of the European powers.

Regardless, the episode in Tahiti is important in revealing Wilkes's character and his attitude toward less modern cultures. Wilkes was as concerned as any Westerner about the proper treatment of sailors on the islands and was quick to punish offenses through force. He believed that Westerners had every right to visit and use the islands and to bring "civilization." Yet, he was equally concerned with protecting the natives against abuse by sea captains

Hut for processing bêche-de-mer, engraving by Agate. After being gathered in shallow water, the sea cucumbers (holothuria) were boiled and then dried in long huts. They were then carried to China for use in the cuisine.

Near such a hut as this, ten crew members of the ship Charles Doggett of Salem, Massachusetts, were slain in 1834. According to the deposition of James Magoun, a survivor, the "tenth (a negro) had been cooked, but the natives had not eaten him, as they fancied that his flesh tasted of tobacco." The other bodies were recovered and buried at sea; however, they refloated and were retaken by the natives. (Wilkes 1845, 3: facing p. 220; Wilkes 1840c)

unwilling to pay for pilotage or for provisions and by sailors bent on violence or sexual license. Wilkes did not expect to change local practices overnight and preferred the route of reason as having the best long-term effects. While generally supportive of the work of the missionaries, who by then had reached much of the Pacific, he also criticized their attempts to exercise too strict control and to manipulate island politics. This attitude of deference to local culture characterized his actions throughout the voyage.

Twice again on other islands Wilkes called councils of chiefs about treatment of American seamen. First at Samoa and later at Fiji, these councils led to negotiating formal commercial regulations. Upon arriving at Apia harbor, Lieutenant Hudson tried a Samoan who had admitted to killing a New Bedford sailor. The chiefs were reluctant to execute him as Hudson wanted, because it was against their custom and because the incident had occurred years earlier, before they had become Christianized. The commanders eventually got their satisfaction by exiling the man to a distant island, but the incident points up the difficulties of applying Western justice to another culture. The situation with a renegade chief named Opotuno was more troublesome: guilty of numerous murders, but feared by the other chiefs, he retreated to a neighboring island and evaded a party Wilkes sent to capture him. Wilkes then turned his attention to negotiating a set of commercial regulations to address such problems in the future.

At this meeting or *fono* in November 1839, the chiefs agreed on sixteen points which protected them from whaling masters and crews by setting payments for services and a course of redress. They in turn committed themselves to uphold law and order, to protect ships and crews wrecked on their shores, and to help capture islanders who murdered foreigners. Wilkes appointed an American consul in Samoa, selecting John C. Williams, the son of a pioneering British missionary and popular merchant who later inaugurated the copra industry in the islands.

Six months later the squadron arrived at Ovalau Island in the Fijis, where the negotiations described above with King Tanoa took place. Once Tanoa

had signed the commercial regulations, other chiefs were induced to sign as the squadron visited and surveyed the rest of the archipelago.

The three months in the Fijis were onerous for the squadron. The surveying boats were attacked and harassed numerous times, leading to several retaliatory acts. Wilkes and Hudson also investigated earlier attacks on American merchantmen and punished the offenders where appropriate. The islands, once a source of sandalwood for the China trade, were now being visited by vessels seeking bêche-de-mer, tortoise shell, and a few other items. But the Fijians were not at all disposed to abide by Western notions of behavior if these ran counter to their traditions—such as claiming all things, or persons, which washed ashore. While Wilkes did not expect the commercial regulations to change all of this immediately, he was satisfied to have made a start "which would make them feel we were desirous of doing them justice." [Wilkes 1845, 3:57] He reported to the secretary of the navy that the islands, now that they were charted, were a potential major whaling ground and the proper standards of behavior for both foreigners and Fijians needed to be established.

Wilkes also appointed a vice-consul at Fiji, select-

Vendovi, drawn by Agate. Squadron members were surprised to learn that the perpetrator of the Charles Doggett *massacre was Vendovi. Charles Pickering wrote in his journal that "on a Botanical excursion. . .we fell in with three men, one of whom was taller than the others, and from his appearance we should have taken him for the fop of the Village. His face was painted a shiny black, except for the lower part of his nose which was vermilion, carefully "squared off," & his hair from behind had much the appearance of an inverted iron pot. This we subsequently found was Vendova . . . ." (Wilkes 1845, 3:120; Pickering 1840)*

In his account of the Expedition, Midshipman George Colvocoresses wrote that Vendovi "is about thirty-five years of age, tall and rather slender, and has a countenance which belies his character—its expression is mild and benevolent." In March 1842, Master's Mate Benjamin Vanderford, who had befriended the chief and spoke Fijian, died as the squadron was crossing the Indian Ocean on the way home. Wilkes noted that "His death produced a great impression upon Vendovi" and that "His own disease, henceforward made rapid strides toward a fatal termination. . . ." (Colvocoresses 1855: 150; Wilkes 1845, 5: 417–18)

Drawn by A.T Agate: J. W. Paradise Sc.

A-9

U.S. Ship Peacock
At Sea July 16 1841

Sir

The following is a list of "Presents
for Natives" now on board this Ship
Viz.

19 Small Axes
13 Accordeons
16 Bunches Blue Beads
3½ pounds Com. Beads
94 Hand Saw Files
216 Small Gimblets
73 Worsted Plaid Shawls
8 Small Fancy do.
22 Jews Harps
4 Pair Carpet Slippers
114 Com. Iron Spoons
4 Plane Irons
200 Com. Clay Pipes
6 Com. Muskets (of but little value)
33 Pocket Knives
31 Boxes Shaving Soap
16 Brass Kettles
350 Assorted Flints
9 M do. Needles
632 Small fish Hooks
18 Small Pocket Compasses
130 Yds Printed Cotton
14 " Unbleached do.
48 Papers "China Rouge"
9 Butchers Knives
51 Whales Teeth
2 Kegs & an fillage Tobacco.

Wm L Hudson Eq
Com. U.S. Ship Peacock

Very respectfully
Y. U. Servt
A. Speiden, Purser

ing David Whippy, an American who had lived there for eighteen years and spoke the language capably.

One of the squadron's most celebrated attempts to punish crimes against American sailors involved the *Charles Doggett* mentioned in the Salem East India Society 1834 memorial. Twelve of the crew had been ashore on Viti Levu Island curing bêche-de-mer. Native hostages were normally kept on board ships when crew members went ashore, but on this particular day the hostage, feigning illness, was allowed off and ten men were killed. Wilkes sent Hudson with the *Peacock* to find and punish the offender, who turned out to be Vendovi, brother of the king of Viti Levu. Hudson captured Vendovi by stratagem, examined him, and, after Vendovi confessed his guilt, determined to take him to America.

Imperial Designs in the Pacific

Signing commercial regulations and appointing American consuls had a significance beyond punishing a few wayward natives who attacked American seamen at scattered spots across the Pacific basin. The presence and activities of this sizeable fleet also impinged upon the emerging imperialism of the European powers in the region.

After the early Pacific explorers had come missionaries, such as John Williams, who reached Samoa in 1816 and opened those islands to Western commerce. While the initial intent was not colonization and empire, as consuls were appointed and as competition began between France and England to capture both trade and souls, the tenor of activities gradually changed.

Consul Moerenhout's squabble with George Pritchard over the Catholic missionaries had its denouement in 1842, when the Society Islands became a French protectorate; Pritchard was eventually transferred to Samoa where he agitated

Presents for natives on board the Peacock *in July 1841. These trade goods were lost with the* Peacock *on the Columbia River bar. (Speiden 1841) Courtesy National Archives.*

unsuccessfully for a British takeover there. Even as the squadron visited the Antipodes, a British governor arrived in New Zealand to make a treaty with the Maori, which began to undermine their sovereignty. Wilkes was alarmed about this development, not because he wanted the United States to become embroiled in a contest for empire, but because it would close off important whaling grounds to American ships. In a letter from Sydney to the secretary of state, he urged that the U.S. consul there, James H. Williams, be made consul general for all of Polynesia in order to ensure American interests were properly protected throughout the Pacific. Joseph Couthouy, the Expedition's conchologist, wrote the secretary of the navy expressing similar fears and noted that the fifty U.S. ships which visited New Zealand in 1839 exceeded the total number of British and French whalers together.

The jealousy among the French, British, and Americans spilled over into the Antarctic discoveries as well. Renowned Captain James Ross of the Royal Navy peevishly complained that Wilkes and the French expedition under Dumont d'Urville were ungentlemanly to explore for new lands along the same route that, as they knew, he was planning to use in the spring of 1840. Wilkes felt no such ill-will against Ross and, disobeying instructions, wrote the Scot after his second Antarctic voyage describing his discoveries and enclosing a map. Ross would have no kindness directed his way and voiced publicly doubts about all of the American's findings because of certain apparent errors on the chart. Wilkes and the Frenchman got into a dispute over who had first seen land. For Wilkes, it was mainly a point of pride; however, Dumont d'Urville had claimed the land in the name of his king, as Ross was also to do.

Apart from questions of sovereignty and political influence, which may not have always amounted to much, events in the Pacific during the mid-nineteenth century were also important for what they represented in terms of cultural penetration. On a number of occasions, Wilkes and Hudson intervened in disputes between the "missionary factions" and opposing groups on various islands—most notably at Tonga where mediation was unsuccessful. The "Christian" King George stalled peace efforts, in the words of Charles Pickering, "to make Converts by the Sword." [Pickering 1840]

Wilkes himself in no way tried directly to advance the Christian cause at Tonga or anywhere else through force or similar means. He approved the "civilizing" of the natives by missionaries where this meant improved safety for commerce; he and Hudson consulted with missionaries before taking certain actions which might jeopardize their safety. Yet Wilkes was remarkably faithful to his instructions to "neither interfere, nor permit any wanton interference with the customs, habits, manners, or prejudices, of the natives of such countries or islands as you may visit; nor take part in their disputes, except as a mediator. . . ." [Wilkes 1845, 1: xxviii]

Wilkes's first act upon leaving Peru in July 1839 had been to issue a general order enjoining "great moderation" in relationships between the squadron and the inhabitants of the Pacific islands and stating that "an appeal will rather be made to their good will than to their fears." [Wilkes 1839] Expedition members were sorely put to the test in Fiji, where they encountered cannibalism; but, except where such acts directly affected foreigners, no attempts were made to stop this practice despite personal feelings of revulsion.

The Uses of Gifts and Weapons

Pomp and circumstance were very much a part of the routine in dealing with the peoples of the Pacific. At every opportunity Wilkes and Hudson would invite chiefs on board, treat them with great ceremony, present them gifts in the name of the president and the American people, feed them, and amuse them with drill demonstrations—to make them feel at once honored and well-disposed to the United States, yet also to impress them with the power of a warship and the respect due Americans.

Such ceremonial gift-giving was only the top tier of a regulated exchange set by the purser. All trade was to be conducted by designated persons on each ship, yet the squadron depended upon barter to procure provisions and scientific specimens;

when the surveying parties were out for extended periods at remote locations, a good deal of impromptu trading must have occurred. William Reynolds summed up the range of barter at Fiji in a letter to his family:

The natives were now permitted to come alongside to trade; they brought out few pigs to dispose of, much to our regret, but of the other things I have mentioned, they had abundance. For bottles, we could get cocoa nuts, yams, bow & arrows & other trifles; red paint was highly valued, and hachets, plane irons, knives, razors, scissors, fish hooks, looking glasses, calico, beads were a stock with which you could buy anything in Fegee. Muskets, powder, lead, whales teeth, & chests with locks were the things most valued, but these are only used as presents. . . . [Reynolds 1840]

But at times gifts were not sufficient to win their way with the natives. Such incidents usually grew out of the islanders' very desire for sailors' clothing and other products of industrialization; theft was usually the motive for killing foreigners. The squadron punished with force such crimes, as well as, occasionally, interference with their surveying or collecting duties. Two or three incidents stand out, which illustrate the conditions under which the men worked and the limits to diplomacy.

The saddest incident for all the Expedition members who left memoirs occurred in July 1840 at Malolo Island in western Fiji. Here, part of a surveying party was bartering for food on shore when they were suddenly attacked and two officers, Lieutenant Joseph Underwood and Midshipman Wilkes Henry, struck down. Wilkes, five miles distant in the *Flying Fish* when the incident occurred, ordered a retaliatory attack on the island.

When the villagers sued for peace the following day, Wilkes required them to provision his ship. "I feel conscious I have done my duty," he wrote his wife, "inflicted severe punishment tempered with mercy and fully avenged the death of Poor Wilkes & Lt. Underwood." [Wilkes 1840a] The Malolo incident cast a pall over the squadron's stay at Fiji. It happened despite Wilkes's strict orders about pre-

Attack at Malolo, July 1840. The frontispiece from George Colvocoresses's book (1855) shows the fatal attack on Lieutenant Joseph Underwood and Midshipman Wilkes Henry at Malolo Island in the Fijis. Henry was the only son of Charles Wilkes's sister Eliza; Wilkes wrote his wife that during the cruise his nephew "had very much improved and was beloved by all the officers men of the Squadron & is regreted." (Wilkes 1840a)

Joseph A. Underwood, by Agate. In a letter to his father, Midshipman William May wrote that Lieutenant Underwood "had not his superior, if equal, in the Navy— he was very talented, spoke fluently French, Spanish & Italian, was a profound mathematician & surveyor—and possessed many other accomplishments, such as drawing, engraving, & music." Underwood was one of a "cabal" of eight or nine officers Wilkes accused of conspiring to undermine his leadership; Wilkes privately expressed the feeling that the Malolo incident was the result of Underwood's overconfidence.

The officers of the squadron erected a monument in Mt. Auburn Cemetery in Cambridge, Massachusetts, in memory of Underwood and Henry, and the officers lost in the Sea Gull in early 1839. (May 1840; Wilkes 1978: 442) Courtesy U.S. Naval Academy Museum.

The burning of Malolo. In retaliation for the attack on squadron members, two landing parties were put ashore while boats armed with blunderbusses stood off to prevent escapes or reinforcements. By the end of the day, an estimated sixty Fijians were dead and wounded and two villages lay in ashes, including a palisaded stronghold set afire with rockets. (Emmons 1840) Courtesy Beinecke Rare Book and Manuscript Library, Yale University.

cautions to be taken while surveying, but perhaps it was inevitable given the frequent hostility the crews encountered.

A second encounter at Drummond Island (Tabiteuea) is more typical of the military engagements undertaken by the Expedition. Kidnappings of sailors were common in the Pacific because a white man's technological skills and other attributes could bring prestige and military advantage to a village. When a crew member of the *Peacock* disappeared on Drummond and attempts to ransom him with tobacco were unsuccessful, Hudson sent an assault party ashore. As it neared land a few shots were fired "and a rocket was discharged, which

took its flight towards the great of them. The latter missle caused great confusion, and many of them turned to seek the shore, but their terror did not last long, and they made another stand," only giving way after a determined attack. The village was burned but the sailor never found. [Wilkes 1845, 5: 56–61]

Rockets were especially frightening to natives, as were other new weapons, which gave the squadron further advantage over their opponents.

Oregon and California

The United States had no territorial ambitions in the Pacific, but the same could not be said of western North America. Wilkes's instructions called for him to survey and examine Oregon and the Columbia River, plus the coast of California, including San Francisco Bay in particular.

Clearly, Wilkes felt he had a role in the United States acquisition of Oregon, yet he played his part very coolly. The territory embraced by present-day Oregon, Washington, Idaho, and British Columbia was, by treaties of 1818 and 1827, to be occupied jointly by the British and Americans. Although the United States had claims based on the discovery of the Columbia River in 1792, the Lewis and Clark expedition, and the Adams-Onís treaty with the Spanish in 1819, in fact the British—through the Hudson's Bay Company—more effectively occupied the entire territory. By 1841, when the Expedition arrived, ten years of organized American immigration to Oregon was just beginning to cause the company enough concern to lead it to institute its own immigration program with Canadian settlers.

John McLoughlin, chief factor of the company, was surprised to see the squadron appear without warning, as he reported to his supervisors. The only indication of its coming was the arrival from Honolulu in spring 1841 of a merchant ship with supplies for the Expedition. In his autobiography, Wilkes wrote that McLoughlin hesitated to give information and assistance at first, but that his own friendly demeanor gradually led the British to believe that the Expedition had no ulterior motives; in any case, he added, they soon learned that the squadron intended to carry out its surveying mission regardless of opposition. Wilkes believed that the treaties gave both sides equal rights to the territory and, further, was "fully satisfied it was to be full part and parcel of our country." [Wilkes 1978: 505–6]

Despite this undercurrent, both parties became quite congenial and helpful to each other. McLoughlin, based at Fort Vancouver on the Columbia, assured that the squadron would be provisioned during its work at Puget Sound; company agents were even to supply the Americans with scarce fresh beef, if they gave it to their own people too, but "it must not appear we do so because others do so." [McLoughlin 1841] When the *Peacock* wrecked on the Columbia bar, the company provided shelter and supplies to the crew and later helped to outfit the replacement ship *Oregon*. McLoughlin wrote to the governors that he sold supplies at a favorable price to avoid charges of gouging.

Hudson returned McLoughlin's favor by sending forty of his shipwrecked crew to help bring in the harvest. Wilkes also carefully avoided direct dealings with the Native Americans, so that McLoughlin could observe that he was "not aware that any one attached to the Expedition traded a Single Skin from the Indians and even Salmon[;] when the parties were in reach of the [company's] Establishment they preferred to get from us than to have any dealings with the natives." [McLoughlin 1943: 41]

American settlers in Oregon—mostly concentrated south of the Columbia—were dissatisfied with their dependence on the Hudson's Bay Company. They were disgruntled that the company bought beaver skins only from their own trappers, not the American missions, and would not sell goods to persons interested in competing with company stores. Wilkes thought this attitude showed "ill grace" considering the "kindest attentions and hospitality" provided them by the company. In the Willamette Valley in June 1841, Wilkes visited a farm where the

people were quite alive on the subject of laws, courts, and magistrates, including governors, judges, &c. I was here informed that a committee had been appointed to wait upon me on my arrival at the mission, to hold a consultation relative to the founding of settled governments.

Upon arriving at the Methodist mission of Jason Lee, the commander heard the committee, but he argued that such moves were premature because Americans were still in the minority and wouldn't control the government, because no crime or other problem needed addressing, and because of the difficulty in determining their boundaries with the company. He "further advised them to wait until the government of the United States should throw

its mantle over them." [Wilkes 1845, 4: 341–44, 348–49, 352–53] Wilkes's advice was taken and, in retrospect, appears to have been sound.

Once American settlers caught "Oregon fever" after 1842 and began coming in greater numbers, the situation took care of itself. Americans in the Willamette Valley did draw up the Champoeg compact for local government in 1843, but it was not until 1845 that American numbers began to overwhelm the Canadians.

Despite his advice to American settlers and his outward demeanor with company officials, Wilkes was studying how United States interests could be protected in Oregon. From Fort Nisqually, he wrote the secretary of the navy:

I shall continue my operations in the waters of this Territory and keep parties engaged in the interior during the time we remain; obtaining as much knowledge of the country as possible, being well aware of the importance of accurate information for the use of the government relative to the value of the country, pending the settlement of the boundary question. [*Wilkes 1841*]

Later he indicated that he had exceeded his instructions by concentrating considerable attention farther north in the area of the Strait of Juan de Fuca and promised a full report upon his return.

The report he handed in the following June argued for an immediate takeover of Oregon by the United States to preempt British expansionism. But Wilkes's message appears to have fallen on deaf ears, for the Tyler administration was more interested in Texas than Oregon. By the Polk administration, however, American immigration exceeded a thousand per year, and even with the distraction of the Mexican War the United States was able to obtain the Oregon territory to parallel forty-nine.

The squadron left Oregon in early autumn to

Cocoanut Grove and Temple, Fakaofo, drawn by Agate. A diplomatic scene takes place in front of a sacred building. The two god images are described in the Narrative *as covered or enveloped in mats. One was fourteen feet high and eighteen inches in diameter, the other four feet high.*

meet the party sent under Lieutenant George Emmons overland to San Francisco Bay. Wilkes arrived in October 1841 "prepared for anarchy and confusion, [but] I was surprised when I found a total absence of all government in California, and even its forms and ceremonies." [Wilkes 1845, 5: 152]

Wilkes's comments were well taken, for the Mexican government then exercised little control over Upper California. Once in San Francisco and uncertain when Emmons's party would arrive from Oregon, Wilkes approached the Mexican military commander of Upper California, General Mariano Guadalupe Vallejo, for provisions. General Vallejo, who maintained a presidio at Sonoma at his own expense, was lord over what David Weber calls a "near-feudal barony" on the California frontier. [Weber 1982: 109] Although he promoted Mexican frontier expansion and opposed American immigration to California, Vallejo received Wilkes hospitably. Wilkes was unable to find all the requested supplies, because these were simply not to be had in California. Fortunately, however, Emmons soon arrived and enough provisions were acquired from an American merchant.

About California Wilkes wrote, "it is very probable that this country will become united with Oregon, with which it will perhaps form a state that is destined to control the destinies of the Pacific." [Wilkes 1845, 4: 171] Although expecting it too would be acquired in time by the United States, Wilkes nevertheless displayed less interest in California than in Oregon. He prepared no special report on California, and except for attempting to purchase supplies and perhaps to drop off mail, the squadron had no apparent contact with the merchant (and later special U.S. agent) Thomas Larkin in Monterrey, who was soon to lead the American separatist movement. It was not for Wilkes to take the kind of precipitate action as Thomas ap Catesby Jones the following year, who, thinking the United States was at war with Mexico, captured Monterrey briefly without orders—or as John C. Frémont during the war itself.

The author acknowledges with gratitude the assistance of William Kane and Benjamin T. Pierce in the research for this chapter.

The Sulu Agreement

Upon leaving California in November 1841, Wilkes had one major diplomatic act yet to perform. While he had permission to touch at Japan and explore the Sea of Japan, shortness of time prevented this; instead, he sailed for Manila and then, in February 1842, south into the Sulu Sea. There he had been instructed to search for a shorter route for vessels engaging in the China trade and to learn about the possibilities for commerce.

A Moslem sultanate had ruled the Sulu archipelago from Soung since the sixteenth century. A year before the Expedition left Norfolk, the secretary of state received a letter from an official of the sultan's court inviting the United States to make a treaty and encouraging American commerce. Wilkes quickly addressed this request after arriving at Soung, concluding an agreement in which the sultan pledged himself to protect commerce in his domain.

Wilkes wrote that the principal value of the agreement would be to remove the danger from pirates and, by allowing passage through the Sulu Sea, to "shorten by several days the passage to Manilla or Canton, and be a great savings of expense in the wear and tear of a ship and her canvass." [Wilkes 1845, 5: 366–67]

Ever mindful of the possibilities for trade, Wilkes recorded a "list of the goods saleable at Sooloo," which included commodities such as rice and lumber, cotton and silk goods and clothing, silver and iron, cutlery and crockery, opium, and "arms of all kinds." [Wilkes 1842] Goods for export from Sulu included items for Asian markets, such as birds' nests and bêche-de-mer, as well as pepper, camphor, and cocoa. Attempts to look around Soung and neighboring areas for further intelligence of this kind were foiled by firm resistance—which the Americans felt was to hide evidence of the piratical activities of the inhabitants. Nonetheless, Wilkes had accomplished his mission and gotten the agreement giving Americans most-favored status. The *Vincennes* left in February bound for home.

Conclusion

The accomplishments of Wilkes and the Exploring Expedition in the field of diplomacy were numerous. Just how significant and lasting these deeds were is hard to gauge in all cases because of the variety of other forces at work. The Sulu agreement and survey opened a new route for American trade with China, soon to expand with the Opium War and its aftermath. In fact, in Singapore Wilkes met commodore Lawrence Kearny on his way to China with the East India Squadron to protect U.S. interests; the United States signed a treaty with that country in 1844.

Wilkes's role in western North America was very different. By all appearances, he was successful in securing the assistance of both British and Mexican authorities in the surveying work. The *Narrative* and other publicity about the voyage doubtless spurred the wave of immigration that was already beginning to Oregon and was about to roll toward California. Intelligence gathered about the West Coast was of great importance to the American government as it negotiated for these lands in ensuing years.

The efforts of the Expedition in the Pacific islands are more difficult to evaluate because of the vast expanse involved. The very presence of a large American squadron must have had a significant effect wherever it went. In specific groups such as Samoa and Fiji the consuls and trade agreements Wilkes left behind promoted U.S. commerce. Wilkes's vision was broad, but the Tyler and Polk administrations did not pursue the larger diplomatic role which Wilkes felt appropriate. Yet, all of the work conducted in the Pacific—surveying, treaty making, collecting—made that area more comprehensible to Americans and encouraged them to expand their activities there regardless of government support.

11 The National Gallery at the Patent Office

The return of collections from the U.S. Exploring Expedition led to Washington's first federally supported museum, in the National Gallery of the Patent Office, and influenced the early development of the Smithsonian Institution. Originally the collections were to have been placed with private institutions, as had been the case three decades before with the gatherings of the Lewis and Clark expedition. But a new approach gained favor as a result of an English scientist's munificent bequest to the United States and the aspirations of prominent officials to enhance the scientific and cultural attributes of the city. By the time the Expedition returned in 1842 the placement of the collections as the core of a museum in the Patent Office was a foregone conclusion that none would have predicted four years before—except perhaps for the chief strategist of this outcome, Secretary of War Joel Poinsett.

Just as the Expedition sailed in 1838, American emissary Richard Rush returned from London with $508,318 in gold coin, the proceeds of an estate left by James Smithson to establish the Smithsonian Institution in Washington "for the increase

Interior of the National Gallery in the early 1850s. From United States Magazine, *October 1856. Courtesy National Portrait Gallery, Smithsonian Institution.*

and diffusion of knowledge." Rush's return sparked an extended debate over possible uses for the bequest, including an agricultural institute, an astronomical observatory, a university, and a library. But Poinsett had a different aim and to bring it about formed an organization in May 1840 called the National Institution for the Promotion of Science. He was a widely traveled soldier-diplomat, familiar with the museums and educational establishments of European capitals, as well as an amateur naturalist who introduced the poinsettia into the United States. His goal was to establish a center in the nation's capital for the scientific and useful arts, embracing an "observatory, a museum . . . a botanic and zoological garden, and the necessary apparatus for illustrating every brand of Physical Science." Poinsett was quick to suggest that his organization care for the collections of the Exploring Expedition in Washington, informing its first annual meeting in January 1841 that he could "not believe that after all the labor, pains, and expense incurred these specimens are not to be brought to Washington, to be arranged and exhibited here." His solution was to apply the interest from the Smithson bequest to his institution to operate a national museum to house these and other government collections. [Goode 1891:290–91]

Poinsett's organization—involving cabinet members and congressmen, seasoned government ad-

J.R. Poinsett

ministrators such as Colonel John J. Abert of the Army Corps Topographical Engineers and Francis Markoe of the State Department, and Washington civic leader Peter Force—combined a variety of talent and political influence. In its first six months the group had announced its goals to scientific and academic bodies at home and abroad; set up committees on publishing and relations with the cabinet and Congress; formed departments in natural history, agriculture, American history and antiquities, and other collecting areas; and developed its strategy for gaining congressional support. Peter DuPonceau, president of the century-old American Philosophical Society in Philadelphia, applauded the auspicious beginnings, certain that Smithson would have approved of the organization. "Congress cannot find a better opportunity to execute the will," he wrote, "than by laying hold of your institution and making it its own." [National Institute 1841–46:12]

The Whig defeat of the Democratic administration of which Poinsett and many of his colleagues were a part did little to slow the momentum. Before leaving Washington Poinsett prevailed upon the secretary of the navy to direct that the Exploring Expedition's collections be placed in the care of the National Institution. On 8 February 1841 the Institution's members were told that 150 boxes were on the way from Philadelphia, and on 3 March an appropriation of $5,000 was made to the navy to facilitate the work. The Exploring Expedition collections were about to arrive. Where they were to be housed was another matter.

Meanwhile, architect Robert Mills had been erecting three stone fireproof buildings for the Treasury, Post Office, and Patent Office. These grand classical revival structures changed the landscape of the city, reflecting the expanding domestic requirements of the nation, as well as the concern that government functions and records be protected in permanent buildings of suitable appearance. In both its legislative history and design, the Patent

Joel R. Poinsett, secretary of war, on the eve of establishing the National Institution for the Promotion of Science. Lithograph by Charles Fenderich, 1838. Courtesy National Portrait Gallery, Smithsonian Institution.

Office Building was uniquely suited for the purposes Poinsett had in mind. A Senate report had urged in 1836 that the building contain displays of patent models as well as manufactures, "specimens of useful and elegant fabrics," possibly "a cabinet of interesting minerals" and American Indian artifacts. What was then contemplated was in effect "a national museum of the arts, . . . inventions and improvements in machinery and manufactures, . . . together with such other objects of interest as might conveniently and properly be placed under the superintendence of the Commissioner." [U.S.Congress 1836:8] This broad mandate was to be stretched to the limits in the years ahead.

When the building was completed in 1840, more than half was designed for exhibitions, including large rooms on the lower two floors devoted to patent models. Above was a grand vaulted room which Mills claimed was "the largest in the United States"[1842] and which Patent Commissioner Henry Ellsworth dubbed the "National Gallery of American Manufactures and Agriculture," an exhibit center for productions and discoveries throughout the expanding nation. Ellsworth promptly invited citizens to exhibit their "choicest specimens," promising to affix "the name and address of manufacturer (with the prices when desired)." [1840] But he was in the anomalous position of having the most spacious hall in the nation with little to put in it. More than seven thousand patent models had burned in 1836, just as construction on the new building had begun. Few of them had been replaced, and Ellsworth's campaign for exhibits of manufactures had just started.

Given the suitability of the building, the lack of alternatives in Washington, and pressure from Poinsett's followers, it was inevitable that the Expedition's holdings would be at least temporarily exhibited in the Patent Office. The National Institution hired geologist Henry King as its curator and began to move into the basement of the building on 12 April 1841. Joining the initial shipment from Wilkes's squadron were other government and private collections, including "Indian Portraits and Curiousities" from the War Department and James Smithson's cabinet of gems, minerals, and personal memorabilia from the Treasury. Chief among the private collections were the holdings of the Washington Museum, whose proprietor John Varden was paid by King in June "to move all my Curiosities, Fixtures, Lampes, etc., to the Hall of the National Gallery." [Varden 1855] Varden came along as well and was to spend most of the next twenty years managing collections at the Patent Office.

Within weeks Markoe wrote Poinsett that "we expect soon to have the fine room in the 3rd story of the Patent Office—273 ft. long." [Markoe 1841] Two events, the arrival of twenty tons of new shipments from the explorers and reports of damage to collections from dampness in the basement, led the Institution to request this prime space, and by midsummer Ellsworth's supervisor, Secretary of State Daniel Webster, had agreed to the move, as long as it did "not interfere with any uses to which the Patent Office is destined by law." [National Institute 1841–46:101] Prophetically, Webster turned over the State Department's historic treaties and archives, including the Declaration of Independence, to Ellsworth, as the federal official legislatively charged with the supervision of collections in the building. Webster was unwilling to consign "state treasures" to the privately controlled National Institution. Ellsworth was to make much of the organization's being national in its name only and having no right to occupy space legally assigned to the Patent Office. But for the moment expediency reigned, and Ellsworth had both the National Institution and the Exploring Expedition smack in the center of the National Gallery.

Ellsworth's next annual report in January 1842 presented what became a standard litany in the years ahead—the present accommodations for extraneous government collections could only be temporary, but wings could be added to the building both to house the National Institute, as it began to call itself in 1842, and to permit lectures and other possible applications of the Smithson bequest. For its part, the Institute's ambition knew no end. King even suggested it gain curatorial control of all collections in the building, including those of the Patent Office, which he hoped would entitle it to support from the Patent Fund. Happily for Ellsworth, this proposal died aborning.

Ensconced in the eastern half of the National Gallery and "looking with some anxiety for additional shipments from the exploring squadron," the Institute issued its own status report on 1 January 1842. Two conditions were necessary for it to perform as curator for the government and to forward its objective of "the increase and diffusion of knowledge among men" (a direct association of the Smithson will with the goals of the Institute). These requirements were an appropriation of $20,000 to arrange the collections during 1842 and "uncontrolled occupation of the whole room." [Goode 1892:348–50] However, after an enormously successful start, which led Poinsett to write that the Institute would have to be "considerably mismanaged not to succeed now" [1842a], it nonetheless foundered, receiving a twenty year charter from Congress but no federal appropriation. Poinsett was "averse to mingle with the heterogeneous materials that compose the Tyler cabinets" [Poinsett 1843], as he later put it, and refused to return to support the Institute more energetically, thinking he could "coax it along for the next three years and then take hold of it in earnest." [Poinsett 1842b]

As to the request for use of the entire gallery, Ellsworth pointedly warned Webster against any further allowances to an organization "not under control of the government," citing his generous provision of space and exhibit cases, as well as his need to present incoming contributions of manufactures, patent models, and "products of the soil," which he planned to arrange "scientifically . . . according to the latitudes." Instead he asked for full control of the hall and its exhibits. The Institute had become a public nuisance. Ellsworth said he had had no idea that "birds & beasts were to be stuffed & prepared in the very Hall itself & still less so, that living animals such as rattlesnakes, foxes, etc., would be kept there." Should the secretary accede to the Institute's request to control the hall,

Section of the New Patent Office and Plan of the National Gallery of American Manufactures and Agriculture circulated by Patent Commissioner Ellsworth. The section indicates the originally intended disposition of space for offices, models, and other exhibitions. Lithograph, December 1840. Courtesy the Columbia Historical Society.

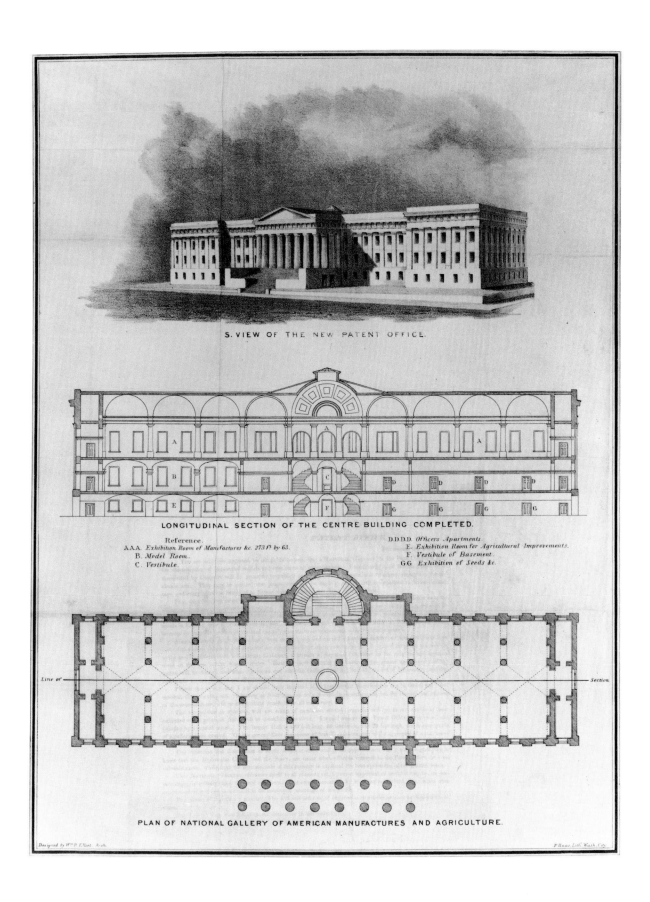

S. VIEW OF THE NEW PATENT OFFICE.

LONGITUDINAL SECTION OF THE CENTRE BUILDING COMPLETED.

Reference.

A.A.A. *Exhibition Room of Manufactures &c. 273 f.t by 63.*
B. *Model Room.*
C. *Vestibule.*

D.D.D.D. *Officers Apartments.*
E. *Exhibition Room for Agricultural Improvements.*
F. *Vestibule of Basement.*
G.G. *Exhibition of Seeds &c.*

Line of — — Section.

PLAN OF NATIONAL GALLERY OF AMERICAN MANUFACTURES AND AGRICULTURE.

Ellsworth would "be driven to the mortifying necessity" of notifying the public of his inability to "receive the numerous articles now in preparation for the Hall of National Industry." [Ellsworth 1842a] If the National Institute wanted a confrontation, Ellsworth was ready.

Poinsett's withdrawal, a mood of fiscal retrenchment dominating the capital, support for alternative plans for the Smithson bequest, and opposition in high places, including Ellsworth's—all affected the Institute's attempts to control the collections. But even more significant a factor was the return in mid-1842 of the scientists of the Exploring Expedition and their intrepid leader, Charles Wilkes. As Navy Secretary Abel P. Upshur considered the mission completed when the squadron returned, Senator Benjamin Tappan led an effort to secure funds for the preservation and publication of the Expedition's discoveries. An appropriation of $20,000 was made in August to transport and prepare the specimens. Congress named its Joint Committee on the Library to oversee the project, and Tappan became its chairman. A related measure stipulated "that until other provision be made by law for the safe-keeping and arrangement of such objects of natural history as may be in possession of the Government, the same shall be deposited in the upper room of the Patent Office, under the care of such person as may be appointed by the Joint Committee on the Library." [Rhees 1901:240] Assignments of collections previously made by administrative action now had legislative authority. One of Wilkes's scientists, Charles Pickering, was chosen as curator, and attention turned from politics and space to the management and exposition of the squadron's specimens.

The first step in preserving the collections had been to return them safely to the United States. Wilkes had written the secretary of the navy in November 1840 of the "utmost care" being taken in the packing and labeling of boxes, barrels, and bundles. Their contents were cataloged on lists certified by the scientists and duplicated for use in checking and unpacking the shipments in the states. A variety of numbering and lettering systems, ink colors, and symbols were used to track the hundreds of containers involved. Typical entries for items shipped aboard the *Lausanne* read "Box, W, No. 23, Curiousities from Fegee" and "Box Z, No. 26, Shells from New Zealand & Hawaiian Group." The scientists also kept detailed numbering systems keyed to field notes for specific items in the packages. Wilkes urged the secretary to secure the collections in a safe and dry place and keep them intact until the squadron returned, when "with the assistance of the Catalogue they can be arranged without difficulty." [Wilkes 1840]

Despite these precautions, the apparent appropriation of collections by the Expedition members themselves was challenged by the National Institute when the first shipments reached Washington in spring 1841. Of twenty tons of incoming shipments, King discovered, "nearly one fourth of the whole is marked private," including the choicest specimens. All such cases, Colonel Abert wrote Poinsett, were "from Peale and no doubt intended for his museum, but it would be a shocking outrage of propriety to countenance the idea that this Expedition was got up and those naturalists paid by the U.S. for their private benefit." Abert also reported finding fresh wood shavings instead of specimens, implying diversion of collections en route. In Peale's favor, Abert acknowledged that the government originally had been "indifferent about the collection and intended to distribute it," but even so, Abert said, the only proper approach was for the government to make the distribution. [Abert 1846] When asked for a ruling, the secretary of the navy unequivocally responded "all specimens collected by officers attached to the Expedition belong solely to the United States." He urged the "proper & early arrangement & preservation," of the collections and "vigilant protection of the rights of original discovery," adding that the scientists "should not be allowed to lose any of the literary reputation which properly attaches itself to their labor." [Badger 1841] The collections were to be kept intact and preserved; the scientists would have their fame through publication of their discoveries in the years to come.

Given the limited capabilities of the Institute's staff, it is fortunate that the bulk of the Expedition's specimens remained packed until its return. During 1841 the only scientifically experienced staff pres-

Patent Office Building, with greenhouse to the rear. Daguerreotype attributed to John Plumbe, Jr., ca. 1846. Courtesy Prints and Photographs Division, The Library of Congress.

ent were naturalist John Kirk Townsend and botanist Thomas Nuttall, both attracted from Philadelphia, which, with the Peale Museum and the Academy of Natural Sciences, was the nation's foremost center for the care and study of natural history collections. Townsend was the chief taxidermist, assisted by an amateur, Richard J. Pollard; Nuttall treated the botanical specimens. King directed the operation, attending to the minerals and shellfish, erecting cases and ordering materials,

including hundreds of assorted glass jars and vials, some with custom-made stoppers to permit suspension of specimens being preserved. Other regulars included Washingtonians Varden, "a good mechanic and arranger," R.J. Falconer, the carpenter, and R.G. Campbell, the messenger and laborer. Salaries ranged from King's $5 a day to $3 for Townsend and Nuttall, and $1.50 for the others. By year's end, with its funds exhausted and collections expanding daily, the Institute had only accomplished work "preliminary to a permanent and scientific arrangement." [Goode 1892:349–50]

Spencer Baird, a gifted young naturalist in Carlisle, Pennsylvania, who was ultimately to become secretary of the Smithsonian Institution, tracked the progress of the Institute through reports from his brother William in Washington. In summer 1841, William wrote that three or four persons "are engaged in stuffing and mounting birds and cleaning shells, minerals, etc. . . . The shelves of one room were piled with bird skins. . . . very few have been mounted . . . not more than 150, principally parrots and pigeons." William considered King "a humbug" but praised Townsend, who mounted specimens "in the most splendid manner," used the most advanced tools, and had developed a safer preserving powder by diluting the arsenic. (Ironically, he died in 1851 at the age of forty-two, a victim of chronic arsenic poisoning.) "Townsend can skin, stuff and sew up a bird, so as to make it look far superior to any I have ever seen, in five minutes. . . ." This would have been an extraordinary pace, considering the Institute's own report that the rate of the preparation of birds was six skins a day for moderate-sized birds in good condition and slower for larger and more complicated specimens. Several months later William mentioned that "some hundreds" of species of birds had been mounted but not yet set up, and the large collection of reptiles and fish, mostly from the expedition, was "so mixed up together in the bottles that there is very little satisfaction in looking at them. The cabinet of animals is very fine and there is a good collection of geological specimens." [Baird 1841–42]

William Baird's compliments notwithstanding, the scientists would have preferred the Institute to have kept hands off and said so emphatically upon their return. As its interest was only in exhibiting the collections, not their study and publication, it disregarded the elaborate record systems made by the scientists in the field. Conchologist Joseph P. Couthouy, for example, found the numbered tin tags that he had applied to specimens preserved in alcohol had been removed when their lead content discolored the specimens. The tags were saved, but Couthouy's key to his research notes was ruined. Many of Dana's Crustacea specimens were

taken from bottles, dried, and pinned up for display to the point of losing scientific value; his numbering system was upset as well. Wilkes reported in his autobiography that many boxes had been opened "and specimens abstracted from them." [p.528] Peale later reported the loss of 180 specimens of birds and the need to reprepare most of the birds and mammals and to rehouse insects that had been "improperly placed, exposed to light and destructive insects." [Peale 1844]

King proved a liability and in September was ousted by the Institute because he had meddled in policy questions and provoked unnecessary scraps with the scientists and Ellsworth. "Moreover," Abert reported to Poinsett, "we look upon him as a mere pretender in the Sciences to which he lays claim—we are glad that we have got rid of him." [1842a] But the Institute's custody of the Expedition's collections was at an end. While it deserved credit for having the collections brought intact to Washington, its mixed record of handling many types of specimens not only frustrated the scientists but damaged its own chance of securing a federal appropriation.

Pickering's appointment in September brought some order. Brackenridge, Dana, and Hale joined him in an initial progress report two months later. Pickering's tally of "Dried Preparations" included 471 birds, 26 quadrupeds, 66 reptiles, and 48 fish. There were also 208 jars of insects and zoological specimens "in spirits" and 895 envelopes consisting of 5,100 larger specimens. Not yet prepared were about 300 bird skins and 20 quadrupeds, "exclusive of an immense number of duplicate specimens," and all of the conchology collections. Neither was Brackenridge's extensive botanical collection arranged, but a "greenhouse 50 feet long, and partitioned into two apartments" was in place behind the Patent Office to accommodate live plants, of which there were 1,600 growing and more sprouting. He asked for a space for summer displays and

Spencer Fullerton Baird at age seventeen. Daguerreotype 29 September 1842. Courtesy Division of Photographic History, National Museum of American History, Smithsonian Institution.

for ornamental trees, "sample fruits, flowers, and esculents." Brackenridge predicted the botanical specimens would lead to improvements in nutrition, medicine, and the arts. His goal was a botanical establishment to rival those of Europe. In a short time Brackenridge's greenhouse and gardens became one of the most popular of the Expedition's displays at the Patent Office. [Goode 1892:351–54]

Dana reported that the Crustacea collection of about 650 species was fully arranged and that more than 350 species of coral were squeezed into two cases. While he had already filled three cases from one package of minerals and geological specimens, there were "yet 7 or 8 boxes untouched." In his opinion, a national museum required "a complete collection of minerals systematically arranged, comprising specimens from all countries, and illustrating fully every branch of science." He also suggested separate cases of geological and mineral specimens for each state of the Union to stimulate pride in the nation's wealth and promote knowledge of its resources. He concluded that twice the space was needed to permit collections from other areas to be added to the nucleus from the Exploring Expedition. Hale's report was an essay on the importance of a newer science—anthropology. Commenting on the need to study the "state of the arts, the daily habits, and the ideas of comfort and prosperity among particular people," he suggested that the Expedition's collections of native manufactures of the New Hollanders and the Fijians would "in a single glance . . . give a clearer idea of the wide difference between these tribes than any description." [Goode 1892:356–59]

In July 1843, Pickering resigned to prepare his report and was replaced by Wilkes, who lost no time in claiming the hall for the Expedition by erecting a sign over its entrance announcing in gold letters: "Collection of the Exploring Expedition." He chided Pickering for leaving unspent $5,300 of the year's $20,000, as funds were "so essential to making the wheels turn around," and set out to reinstall the hall. Cases were to be arranged scientifically and placed to permit inspection "in the best possible light." There would be an end to juxtapositions of "teapots, sugar dishes and pots . . . with shells, birds, or corals," and the contents of each

case would be cataloged. Wilkes told Tappan of friendly discussions with Ellsworth, who now was assigned all the other government collections in the hall. At the latter's suggestion, Wilkes retained Varden as custodian. "Ellsworth has great confidence in him, and thought him the most trustworthy and honest" man available. [Wilkes 1843] Next he thwarted the "odious habit" of tobacco spitting by ordering keepers to follow with a sponge "any one who was . . . using the 'weed,'" counting on disapproval from ladies accompanying the male offenders to assist. [Wilkes 1978:529] Wilkes also took a hard line toward the National Institute, refusing to allow his federally paid staff to assist with its private collections. The Captain had taken command. Thereafter the Institute had little say regarding the use of the hall and was relegated to a handful of exhibit cases and one or two rooms in the basement of the building until its charter expired in 1862.

Varden was the glue between Wilkes, Ellsworth, and the National Institute, serving on all three payrolls, including $10 per month from the National Institute. When the Institute's till was empty Varden would dun members for back dues, until he covered his own meager salary. The Library Committee paid him $50 per month, plus reimbursements for approved expenses, and the Patent Office alloted him $25 per quarter beginning in 1845 to care for the government collections unrelated to the Exploring Expedition. Beginning in 1854, when the commissioner of patents was assigned custody of all the collections, Varden received $900 per year as curator of the National Gallery.

Varden was hardworking, eager to please his superiors, and dedicated to the collections. Above all, he was loyal. His letter of 3 November 1846 is typical of his periodic assertions of faithfulness, when he assured Wilkes of his "constant Studey to attend to my known Duty and to do Whatever was required of me without the least Partialety keeping in View my own accountability to those placed above me." Wilkes thought him a bit dense about getting things right the first time, but Varden was savvy enough to survive. As Wilkes's proxy in the building, Varden carried out administrative chores along with curatorial tasks. Over a six-week period in 1843 he recruited and directed about two dozen workers in a crash project to clean and reorganize the hall for Wilkes. Varden also served the employees' interests, vouching to a local storekeeper for advances in groceries. Keeping accounts was another matter, as numbers were not his forte. Time and time again Wilkes and his clerk, Frederick D. Stuart, chastized Varden for mistakes in bills presented to the Treasury Department and for insufficient justification.

Wilkes used all the space he could scrounge from Ellsworth for preparing the Expedition's collections for publication and exhibition. While most of the National Gallery was eventually devoted to exhibitions, an alcove was set off for the herbarium, and a workroom was prepared for Peale, equipped with a copper boiler to prepare birds and other specimens. In the basement was a carpenter's shop for constructing cases and shelving, and outside were the greenhouse and horticultural gardens. To accommodate the expanding collections of plants, the fifty-foot greenhouse erected in 1842 was extended by twenty feet in 1843 and another seventy-eight feet in 1844. A glass-lined planting bed was constructed in 1845, the same year a stove was added to Brackenridge's alcove inside the building, to maintain steady temperatures during the winter.

The supplies for the greenhouse were of a class and magnitude of their own. An order for soil included two loads of gravel from Rock Creek, six of compost from Sixth Street, one of black soil from the country, three of manure, and two of sand. Repeated orders included those for a half boatload of vegetable manure, barrels of lime, flower and watering pots, ten loads of expended tanner's bark, six pounds of fumigating tobacco, and, in winter, twelve tons of anthracite coal. Supplies for the inside operations included lumber and glass for cases; mounting wire for specimens and straw for stuffing the skins of elephant seals; sewing twine and supplies; arsenic for preserving potions; linseed oil, varnish, rosin, and camphor; and parchment, stationery supplies, and paints, including naples yellow, antwerp blue, cobalt, vermilion, and indian red, for illustrating specimens. Large purchases included four hundred bird stands and one thousand plaster casts for arranging the corals. Although

most purchases were made locally, special orders were regularly placed with vendors in Boston, Philadelphia, and Baltimore.

Patent Commissioner Ellsworth reported early in 1844 that the Exploring Expedition's items had "been newly classified and re-arranged under the direction of Wilkes, so that they now present to the visitor a gratifying and instructive exhibition of the curiousities of nature and art." [U.S. Patent Office 1844:2] That May, Gideon Printers of Washington delivered one hundred copies of the "Plan of the National Gallery Containing the Collections of the Exploring Expedition," fifty of them mounted on cardboard, as well as a variety of labels to affix to cases and shelves. The plan was arranged according to case, describing not only the Expedition's collections but also those from government surveys by John C. Frémont and David Dale Owen; Smithson's memorabilia; the Declaration of Independence, relics of George Washington, and historic treaties; two cases of American manufactures; and a small number of exhibits from the National Institute. More than two-thirds of the sixty-three cases were devoted to the Exploring Expedition. All were numbered and described on the cards, which were made available to visitors as guides to the room and were periodically replaced as they became worn. On walls surrounding the room were forty-five paintings including a variety of copies of European masterworks deposited by Varden, Mrs. Poinsett, and others, as well as ten portraits of North American Indians transferred from the War Department. In addition, Washington guidebooks of the late 1840s indicate the presence of numerous other paintings and collections not reflected on this plan.

There was also a room guarded by R.K. Watts containing jewels and other valuable articles from the State Department. It is unclear where this room was located, possibly one of the four small alcoves at the ends of the hall not assigned to other collections on the plan. Ellsworth had argued effectively for guards to protect these collections when he took responsibility for them, reminding Congress in his annual report for 1841 of "the late robbery of the jewels," and the risk in relying on "bolts and bars, as ingenuity and depravity seem to defy the strength of metals." [U.S. Patent Office 1842] He demanded protection by humans as well as devices, and guards were thereafter posted over the various collections. Varden later successfully argued as well for a "dog watch" for the evening and early morning hours, when he thought the Expedition's holdings particularly vulnerable. When Ellsworth was assigned custody of all the collections in 1854, the $3,080 appropriation provided for a night watchman specifically for the hall. Despite these precautions there were periodic incidents over the years. The jewels stolen in 1841, by the way, were recovered through the offer of a reward.

The various exhibitions in the Patent Office were a great public success. John Ketchum summed it up in the summer of 1844: "Everything almost in the wide world is here by sample . . . I could spend a week in the Patent Office with great interest." Local guidebooks promoted the building's displays, although most reflected the ambition of local boosters of the foundering National Institute and credited it with custody of all the collections, as if nothing had changed in the Institute's status over the decade. Robert Mills's 1847 guidebook was more balanced, ascribing to the Exploring Expedition 2,576 ethnological specimens on view, 3,130 of mammalia and birds representing 846 species, the herbarium of 10,000 species and thousands of other items in various scientific classes. Patent models were presented in twenty-one classes including "Agriculture, its instruments and operations; Fire arms and implements of war; and Wearing apparel for the toilet." [Mills 1847] The exhibitions were so popular that Varden urged Wilkes to employ a man to clean the hall, "where so many thousands are constantly visiting." [Varden 1845a] The attendance was upwards of a hundred thousand annually.

Varden took many measures to manage the collections, reporting to Wilkes in 1847 that "nothing has ever left this place belonging to the U.S. Ex Collection without an order from some one in authority and a receipt." [Varden 1847a] Typical transactions involved items needed by scientists working on their manuscripts in other cities and by Drayton, who was preparing illustrations in Philadelphia and Boston. Varden prepared his own catalogs to keep track of items not assigned to the scientists, including the historic collections, deposits of man-

ufactures, and holdings of the National Institute. Certain collections proved more difficult to control than others. Brackenridge's live exotic plants were in such great demand that Wilkes had to order that "no flowers & plants should be cut or given away under any call for them by those in official station" and then to stand behind Brackenridge despite pressure from congressmen and "even Mrs. Tyler, the President's lady." [Wilkes 1978:529] Senator Tappan, a collector of minerals and shells, posed another problem, reportedly pressuring the scientists to identify his own shell collections and Varden for access to the tens of thousands of duplicates stored in the basement. Tappan had been permitted by the Library Committee in 1844 to have single duplicates of items in the shell collections, a privilege Congressman George P. Marsh told the patent commissioner in 1845 invited "much danger of abuse" and required that Tappan's selections be carefully listed by an appropriate official. Tappan's collecting interests caused continuing frustrations for the Expedition's staff even after his authority was rescinded two years later.

By the mid-1840s the National Gallery overseen by Varden had taken on all the basic functions of today's museum, albeit in an elemental form, ranging from recording and physically protecting collections to seeing to their use for research and public enlightenment. The government's first attempt to manage a museum was underway, in a remarkably short time and on a dramatic scale, in no small measure because of the impetus provided by the Expedition's collections, the timely availability of the Patent Office Building, the responsible concern for protecting the collections evidenced by Ellsworth and Wilkes, and the National Institute's drive to secure the Smithson bequest for a national museum.

The law creating the Smithsonian Institution in 1846 both reflected this recent history and posed a solution to the patent commissioner's need to reclaim his space. Like that of the National Insti-

Plan of the National Gallery containing the collections of the Exploring Expedition. The plan reveals the range of collections then on exhibit. Lithograph, between 1844 and 1849. Courtesy Smithsonian Institution Archives.

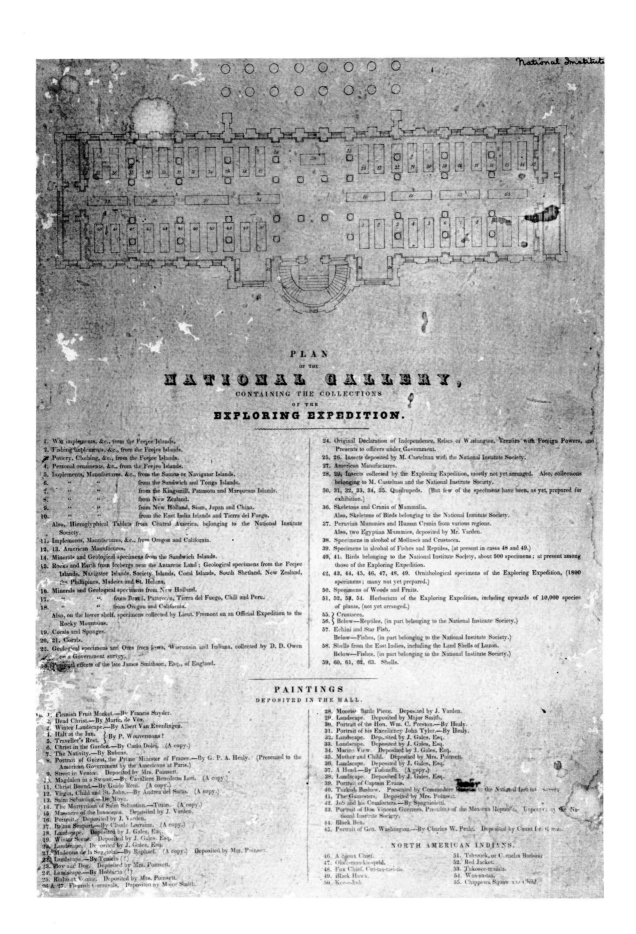

National Institute

PLAN
OF THE
NATIONAL GALLERY,
CONTAINING THE COLLECTIONS
OF THE
EXPLORING EXPEDITION.

1. War implements, &c., from the Feejee Islands.
2. Fishing implements, &c., from the Feejee Islands.
3. Pottery, Clothing, &c., from the Feejee Islands.
4. Personal ornaments, &c., from the Feejee Islands.
5. Implements, Manufactures, &c., from the Samoa or Navigator Islands.
6. " " " from the Sandwich and Tonga Islands.
7. " " " from the Kingsmill, Paumotu and Marquesas Islands.
8. " " " from New Zealand.
9. " " " from New Holland, Siam, Japan and China.
10. " " " from the East India Islands and Tierra del Fuego.
    Also, Hieroglyphical Tablets from Central America, belonging to the National Institute Society.
11. Implements, Manufactures, &c., from Oregon and California.
12, 13. American Manufactures.
14. Minerals and Geological specimens from the Sandwich Islands.
15. Rocks and Earth from Icebergs near the Antarctic Land; Geological specimens from the Feejee Islands, Navigator Islands, Society Islands, Coral Islands, South Shetland, New Zealand, the Phillipines, Madeira and St. Helena.
16. Minerals and Geological specimens from New Holland.
17. " " from Brazil, Patagonia, Tierra del Fuego, Chili and Peru.
18. " " from Oregon and California.
    Also, on the lower shelf, specimens collected by Lieut. Fremont on an Official Expedition to the Rocky Mountains.
19. Corals and Sponges.
20, 21. Corals.
22. Geological specimens and Ores from Iowa, Wisconsin and Indiana, collected by D. D. Owen on a Government survey.
23. Personal effects of the late James Smithson, Esq., of England.

24. Original Declaration of Independence, Relics of Washington, Treaties with Foreign Powers, and Presents to officers under Government.
25, 26. Insects deposited by M. Castelnau with the National Institute Society.
27. American Manufactures.
28, 29. Insects collected by the Exploring Expedition, mostly not yet arranged. Also, collections belonging to M. Castelnau and the National Institute Society.
30, 31, 32, 33, 34, 35. Quadrupeds. (But few of the specimens have been, as yet, prepared for exhibition.)
36. Skeletons and Crania of Mammalia.
    Also, Skeletons of Birds belonging to the National Institute Society.
37. Peruvian Mummies and Human Crania from various regions.
    Also, two Egyptian Mummies, deposited by Mr. Varden.
38. Specimens in alcohol of Molluscs and Crustacea.
39. Specimens in alcohol of Fishes and Reptiles, (at present in cases 48 and 49.)
40, 41. Birds belonging to the National Institute Society, about 500 specimens; at present among those of the Exploring Expedition.
42, 43, 44, 45, 46, 47, 48, 49. Ornithological specimens of the Exploring Expedition, (1800 specimens; many not yet prepared.)
50. Specimens of Woods and Fruits.
51, 52, 53, 54. Herbarium of the Exploring Expedition, including upwards of 10,000 species of plants, (not yet arranged.)
55. } Crustacea.
56. } Below—Reptiles, (in part belonging to the National Institute Society.)
57. Echini and Star Fish.
    Below—Fishes, (in part belonging to the National Institute Society.)
58. Shells from the East Indies, including the Land Shells of Luzon.
    Below—Fishes, (in part belonging to the National Institute Society.)
59, 60, 61, 62, 63. Shells.

PAINTINGS
DEPOSITED IN THE HALL.

1. Flemish Fruit Market.—By Francis Snyder.
2. Dead Christ.—By Martin de Vos.
3. Winter Landscape.—By Albert Van Everdingen.
4. Halt at the Inn. } By P. Wouvermans ?
5. Traveller's Rest. }
6. Christ in the Garden.—By Carlo Dolci. (A copy.)
7. The Nativity.—By Rubens.
8. Portrait of Guizot, the Prime Minister of France.—By G. P. A. Healy. (Presented to the American Government by the Americans at Paris.)
9. Street in Venice. Deposited by Mrs. Poinsett.
10. Magdalen in a Swoon.—By Cavaliere Benedetto Latti. (A copy.)
11. Christ Bound.—By Guido Reni. (A copy.)
12. Virgin, Child and St. John.—By Andrea del Sarto. (A copy.)
13. Saint Sebastian.—De Moye.
14. The Martyrdom of Saint Sebastian.—Titian. (A copy.)
15. Massacre of the Innocents. Deposited by J. Varden.
16. Portrait. Deposited by J. Varden.
17. Italian Seaport.—By Claude Lorraine. (A copy.)
18. Landscape. Deposited by J. Gales, Esq.
19. Winter Scene. Deposited by J. Gales, Esq.
20. Landscape. Deposited by J. Gales, Esq.
21. Madonna de la Seggiola.—By Raphael. (A copy.) Deposited by Mrs. Poinsett.
22. Landscape.—By Teniers (?)
23. Boy and Dog. Deposited by Mrs. Poinsett.
24. Landscape.—By Hobbima (?)
25. Rialto at Venice. Deposited by Mrs. Poinsett.
26 & 27. Flemish Carousals. Deposited by Major Smith.

28. Moorish Battle Piece. Deposited by J. Varden.
29. Landscape. Deposited by Major Smith.
30. Portrait of the Hon. Wm. C. Preston.—By Healy.
31. Portrait of his Excellency John Tyler.—By Healy.
32. Landscape. Deposited by J. Gales, Esq.
33. Landscape. Deposited by J. Gales, Esq.
34. Marine View. Deposited by J. Gales, Esq.
35. Mother and Child. Deposited by Mrs. Poinsett.
36. Landscape. Deposited by J. Gales, Esq.
37. A Head.—By Tofanelli. (A copy.)
38. Landscape. Deposited by J. Gales, Esq.
39. Portrait of Captain Evans.
40. Turkish Bashaw. Presented by Commodore Reed to the National Institute Society.
41. The Gamesters. Deposited by Mrs. Poinsett.
42. Job and his Comforters.—By Spagnoletti.
43. Portrait of Don Vincent Guerrero, President of the Mexican Republic. Deposited by the National Institute Society.
44. Black Ben.
45. Portrait of Gen. Washington.—By Charles W. Peale. Deposited by Count de Menou.

NORTH AMERICAN INDIANS.

46. A Sioux Chief.
47. Okee-man-kie-quid.
48. Fox Chief, Cut-tan-tas-tia.
49. Black Hawk.
50. Kee-o-kuk.

51. Tshusick, or Cornelia Barbour.
52. Red Jacket.
53. J'akosce-matila.
54. Waa-pa-taa.
55. Chippewa Squaw and Child.

tute, the Smithsonian's governing body, the Board of Regents, included high government officials—the chief justice, vice-president, and three members of each house of Congress—and private individuals. Two of the six private members were to be selected from members of the National Institute residing in Washington, a small success after the Institute's long struggle. The bill also allowed for the possible construction of the Smithsonian building adjacent to the Patent Office along Seventh Street. There were many provisos attached to this prospect, however, including concurrence by the commissioner of patents, whose constituents had long resented the intrusion of extraneous collections. Instead, the Smithsonian was placed on the Mall, and the Patent Office began to lobby for it to take the government and National Institute collections. Nearly a decade passed before completion of the Smithsonian building permitted transfer of the collections, and then only after the Smithsonian received a federal payment for their care.

Another pressure for the removal of the collections was the establishment in 1849 of the Department of the Interior to consolidate numerous domestic functions of government. The Mexican War had resulted in an increase of the nation's land area by a third, and settlement was rapidly moving beyond the Mississippi into western territories. The expanding business of the General Land Office, Pension Office, Bureau of Indian Affairs, and the Census was to be accommodated in wings to be added to the Patent Office Building. These were constructed along Seventh and Ninth Streets respectively and occupied as soon as space was available beginning in 1853. Additionally, during the 1840s the collection of patent models had increased enormously, quadrupeling in number to 17,257 since the arrival of the squadron's shipments in 1841. Less than a fifth of these models were exhibited, and the commissioner now demanded return of both the space and cases provided the Expedition's collections in the National Gallery. Even then, his 1850 annual report indicated, more than four thousand models would be without cases. Another thirty-three thousand models would arrive during the decade. The obvious conclusion was that the government collections had to go.

In May 1850 a $5,000 appropriation was made to relocate the greenhouse, and by the end of the year construction was underway at the foot of Capitol Hill near the site of today's United States Botanic Gardens. Brackenridge fretted all year at the slow pace of the work, pressed by the speed of construction at the Patent Office on the one hand, fearful of damaging winter frosts on the other. Concerned that "too many have got a finger in the pie" and beset with "a parcel of lazy mechanics," he was unable to move until winter, after some of the plants had suffered. [Brackenridge 1850] While the greenhouse collections were on their way out, relocation of the other collections was still several years ahead.

By the mid-1850s it appeared that the rest of the Expedition's collections were headed inexorably to the Smithsonian Institution. The question was when and under what terms. Completion of portions of the Smithsonian's building had begun to provide space for collections, and Spencer Baird was now on hand to acquire and arrange them. It seemed natural to many in Congress and to the patent commissioner that the Institution take them over. Joseph M. Henry—once said to have called the government collections an "Elephant's Foot" [Wilkes 1848]—however, refused to expend the private Smithsonian trust on their care and agreed to take them only when an allowance of $4,000 per year was approved.

Henry received the Smithson cabinet and memorabilia in January 1857, and later that year $15,000 was provided for new cases and for the transfer and arrangement of other collections. The arduous task of packing the specimens began, with John Varden front and center. For the next year, his day book reported packing as a constant chore. While delegations of Indians and other visitors came and went, Varden packed: 13 December, shells in pill boxes; 4 January 1858, shells in square boxes; 15 January, shells in cotton and wooden trays; 5 April, shells in small boxes, "a grate many visitors, being Easter Monday"; 21 May, Crustacea to Smithsonian; 4 June, finish packing shells; 8 and 9 June, Baird brothers direct packing of minerals and fossils, and Henry checks progress. Next were the birds. The contents of half the hall's cases were moved by mid-June, and Varden completed the job and his career in the museum at the Patent Office on 4 November: "To The Patent Office. Packed all my things . . . & remaining things for the National Gallery & sent to Smithsonian Institution. I feel unusually tired and almost worn out with hard work and shall not do any moor this day." [Varden 1857–63]

The "temporary" residence of the Exploring Expedition's collections at the Patent Office had come to an end. Their tenure there marked a noble beginning for the care of government collections in the capital—brought about by a combination of necessity, local and national chauvinism, accident, and design. Poinsett and his National Institution for the Promotion of Science launched the process with their crusade for a national museum and the Smithson bequest. Wilkes and the scientists brought professionalism and discipline, and Varden and his stalwart crew did the work. For its breadth and scale the museum enterprise was unique in the land. Its mark on the nation's capital was indelible, leaving no doubt that a national museum would be a permanent fixture of the city.

12 The Exploring Expedition and the Smithsonian Institution

While the Wilkes Expedition was wending its way around the globe and in the period immediately after its return to the United States, a quiet cultural and administrative drama was unfolding. Interested parties inside and outside of Washington debated the fate of an unexpected bequest of half a million dollars in gold from a little-known Briton, James Smithson. In 1846 two key events occurred. On 10 August the statute establishing the Smithsonian Institution became law, and on 3 December the Board of Regents of the Institution voted to offer the secretaryship (the executive head of the organization) to Joseph Henry, the professor of natural philosophy (i.e., physics) at the College of New Jersey (now Princeton University). As the Institution's first secretary, serving until his death in 1878, Joseph Henry shaped Smithson's legacy in ways still visible. To a great extent his views and actions determined the fate of the collections brought back by the Expedition: specifically, that they would largely end up in a part of the Smithsonian Institution formerly designated the National Museum and that the National Museum would have what we would now call a basic scientific research function

Joseph Henry as he looked when he was elected Secretary of the Smithsonian. Daguerreotype, ca. 1845. Courtesy Chicago Historical Society.

as well as a mandate for the popular diffusion of knowledge.

Henry was one of the few American scientists of that era with an international reputation. A fine experimental physicist best known for work on electricity and magnetism, he was admired and respected by a small, influential circle of scientists and concerned politicians who had faith in Henry's ability to preserve the bequest from unworthy uses and to do justice to the vaguely defined intentions of Smithson. Henry originally came from Albany, New York. Around age twelve, he left school and was apprenticed to a silversmith and watchmaker. In a few years Henry developed an enthusiasm for the theater and considered acting as a future career. But he had encountered science in his reading and in 1819, at age twenty-two, he enrolled at the Albany Academy to make up his educational deficiencies, determined to become a scientist. Henry soon became the professor of mathematics and natural philosophy at the Albany Academy. While occupying that post, he began the researches that won him renown in his day and later the honor of having the unit of inductance designated the Henry. Significantly for his later career in Washington, the young Henry was a curator of the Albany Lyceum of Natural History. He also acted as the librarian both of the Lyceum's successor, the Albany Institute, and the Albany Academy. From his

Exterior of the Smithsonian Building from the northeast, ca. 1862. Photograph by A. J. Russell. Courtesy Smithsonian Institution Archives.

surviving library, we know that even at this early point in his career, he was an avid reader and collector of books.

At Princeton from 1832 to 1846 Henry's research added to his reputation at home and abroad. Personal contacts convinced many of his integrity and ability to lead. Less visible to his contemporaries were continuing interests important for his course as secretary of the Smithsonian Institution. His natural history interests at Albany were manifested in Princeton in his giving a course in geology that combined a concern for the physical phenomena with careful treatment of the fossil record. The growth in the library holdings of Princeton were in part a result of his recognition of the need for reference materials.

When Henry accepted the call from the Board of Regents at the end of 1846, he brought strongly held views about the future program of the new organization. To Henry and at least some of the regents, his role was to save the good name of the country and to carry out Smithson's intent in the face of conflicting, unrealistic, and unworthy claims upon the bequest.

The language of Smithson's will and the history of the bequest in the United States from 1835 (when its existence became known) to 1846 created serious problems of policy and administration. Smithson's will of 1826 specified that if his heir, a nephew, died without issue, then his estate was bequeathed "to the United States of America, to found at Washington, under the name of the Smithsonian Institution, an establishment for the increase & diffusion of knowledge among men." [Rhees 1901:6] So little has survived about James Smithson that attempts at determining his exact objective are necessarily speculative. Even Henry, who had access to Smithson's effects before their destruction by fire in 1865, wrote letters to Britain in a futile effort to find out more about the man and his intentions. Possibly the terseness of the clause simply reflected Smithson's belief in the improbability of the contingency and the self-evident, to him, meaning of the words.

Although many individuals in the United States had strong opinions, no preponderance of belief, yet alone unanimity, about what Smithson meant was ever attained in the years before the Civil War. By patience, by adroit compromise or evasion of other viewpoints, and by sheer toughness under pressure, Henry steered the Smithsonian more or less down the path he developed in 1846 and 1847.

Whatever Smithson's intent, the Congress made two very explicit statements about the Smithsonian Institution's program in the act of establishment. First, the building housing the Institution should include "suitable rooms or halls, for the reception and arrangement, upon a liberal scale, of objects of natural history, including a geological and mineralogical cabinet; also a chemical laboratory, a library, a gallery of art, and the necessary lecture rooms." [Rhees 1901:432] Second, "All objects of natural history, plants, and geological and mineralogical specimens, belonging, or hereafter to belong, to the United States, which may be in the city of Washington," should be turned over to the Smithsonian "as suitable arrangements can be made for their reception." [Rhees 1901:433] Rather naturally, these statements were widely interpreted to mean that the Wilkes Expedition material would ultimately be turned over to the Smithsonian Institution for its museum.

One man willing to challenge that assumption was Joseph Henry. One of his first acts as secretary in December 1846 was to reject the Wilkes collections. He argued that Congress had ordered the Smithsonian Institution to do much more than was

possible with its income. Properly caring for the Wilkes collections was expensive, costing approximately $25,000 out of an annual budget of $30,000, and the return would be small. Since "a collection of curiosities at Washington is a very indirect means of increasing or diffusing knowledge" [Henry 1846] the establishment of a museum to house the Wilkes material should have a very low priority. A museum necessitated the expenditure of money on a building, something Henry wished to avoid. The bequest should be used to support science, not to purchase bricks. He expanded his argument in 1849, contending that although Congress had, in the 1846 law, given the Wilkes collections to the Smithsonian Institution, the regents were not obligated to accept them. The funds of the Institution could be better spent on collecting new objects and thus expanding knowledge than on the preservation of material "from which the harvest of discovery has already been fully gathered." Rather, let the government of the United States preserve the specimens as "a memento of the science and energy of our navy." As for the obvious compromise, which was to have the government supply the Smithsonian with an annual appropriation to take care of the collections, leaving the Smithson bequest free for supporting other activities, Henry again said no. This would force the Smithsonian to become an annual "supplicant for government patronage, and ultimately subject it to political influence and control." [Smithsonian Regents 1853:174] Good science and political control did not mix.

Henry's attitude toward the Wilkes collections was a reflection of his effort to make the Smithsonian the first governmental bureau with a mandate to increase knowledge without a corresponding mandated mission (the second, the National Science Foundation, did not appear for another century). Other government agencies did do basic research—the Naval Observatory and the Coast Survey, for example—but the research was justified by specific, practical missions. In contrast, Henry wanted to stimulate research through cash awards, the direct support of research, and the publication of contributions to knowledge.

Yet despite Henry's apparent hostility to the Wilkes collections, these specimens and the whole area of natural history were less controversial, less subject to bitter acrimony, in Henry's tenure than the problem of the Institution's library. As a result, the Smithsonian today has the National Museum of Natural History, but its extensive library was transferred to the Library of Congress in 1866.

That museums are part of the Smithsonian, despite Henry's initial attitude, can be credited to three things: first, Henry's sympathy to natural history research, as differentiated from natural history museums; second, the arrival of Spencer F. Baird as assistant secretary; third, the great flood of government collections during the 1850s and Henry's recognition that, unlike the situation regarding the library, there was no proper alternative depository for these specimens except the Smithsonian.

It is important to remember that Henry had experience with natural history cabinets in Albany and to realize that he explicitly included descriptive natural history as one of the fields that the Smithsonian should support, along with meteorology, experimental physics and chemistry, the gathering of statistical data in both the natural and social sciences, history, and ethnology. But Henry drew a distinction between research collections and museums. The former were a tool in the active expansion of human knowledge. Their scope was national or international. In contrast, museums were at best passive diffusers of knowledge, serving local needs. The Smithson bequest was too important and too special to be used in that manner. With this goal in mind, Henry announced in 1850 that he was determined to limit the natural history holdings "to objects of a special character, or to such as may lead to the discovery of new truths, or which may serve to verify or disprove existing or proposed scientific generalizations." Funds would not be expended on "the reproduction of collections of objects which are to be found in every museum of the country." [Smithsonian Regents 1853:194] Any assistant Henry obtained to aid in the Smithsonian's activities in the field of natural history would thus have to be on the forefront of research. In Spencer F. Baird he found such a man.

Baird was born in Reading, Pennsylvania, in 1823. When he was ten, his widowed mother moved the family to Carlisle, Pennsylvania, nearer her own

family and the site of Dickinson College, which Baird attended from 1836 through 1840. There he acquired the typical antebellum liberal arts education, characterized by breadth but not depth. While better educated than Henry in the most general sense, he had had comparatively little more preparation for a scientific career. He was concurrently developing an expertise as a field naturalist, but under the tutelage of his elder brother William, a respected amateur ornithologist, not at Dickinson. When William moved to Washington, D.C., in 1840, Baird found other sponsors and teachers. In June of that year he initiated a correspondence with John J. Audubon, impressing the artist-naturalist with his talent and obtaining an invitation to collect for Audubon. Three months later, Baird expanded his contacts in science even further by a visit to the Academy of Natural Sciences of Philadelphia, where he met most of the leading Philadelphia naturalists not on the Wilkes Expedition, and developed a network for the exchange of specimens. In 1841 Baird enrolled in the College of Physicians and Surgeons in New York City, ostensibly to study medicine. In fact, in the three months he was a student, he attended the science lectures (chemistry, botany, and anatomy) but ignored those lectures dealing with medical topics. Much of his time in New York was spent in the company of Audubon and other naturalists. It was soon obvious that Baird was not going to earn his living as a physician.

What was not so obvious was how he would support himself if dedicated to natural history. Fortunately, from 1842 through 1846 he was able to live off the bounty of his family while ever expanding his relationships with the American scientific community. By the end of this period, while he was still in his early twenties, Baird was in correspondence with some two hundred naturalists and collectors. Trips to Philadelphia and New York became commonplace. Boston and New Haven were also visited. It can be safely said that he knew almost everybody worth knowing in American natural history. Perhaps most important for the future, at least as a foreshadowing, was his stay with his brother William in Washington from November 1843 through January 1844. During this trip he met James Dwight Dana and assisted him with the

Great Hall of the Smithsonian Building as it looked in the early 1860s. Woodcut from William J. Rhees, An Account of the Smithsonian Institution *(Philadelphia, 1865), p. 20. Courtesy Smithsonian Institution Libraries.*

Crustacea collections of the Wilkes Expedition, turning him into a strong ally. Finally, in 1846, Baird received a salaried professorship of natural history at his alma mater. He remained at Dickinson until the call from the Smithsonian in 1850.

Henry was not unaware of Baird's existence. Dana had recommended Baird for a position as an assistant soon after the Smithsonian was organized. Baird had written Henry in February 1847, announcing his candidacy for the post of curator and offering both himself and his collections. At that time Baird carefully mentioned some of his friends and correspondents in the scientific world, many of whom were known to Henry personally. He also emphasized his dedication to scientific research, his accomplishments to date, and the publications that would see light in the future. The case was made that Baird was both an experienced field naturalist and familiar with the international literature. During the next three years Baird kept himself in Henry's eye, both directly and through the efforts of his friends and fellow scientists. Ultimately, when Henry finally decided in 1850 that the natural history activities of the Smithsonian, as well as the international exchange and the publication program, had reached a level where an assistant with responsibility for these areas was necessary, he chose Baird over the much more experienced naturalist Titian Peale.

Henry's reasoning in selecting Baird over Peale is revealing of Henry's priorities. If he simply wanted someone to run a natural history museum or take care of specimens, he might well have selected Peale. But Henry still rejected the idea of accepting the Wilkes collections and having a museum. The assistant secretary was also to have responsibility for the international exchange and the publication program. Such responsibilities necessitated a facility in languages and experience in the oversight of publications. Baird had that facility and that experience. Indeed, although Henry did admire Baird's scientific accomplishments, and had stated that he wanted "an original investigator and not a mere curator of a museum," [Henry 1849] he explicitly claimed that Baird "was not appointed on account of his capability as a naturalist." [Henry 1850] It was his other skills and experience that were essential. That Baird also personally owned a natural history cabinet which filled two boxcars, and would be donated to the Smithsonian was probably incidental to Henry's decision, and to the future of the Smithsonian.

When Baird arrived at the Smithsonian, Henry had already initiated a program of support of natural history research and the acquisition of research collections. Some of this material was purchased from collectors; some was acquired at the cost of transportation. In any case, the acquisition was planned, not accidental. Very specific specimens were obtained. Baird greatly expanded this activity. He also facilitated the Smithsonian's cooperation with the government's massive program of exploration of the West in the 1850s to ensure that one of its fruits would be more exact knowledge of the flora and fauna of the United States.

The period between the Mexican War and Civil War was one of a "grand national reconnaissance of the entire trans-Mississippi country." [Goetzmann 1972:303] The Army Corps of Topographical Engineers surveyed possible railroad routes to the Pacific Ocean, possible supply routes for armies operating against the Mormons in Utah, transportation routes for troops fighting the Sioux in the Dakotas, and the Mexican boundary. Whatever the primary mission of the survey teams, they were all accompanied by naturalists, brought back specimens, and published reports. No doubt learning from both their own past experience and those of the Wilkes Expedition, these army surveys were generally charac-terized by cooperation between the civilian and military components, as well as rapid publication of results.

The Smithsonian's initial role was to supply the expeditions with "all necessary instruments and apparatus for natural history research, much of it contrived with special reference to the exigencies of the particular service involved." [Smithsonian Regents 1853:50] In those cases where expedition personnel were unfamiliar with the fundamentals of natural history collecting, instruction was provided. The Smithsonian also disseminated the collected specimens to the appropriate scientists and artists. All this was done at the government's expense, the Smithsonian acting as supervisor without having to commit its slender resources.

In terms of the number of specimens, the return from these surveys of the 1850s dwarfed all predecessors, including the Wilkes Expedition. Exact figures are impossible to determine, because Baird reported donations and additions by jars, with the number of specimens per jar not stated beyond the term "considerable." In addition, the Smithsonian always had a major backlog of material received but not recorded. Some sense of the quantity may be deduced from Henry's 1855 claim of having the finest collection of American fauna in the world. Yet over the next two years the number of recorded specimens doubled. When the Smithsonian acquired the Wilkes collections in 1858, Henry reported that they only made up one-fifth of the natural history holdings of the Smithsonian at that time.

In fact, the Smithsonian was only receiving a proportion of the specimens gathered during these surveys. Some were being sent directly to the leading researchers in the respective fields, such as the paleontologist Joseph Leidy at the Academy of Natural Sciences of Philadelphia, or the botanists John Torrey or Asa Gray, neither man directly affiliated with the Smithsonian nor a resident of Washington.

Thus, if the presence of the Wilkes material at the Patent Office represented a problem for the American government, it was minor compared to the scale of the problem created by this new and larger influx of government collections. It was nec-

"Laboratory of Natural History" as it looked in the early 1860s. Woodcut from William J. Rhees, An Account of the Smithsonian Institution *(Philadelphia, 1865), p. 21. Courtesy Smithsonian Institution Libraries.*

essary to find a home for them. The obvious solution was the Smithsonian. This time Henry agreed, bowing to the inevitable, even accepting the Wilkes collections, while always attempting to keep his options open. He never lost his fear that the costs of exhibition might overwhelm the research efforts of the Smithsonian, which he felt was its reason for existence. Neither did he ever concede that the solution was anything but temporary.

The first indication that Henry was willing to modify his position on the Wilkes collections appeared in 1853, perhaps not coincidentally the same year that the first major influx of specimens from

the army surveys began streaming eastward. Thereafter, the fate of the army and navy specimens and that of the National Museum became intertwined.

In the same annual report that Henry announced that the Institution was taking "temporary" charge of specimens from the army surveys, he reported a suggestion by the commissioner of patents that a portion of the Smithsonian building be purchased to store the Wilkes collections. Since Henry viewed the "castle" on the Mall as an expensive white elephant foisted on the Smithsonian over his loud objections, he responded to the commissioner's suggestion with enthusiasm. He even offered the

Smithsonian's services as the supervisor of the resulting National Museum and promised that the army survey collections would be turned over to the museum as soon as they had been scientifically described. It is important to note that Henry was not envisioning the National Museum as a function of the Smithsonian, but rather the Smithsonian as an independent operator of the National Museum. With the museum taking the fiscal responsibility for preserving the natural history specimens gathered by agents of the government, the Smithsonian would be free to continue to concentrate on the increase and diffusion of basic research.

By 1856 the flood of specimens from the army in the West made the situation acute. In 1854, for example, four surveys were examining possible routes for a Pacific railroad, each accompanied by a scientific corps. Henry could not, in good conscience, refuse to accept the fruits of these surveys. There was no alternative home for them, and he could not allow this potential treasure trove of scientific information to be destroyed through neglect. One stopgap measure was to send specimens to researchers outside Washington rather than require them to come to the specimens. This made it easier for scientists to conduct their research and, at the same time, reduced the pressures on the limited space at the Smithsonian. But a dark future seemed inevitable. The influx of government specimens into the Smithsonian would continue, making the Institution the home of the National Museum in fact, if not in law. Rather than let that happen, and see the Smithson bequest be swallowed up by the costs of maintaining the collections, Henry called for the adoption of the suggestion by the commissioner of patents. Let Congress establish a National Museum in the Smithsonian building. Designate the Smithsonian "curator" of that museum. Charge the expenses of maintaining these national collections to the federal government. The Wilkes collections could come over to the Smithsonian, as long as Congress appropriated funds for their care.

This Congress did on 3 March 1857, providing $15,000 for the construction and erection of exhibit cases, $2,000 to cover the cost of moving the specimens, and an annual appropriation of $4,000. The specimens were installed in July 1858. The next year the *Guide to the Smithsonian Institution and National Museum* was published, and the words "National Museum of the United States" appeared over the entry to the Great Hall of the Smithsonian building.

In terms of public exhibition, a great milestone had been reached. Before the Wilkes collections came in 1858, the Smithsonian had not displayed natural history specimens. Specimens were accessible to anyone with a serious need to examine them, but they were not available for the satisfaction of the idle curiosity of the casual visitor. Henry's excuse was the lack of funds. He was very conscious of the need to exhibit specimens properly to the public, if they were to be exhibited at all. Of course, he had hoped not to exhibit at all.

As was indicated earlier, Henry did not believe that the establishment of the National Museum in the Smithsonian building marked the eternal marriage between the museum and the Smithsonian. He hoped, even assumed, that the arrangement was only temporary. Indeed, the high quality of the public exhibition set up in the Great Hall was not a reflection of Henry's dedication to exhibits, but part of his plan to get rid of the museum. He believed that if he made the museum popular, Congress would rush to relieve the Smithsonian from the expense and even the care of the collections. Henry's true attitude toward public show was presented in a letter to his friend Asa Gray: "It does not become the dignity of the Institution to do any thing for popular effect on its own account but as the custodian of the government property it will be obliged to do something in the way of display." [Henry 1857]

Henry's vision of the National Museum was also much narrower than the present National Museum of Natural History. Citing the limited funds available, Henry declared that unless other sources of revenue were provided beyond the $4,000 appropriation, the Smithsonian would confine the scope of the collections of the museum to North America. Within that limitation, however, the collection would be as complete as possible. Ideally, visitors would be able to see "a full series of natural objects belonging to each State." [Smithsonian Regents

Photograph of the Great Hall of the Smithsonian Building, ca. 1872. Courtesy Smithsonian Institution Archives.

West Range of the Smithsonian Building, looking toward the Library, ca. 1862. The photograph is attributed to Titian Ramsay Peale. Courtesy Smithsonian Institution Archives.

1858:55] The more exotic flora and fauna would have to be ignored. Not that the navy, merchant marine, government officials, and American travelers abroad could not be persuaded to collect specimens. Henry was sure they could. But there was simply neither room nor money for the preservation of the exotica.

Although the arrival of the Wilkes collections represented a clear milestone in the history of the Smithsonian's exhibition policy, it was less significant from an intellectual perspective, at least to Henry. Quantitatively, the material from the Patent Office was simply not that important—it represented only one-fifth of the natural history holdings of the Smithsonian in 1858. Viewed qualitatively, the problem was that the bulk of the Wilkes material came from outside North America, outside the geographical limitation Henry had imposed in order to avoid dissipating the resources of the Institution. The value of the Wilkes collections was further lessened because so much of the material had already been worked up. It was far better, in Henry's mind, to concentrate on specimens that had not yet been examined.

The ensuing history of the National Museum during Henry's tenure as secretary was one of growth on one hand, and, on the other, Henry's efforts to separate the Smithsonian from the museum and prevent these huge collections from ultimately constricting the Smithsonian's ability to do what it did best and uniquely in nineteenth-century America, support scientific research. In fact, Henry was able to win a number of victories on the fiscal front. The appropriation by Congress for the museum did increase over the years. By 1874 it had reached $15,000 for the preservation of the collections, the same amount for fitting out the halls, and $12,000 for steam-heating the museum. The government was paying for the upkeep of the museum (with the exception, as Henry was fond of pointing out, of rent for the space it was occupying in the Smithsonian's building), although Henry was not happy with the political lobbying necessary to persuade the government to meet its obligation.

Victories of this sort were not enough, however. Henry's conception of the Smithsonian was about to be doomed by circumstance. If the explosive increase in government collections during the 1850s threatened Henry's concept and forced a compromise, the Centennial of 1876 shattered it. The massive government exhibits were to be put on display in Washington at the close of the exposi-

tion. To increase the burden on the Smithsonian even more, many of the foreign and state exhibits were also donated to the National Museum. It was obvious that more space was absolutely necessary. The best solution appeared to be the construction of a separate building for the National Museum. Henry, ever the optimist, hoped that such a building would divorce the Smithsonian and the National Museum. But by the time Congress appropriated one-quarter of a million dollars for the new building (now known as the Arts and Industries Building), Henry was dead and Baird was his successor. The new secretary had no intention of giving up the National Museum.

The changes wrought on Henry's concept did not end with Baird's commitment to the museum. Henry, the physicist, had had a broad vision of the scientific needs of the nation. Under him, the Smithsonian showed no favoritism regarding disciplines. Meteorology, natural history, archeology, and anthropology were all supported. In contrast, Baird tilted the Smithsonian's programs away from the physical sciences and toward the biological. The balance temporarily disappeared. The Smithsonian became identified in the public mind more with the museum than with grants to scientists.

Within that museum, the Wilkes collections have remained as a symbol of the support of the federal government for exploration, exhibition, and research. In its time the Wilkes Expedition represented a major allocation of resources; it demonstrated that American science had come of age. Since then there have been many expeditions, many exhibitions, and much research. Today the Wilkes collections are but a tiny fraction of the holdings of the Smithsonian. We have come very, very far.

The following drawings are by Expedition artist Alfred T. Agate. They are part of a collection of his drawings and engravings that were purchased in 1945 by the Naval Historical Foundation from Elizabeth A. Duhamel, whose mother had been briefly married to Agate upon his return from the Expedition. Their marriage ended within a few months and without issue because of his untimely death at the age of 33. These drawings are significant not only because they form the basis for many of the illustrations that were published in the official narrative, but also because they include additional firsthand depictions of personnel, vessels, and scenes associated with the U.S. Exploring Expedition. The drawings are reproduced through the courtesy of Captain David A. Long, USN Retired, the Executive Director of the Naval Historical Foundation, who brought them to the attention of the editors of this volume, while the publication was in press. The photographs themselves are by Charles Phillips.

Characteristics of Selected Exploring Vessels

Year of Launch	Name	Type	Displacement	Length (BP)	Beam	Depth in Hold	Guns	Speed (knots)	Crew	Original Purpose
International Vessels										
1768	Endeavour	bark	369 t	98′	29′	13.5′	6	—	—	collier
	Descubierta	corvette	306 t	109′	28.5′	13.8′	16	—	104	corvette
	L'Astrolabe	corvette	380 t	94′	29′	13′	10	—	98	horse transport
1826	Erebus	bomb ketch	378 t	106′	29′	—	—	—	—	bomb ketch
Exploring Expedition Vessels										
1826	Vincennes	sloop of war	700 t	127′	34.75′	16.5′	10	10.5	190	sloop of war
1828	Peacock	sloop of war	559 t	118′	31.5′	15.5′	10	11	130	sloop of war
1836	Porpoise	brig	224 t	88′	25′	11′	4	10	65	brigantine
	Relief	storeship	468 t	109′	30′	12′	6	8.5	75	storeship
	Oregon	transport	250 t	85′	22′	11′	2	—	—	merchant brig
	Sea Gull	tender	110 t	73.5′	20.5′	9.75′	2	—	15	pilot schooner
	Flying Fish	tender	96 t	70.25′	19.75′	8′	2	—	15	pilot schooner

This Appendix was compiled by Philip K. Lundeberg

William L. Hudson

Iron Men and Wooden Ships: A Chronology, 1838–1842

This chronology lists the dates, times, positions, places, and events as reported by Charles Wilkes in his five-volume *Narrative of the United States Exploring Expedition* (Philadelphia: Lea and Blanchard, 1845) as compiled from the chart showing the track of the *Vincennes* during the Expedition. The *Vincennes* may, or may not, have been in company with other ships of the squadron. Each ship was given individual instructions on surveys to be performed, on when and where to rendezvous, and on other details of the overall purpose of the expedition, after which each proceeded independently to carry out those instructions. Thus, while there were occasions when all ships engaged in a common endeavor, the individual commanders, William L. Hudson, the *Peacock*, Cadwalader Ringgold, the *Porpoise*, R.F. Pinkney, the *Flying Fish*, and James W.E. Reid, the *Sea Gull* until lost at sea, did their share in contributing to the success of the Expedition.

Heroics and hard work were commonplace under sail. Men fell ill, were injured, and some died, to be buried at sea or interred on some unnamed island. Yet at no time did these truly "iron men" shirk their duty as they strove to complete what was to become the last great circumnavigation of the globe under sail.

This appendix was compiled by Commander Bernard M. Kassell, USN (Ret)

Vincennes

1838

18 August	Departed Norfolk, Virginia
25 August	On course to Madeira
26 August	Parted company with *Peacock* and *Flying Fish*
1 September	38°30'N, 47°30'W
8 September	37°17'N, 34°08'W
10 September	38°N, 25°W
16 September	Arrived Funchal, Madeira
25 September	Departed Funchal, Madeira
7 October	Anchored Porto Praya Bay, Cape Verde Islands
	Departed Cape Verde Islands
10 October	11°30'N, 24°W
20 October	7°N, 21°W
24 October	5°4'N, 21°25'W
1 November	3°N, 13°30'W
5 November	Crossed the equator southbound in 17°W
7 November	3°30'S, 18°20'W at 1200 hours
10 November	3°S, 20°30'W
13 November	6°15'S, 24°25'W
16 November	Crossed magnetic equator in 13°30'S, 30°18'W, variation 10°30'W
20 November	15°S, 31°W
22 November	Made Cape Frio, Brazil
23 November	Arrived Rio de Janeiro, Brazil

1839

6 January	Departed Rio de Janeiro, Brazil
10 January	25°S, 43°30′W
18 January	78 miles off the mouth of Rio la Plata
20 January	40°S, 55°W
25 January	Arrived Rio Negro, Argentina
3 February	Departed Rio Negro, Argentina
10 February	48°S, 60°W
13–16 February	Enroute Orange Harbor, Tierra del Fuego, via Staten Land, Cape St. Diego, Tierra del Fuego, Straits of LeMaire, Hermit Island, and Nassau Bay
18 February	Arrived Orange Harbor, on west side of Nassau Bay, 55°30′50″S, 68°00′23″W

First Antarctic Expedition

25 February	0700 hours Wilkes, embarked in *Porpoise*, departed Orange Harbor with *Sea Gull* in company, *Peacock* and *Flying Fish* following

1 March	First ice islands made. At 1200 hours made land, Ridley's Island
3 March	Enroute for Palmer's Island. At 0630 hours sighted Mount Hope, east point of Palmer's Land, in 63°25′S, 57°55′W
5 March	*Sea Gull* ordered to return to Orange Harbor via Deception Island. Decided to return to Orange Harbor as soon as possible in view of conditions
14 March	Made land
16 March	Off Straits of LeMaire
17 March	Put into Good Success Bay to wait out storm
20 March	Put to sea to ride out storm
25 March	Returned to Good Success Bay
28 March	Departed for Orange Harbor
30 March	Arrived Orange Harbor End of First Antarctic Expedition
17 April	Departed Orange Harbor for Valparaiso, Chile
21 April	Lost sight of land, passing to northward of Diego Ramieres Island

28 April	56°30′S, 78°30′W
30 April	43°S, 76°W
10 May	Island of Mocha
13 May	36°S
15 May	Arrived Valparaiso, Chile
6 June	Departed Valparaiso for Callao, Peru
May	*Sea Gull* presumed lost at sea with all hands between Orange Harbor and Valparaiso, Chile
12 June	28°34′S, 74°40′W
20 June	Arrived San Lorenzo Island. *Relief* smoked to destroy rats. Marines punished by lashing; that became one reason for court-martial of Wilkes upon return
30 June	Departed San Lorenzo Island for Callao, arriving same day
8 July	Private Benjamin Holdien, Marine Corps, died of smallpox. Interred San Lorenzo Island

*Beginning of Survey of Western Pacific**

13 July	Departed Callao, Peru, for Paumotu (Tuamotu) Group, or Cloud of Islands. Enroute for Minerva or Clermont de Tonnerre (Reao) Island. General order on behavior issued
20 July	16°30′S, 92°W
24 July	15°35′S, 99°39′W
30 July	17°36′S, 113°29′W
1 August	17°S, 114°W
7 August	18°14′S, 125°W
10 August	18°S, 131°W
12 August	Corporal Alexander Ogle, Marine Corps, died of inflammation of the brain and was buried at sea with honors
13 August	Made Clermont de Tonnerre, SE point 18°32′49″S, 136°21′12″W
16 August	Serle Island (Pukarua), SE end 18°21′10″S, 137°04′10″W
19 August	Henuake or Honden or Dog (Pukapuka) Island, center 14°55′40″S, 138°47′36″W
23 August	Made Disappointment Islands, Wytoohee (Napuka) and Otooho (Tepoto)
29 August	Uncharted island, center in 15°42′25″S, 144°38′45″W, named King's (Taiaro) Island for man at masthead who first sighted it
30 August	En route for Raraka. Uncharted island sighted en route

_____

* Modern names, where known, are in parentheses.

30 August	Arrived Raraka, 16°06′25″S, 144°57′40″W
2 September	Arrived Vincennes (Kauehi) or Kawahe Island, 15°59′48″S, 145°09′30″W
4 September	Waterlandt Island or Wilson's or Manhii (Manihi) Island, 14°26′22″S, 146°04′20″W, surveyed 5 and 6 September
9 September	Metia or Aurora (Makatea) Island, 15°49′35″S, 148°13′15″W
9 September	Departed for Tahiti, Society Group
10 September	Arrived Tahiti, Matavai Bay
22 September	Departed Matavai Bay for Papieti (Papeete) Harbor
25 September	Departed Papieti (Papeete) Harbor for Eimeo (Moorea)
29 September	Departed Society Group
30 September	Landed on Bellinghausen's Island, departed same day for Rose Island in the Samoan Group
1 October	16°S, 156°W
7 October	Arrived Rose Island, departed same day

8 October	Arrived Manua (Manu'a) Island, departed same day; arrived Oloosinga (Olosega) Island, departed same day for Tutuila
11 October	Arrived Tutuila. Surveys and exploration included islands of Upolu, Manono, and Savaii
25 October	Departed Tutuila for survey Apia, Upolu
10 November	Departed Apia for Sydney, Australia
11 November	Out of sight of Savaii Island, Samoan Group
12 November	Uea or Wallis Island, 13°24′S, 176°09′22″E
13 November	Hoorn Island. Passed 60 miles west of Feejee (Fiji) Group Crossed International Date Line, dropped 14 November 1839
18 November	Matthews Rock, height 1,186′, 22°27′S, 172°10′33″E
20 November	26°S, 170°E
24 November	Electrical storm during which St. Elmo's fire was observed
29 November	Arrived Port Jackson, Sydney, New South Wales, New Holland (Australia) and anchored at 2200 hours with *Peacock*
30 November	*Porpoise* and *Flying Fish* arrive

Second Antarctic Expedition

26 December	Departed Sydney for Antarctica at 0600 hours. Two stowaways found on board and taken on as hands
31 December	43°S

1840

2 January	Lost sight of *Flying Fish* in 48°S and not seen again until return
3 January	Lost sight of *Peacock*
6 January	53°30′S, 157°35′E
7 January	54°20′S, 160°47′E. Unable to make Macquairie Island. Stood for Emerald Island
8 January	55°38′S, 162°13′E
9 January	57°15′S, 162°30′E. Emerald Island not sighted
10 January	First iceberg sighted in 61°08′S, 162°32′E
11 January	64°11′S, 164°30′E
15 January	*Peacock* and *Porpoise* once again in company with *Vincennes*

16 January	Date of discovery claimed for squadron. 157°46′E
19 January	66°20′S, 154°30′E. Sun and moon both appeared above the horizon at the same time
20 January	*Peacock* observed conflict as a "killer" whale hung onto another whale's lower jaw
24 January	*Peacock* suffered heavy damage to rudder in 65°55′20″S, 151°18′45″E and is ordered to proceed to Sydney for repairs
	Disappointment Bay, 67°04′30″S, 147°30′E. *Porpoise* and *Vincennes* in company
29 January	63°30′S, 140°E
30 January	Gave the land the name of the Antarctic Continent. 66°45′S, 140°02′30″E
31 January	Medical officers concerned about health of crews
7 February	Cape sighted in 64°49′S, 131°40′E named Cape Carr for First Lieutenant of *Vincennes*
8 February	65°03′S, 127°07′E
10 February	65°27′S, 122°35′E
12 February	64°57′S, 112°16′12″E
13 February	65°57′S, 106°40′E
14 February	65°59′40″S, 106°18′42″E
15 February	64°06′S, 104°E
16 February	64°21′S, 99°E
17 February	64°01′S, 97°37′E
19 February	63°02′S, 101°E
21 February	Ice exploration terminated. Sets course to north
1 March	50°S, 132°E
10 March	36°S, 148°E
11 March	Arrived Sydney
19 March	Departed Sydney at 1500 hours for Tongataboo via New Zealand
25 March	34°24′S, 160°26′E
29 March	North Cape, New Zealand
30 March	Anchored in Kawa-Kawa River, Bay of Islands, New Zealand
6 April	*Vincennes, Porpoise,* and *Flying Fish* depart Bay of Islands for Tongataboo
11 April	29°S, 178°W
14 April	Sunday Island, 29°12′S, 178°15′W
20 April	24°26′S, 174°47′30″W
24 April	Tongataboo and Eooa of Hapai Group (Friendly Isles of Cook)
1 May	*Peacock* rejoined squadron after repairs in Sydney
4 May	Departed Nukualofa, Tongataboo

5 May	Sighted Turtle Island, 19°50′S, 178°37′13″W	14 July	Burned town of Tye in retaliation for natives having stolen a boat and removing contents valued at over $1,000
6 May	Extensive surveys in Feejee (Fiji) Group began		
17 May	Private David Bateman, Marine Corps, assigned to *Porpoise* but transferred to *Vincennes*, died of lung ailment	16 July	Conducted survey of Anganga Island
		24 July	Battle on Malolo Island. Lieutenant Joseph A. Underwood and Midshipman Wilkes Henry, the commander's nephew, were killed and buried on an island about 10 miles from Malolo. Wilkes named the group, six in all, the Underwood Group, and the burial island Henry Island
9 June	*Porpoise* rejoined squadron at Somu-somu, having been detached since 8 May off Fulanga Island to survey eastern islands		
18 June	Anchored Levuka, 17°40′46″S, 178°52′40″E		
28 June	Departed Levuka	31 July	Vatulele and Mbenga islands surveyed
5 July	Anchored Mbua Bay, 16°39′24″S, 178°31′30″E	1 August	Kantavu Island, 18°58′34″S

4 August	Ovolau Island, 17°40′46.79″S, 178°52′40.78″E, selected as site of a laboratory and as a point of departure for extensive area surveys and exploration
11 August	End of observations in Feejee (Fiji) Group. Under way northbound for Oahu, Sandwich (Hawaiian) Islands
13 August	Passed from east to west longitude. Changed dates
14 August	Ships parted company for independent surveys
16 August	5°41′S, 175°46′W
18 August	Second anniversary of sailing from Hampton Roads, Virginia
19 August	Kemin's or Gardner's Island, 4°37′42″S, 174°40′18″W
	Uncharted island sighted in 3°35′10″S, 174°17′26″W. Named M'Kean's Island for first man who sighted it.
26 August	Uncharted island sighted in 4°29′48″S, 172°20′52″W. Named Hull's Island for outstanding U.S. Navy officer
28 August	Enderbury's Island sighted in 3°08′S, 171°08′30″W
1 September	3°30′S, 170°W
4 September	Crossed the equator in 167°45′30″W
7 September	Crossed the magnetic equator in 7°10′N, 162°25′W
10 September	8°N, 161°10′W
17 September	21°33′N, 161°37′W, 200 miles west of Oahu, Hawaiian Islands
20 September	Kauai sighted
23 September	Made Oahu
24 September	Anchored in Honolulu roads at 0830 hours
25 September	Stood into harbor and moored to buoys
30 September	*Peacock* arrived
8 October	*Porpoise* arrived, 30 days out of Samoan Islands
	Wilkes now deemed it too late in the year to begin operations off the northwest coast of the United States. *Peacock*, Hudson, therefore was ordered to return to the Samoan Group, visit Ellice and Kingsmill, and rejoin the squadron at the Columbia River at the end of April 1841. *Porpoise*, Ringgold, was ordered back to the Paumotu Group, afterward to touch Tahiti, Penrhyn, and Flint, and return to Oahu before 1 April 1841. *Vincennes* was to visit Hawaii, the Marquesas, and return to rendezvous with *Porpoise* for voyage to the northwest coast of the United States. *Flying Fish*, Sinclair, was to accompany *Peacock*

16 November	*Porpoise* departed for Paumotu Group
	The end of November was the ". . . eve of sailing to examine parts of the ocean of great interest to that important branch of national industry, the whale-fishery. . . ." (*Narrative*, IV, 103)
2 December	*Peacock* and *Flying Fish* departed to middle and extreme western part of the cruising ground of U.S. whale-ships
3 December	*Vincennes* began exploration of Hawaiian Islands lasting into 1841

1841

19 March	*Vincennes* returned to Honolulu to make preparations for departure to the Columbia River
24 March	*Porpoise* arrived Honolulu after a voyage that lasted 4 months and 9 days, only 8 of which were spent in port
5 April	Departed Honolulu for the United States at 1130 hours
10 April	25°N, 162°W
12 April	25°N, 160°W
20 April	35°N, 153°W
28 April	Made Cape Disappointment at 0600 hours, 22 days out of Oahu
1 May	Well inside Strait of Juan de Fuca
2 May	Anchored Port Discovery
6 May	Departed Port Discovery
7 May	Port Townsend
8 May	Port Lawrence
11 May	Fort Nisqually. Wilkes departed *Vincennes* for inland exploration
16 June	Wilkes returned to *Vincennes*
17 June	Under way for Port Lawrence
	At this point a major concern was the whereabouts of *Peacock* and *Flying Fish*, now three months overdue
19 June	Anchored off Port Lawrence
20 June	Anchored in New Dungeness Roads and joined by *Porpoise*
4 July	Point Roberts
27 July	Advised of loss of *Peacock* on bar at the mouth of the Columbia River
2 August	Lunar eclipse
6 August	Cape Disappointment. *Flying Fish* joined at 1200 hours. Captain Hudson reported on board to tell of loss of *Peacock*, which struck the bar at approximately 1205 hours on 18 July and was finally abandoned without loss of life at 1700 hours on 20 July

7 August	Wilkes decided to shift his pennant to *Porpoise* then take boats from *Flying Fish* and *Peacock* to survey the Columbia River. Ringgold to take *Vincennes* to San Francisco and survey Sacramento River	20 October	*Oregon* made safe arrival
		28 October	Preparations were begun for departure from San Francisco for Hawaiian Islands on first fair wind
	Arrangements made to purchase brig *Thomas H. Perkins*, located in Astoria, to replace *Peacock*	1 November	Under way but encountered heavy swells and had to anchor. At 0330 hours on 2 November Private Joseph Alshouse, Marine Corps, was hit by a falling spar and died a few hours later
9 August	Began survey		
10 August	Brig purchased for the United States for $9,000 and renamed *Oregon*, Hudson in charge	5 November	33°N, 126°W
		7 November	26°N, 134°W
		10 November	21°N, 141°W
18 August	*Porpoise* and *Oregon* departed Astoria with *Flying Fish* in company	14 November	25°48′N, 151°36′W
		16 November	Maui made
1 October	Returned to Astoria	17 November	Anchored off Honolulu at 1000 hours. *Porpoise* anchored at 1400 hours, *Flying Fish* at 1700 hours. *Oregon* joined on 18 November
5 October	Departed Astoria and crossed bar bound for San Francisco at 1530 hours		
15 October	Wilkes in *Porpoise* parts company with *Oregon* and heads south	19 November	Squadron moored in Honolulu Harbor
		27 November	Squadron departed Hawaiian Islands at 2000 hours under the following order:
19 October	Arrived in Sausalito Bay at 1500 hours and anchored near *Vincennes*, which had arrived at Yerba Buena on 14 August to begin survey of Sacramento River		*Porpoise* and *Oregon* were to sail a WNW course from the Hawaiian Islands until into the Japan Current,

thence through the China Sea to Singapore

Vincennes and *Flying Fish* were to sail to Manila via Strong and Ascension islands, thence to Singapore

Estimated time of arrival in the United States was 31 May 1842, requiring that a 142-day passage be made in six months

29 November	Ordered *Flying Fish*, Acting-Master S. R. Knox, to proceed to Strong and Ascension islands, thence to Manila, with an estimated time of arrival 19 January 1842
30 November	*Vincennes* proceeded unaccompanied
1 December	19°19′N, 165°25′W. Maloon's Island not sighted
	19°17′N, 166°48′W. Charted island not sighted
3 December	18°20′N, 170°30′W. Reported shoal not found
	16°10′N, 173°15′W. Jane's Island not sighted
6 December	15°N, 175°W. Gaspar Island not sighted
7 December	Crossed the International Date Line, dropped a day and passed into east longitude
14 December	15°N, 174°50′E
15 December	16°N, 171°42′E. Reported island not found
	16°51′N, 169°33′E. Cornwallis Island not sighted
20 December	Wake Island
27 December	19°13′N, 163°30′E. Halcyon Island not sighted
	18°21′N, 155°19′E. Folger's Island not sighted
29 December	Made Grigan, the northernmost of the inhabited Ladrone of Marian islands at 0700 hours. Assumption Island at 2400 hours

1842

1 January	Enroute to Cooper's Island. 19°N, 154°E
4 January	20°11′N, 131°54′E. Abajos Shoal not found
8 January	Sabtang. 20°18′N, 121°50′30″E Departed Pacific Ocean
12 January	Approached Manila. *Flying Fish* arrived at 1530 hours Anchored 8 miles from Manila after dark
13 January	Anchored in 6 fathoms in roadstead by 0900 hours

21 January	Departed Manila southbound for Straits of Mindoro *Flying Fish* in company
22 January	Dispatched *Flying Fish* to survey Apo Shoal between Palawan and Mindoro Passed entrance to Straits of San Bernadino British and Spanish charts useless
27 January	Continued survey of Panay coast
31 January	Anchored Caldera, Mindanao
1 February	Anchored off Sangboys Island for the night
2 February	Under way westbound
4 February	Towed by boats into Bay of Soung, Sooloo Island, 6°01′N, 120°55′51″E
6 February	Departed Straits of Balabac
7 February	7°03′30″N, 118°37′E
8 February	Mangsee Islands at 0900 hours
13 February	Reported Viper Shoal not found
18 February	Straits of Singapore
19 February	Anchored in Singapore Roads at 1700 hours *Porpoise* had arrived on 22 January *Oregon* had arrived on 22 January *Flying Fish* had arrived on 16 February *Flying Fish* in no condition to continue Decision made to sell the ship, which was done at public sale for $3,700
26 February	Underway at 0500 hours with *Porpoise* and *Oregon*. *Vincennes* to stop at Cape

of Good Hope for bread. *Porpoise* and *Oregon* to proceed to Rio de Janeiro for bread as well as for further observations and additional specimens of natural history

Passage made through Straits of Rio

28 February	Passed Linten Island enroute Straits of Banca
1 March	Approached north entrance to Straits of Banca
2 March	Transited Straits of Banca
3 March	Anchored near Two Brothers
4 March	George Porter died during the night. Buried at sea with customary ceremony and honors
5 March	Arrived at Hout's Island, the entrance to Straits of Sunda
6 March	Stood into Indian Ocean
7 March	Homeward bound
	Vincennes parted with *Porpoise,* Ringgold, and *Oregon,* Carr, as per previous instructions. Both were deemed too slow to be kept in company any longer
10 March	14°S, 100°E
12 March	17°S, 98°E
20 March	21°S, 80°E
23 March	Benjamin Vanderford, Master's Mate, died. A former commander of various ships out of Salem, he was a friend of Vendovi and the only man on board who could converse with him
24 March	Vanderford committed to the deep
25 March	23°S, 68°E

25–30 March	Fine weather. Making good 250 miles per day
12 April	Arrived off False Bay
14 April	Anchored in Table Bay, Capetown
17 April	Departed Capetown
19 April	Joseph Sylva (boy) died. Committed to the deep
	Enroute St. Helena. Wilkes hoped to intercept the two brigs and if bread was available proceed directly to the United States with them
30 April	23°S, 2°40'E
1 May	Arrived St. Helena. Brigs had sailed shortly before in good shape
3 May	Departed St. Helena
9 May	Crossed magnetic equator in 9°20'S, 16°40'W
10 May	9°S, 17°W
16 May	Crossed equator in 30°30'W
20 May	4°N, 32°W
26 May	16°N, 48°31'W
2 June	29°N, 68°W
10 June	Pilot anchored ship off Sandy Hook at 1200 hours, cleared quarantine, then proceeded to anchor off the battery where Wilkes turned the ship over to Captain Hudson who took it into the navy yard. Wilkes disembarked from *Vincennes*
	Vendovi was taken to the Naval Hospital New York where he soon died
	Porpoise and *Oregon* arrived in New York within a few days of each other

Landings of the Vessels of the U.S. Exploring Expedition

Flying Fish

No journal in National Archives before September 15, 1839

1839

September 15–October 11	Society Islands
October 18–November 12	Samoan (Navigator) Islands
November 29–December 26	Sydney Harbor, New South Wales

1840

March 9–April 6	Bay of Islands, New Zealand
April 22–May 4	Tonga (Friendly) Islands
May 5–August 16	Fiji Islands
September 19–	Hawaiian Islands

No journal in National Archives after October 1840

Oregon

1841

August 18–October 10	Columbia River
October 19–November 1	San Francisco Bay
November 18–27	Honolulu Harbor

1842

January 22–February 26	Singapore Roads
April 24	St. Helena Island
May 13–22	Rio de Janeiro Harbor

For the landings of the *Vincennes*, see Appendix 2. Appendix 3 was compiled by the staff of the National Archives.

Peacock

1838

September 18–25	Funchal Roads, Madeira Islands
October 5–7	Praia Harbor, Cape Verde Islands
November 21–December 16	Rio de Janeiro Harbor
December 26–January 6, 1839	Rio de Janeiro Harbor

1839

January 26–February 3	Mouth of Rio Negro, Argentina
February 19–25	Orange Harbor, Tierra del Fuego
April 21–June 6	Valparaiso Harbor, Chile
June 20–July 13	Callao Roads, Peru
August 14–September 7	Paumotu (Low) Archipelago
September 8–	Society Islands
?–November 12	Samoan (Navigator) Islands
November 29–December 26	Sydney Harbor, New South Wales

1840

February 21–March 30	Sydney Harbor, New South Wales
April 30–May 5	Tonga (Friendly) Islands
May 6–August 11	Fiji Islands
September 24–December 3	Hawaiian Islands
December 11–14	Washington Island
December 20	Jarvis Island

1841

January 9	Enderbury Island
January 18–February 3	Union Islands
February 5–March 6	Samoan Islands
March 14–24	Ellice Islands
April 3–May 1	Gilbert (Kingsmill) Islands
May 2–9	Marshall Islands
June 14–21	Honolulu Harbor
July 18	Bar of the Columbia River

Porpoise

1838

September 17–25	Funchal Roads, Madeira Islands
October 6–7	Praia Harbor, Cape Verde Islands
November 24–January 6, 1839	Rio de Janeiro Harbor

1839

January 26–February 3	Mouth of Rio Negro, Argentina
February 18–25	Orange Bay, Tierra del Fuego
March 19–26	Good Success Harbor, Tierra del Fuego
May 16–26	Valparaiso Harbor, Chile
June 11–July 13	Callao Roads, Peru
August 14–September 7	Paumotu (Low) Archipelago
September 8–28	Society Islands
October 7–12	Samoan Islands

No journal in National Archives, November 23, 1839–November 15, 1840

1840

November 16	Honolulu
December 11–January 19, 1841	Paumotu (Low) Archipelago

1841

January 21–29	Society Islands
February 16	Penrhyn Island
March 24–April 5	Hawaiian Islands
April 30–August 4	Puget Sound
August 6–October 5	Columbia River
October 18–November 1	San Francisco Bay
November 17–27	Honolulu Harbor

1842

January 22–February 26	Singapore Roads
April 24	St. Helena Island
May 12–22	Rio de Janeiro Harbor

Relief

1838

October 18–21	Praia Harbor, Cape Verde Islands
November 27–December 20	Rio de Janeiro Harbor

1839

January 22–23	Good Success Bay, Tierra del Fuego
January 30–February 26	Orange Bay, Tierra del Fuego
April 15–May 1	Valparaiso Harbor, Chile
May 12–July 16	Callao Roads, Peru
September 5–19	Honolulu Harbor
October 31–November 19	Sydney Harbor, New South Wales

1840

January 27–February 3	Rio de Janeiro Harbor

Sea Gull

No journal in National Archives before February 19, 1839

1839

February 19–25	Orange Harbor, Tierra del Fuego
March 10–13	Pendulum Cove, Tierra del Fuego

No journal in National Archives after March 24, 1839

References

General Sources

References cited by more than one author are listed in this section. References pertinent to only one chapter are grouped by chapter in the sections that follow.

Bartlett, Harley Harris
    1940   The Reports of the Wilkes Expedition, and the Work of the Specialists in Science. *Proceedings of the American Philosophical Society* 82: 601–705.

Gilman, Daniel C.
    1899   *The Life of James Dwight Dana.* New York and London: Harper and Brothers.

Haskell, Daniel C.
    1942   *The United States Exploring Expedition 1838–1842 and Its Publications 1844–1874.* New York: New York Public Library. Reprinted by Greenwood Press, 1968.

Pickering, Charles
    Journal. Massachusetts Historical Society. Copy at the Philadelphia Academy of Natural Sciences.

Poesch, Jessie
    1961   *Titian Ramsay Peale 1799–1885 and His Journals of the Wilkes Expedition.* Philadelphia: American Philosophical Society.

Rhees, William Jones, ed.
    1901   *The Smithsonian Institution: Documents Relative to Its Origin and History, 1835–1851.* Vol. 1. Washington: U.S. Government Printing Office.

Stanton, William
    1975   *The Great United States Exploring Expedition of 1838–1842.* Berkeley, Los Angeles, London: University of California Press.

Tyler, David B.
    1968   *The Wilkes Expedition, The First United States Exploring Expedition (1838–1842).* Philadelphia: American Philosophical Society.

Wilkes, Charles
    1844   *Narrative of the United States Exploring Expedition.* 5 vols. Philadelphia: C. Sherman.

    1845   *Narrative of the United States Exploring Expedition During the Years 1838, 1839, 1840, 1841, 1842.* 5 vols. Philadelphia: Lea and Blanchard.

    1978   *Autobiography of Rear Admiral Charles Wilkes, U.S. Navy 1798–1877.* William James Morgan, David B. Tyler, Joye L. Leonhart, and Mary F. Loughlin, eds. Washington: Naval History Division, Department of the Navy.

Chapter 1

Reynolds, William
    Letters to various members of his family as follows. William Reynolds Collection, Franklin and Marshall College.

    1838a 12 August 1838

    1838b 30 August 1838

    1838c 3 September 1838

1838d 25 November 1838

1838e 19 December 1838

1839a 2 June 1839

1839b 6 July 1839

1840a 4 March 1840

1840b 21 September 1840

1840c 29 November 1840

1841 11 November 1841

Wilkes, Charles
  1861 Letter to Mary Lynch Wilkes, 15 November
        1861. Gilbert Wilkes, Martinsburg, W. Va.

Chapter 2

Dana, James D.
  1846 Letter to Asa Gray, 12 February 1846. Archives
        of the Gray Herbarium Library, Harvard Univer-
        sity.

Gray, Asa
  1854 *Botany*. Vol. 15. *U.S. Exploring Expedition.*
        Philadelphia: C. Sherman.

Reynolds, Jeremiah N.
  1827 *Remarks on a Review of Symmes's Theory.*
        Washington: Gales and Seaton.

Rich, William
  1844 Letter to Charles Wilkes, 9 December 1844,
        Benjamin Tappan Papers, Library of Congress.

Wilkes, Charles
  1847 Letters to James A. Pearce, 19 March and 5
        April 1847. Letterbook, Charles Wilkes Papers,
        Library of Congress.

1861 Copy of letter to John Torrey, 16 March 1861. Charles Pickering Papers, Huntington Library.

For other sources, see the version of this chapter aimed at specialists in the history of botany: William Rich of the Great Exploring Expedition and How His Shortcomings Helped Botany Become a Calling. *Huntia* 8(1), 1985.

Chapter 3

Agassiz, Louis
1855 Synopsis of the Ichthyological Fauna of the Pacific Slope of North America. *American Journal of Science and Arts* 2d series 19 (55):71–99, 215–31.

Allen, J.A.
1880 *History of North American Pinnipeds.* U.S. Geological Survey Miscellaneous Publication 12.

Amadon, David
1942 Birds Collected during the Whitney South Sea Expedition. L Notes on Some Non-Passerine Genera. *American Museum Novitates* 1176. pp. 1–21.

Baird, S. F.
1858 *Herpetology.* Vol. 20. *U.S. Exploring Expedition.* Philadelphia: C. Sherman & Son.

Bonaparte, Charles Lucien
1850 *Conspectus Generum Avium.* Part 1. Lugduni Batavorum: E. J. Brill.

Cassin, John
1858 *Mammalogy and Ornithology.* Vol. 8 and Atlas. *U.S. Exploring Expedition.* Philadelphia: C. Sherman & Son.

Dall, William Healey
1915 *Spencer Fullerton Baird, A Biography.* Philadelphia and London: J. B. Lippincott Co.

Fowler, Henry W., and Barton A. Beach
1924 Descriptions of Eighteen New Species of Fishes from the Wilkes Exploring Expedition, Preserved in the United States National Museum. *Proceedings of the United States National Museum* vol. 63, number 2488, article 19.

Fowler, Henry W.
1940 The Fishes Obtained by the Wilkes Expedition, 1838–1840. *Proceedings of the American Philosophical Society* 82:733–800.

Gill, Theodore
1866 Prodrome of a Monograph of the Pinnipeds. *Proceedings of the Essex Institute* 5 (1):1–13.

Girard, Charles
1858 *Herpetology. U.S. Exploring Expedition.* Philadelphia: J. B. Lippincott & Co.

Goode, George Brown
1891 The Published Writings of Dr. Charles Girard in Bibliographies of American Naturalists. *Bulletin of the United States National Museum* 41.

Hartlaub, G.
1852 R. Titian Peale's Vögel der "United States Exploring Expedition" im Auszuge mitgetheilt und mit kritischen Anmerkungen. *Archiv für Naturgeschichte* 18:93–138.

Jardine, Sir William
1852 Ornithology of the United States Exploring Expedition. *Contributions to Ornithology* 1852 (part 4): 89–90.

Peale, Titian Ramsay
1831 *Circular of the Philadelphia Museum Containing Directions for the Preparation and Preservation of Objects of Natural History.* Philadelphia: James K. Jun. and Co.

1848 *Mammalia and Ornithology.* Vol. 8. *U.S. Exploring Expedition.* Philadelphia: C. Sherman.

1978 *Mammalia and Ornithology,* with an Introduction by Kier B. Sterling. Reprint ed. New York: Arno Press.

Poole, Arthur J., and Viola S. Schantz
1942 Catalog of the Type Specimens of Mammals in the United States National Museum, Including the Biological Survey's Collection. *Bulletin of the United States National Museum* 178.

Stone, Witmer
1901 John Cassin. *Cassinia* 5:1–7.

Chapter 4

Agassiz, Louis
1862 *Contributions to the Natural History of the United States.* Vol. 4. Boston: Little, Brown and Co.

Couthouy, J.P.
Journal. Boston Museum of Science.

Dall, William Healey
1888 Some American Conchologists. *Proceedings of the Biological Society of Washington* 4:94–134.

Dana, James D.
1852 [1853],
1855 *Crustacea.* Vol. 13–14. *U.S. Exploring Expedition.* Philadelphia: C. Sherman.

274

Gould, Augustus A.
  1852, *Mollusca and Shells.* Vol. 12. *U.S. Exploring*
  1857 *Expedition.* Philadelphia: C. Sherman.

Johnson, Richard I.
  1964 *The Recent Mollusca of Augustus Addison*
     Gould. United States National Museum Bulle-
     tin 239.

Milne Edwards, Henri, and Haime, Jules
  1850 *A Monograph of the British Fossil Corals. Intro-*
     duction. London: Palaeontographical Society.

  1857 *Histoire Naturelle des Coralliaires ou polypres*
     proprement dits. Vol. 1. Paris: Librairie Encly-
     clopedique de Roret.

Chapter 5

Couthouy, Joseph P.
1842 Remarks Upon Coral Formations in the Pacific; With Suggestions as to the Causes of their Absence in the Same Parallels of Latitude on the Coast of South America. *Boston Journal of Natural History* 4(1): 66–105, 137–62.

Cox, Allan, and Engebretson, David
1985 Change in motion of the Pacific plate at 5 Myr BP. *Nature* 313:472–74.

Dana, James D.
1837 *A System of Mineralogy.* New Haven: Durrie & Peck and Herrick & Noyes.

1849 *Geology.* Vol. 10 *U.S. Exploring Expedition.* Philadelphia: C. Sherman. With Atlas, New York: Geo. P. Putnam.

1872 *Corals and Coral Islands.* New York: Dodd & Mead.

1890 *Characteristics of Volcanoes.* New York: Dodd, Mead and Co.

Darwin, Charles
1846 *Geological Observations on South America.* London: Smith, Elder and Co.

1851 *Geological Observations on Coral Reefs, Volcanic Islands, and on South America.* Part I: *The Structure and Distribution of Coral Reefs* [1842]. Part II: *Geological Observations on Volcanic Islands* [1844]. London: Smith, Elder and Co.

Decker, Robert W., and Christiansen, Robert L.
1984 Explosive Eruptions of Kilauea Volcano, Hawaii. In *Explosive Volcanism: Inception, Evolution, and Hazards,* F. R. Boyd, Jr., ed., pp. 122–32. Washington: National Academy Press.

Hoare, Michael E.
1969 The Challenge of Science Accepted in New South Wales. *Records of the Australian Academy of Sciences* 1(4):32–37.

Jackson, Everett D., and Koisumi, Itaru, et al.
1980 *Initial Reports of the Deep Sea Drilling Project,* Vol. 55. Washington: U.S. Government Printing Office.

Jackson, Everett D., and Shaw, Herbert R.
1975 Stress Fields in Central Portions of the Pacific Plate: Delineated in Time by Linear Volcanic Chains. *Journal of Geophysical Research* 80 (14):1861–74.

Jarrard, Richard D., and Claque, David A.
1977 Implications of Pacific Island and Seamount Ages for the Origin of Volcanic Chains. *Reviews of Geophysics and Space Physics* 15 (1):57–76.

Lindren, Waldemar, and Turner, H.W.
1895 U.S. Geological Survey Folio 17, Marysville Folio, California. Washington: U.S. Government Printing Office.

Martin, Margaret Greer, ed.
1979 *The Lymans of Hilo.* Rev. ed. Hilo: Lyman House Memorial Museum.

Moore, James G., and Moore, George W.
1984 Deposit from a Giant Wave on the Island of Lanai, Hawaii. *Science* 226(4680):1312–15.

Morgan, W.J.
1972a Plate Motion and Deep Mantle Convection. Geological Society of America Memoirs 132:7–22.

1972b Deep Mantle Convection Plumes and Plate Motions. American Association of Petroleum Geologists Bulletin 56:203–13.

Natland, James H.
1980 The Progression of Volcanism in the Samoan Linear Volcanic Chain. *American Journal of Science* 280–A:709–35.

Natland, James H., and Turner, Donald L.
1985 Age Progression and Petrological Development of Samoan Shield Volcanoes: Evidence from K/Ar Ages, Lava Compositions, and Mineral Studies.

Prendergast, Michael L.
1978 James Dwight Dana: The Life and Thought of an American Scientist. Ann Arbor: University Microfilms International.

Scott, G.A.J., and Rotondo, G.M.
1983 A Model for the Development of Types of Atolls and Volcanic Islands on the Pacific Lithospheric Plate. Atoll Research Bulletin 260: 1–33.

Williams, Howell
1929 Geology of the Marysville Buttes, California. University of California Publications, Bulletin of the Department of Geological Sciences 18:103–220.

1942 *The Geology of Crater Lake National Park, Oregon.* Carnegie Institution of Washington Publication 540.

Williams, Howell, and Curtis, G.H.
1977 *The Sutter Buttes of California.* University of California Publications in Geological Sciences, Vol. 116.

Wilson, J.T.
1963a A Possible Origin of the Hawaiian Islands. *Canadian Journal of Physics* 41:863–70.

1963b Evidence from Islands on the Spreading Ocean Floors. *Nature* 197:536–38.

Chapter 6

Clunie, Fergus
1983 Ratu Tanoa Visawaqa's Breastplate. *Domodomo* 1:123–25.

Jirokichi
Bantan: Adventures in Foreign Lands. Bishop Museum Library, Honolulu.

Judd Papers
The Papers of J. P. Judd. Bishop Museum Library, Honolulu.

Kaeppler, Adrienne L.
1978 *"Artificial Curiosities" Being an Exposition of Native Manufactures Collected on the Three Pacific Voyages of Captain James Cook, R.N.* Honolulu: Bishop Museum Special Publication 65.

Mountford, Charles P.
1963 Australian Aboriginal Skin Rugs. *Records of the South Australian Museum* 14:525.

Sellers, Charles Coleman
1979 *Mr. Peale's Museum.* New York: W. W. Norton & Company.

Stewart, T. D.
1978 The Skull of Vendovi: A Contribution of the Wilkes Expedition to the Physical Anthropology of Fiji. *Archaeology and Physical Anthropology in Oceania.* Vol. 13 (2 & 3): 204–14.

Chapter 7

Anderson, Rodger C.
1952, *Catalogue of Ship Models.* Greenwich: National
1958 Maritime Museum.

Bauer, K. Jack
1969 *Ships of the Navy, 1775–1969.* Troy, N.Y.: Rensselaer Polytechnic Institute.

Beaglehole, J.C.
1961 *The Journals of Captain James Cook.* 2 vols. Cambridge: Hakluyt Society.

Bellec, Francois
1983 Le Naufrage de l'Expedition Lapérouse. *Neptunia* 149:1–11, 150:1–14.

Chapelle, Howard I.
1935 *The History of American Sailing Ships.* New York: W. W. Norton.

1949 *The History of the American Sailing Navy.* New York: W. W. Norton.

College, J.J.
1969 *Ships of the Royal Navy: An Historical Index.* 2 vols. New York: Augustus M. Kelley.

Congreve, Sir William
1814 *The Details of the Rocket System.* London: J. Whiting.

Cutter, Donald C.; de Iglesias, Mercedes Palau; Polese, Richard; and Weber, Michael
1977 *The Malaspina Expedition: "In Pursuit of Knowledge."* Santa Fe: Museum of New Mexico Press.

Dodge, Ernest S.
1965 *New England and the South Seas.* Cambridge: Harvard University Press.

1971 *Beyond the Capes: Pacific Exploration from Captain Cook to the "Challenger." (1776–1877).* Boston and Toronto: Little, Brown and Co.

Dumont d'Urville, Jules S.C.
1841– *Voyage au Pole Sud et dans l'Océanie sur les*
46   *Corvettes "L'Astrolabe" et "La Zélée" . . . 1837–1838–1839–1840.* 10 vols. Paris: Gide.

1883 *Voyage de la Corvette "L'Astrolabe" Executée Pendant les Annees 1826–1827–1828–1829. . . .* 5 vols. Paris: J. Tastu.

Emmons, George F.
1850 *The Navy of the United States, . . . 1775 to 1853. . . .* Washington: Gideon and Company.

Friis, Herman R.
1967 *The Pacific Basin: A History of Its Geographical Exploration.* New York: American Geographical Society.

Hobbs, Richard R.
1968 The Congreve War Rockets, 1800–1825. *United States Naval Institute Proceedings* 94(3):80–88.

Johnson, Robert E.
1963 *Thence Round Cape Horn.* Annapolis: United States Naval Institute.

Norman, Henderson Daingerfield
1939 The Log of the *Flying Fish. United States Naval Institute Proceedings* 65(3):363–69.

Palmer, James C.
1843 *Thulia: A Tale of the Antarctic.* New York: Samuel Colman.

Peterson, Harold L.
1967 *Pageant of the Gun.* Garden City, N.Y.: Doubleday.

Ross, Sir James Clark
1847 *A Voyage of Discovery and Research in the Southern and Antarctic Regions, During the Years 1839–43.* 2 vols. London: John Murray.

Serrano, Carmen Sotos
1982 *Los Pintores de la Expedition de Alejandro Malaspina.* 2 vols. Madrid: Real Academia de la Historia.

Shelton, R.A.
1969 *Captain James Cook After Two Hundred Years.* London: The British Museum.

Smith, Merritt Roe
1977 *Harpers Ferry Armory and the New Technology: The Challenge of Change.* Ithaca: Cornell University Press.

Taillemite, Etienne
1981 French Contribution to the Discovery of the Pacific. *International Congress of Maritime Museums, Fourth Conference Proceedings,* Paris.

U.S. Navy Department, Naval History Division
1959– *Dictionary of American Naval Fighting Ships.* 8
81   vols. Washington: Government Printing Office.

Vaughan, Thomas; Crownhart-Vaughan, E.A.P; and de Iglesias, Mercedes Palau
1977 *Voyages of Enlightenment: Malaspina on the Northwest Coast, 1791-1792.* Portland: Oregon Historical Society.

Waite, Arthur H.
n.d. *National Maritime Museum Catalogue of Ship Models to 1815.* Greenwich: National Maritime Museum.

Ward, R. Gerald
  1966   *American Activities in the Central Pacific,*
          1790–1870. Ridgewood, N.J.: Gregg Press.

Unpublished sources

James Barron Papers, 1833–43. G. W. Blunt White Library, Mystic Seaport, Inc., Mystic, Conn.

Warship Draughts, Bureau of Construction and Repair, U.S. Navy Department, Record Group 45 U.S. National Archives

Chapter 8

Bancroft, George
  1845   Letter to Benjamin Tappan, 29 September 1845.
          Benjamin Tappan Papers, Library of Congress.

Bancroft, H.H.
  1884   *History of the Northwest Coast.* 2 vols. San
          Francisco: A. L. Bancroft & Co.

Boggs, S. Whittemore
  1938   American Contributions to Geographical
          Knowledge of the Central Pacific. *Geographical*
          Review 28:178–92.

Cooley, Mary E.
  1940   The Exploring Expedition in the Pacific. *Pro-*
          ceedings of the American Philosophical Society
          82(5):707–19.

Drayton, Joseph
  1843   Letter to Benjamin Tappan, 22 April 1843. Ben-
          jamin Tappan Papers, Library of Congress.

Field, Admiral M.
  1920   *Hydrographical Surveying, A Description of*
          Means and Methods Employed in Constructing
          Marine Charts. 4th ed. London: John Murray,
          Albemarle Street.

Finlay, A.G.
  1851   *Directory for the Navigation of the Pacific*
          Ocean.

Henry, John Frazier
  1982   The Midshipman's Revenge. *Pacific Northwest*
          Quarterly 73:156–64.

Jeffers, William N.
  1871   *Nautical Surveying.* New York: D. Van Nos-
          trand.

Reisenberg, Felix
  1940   *The Pacific Ocean.* New York: Whittlesey
          House, McGraw-Hill Book Co.

Reynolds, Jeremiah N.
  1835   *Pacific Ocean and South Seas.* 23d Cong., 2d
          sess., House Document 105, serial 273.

  1841   *Pacific and Indian Oceans: or, The South Sea*
          Surveying and Exploring Expedition. . . . New
          York: Harper & Brothers.

Reynolds, William
  1840   Letter to his family, 21 September 1840. Wil-
          liam Reynolds Collection, Franklin and Mar-
          shall College.

Stuart, Frederick D.
  1856   Letter to Charles Wilkes, 9 January 1856. Gen-
          eral Correspondence, Charles Wilkes Papers,
          Library of Congress.

Tappan, Benjamin
  1846   Volume 21, May 15, 1846. Benjamin Tappan
          Papers, Library of Congress.

Weber, Gustavus A.
  1926   *The Hydrographic Office, Its History, Activities*
          and Organization. Baltimore: The Johns Hop-
          kins University Press.

Wilkes, Charles
  1843   Letter to Benjamin Tappan, 4 April 1843. Benja-
          min Tappan Papers, Library of Congress.

  1844   *Synopsis of the Cruise of the U.S. Exploring*
          Expedition. Washington: Peter Force.

Chapter 9

Published sources

Bixby, William
  1966   *The Forgotten Voyage of Charles Wilkes.* New
          York: David McKay Co.

Borthwick, Doris Esch
  1965   Outfitting the United States Exploring Expedi-
          tion: Lieutenant Charles Wilkes' European
          Assignment, August–November, 1836. *Proceed-*
          ings of the American Philosophical Society
          109(3):159–72.

Dick, Steven J.
  1980   How the U.S. Naval Observatory Began, 1830–
          65. *Sky and Telescope* 60(6):466–71.

Henderson, Daniel
  1953   *The Hidden Coasts.* New York: William Sloane
          Associates

Jeffries, William W.
  1945   The Civil War Career of Charles Wilkes. *Journal*
          of Southern History 3(2):324–48.

Jenkins, John S.
  1850   *Voyage of the U.S. Exploring Squadron, Commanded by Captain Charles Wilkes. . . .* Hudson, N.Y.: P. S. Wynkoop.

Malone, Dumas, ed.
  1943   Charles Wilkes. *Dictionary of American Biography.* Vol. 20. New York: Charles Schribner's Sons.

Silverberg, Robert
  1968   *Stormy Voyager: The Story of Charles Wilkes.* New York: J. B. Lippincott Co.

Smucker, Samuel M.
  1858   *The Life of Dr. Elisha Kent Kane, and of other Distinguished American Explorers. . . .* Philadelphia: J. W. Bradley.

Stanley, Albert A.
  1976   Hassler's Legacy. *NOAA* [National Oceanic and Atmospheric Administration] 6(1).

Stanton, William
  1975   *The Great United States Exploring Expedition of 1838–1842.* Berkeley, Los Angeles, London: University of California Press.

Warren, Gordon H.
  1981   *Fountain of Discontent: The Trent Affair and Freedom of the Seas.* Boston: Northeastern University Press.

Weber, Gustavus A.
  1926   *The Naval Observatory: Its History, Activities and Organization.* Baltimore: The Johns Hopkins University Press.

Unpublished sources

Charles Wilkes Papers, Manuscript Division, Library of Congress.

Records of the Hydrographic Office, Record Group 37, National Archives.

Z Files, Operational Archives Branch, Naval Historical Center.

Chapter 10

Charles Wilkes's despatches to the secretary of the navy are among the principal manuscript sources for this chapter. These are collected, together with other papers, in the Letters Relating to the Wilkes Exploring Expedition, rolls 1–6, *Records of the United States Exploring Expedition Under the Command of Lieutenant Charles Wilkes, 1836–1842,* National Archives Microfilm Publication M75. Another sizeable body of Wilkes material is found at the National Archives [hereafter cited as NA] in the Area Files, Naval Records Collection of the Office of Naval Records and Library, Record Group 45. The area files consist of miscellaneous papers received from private hands and are arranged by geographic area of subject; of most interest are areas 4 (the Atlantic), 9 (eastern Pacific), and 10 (western Pacific). Letters from the Secretary of the Navy to Officers, 1837–38 (RG 45), were also consulted.

State Department records include diplomatic and consular correspondence—most particularly, Despatches from U.S. Ministers to Brazil, 1838–1839 (M121, roll 13); Despatches from U.S. Ministers to Chile, 1839 (M10, roll 5); and Consular Despatches, Society Islands, 1836–1841 (M465, roll 1). Also consulted were Miscellaneous Correspondence 1837–1840 (M179, rolls 83 and 90); Applications and Recommendations, Van Buren, Harrison, Tyler Administrations, 1836–1840 (RG 59); and the List of Consular Officers (M587).

Other important depositories include the Wilkes Family Papers in the Manuscript Department of Duke University Library; the Papers of Charles Wilkes, 1837–1847, in the Kansas State Historical Society, Topeka (Microfilm MS–53s); and the Charles Wilkes Family Papers, Manuscript Division, Library of Congress. Because Charles Wilkes kept most diplomatic activities in his own hands, the papers of most other Expedition members are less useful. Perhaps most valuable are the William Reynolds Papers at Franklin and Marshall College, Lancaster, Pennsylvania; and the journal of William Hudson, volume 1 of which is located at the American Museum of Natural History, New York. Other manuscript sources and specific quotations from the sources mentioned above are cited below.

Agreement Made by the Sultan of Sooloo at Soung, 5 February 1842.
    1842   Box 21, Charles Wilkes Family Papers, Manuscript Division, Library of Congress.

Amilbahar, Datu
    [1836] Letter to G.E. Ward, undated. Box 1, Area File 10, RG 45, NA.

Blackler, Samuel
    1840   Despatch, 31 October; also, letter from Buareia to secretary of state, 20 January 1841, and letter from Oliver Potter to secretary of state, 20 May 1841. Roll 1, M465, Consular Despatches, Society Islands, NA.

Colvocoresses, George M.
    1855   *Four Years in the Government Exploring Expedition; commanded by Captain Charles Wilkes. . . .* 5th ed. New York: J.M. Fairchild & Co.
Commercial Regulations made by the principal Chiefs of the Samoa group of islands after full consideration in Council on the 5th day of November / 39

    1839   Coe Collection, Beinecke Rare Book and Manuscript Library, Yale University Library.

    1853   Box 1, Area File 9, RG 45, NA.

Congreve, William
    1814   The Details of the Rocket System: showing the various applications of this weapon, both for sea and land service, and its different uses in the field and in sieges; illustrated . . ., with General Instructions for its application, and a demonstration of the comparative economy of the system. Reprint. Ottowa: Museum Restoration Service, 1970.

Drury, Clifford M.
    1973   *Marcus and Narcissa Whitman and the Opening of Old Oregon.* Glendale, Calif.: The Arthur H. Clark Co.

East India Marine Society, Salem, Mass.
    1834   Memorial . . . praying that an expedition be fitted out by the government to make a voyage of discovery and survey to the south seas. 16 December 1834. 23 Cong., 2 sess. Doc. 75.

    1836   Report of the . . . to the secretary of the navy, 3 November. Folder 5, box 2, Wilkes Family Papers, Duke University Library.

Emmons, George Foster
    1840   Journal. Western Americana Collection, Beinecke Rare Book and Manuscript Library, Yale University Library.

Eyde, Richard
    1985   William Rich of the Great Exploring Expedition and How His Shortcomings Helped Botany Become a Calling. *Huntia* 8(1).

Hudson, William
    1840   Letter to King Tuindrekote, Rewa, Fiji, 21 May. Box 1, Area File 9, RG 45, NA.

Jones, Thomas ap Catesby
    1837   South Sea Surveying and Exploring Expedition. Suggestions Furnished by Commodr Thos. ap Catesby Jones, June 1st 1837. Roll 2, M75, Letters Relating to the Wilkes Exploring Expedition. NA.

Jornal do Comercio (Rio de Janeiro)
    1839

Karsten, Peter
    1972   *The Naval Aristocracy: The Golden Age of Annapolis and the Emergence of Modern American Navalism.* New York: The Free Press.

Lang, Charles R., et al.
    1838   Letter to the secretary of state, 18 June. Roll 1, M465, Consular Despatches, Society Islands, Department of State, NA.

Larkin, Thomas O.
    1953   *The Larkin Papers: Personal, Business, and Official Correspondence of Thomas Oliver Larkin, Merchant and United States Consul in California.* George P. Hammond, ed. 10 vols. Berkeley: University of California Press.

McLoughlin, John
    1841   Letter to A.C. Anderson, 15 June. MS-319, Western Americana Collection, Beinecke Rare Book and Manuscript Library, Yale University Library.

1842   Letter to the Governor, Deputy Governor, and Committee, 4 November. Pages 97–98 in *The Letters of John McLoughlin from Fort Vancouver to the Governor and Committee. Second series, 1839–1844.* E.E. Rich, ed. London: The Hudson Bay Record Society.

Marcy, W.L.
1854   Letter to James C. Dobbin, 21 September; also, Dobbin to Bladin Dulany, 16 October. Box 2, Area File 9, RG 45, NA.

Masterman, Sylvia
1934   *The Origins of International Rivalry in Samoa 1845–1884.* London: George Allen & Unwin.

May, William
1840   Letter to Frederick May, 23 October. Box 1, Area File 9, RG 45, NA.

El Mercurio (Valparaiso)
1839   Article on presidential banquet, 24 May. Other references to Expedition occur between April and June.

Merk, Frederick
1966   *The Monroe Doctrine and American Expansionism 1843–1849.* New York: Alfred A. Knopf.

Miller, Hunter
1931   *Treaties and Other International Acts of the United States of America.* 8 vols. Washington: Government Printing Office.

Paullin, Charles Oscar
1967   *Diplomatic Negotiations of American Naval Officers, 1778–1883.* Baltimore, 1912. Reprinted, Gloucester, Mass.

Phillips, S.C.
1837   Letter to the secretary of state, 1 July. Roll 83, M179, Miscellaneous Correspondence, Department of State, NA.

Reynolds, William
1840   Letter to his family, 21 September. William Reynolds Papers, Franklin and Marshall College, Lancaster, Pennsylvania.

Rogers, N.L., & Brothers
1838   Letter to Charles Wilkes, 16 July. Papers of Charles Wilkes, 1837–47; Microfilm MS–53s; Kansas State Historical Society, Topeka.

Ross, James Clark
1847   *A Voyage of Discovery and Research in the Southern and Antarctic Regions, during the Years 1839–43.* 2 vols. London: J. Murray.

Speiden, William
1841   Memorandum to William Hudson listing "Presents for Natives," 16 July. Box 1, Area File 9, RG 45, NA.

U.S. Department of the Navy.
1838   Instructions, from the secretary of the navy to Charles Wilkes, 11 August. Pages 402–12, Letters from the Secretary of the Navy to Officers, 1837–38, RG 45, NA.

Weber, David J.
1982   *The Mexican Frontier, 1821–1846: The American Southwest Under Mexico.* Albuquerque: University of New Mexico Press.

Wilkes, Charles
1839   General Order, 13 July. Box 1, Area File 9, RG 45, NA.

1840a   Letter to Jane Wilkes, 10 August. Folder 1, Box 4, Wilkes Family Papers, Manuscript Department, Duke University Library, Durham.

1840b   Despatch 66, 10 August. Roll 6, M75, Letters Relating to the Wilkes Exploring Expedition, NA.

1840c   Despatch, 11 August. Roll 6, M75, Letters Relating to the Wilkes Exploring Expedition, NA.

1841   Despatch, 15 May. Roll 6, M75, Letters Relating to the Wilkes Exploring Expedition, NA.

[1842] List of the goods saleable at Sooloo, undated. Box 1, Area file 10, RG 45, NA.

Chapter 11

The *Bulletin of the Proceedings of the National Institute for the Promotion of Science* is the chief source for documents related to the early activities of the Institute. In addition, an invaluable account of the relationships between the Institute, the Patent Office, and the Exploring Expedition, in the context of the establishment of the Smithsonian Institution, is given in G. Brown Goode's "The Genesis of the National Museum," listed below, which presents documentary material from the collections of the Smithsonian Institution Archives. Rhees's *Documents,* listed above under General Sources in these references, is the main source for statutory and appropriation data.

The principal manuscript collections used at the Smithsonian Institution Archives (SIA) were those of the National Institute (Record Unit 7058), John Varden (Record Unit 7063), United States Exploring Expedition (Record Unit 7186), William Dunlop Brackenridge (Record Unit 7189), and Spencer F. Baird (Record Unit 7002). Requisitions, account registers, invoices, and various documents contained in the National Institute papers, particularly in Box 14, provided data about administrative relationships, practices, and purchases. Shipping documents are located in the same box and in Box 2 of the U.S. Exploring Expedition papers. Other letters and documents quoted from these and from the Varden, Brackenridge, and Baird papers are itemized below.

Other manuscript holdings consulted were the Joel R. Poinsett Papers and the Poinsett papers in the Henry D. Gilpin Collection, both at the Historical Society of Pennsylvania (HSP); the Benjamin Tappan Papers, the John J. Abert Papers, and the Edmund Burke Papers at the Manuscript Division of the Library of Congress (LC), and the records of the Department of State and the United States Exploring Expedition located at the National Archives.

Abert, John J.
1841a Letter to Joel R. Poinsett, 6 May 1841. Poinsett Papers, HSP.

1841b Letter to Joel R. Poinsett, 12 July 1841. Poinsett Papers, Gilpin Collection, HSP.

1842a Letter to Joel R. Poinsett, 9 November 1842. Poinsett Papers, HSP.

1842b Letter to Joel R. Poinsett, 23 August 1842. Poinsett Papers, Gilpin Collection, HSP.

Badger, George E.
1841 Letter to J. Abert, A.O. Dayton, and F. Markhoe, 17 May 1841. Folder 2, Box 9, RU 7058, SIA.

Baird, William M.
1841a Letter to Spencer F. Baird, 2 July 1841. Box 38, RU 7002, SIA.

1841b Letter to Spencer F. Baird, 24 August 1841. Box 38, RU 7002, SIA.

1842a Letter to Spencer F. Baird, 1 February 1842. Box 38, RU 7002, SIA.

1842b Letter to Spencer F. Baird, 23 November 1842. Box 38, RU 7002, SIA.

Brackenridge, William D.
1844 Request for payment for J.R. Wroe, September 1844. Folder 3, Box 14, RU 7058, SIA.

1850a Letter to John Torrey, 3 August 1850. Box 1, RU 7189, SIA.

1850b Letter to John Torrey, 17 September 1850. Box 1, RU 7189, SIA.

1850c Letter to John Torrey, 20 December 1850, Box 1, RU 7189, SIA.

Ellsworth, Henry L.
1840 Letter to the *National Intelligencer*, 21 November 1840

1841 Letter to John J. Abert and Peter Force, 21 June 1841. Folder 2, Box 9, RU 7058, SIA.

1842a Letter to Daniel Webster, 18 April 1842. Benjamin Tappen Papers, LC.

1842b Letter to Daniel Webster, 12 November 1842. *Miscellaneous Letters of the Department of State, 1789–1906.* National Archives Microfilm Publication M179.

Ewing, Thomas
1841 Letter to J.J. Abert, A.O. Dayton, and F. Markoe, 9 June 1841. Box 1, RU 7058, SIA.

Goode, G. Brown
1892 The Genesis of the National Museum. *Report of the U.S. National Museum.* Washington: U.S. Government Printing Office.

Ketcham, John L.
1844 Letter to Jane M. Ketcham, 15 June 1844. Ketcham Collection, Indiana Historical Society.

King, Henry
1841a Letter to William Muzzey, 24 April 1841. Folder 1, Box 14, RU 7058, SIA.

1841b Letter to William Muzzey, 28 April 1841. Folder 1, Box 14, RU 7058, SIA.

1841c Draft of letter to George E. Badger, 9 May 1841. Folder 2, Box 9, RU 7058, SIA.

1841d Letter to Joel R. Poinsett, 14 December 1841. Poinsett Papers, HSP.

Markoe, Francis
1841 Letter to Joel R. Poinsett, 30 June 1841. Poinsett Papers, HSP.

Marsh, George P.
1845 Letter to Edmund Burke, 21 June 1845. Burke Papers, LC.

Mills, Robert
1842 *Guide to the National Executive Offices and the Capitol of the United States.* Washington: P. Force, Printer.

1847– *Guide to the National Executive Offices and*
48   *the Capitol of the United States.* Washington: P. Force, Printer.

National Institute for the Promotion of Science
1841– *Bulletin of the Proceedings.* Washington: Gales
46 and Seaton. Photocopied and bound, Smithsonian Libraries, 1966.

Peale, Titian R.
1844 Letter to Charles Wilkes, 9 December 1844. Benjamin Tappan Papers, LC.

Poinsett, Joel R.
1842a Letter to Gouverneur Kemble, 12 January 1842. Poinsett Papers, Gilpin Collection, HSP.

1842b Letter to Gouverneur Kemble, 24 May 1842. Poinsett papers, Gilpin Collection, HSP.

1843 Letter to Gouverneur Kemble, 24 May 1843. Poinsett Papers, Gilpin Collection, HSP.

Smithsonian Institution
1854– *Annual Report of the Board of Regents.* Wash-
58 ington: Smithsonian Institution.

[unknown]
[1844– Plan of the National Gallery containing the
49] Collections of the Exploring Expedition. Washington: J. & G.S. Gideon, Printers.

U.S. Congress
1836 *Report of the Select Committee on the Patent Office,* 28 April 1836. 24th Cong., 1st sess. Senate Report 338.

U.S. Exploring Expedition
1845– Requisitions and orders. Box 14, RU 7058, SIA.
54

U.S. Patent Office
1842 *Report from the Commissioner of Patents for 1841,* 8 March 1842. 27th Cong., 2d sess., Senate Document 169.

1843 *Report of the Commissioner of Patents for 1842,* 1 February 1843. 27th Cong., 3d sess., House Document 109.

1844 *Report of the Commissioner of Patents for 1843,* 27 February 1844. 28th Cong., 1st sess., Senate Document 150. Washington: Blair & Rives.

1845 *Report of the Commissioner of Patents for 1844,* 30 January 1845. 28th Cong., 2d sess., Senate Document 75.

1846 *Report of the Commissioner of Patents for 1845,* 20 April 1846. 29th Cong., 1st sess., Senate Document 307. Washington: Ritchie & Heiss.

1851 *Report of the Commissioner of Patents for 1850,* 31st Cong., 2d sess., Ex. Doc. 32. Washington: Office of Printers to House of Representatives.

Varden, John
1842–56 Account book. Box 16, RU 7058, SIA.

1845a Letter to Charles Wilkes, 28 March 1845. Folder 2, Box 14, RU 7058, SIA.

1845b Letter to John Sexsmith, 20 May 1845. Folder 2, Box 14, RU 7058, SIA.

1846 Letter to Charles Wilkes, 3 November 1846. Folder 2, Box 14, RU 7058, SIA.

1847a Letter to Charles Wilkes, 5 January 1847. Folder 2, Box 14, RU 7058, SIA.

1847b Letter to Joseph T. Barkley, 9 June 1847. Folder 2, Box 14, RU 7058, SIA.

[1855] List of specimens. Box 1, RU 7063, SIA.

1857–63 Diary. Box 1, RU 7063, SIA.

Webster, Daniel
1841 Letter to Henry L. Ellsworth, 11 June 1841. *Domestic Letters of the Department of State, 1784–1906.* National Archives Microfilm Publication M40.

Wilkes, Charles
1840 Letters to James K. Paulding, 9 November 1840, nos. 77 and 79, *Records of the United States Exploring Expedition Under the Command of Lieutenant Charles Wilkes, 1838–1842.* National Archives Microfilm Publication M75.

1843 Letter to Benjamin Tappan [August] 1843. Tappan Papers, LC.

1848 Letter to Benjamin Tappan, 30 November 1848. Tappan Papers, LC.

Chapter 12

Baird, Spencer F.
1847 Draft of letter to Joseph Henry, 25 February 1847. Baird Papers, Smithsonian Institution Archives.

Deiss, William A.
1980 Spencer F. Baird and His Collectors. *Journal of the Society for the Bibliography of Natural History* 9 (4):635–45.

1985   The Making of a Naturalist: Spencer F. Baird, the Early Years. *From Linnaeus to Darwin: Commentaries on the History of Biology and Geology.* London: Society for the History of Natural History. In press.

Goetzmann, William H.
1972   *Exploration and Empire: The Explorer and the Scientist in the Winning of the American West.* New York: Vintage Books.

Henry, Joseph
1846   Letter to Harriet Henry, 22 December 1846, Family Correspondence; draft of letter to Eliphalet Nott, 26 December 1846; draft of letter to Smithsonian Institution Regent, 28 December 1846. Henry Papers, Smithsonian Institution Archives.

1849   Retained copy of letter to George P. Marsh, 1 August 1849. Henry Papers, Smithsonian Institution Archives.

1850   Letter to Harriet Henry, 19 July 1850. Family Correspondence, Henry Papers, Smithsonian Institution Archives.

1857   Letter to Asa Gray, 6 April 1857. Gray Herbarium Library.

Hafertepe, Kenneth
1984   *America's Castle: The Evolution of the Smithsonian Building and Its Institution, 1840–1878.* Washington: Smithsonian Institution Press.

Reingold, Nathan
1973   The New York State Roots of Joseph Henry's National Career. *New York History* 54:133–44.

Smithsonian Institution, Board of Regents
1853–   *Annual Report.* Washington: Smithsonian Insti-
78   tution. The 1853 *Annual Report* reprints all the *Annual Reports* from 1847 through 1852.

Acknowledgments: The Story of the Ex. Ex. Ex.

Planning for "Magnificent Voyagers" began more than seven years before it opened on 13 November 1985 in the Thomas M. Evans Gallery of the National Museum of Natural History. The idea grew out of a request to Herman J. Viola by Charlene James-Duguid, Manager of the Smithsonian's National Associates Lecture and Seminar Program, for a small exhibit to complement a show at the Bernice P. Bishop Museum in Honolulu on the Pacific voyages of Captain James Cook, R.N. The result was a display of Pacific artifacts collected by the U.S. Exploring Expedition of 1838–42, which Viola brought to the Bishop Museum in January 1978. The exhibit demonstrated changes in the material culture of the Pacific islanders during the sixty years between the British and American expeditions.

Interest in the display was so great, however, that Viola, Director of the Smithsonian's National Anthropological Archives, continued to research the Wilkes Expedition. He eventually developed a slide lecture on the story, which he presented one evening at the Smithsonian. The following day, he was approached by George Watson, then a specialist on birds in the Department of Vertebrate Zoology, who suggested they collaborate on a major exhibition to focus on the importance of the U.S. Exploring Expedition in the history of American science, partic-

ularly its little-known role in establishing the National Museum.

Clearly it was an idea whose time had come, because Viola and Watson easily formed a core planning committee of curators in the Museum of Natural History eager to work on such an exhibit. First to agree was Frederick M. Bayer, a specialist on corals in the Department of Invertebrate Zoology. Bayer had long been a student of the Wilkes Expedition. In fact, he possessed a remarkably complete collection of publications dealing with it. Another early member of the team was Adrienne Kaeppler. Formerly of the Bishop Museum, she had just joined the staff of the Anthropology Department as Curator of Oceanic Ethnology and was already planning to study and catalog the large ethnographic collection assembled by the Exploring Expedition. Assisting her in this herculean task was Jane M. Walsh, her research associate.

The next step was to get formal approval for the exhibition. It was obvious even at this early stage that telling the story of the Expedition and its scientific achievements would require a large and complex exhibit, meaning a sizeable commitment by the Smithsonian of space and funds. Fortunately, the Evans Gallery had been recently installed on the ground floor of the Museum of Natural History, with twelve thousand square feet intended for temporary exhibits. Acting for the planning committee, Viola in August 1981 formally suggested an exhibit tentatively titled: "Genesis of the National Museum: The U.S. Exploring Expedition" to Richard S. Fiske, Director of the National Museum of Natural History. Viola outlined the history of the Expedition, reviewed its importance to American science as well as the Smithsonian, and noted that the exhibit would represent virtually every department in the Museum. Fiske could not have been more enthusiastic about the proposal, because it was an ideal way to commemorate the seventy-fifth anniversary of the Natural History Building only four years away. The exhibit was promptly scheduled for November 1985.

At the time, four years seemed more than adequate to the committee members, who little appreciated the immense task ahead. They called themselves the "Ex. Ex. Ex.," for Exploring Expedition Exhibition, because the original abbreviation "Ex.Ex." appears on the old labels of Expedition specimens and was used so frequently in correspondence by Wilkes and his fellow explorers. The first challenge was to expand the planning committee, for experts in many areas were needed to ensure the accuracy of all the topics the exhibition would be expected to cover. Absolutely essential were specialists in the scientific collections that survived the Expedition. With anthropology, invertebrate zoology, and vertebrate zoology covered by Kaeppler, Bayer, and Watson, the committee needed two natural history specialists: a botanist and a mineralogist. After only a minimum of persuasion, Daniel E. Appleman, a geologist in the Department of Mineral Sciences, accepted the exhibit's greatest challenge—to illustrate the monumental accomplishments of Expedition mineralogist James Dwight Dana. Richard H. Eyde, a specialist on fruits and flowers in the Department of Botany, agreed to tackle a challenge almost as formidable—to identify the contributions of the Expedition's plant collectors. It soon became evident, however, that Eyde was as much a historian as a botanist. Indeed, he began as the committee's most reluctant member and emerged as its most zealous.

Although the committee members were planning an exhibition primarily on the history of natural history, they realized they would need historians knowledgeable about the U.S. Navy in the age of sail. Three scholars eventually filled this gap. Two came from the National Museum of American History: Philip K. Lundeberg served as the specialist on ships and logistics; Harold D. Langley provided assistance, when his schedule permitted, on life at sea. The third naval historian was Joye L. Leonhart, an editor in the Historical Research Branch of the Naval Historical Center, who took responsibility for interpreting the complex personality of Charles Wilkes in the exhibit and book. She proved to be a wonderful addition to the team because she had been one of the editors of the Wilkes autobiography and because she became the liaison between the planning committee and Rear Admiral John Kane, Director of the Naval Historical Center, who wholeheartedly endorsed the exhibition. Largely through his efforts, the Navy arranged for a surveying and hydrographic charting vessel to be docked and available for public viewing at Alexandria, Virginia, thereby enabling visitors to the exhibition to compare the mapping and surveying techniques of a century ago to those used by the modern navy.

Since its surveys and maps are among the Expedition's most impressive legacies, they obviously merited a prominent place in the exhibition, but this was one topic that could not be covered by someone from the Smithsonian's community of scholars. What could have been a serious problem, however, became one of the exhibition's strengths when Viola prevailed on Ralph Ehrenberg and John Wolter of the Geography and Map Division of the Library of Congress (with technical assistance by Captain Charles Burroughs of the National Oceanic and Atmospheric Administration in the interpretation of contemporary methodologies of surveying and charting) to fill this void. Inevitably, the scope of their participation grew dramatically as the magnitude and importance of the Expedition's surveying and mapping activities became clear to both them and the planning committee. The result, as reflected in their chapter in this publication, was a major contribution to the history of American cartography.

Like the original expedition, which grew from

one ship to six, the planning committee of the Ex. Ex. Ex. continued to expand as the need arose for additional specialists. The history of science was one such area, and it was superbly covered by Nathan Reingold and his assistant, Marc Rothenberg, editors of the *Joseph Henry Papers*; they were responsible for explaining the role the Expedition collections played in establishing the National Museum at the Smithsonian Institution.

Three other key members of the planning committee were Jeffrey Stann, Deputy Director of the Office of Membership and Development, Douglas E. Evelyn, Deputy Director of the Museum of American History, and Ellen Wells, the Rare Book Librarian at the Smithsonian. Stann researched the diplomatic aspects of the Exploring Expedition; Evelyn assumed the task of telling the story of the Expedition collections while they were housed in the Patent Office Building; and Wells developed that part of the script relating to the official publications of the Exploring Expedition.

For approximately one year, the committee members operated independently as they delved into known research collections and sought information and artifacts that may have eluded earlier scholars. Their research was greatly facilitated by the two archivists on the planning committee: William A. Deiss of the Smithsonian Institution Archives and Elaine C. Everly of the National Archives. Deiss was particularly effective in helping obtain the scientific instruments used in the exhibition.

During this period considerable time was spent locating descendants of Expedition members—sailors as well as scientists—in the hope of finding treasures still in private custody. It was time well spent. Indeed, the world seemed to abound with descendants of Charles Wilkes. (The clan is so extensive and so interested in its history that it publishes the newsletter *Kith and Kin*.) One of the first contacted was Caroline Wilkes of Bethesda, Maryland. She not only contributed Wilkes memorabilia to the exhibition, but she also served as the committee's liaison with other members of the family, one of whom was Gilbert Wilkes III of Martinsburg, West Virginia, a great-great-grandson of the Expedition commander. He donated a number of items essential to the exhibition and book, including

correspondence, publications, photographs, and a portrait of John Deponthieu Wilkes, the father of Charles Wilkes. Gilbert Wilkes also seemed to delight in the controversial image of his illustrious ancestor.

Perhaps the most exciting discovery was made by Eyde, who was relentless in his search for information about the obscure botanist, William Rich. Not even the date or place of his death was known. No matter. After an investigation that would have flattered Sherlock Holmes, Eyde found a Rich relation, Helen Caulfield Madine, living in Fincastle, Virginia. She did not even know of this particular kinsman or the Exploring Expedition. Nonetheless, she and her family opened their door—as well as their attic and basement—to the committee's botanist-turned-historian. Caught up in the excitement of the search, the family and Eyde found a trove of memorabilia relating to Rich's Expedition service. A note tucked into a pack of old valentines revealed that he had died in Washington, D.C., and was buried in Congressional Cemetery.

A year of such enterprise produced a mountain of data, which required the attention of someone who could both organize what had already been found and coordinate the continuing research efforts of this diverse committee. Once again, Viola found the ideal person—Sharon Galperin, a professional librarian and meticulous researcher who eventually rivaled the committee members in her breadth of knowledge about the Expedition and the available resources. Besides serving as the committee's "den mother," she did an amazing amount of original research and at the same time directed a corps of volunteers and interns who investigated specialized topics important to the exhibition and book. One volunteer, Bert Kassell, a retired Navy officer, painstakingly plotted the entire route of the U.S.S. *Vincennes* as recorded in the official narrative published by Wilkes. The chronology is published here.

By January 1984, when Galperin left the Smithsonian to resume her career as a librarian, the bulk of the research had been completed and the planning had moved to a new plateau, namely translating research notes into an integrated exhibit script. The committee now needed someone expert in managing all phases of exhibit work, someone who could reconcile the differing perspectives of designers and curators, balance the requirements of borrowers and lenders, and direct the efforts of scores of workers and supporters. The committee needed the proverbial person who could walk on water without getting damp, and it found her in Carolyn Margolis. She accepted the position of Exhibit Manager in March 1984, becoming, in effect, the committee's quartermaster. Margolis had to assemble the specimen list—at first more than two thousand objects before it was whittled to half that number; she had to work out loan agreements with the more than forty institutions and individuals who promised material to the show; and she had to supervise docents as well as serve as the liaison with the firm commissioned to design the installation. In fact, she cheerfully accepted any assignment handed her, including a few normally left untouched by ten-foot poles.

Difficult as it was, her task would have been even more onerous had it not been for the excellent working relationship that emerged between her, editor Susan Voss of the Department of Exhibits, and Richard Molinaroli, who designed the exhibit. This talented team transformed an astonishing variety of information, biological specimens, maps, drawings, and artifacts into a visual and intellectual whole that brings the Exploring Expedition to life.

The exhibition and book benefited from the assistance and advice of many other persons. Special thanks go to Sheila Mutchler, Special Exhibits Coordinator and a member of the planning committee; Martha Cappelletti of SITES; Joan Madden and Laura McKie of the Office of Education; and photographers Roy E. "Chip" Clark, Vic Krantz, and Harold Dougherty. Elsewhere in the Museum of Natural History continuing support came from Phil Angle, Judy Cash, Dave Carlin, Bruce Daniels, Edith Dietze, Harold Dougherty, Gary Gautier and his ADP staff, Frank Greenwell, Ives Goddard, Catharine Hawks, Cathy Kerby, Constance Lee, Joan Miles, Jane Norman, Laurence O'Reilly, Donald Ortner, Ron Heyer, Carolyn Rose, Gail Simplicio, Victor Springer, T. Dale Stewart, Marjory Stoller, William C. Sturtevant, Wayne Suttles, Cathy Valentour, Sara Wolf, Michele Austin, John Hyltoft, George Zug, Richard Zusi; interns Molly Coxson, Desmond Tatana Kahotea, Gaye Lowenstein, Mina Takahashi, and Laura Wynn; and the staff of the National Anthropological Archives, especially Demetrius Adams, Cathy Creek, and Vyrtis Thomas.

Gary Kulik, Art Molella, Deborah Warner, and Carlene Stephens of the National Museum of American History gave needed assistance and opened their collections to the committee, and liaisons Harry Rubenstein and Harold Ellis made everything work smoothly. Thanks also to Harry Hunter, James Knowles, Michele Sengsourinh, Sal Cillela, Walter Sorrell, Jim Mahoney, Susan Francis, Susan Wallace, Hannelore Aceto, James Goode, Harry Heiss, Jack Marquardt, Janette Saquet, Barbara Veloz, Mary Ellen McCaffrey, Wilcomb Washburn, and Wendy Reaves Wick. Invaluable expertise on the ship models came from Dr. William Brown, Charles J. Newcomb, John Morgen, and Dana Wegner and Colan Ratliff of the Naval Ship Research and Development Center.

At the Library of Congress thanks go to James Gilreath, Dorothy Lee, John McDonough, and the staffs of the Manuscript Division and Geography and Map Division Reading Rooms. Greatly appreciated assistance was also received from Robert Peck and Sylva Baker of the Philadelphia Academy of Natural Sciences; Paul Beelitz, Mary Genett, and Nina Root of the American Museum of Natural History; Sharon E. Knapp of Duke University; Fergus Clunie of the Fiji Museum; Charlotte Brown of Franklin and Marshall College; Bereta Due, Poul Mørk, and Lise Rishøj Pedersen of the National Museum of Denmark; William A. Stanley of the National Oceanic and Atmospheric Administration; Peter Fetchko, Libby Ingalls, Will Phippin, and A. Paul Winfisky and staff of the Peabody Museum, Salem; Dr. George Miles of the Beinecke Library and Judith Schiff of the Sterling Library, Yale University; Richard Beidleman; William Goetzmann; Amy Myers; William Stanton; and Ellis Yochelson.

Without the contributions of our lenders, the show would never have been possible. All were exceedingly helpful, especially James Zeender of the National Archives and Records Administration. Quite a few others also went the extra mile, including J.W. Henderson, Anne Cleaver, Harold Colvorcoresses, and James and Helen Madine. Thanks too to editor Jan S. Danis, who gave indispensable help with the book and to Molly Ryan who drew several of the maps. In addition, at the Smithsonian Institution Press, thanks go to Felix Lowe, Carol Beehler, Kathleen Brown, and Jeanne Sexton whose efforts, talents, and patience made this book a reality.

An exhibition of this size needs the support of so many people, but one group worked untiringly for no reward or credit, our industrious volunteers and interns. Some stuck with Wilkes for years, bringing to the exhibition and book a range and depth the project would have otherwise sorely missed. Thanks for the hard work and devotion of the following: Amy Hollengreen, Elizabeth Stoller, Jill Abraham, Kevin S. Baldwin, Nina Beasley, Kathleen Campisano, Molly Coleman, Neela D'Sousa, Nancy Edelman, Scott Edwards, Mina Eggerton, William Kane, Liz Knapp, Paul Martinovich, Gertrude Matloff, Beatrice Meyerson, Benjamin Pierce, Paul Ruther, Donna Sangimino, Eleanor Schwartz, Stacy Sterling, and Sarah Stromayer. And deepest gratitude to one very special volunteer, Rita Bahl, who was really the "assistant project manager." Without her invaluable help some tasks would never have been completed, nor would the entire project have run as smoothly as it did.

Perhaps it comes as no surprise that financing the exhibition was worrisome. The fact that the exhibition kept growing was a major part of the problem. The more research that was done, the greater its scope came to be and the cost grew accordingly. Fate smiled on the exhibition when, early in the planning, Al Greenstein and Anna Arrington of ARCO recognized its importance. Thanks to their interest, the ARCO Foundation awarded the Smithsonian Institution a major grant that was used to hire consultants and a designer, to finance research trips by committee members, and generally to underwrite the costs of developing the Ex. Ex. Ex. Major support for the exhibition and book has been provided from the Associates and other auxiliary activities of the Smithsonian through the Special Exhibition Trust Fund, by the Atlantic Richfield Foundation, and by Federally appropriated funds for the National Museum of Natural History.

Ironically, it took about the same length of time to plan and install the exhibition as it took for the Wilkes Expedition to complete its epic voyage of enterprise and discovery. The planning committee hopes that its efforts do justice to both the seventy-fifth anniversary of the Natural History Building and to the great U.S. Exploring Expedition.

HJV

Index

A Woman
of
Matea I.

N 23

Lenders to the Exhibition

Alexander Turnbull Library
Wellington, New Zealand

American Philosophical Society
Philadelphia, Pennsylvania

Archives and Special Collections Department
Franklin and Marshall College
Lancaster, Pennsylvania

Dr. Frederick Bayer
Department of Invertebrate Zoology
Natural History Building

Bernice Pauahi Bishop Museum
Honolulu, Hawaii

Boston Athenaeum
Boston, Massachusetts

Dr. William Brown
Chicago, Illinois

Anne (Mrs. William J.) Cleaver
Westfield, Indiana

The Columbia Historical Society
Washington, D.C.

Harold Colvocoresses
Hartford, Connecticut

Department Library Services
American Museum of Natural History
New York, New York

Betty Wilkes Dewey
Summerville, South Carolina

Fiji Museum
Suva, Fiji

The George Peabody Library of the Johns Hopkins
University
Baltimore, Maryland

Hawaii Volcanoes National Park
National Park Service, Hawaii

J. Welles Henderson Collection
Philadelphia, Pennsylvania

The Historical Society of Pennsylvania
Philadelphia, Pennsylvania

Joseph Henry Papers, Smithsonian Institution
Washington, D.C.

Library of the Academy of Natural Sciences of
Philadelphia
Philadelphia, Pennsylvania

The Library of Congress, Washington, D.C
Geography and Map Division
Manuscript Division
Prints and Photographs Division
Rare Book and Special Collections Division

William Henri MacHendrick
Rochester, Massachusetts

James and Helen Madine
Fincastle, Virginia

Mission Houses Museum
Honolulu, Hawaii

Mitchell Library, State Library of New South Wales
Sydney, New South Wales, Australia

National Academy of Design
New York, New York

The National Archives
Washington, D.C.

National Museum of American History
Division of Armed Forces History
Division of Ceramics and Glass
Division of Community Life
Division of Costume
Division of Domestic Life
Division of Extractive Industries
Division of Mathematics
Division of Mechanisms
Division of Musical Instruments
Division of Photographic History
Division of Physical Sciences
Division of Political History
Division of Textiles
Division of Transportation
National Numismatics Collection

The National Museum of Denmark
Copenhagen, Denmark

National Oceanic and Atmospheric Administration
United States Department of Commerce
Rockville, Maryland

National Portrait Gallery, Smithsonian Institution
Washington, D.C.

Naval Historical Center
Washington, D.C.

Naval Historical Foundation
Washington, D.C.

The Naval Sea Systems Command
Washington, D.C.

New England Historic Genealogical Society
Boston, Massachusetts

New Haven Colony Historical Society
New Haven, Connecticut

The New-York Historical Society
New York, New York

Oregon Historical Society
Portland, Oregon

Peabody Museum of Archaeology and Ethnology, Harvard
University
Cambridge, Massachusetts

Peabody Museum of Salem
Salem, Massachusetts

Philadelphia Museum of Art
Philadelphia, Pennsylvania

Smithsonian Building

Smithsonian Institution Archives
Washington, D.C.

Smithsonian Institution Libraries
Washington, D.C.

Mrs. C. W. Styer
Clover, South Carolina

U.S. Naval Academy Museum
Annapolis, Maryland

University Museum of Archaeology and Anthropology
Cambridge, University

The University Museum
University of Pennsylvania
Philadelphia, Pennsylvania

Caroline Woolsey Wilkes
Rockville, Maryland

Gilbert Wilkes III
Martinsburg, West Virginia

Wilkes Family Papers, Manuscript Department
Duke University Library
Durham, North Carolina

Yale University, New Haven, Connecticut
Beinecke Rare Book and Manuscript Library
Sterling Memorial Library
Yale University Art Gallery

Photographic Credits

Additional credits not listed in the captions.

American Museum of Natural History, Department Library Services:
pages 46 (neg. no. 323811) and 102, top (neg. no. 329197), photographed by L. Boltin; page 103 (neg. no. 2641(2)), photographed by O. Bauer.

Boston Athenaeum: page 73, George M. Cushing, photography.

T. Lawrence Mellichamp, University of North Carolina at Charlotte: page 33.

Peabody Museum of Salem:
cover and pages 131 and 151, photographed by Mark Sexton

Charles H. Phillips Photographer:
pages 1, 17, 19, 24, 35, 42, 45, 49, 54, 55, 60, 61, 63 (top and bottom), 64, 65, 67, 70, 75, 77, 118, 124, 132, 133 (baskets), 140, 141, 144, 175, 220, 222, 304.

This book was produced by the Smithsonian Institution Press
Set in Trump Mediaeval by Graphic Composition, Inc., Athens, Georgia
Printed by W.A. Krueger Company, New Berlin, Wisconsin
on 80 lb. Consoweb Brilliant Dull
with Rainbow Colonial jade endsheets
Edited by Jeanne M. Sexton
Designed by Carol Hare Beehler

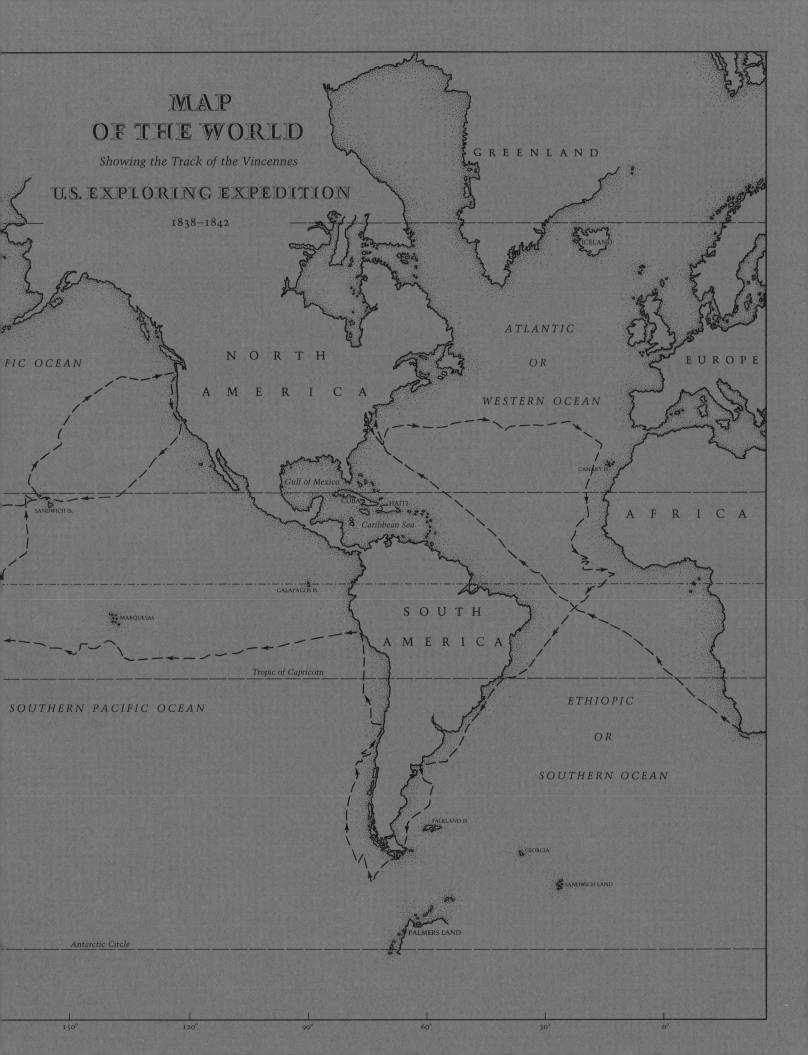